Religion and Empire

NEW STUDIES IN ARCHAEOLOGY

Religion and Empire

The dynamics of Aztec and Inca expansionism

GEOFFREY W. CONRAD

ARTHUR A. DEMAREST

CAMBRIDGE
UNIVERSITY PRESS

CAMBRIDGE UNIVERSITY PRESS
Cambridge, New York, Melbourne, Madrid, Cape Town, Singapore, São Paulo

Cambridge University Press
The Edinburgh Building, Cambridge CB2 2RU, UK

Published in the United States of America by Cambridge University Press, New York

www.cambridge.org
Information on this title: www.cambridge.org/9780521243575

First published 1984
Reprinted 1988, 1990, 1993, 1995, 1998, 1999, 2001, 2002

A catalogue record for this publication is available from the British Library

Library of Congress Catalogue Card Number: 83-14414

ISBN-13 978-0-521-24357-5 hardback
ISBN-10 0-521-24357-2 hardback

ISBN-13 978-0-521-31896-9 paperback
ISBN-10 0-521-31896-3 paperback

Transferred to digital printing 2005

TO OUR FAMILIES

CONTENTS

ILLUSTRATIONS

viii

Tables

ACKNOWLEDGEMENTS

No book comes into the world solely through the efforts of its authors. Four years have passed since the idea for *Religion and Empire* first took form, and in that time we have managed to accumulate considerable debts of gratitude to a number of individuals. It is with pleasure that we now publicly acknowledge those debts.

Three individuals at Cambridge University Press have been especially important in making this work possible. Robin Derricourt saw potential value in this book when it existed only as an outline. Katharine Owen and Caroline Murray helped to transform our manuscript into a finished volume. We are most grateful for their advice, enthusiasm, and support.

Drafts of the manuscript benefited from readings by a number of friends and colleagues. Gordon R. Willey, C. C. Lamberg-Karlovsky, Jeremy Sabloff, and several anonymous reviewers offered useful comments. Rita Wright's insightful criticisms of an earlier version of Chapter 5 were particularly valuable. As always, Patricia Anawalt gave both advice and encouragement. Some of these readers disagreed with our conclusions, but nonetheless took the trouble to suggest ways in which our arguments could be expressed more effectively. We are deeply grateful for their help.

The text includes a fair number of quotations from sixteenth- and seventeenth-century chroniclers, all of which have been translated into English. Good published translations have been used when available; where none is cited, the translation is our own. Judith Conrad of the Department of Modern Languages, Boston University, helped to render several extremely convoluted passages into better English (and refrained from snickering at her older brother's versions).

Figures 4 (top), 5, 6, 8 (top), 9, 10 (top), 15, 16 (bottom), 20, 23 (bottom), 24, and 26 were drawn by L. E. Demarest. We realize how exasperating it must have been for him to deal with two authors – one of them his own son – who seemed incapable of providing anything other than the most cryptic instructions. We appreciate his tolerance as much as his ingenuity and skill.

Figures 1, 2, 7, 11, and Tables 1 and 2 were prepared by Ann Hatfield and Nancy Lambert-Brown. Credits for the other illustrations are listed below.

Although it may seem strange to acknowledge it here, we owe a great debt to each other. Co-authoring has been a sometimes frustrating but highly rewarding experience. This book was jointly authored in every sense of the word; our names are merely listed on the title page in alphabetical order. Drafts of each chapter passed back and forth between us so many times that, even in the case of individual sentences, we would be hard put to say who wrote what. We have had four years of intellectually stimulating discussions, heated debates, snide remarks penciled in the margins of drafts, and mutual support. What has emerged is, we believe, a better book, and certainly a stronger friendship.

Neither one of us could have persevered through the writing and rewriting without the strong and constant support of our wives, Karen Conrad and Mary Demarest. For Karen, Mary, and our growing families, *Religion and Empire* has been the cause of late nights, interrupted meals, and benign neglect when attention would have been better. Somehow they have borne it all with love, forebearance, and forgiveness.

Finally, we must give credit to someone without whom this book simply would not exist. Throughout the writing of the book, Mary Demarest has put the text into a word processor, thereby allowing both constant rewriting and eventually the generation of the computer tape that actually set the type. Mary has coped with four years of illegible handwriting, contradictory instructions, and endless revisions, enduring it all with infinite patience, tolerance, and enthusiasm. Indeed, it has become a standing joke between us that the authorship line should read: "by Mary Demarest, with an incredible amount of harassment from Geoff and Arthur". While originally said in jest, that statement does embody a certain essential truth. We acknowledge that truth with gratitude and affection.

Thanks are due to the following for permission to reproduce illustrative material.

Figure 3. Radin, Paul, *The Sources and Authenticity of the History of the Ancient Mexicans*. University of California Publications in American Archaeology and Ethnology, vol. 17, no. 1. Copyright © 1920 by the University of California Press.

Figure 4 (bottom). Prescott, W. H., *The Conquest of Mexico*. (Henry, Holt, and Company, 1922). Drawing by Keith Henderson, copyright © 1922 by Chatto and Windus.

Figure 8 (bottom left and right). *Florentine Codex: General History of the Things of New Spain*, vol. 3. Translated by C. E. Dibble and A. J. O.

Anderson. Copyright © 1950 by the School of American Research and the University of Utah Press.

Figure 12. Steward, Julian H., and Louis C. Faron, *Native Peoples of South America*. Copyright © 1959 by McGraw-Hill Book Company. (Border and insert map added.)

Figure 13. *The Atlas of Archaeology*, K. Branigan, consultant editor. Copyright © 1982 by Macdonald & Co. (Publishers) Ltd. United States edition by St Martin's Press, Inc. (scale added).

Figure 14. Courtesy of Alan L. Kolata.

Figure 16 (top). Squier, Ephraim George, *Peru: Incidents of Travel and Exploration in the Land of the Incas* (1877); reprinted 1973 by AMS Press, Inc.

Figures 16 (bottom), 19 (top). Demarest, Arthur A., *Viracocha: The Nature and Antiquity of the Andean High God*. Peabody Museum Monograph no. 6. Copyright © 1981 by the President and Fellows of Harvard College.

Figures 17, 18, 19 (bottom), 22. Guaman Poma de Ayala, Felipe, *Nueva Corónica y Buen Gobierno...* (ca. 1610–15). Copyright © 1936 by the Institut d'Ethnologie, Paris; reprinted 1968.

Figure 21. Hemming, John and Edward Ranney, *Monuments of the Incas* (Little, Brown and Company, 1982). Drawing courtesy of John Hemming.

Figure 23 (top). Townsend, Richard Frazer, *State and Cosmos in the Art of Tenochtitlan*. Dumbarton Oaks Studies in Pre-Columbian Art and Archaeology, number 20, Copyright © 1979 by the Trustees for Harvard University.

Figure 25. Sanders, William, and Barbara Price, *Mesoamerica: The Evolution of a Civilization*. Copyright © 1968 by Random House.

Illustrations in Figures 4 (top), 5, 6, 8 (top), 9, 10 (top), 15, 16 (bottom), 20, 23 (bottom), 24, and 26 were drafted by L. E. Demarest. Copyright © 1983 by the artist.

The following gave permission for the reproduction of textual material.

University of Oklahoma Press: Selections from *The Aztecs: People of the Sun*, by Alfonso Caso. Copyright © 1958 by the University of Oklahoma Press.

Viking Penguin Inc.: Selections from *The Aztecs: The History of the Indies of New Spain*, by Fray Diego Durán. Translated, with notes, by Doris Heyden and Fernando Horcasitas. Translation copyright © 1964 by the Orion Press, Inc.

Lawrence and Wishart: Quotation from *A Contribution to the Critique of Political Economy*, by Karl Marx. Copyright © 1971 by Lawrence and Wishart.

I
Introduction

A line of men moves slowly up a steep staircase toward the summit of a pyramid. As each man reaches the top, he is seized and pinioned across an altar. A priest approaches, holding a stone-bladed knife with both hands. Raising the knife above his head and concentrating his strength in the blade, the priest intones a prayer, then plunges the knife downward. The man on the altar dies in a shower of his own blood. His heart is torn out and placed in a bowl. His body is carried to the edge of the steps and dropped. As it rolls and bounces toward the bottom, another man is brought forward and stretched across the altar. Hundreds of people have perished since this ceremony started; hundreds more will die before it ends.

Beside the pyramid stands a rack displaying the skulls of tens of thousands of previous victims. Like the broken bodies accumulating at the foot of the staircase, the skulls are those of captives taken in battle. They have been sacrificed to feed the sun. If the sun is not nourished with the vigorous blood of warriors, he will grow too weak for his daily struggle against the forces of darkness, and the universe will be destroyed.

Today the sun is bright and strong, obviously fit for combat. But what of tomorrow? next week? next year? The threat of destruction never passes, and the demand for blood is unrelenting.

* * * * *

An old man sits unmoving in a dimly lighted room. Everything about him attests to his wealth and power. The clothing he wears and the room's furnishings are of the finest quality. Servants come and go, attending to his wishes. Several aides are conferring with him, their voices subdued and postures deferential. One of them asks questions and the others answer; the old man himself does not speak aloud. The interrogation concerns the crops growing on his farmlands and the preparations under way at one of his country estates, where he plans to spend the summer. Everyone can sense that he is deeply pleased, even though he does not smile or shift his gaze as he listens. Instead, he remains aloof and dignified, the perfect image of lordliness.

1

Indeed, this awesome elder is a king. He claims to be descended from the sun, and his subjects revere him as a god. He has been married several hundred times, but his first and most important wife is his sister. At the moment his happiness stems from the impending visit of his favorite son, the one he has chosen to inherit the throne.

This aged and incestuous ruler, presently conducting a normal day's business, has been dead for thirty-five years. His son, who succeeded him and will dine with him tonight, died three years ago.

* * * * *

Living men die to feed the sun, and dead men live to rule a nation. Surely we have wandered into the realm of nightmares, where everything familiar turns grotesque, and what we hope not to dream about comes to pass.

Quite the contrary. While the events described above are generalized reconstructions, they lie well within the limits of documented fact. Each episode is drawn from a culture that existed less than five hundred years ago. The scene of human sacrifice and skulls mounted on a rack portrays the Mexica Aztecs of Mexico.[1] The vision of a living corpse sitting in his palace depicts the Incas of Peru. As bizarre as these images may seem to twentieth-century Western minds, they were everyday realities for the Mexica and Inca, the two great imperial powers of the Americas on the eve of European discovery.

For sheer historical drama, few ancient civilizations can match the Mexica and Inca. Both cultures emerged during the thirteenth and fourteenth centuries A.D.—times of turmoil in Mesoamerica and the Central Andes.[2] Throughout this period powerful regional states clashed in contests for political and economic supremacy. In these viciously combative settings the Mexica and Inca appeared as small societies with unsophisticated cultures. Ignored or scorned by their potent and prestigious neighbors, they seemed destined to perish as obscure, almost accidental victims in the struggles of the mighty.

Yet the Mexica and Inca not only survived the bitter conflicts surrounding them, they prevailed. In the early 1400s these two peoples, hitherto so backward and unpromising, suddenly transformed themselves into the most efficient war machines in New World prehistory. Their armies began to march outward in campaigns of conquest. By 1500 they dominated the largest states ever formed in the native Americas—the Aztec and Inca Empires. From the depths of insignificance the Mexica and Inca had vaulted to unrivaled heights of power and affluence.

Still the dramas were unfinished. Only a few decades later, in final acts worthy of Sophocles or Shakespeare, each empire collapsed. In both cases the fall was so swift as to be measured in months. Ostensibly the Aztec and Inca Empires were destroyed by military force, but their defeats had a wildly improbable air. The conquering armies contained only a few *hundred* Spanish adventurers. In lands where soldiers could be mustered by the tens of thousands, the invading forces were so puny that they should have been negligible.

The significance of these events extends far beyond their histrionic quality. For archaeologists and anthropologists, the Mexica and Inca raise a series of highly important questions. Why were vast empires formed in Mesoamerica and the Central Andes in late prehistoric times? Why were the Mexica and Inca the peoples who formed them? Why did their empires collapse with such stunning rapidity? And finally, what do the rise and fall of the Aztec and Inca Empires tell us about the evolution of culture in general? It is these questions that we are setting out to answer.

Religion and empire

Our two opening vignettes are directly relevant to the problems posed above, for those episodes are glimpses into the state religions of the Mexica and Inca peoples. Massive human sacrifice to feed the sun and the treatment of dead kings as living beings may strike us as irrational in the extreme, but they were completely logical in their own ideological contexts. Furthermore, these practices and the beliefs underlying them were deeply implicated in the rise and fall of the Aztec and Inca Empires. The historical and anthropological questions we have asked cannot be answered without a consideration of Mexica and Inca religion.

No doubt these claims will seem surprising to many readers. In general, contemporary archaeology takes a limited approach to prehistoric ideologies. Most archaeologists simply disregard the topic. This neglect stems from a widespread view of religion as an essentially conservative force serving to maintain the status quo. Religious beliefs, runs the argument, are passive elements that react to other factors; they are non-causal and 'epiphenomenal'. Therefore, ideology can be safely ignored in studies of prehistoric culture change.

Archaeologists who disagree with this position in the abstract have had little success in providing counter-examples. Most archaeological investigations of religion have been iconographic analyses of prehistoric art styles. Despite the dangers inherent in the attempt to link symbols with their referents—the connections can be highly esoteric—iconographic studies have sometimes provided convincing identifications of specific deities or beliefs. However, the gods or concepts so identified have been isolated particulars whose relations to other aspects of culture remain vague. Hence ideology does indeed tend to appear as passive and static, even in the works of scholars who profess otherwise.

We contend that religion can in fact be a dynamic element in cultural transformations, and that the Mexica and Inca are concrete examples of such a process. In so doing we are trying to redress current inadequacies in archaeological explanations of culture change, but we are not proposing religion as a universal 'prime mover'. Instead, we are explicitly advocating a multicausal view of cultural evolution.

In brief, we will argue that manipulations of traditional religious concepts and rituals played crucial roles in the rise and fall of the Aztec and Inca Empires. In the second quarter of the fifteenth century Mexica and Inca leaders instituted specific ideological reforms. While these changes were intended to serve certain limited purposes, they also proved to be highly effective adaptations to the natural and cultural environments of Mesoamerica and the Central Andes, at least in the beginning. The new state religions gave the Mexica and Inca decisive advantages over their competitors and enabled both peoples to conquer vast territories in a remarkably short time. However, in the long run the very same ideological factors created internal cultural stresses—economic and political strains—that could not be resolved. In less than a century the problems had reached the point of crisis, and what the Spaniards toppled were two states destroying themselves from within.

After presenting the basic data, we will develop our models of 'ideological adaptation and maladaptation' by examining other hypotheses that have been advanced to explain the origins of the two empires. All of them are ultimately inadequate, and we will try to identify exactly where each one goes wrong. We will also pay close attention to the Mexica and Inca collapses, events which most archaeologists seem content to treat in purely descriptive terms. Our goal is to explain both the origins and the collapses in a manner that incorporates the strong points of previous hypotheses while avoiding their flaws and limitations.

Some basic definitions

Up to this point we have been scattering the words 'religion', 'ideology', and 'empire' around without defining them. We cannot continue to be so cavalier; vague terms lead only to confusion. On the other hand, overly specific definitions distort reality by creating artificially sharp distinctions between overlapping and interlocking cultural phenomena. We want to find a middle ground for our terms: precise enough to be meaningful, but not so precise as to be deceptive.

Religion and ideology are perhaps the most difficult terms to define. One source of confusion is that there are many kinds of ideology (e.g., political ideology or religious ideology). Throughout this work, whether explicitly stated or not, when we refer to ideology we invariably mean *religious* ideology—including not only formal religion, but also the various metaphysical beliefs, values, and behaviors that lie outside of the guidance of formalized religious institutions or dogmas. In this sense an *ideology* is a set of interrelated ideas that provides the members of a group with a rationale for their existence. It tells the members who they are and explains their relations to one another, to people outside the group, to the natural world, and to the cosmos. It also establishes rules for acting in accordance with those relationships. A formal *religion* is a particular kind of religious ideology, one based on beliefs in supernatural beings or forces, with a more standardized presentation of these beliefs and, generally, an institutional structure.

For the Mexica and Inca we can in many instances use the words religion and ideology interchangeably. In the modern world there are political and philosophical ideologies that are wholly divorced from religion. Such was not the case in native Mesoamerican and Central Andean civilizations, for which ideology was ultimately religious. In Mexica and Inca culture religious, political, and philosophical thought formed an integrated whole united by belief in a supernatural order. Sometimes subdivision of that whole into discrete categories can result in misleading impositions of modern Western ideology on native systems of belief.[3] Therefore, analyses of the Precolumbian ideologies must proceed with extreme caution and a constant awareness of the continuity and unity of Precolumbian belief systems.

We define an *empire* as a state encompassing a large territory and incorporating a number of previously autonomous, culturally hetero-geneous societies, one of which dominates the others. The dominant society, which has achieved its position by military force, exploits resources formerly controlled by the subordinate societies. While this definition of empire implies some sort of overarching administrative framework, that framework may take various forms, and it may be tightly organized or relatively loose. The exploitation of conquered peoples and territories may be continuous or sporadic.

We have added these qualifications because persons whose notions have been shaped by Old World examples may find that the Mexica state does not quite fit their concept of empire. 'Aztec Empire' is a traditional name in New World archaeology, and we think it is appropriate. The Mexica Aztecs did extend their authority over a vast territory, conquer other societies, and exploit their defeated enemies. Nonetheless, their provincial administrative system was very loose, and some readers may favor the designations 'macro-state' or 'hegemony'. Those who do should feel free to make the substitution. We will use these terms ourselves as synonyms for 'empire'.

Documentary sources

Most of our primary data on the Mexica and Inca are drawn from so-called 'ethnohistorical' documents, written accounts dating to the sixteenth and seventeenth centuries. These documents fall into three broad categories: Spanish chronicles, official administrative records, and the works of native Mesoamerican and Andean authors. The classes overlap with one another, and the divisions are to some extent arbitrary. Here we wish only to give a brief characterization of the sources, and precise distinctions are unnecessary.

The chronicles are descriptive accounts of Aztec and Inca history and culture written by Spaniards of varying backgrounds. Many of the earliest chroniclers were conquistadors.[4] Some of them had taken part in the first battles in Mexico and Peru; others had arrived shortly thereafter and had done their fighting elsewhere. Examples of these conquistador-authors include Bernal Díaz del Castillo and Andrés de Tapia in Mexico, along with Pedro Pizarro and Pedro de Cieza de León in Peru. Other chroniclers were officials of the Colonial governments (e.g., Francisco López de Gómara in Mexico; Juan Polo de Ondegardo and Pedro Sarmiento de Gamboa in Peru). Still others were priests (Bernardino de Sahagún, Diego Durán, Miguel Cabello Valboa, Bernabé Cobo, etc.).

The second group of sources, official records, consists of reports and other documents prepared for Colonial civil and religious administrations. This body of evidence includes such items as the reports of census-takers (the Mexican and Andean *Relaciones Geográficas*, Alonso de Zorita, Iñigo Ortiz de Zúñiga, etc.). There are also descriptions of local religious beliefs and rituals submitted by parish priests engaged in the attempt to convert the natives to Christianity (e.g., Francisco de Avila, Pablo Joseph de Arriaga, etc.). In addition, archives in Mexico, Peru, and Spain contain huge numbers of depositions taken in legal cases—disputes over land tenure, rights to irrigation water, and so on. These legal papers contain valuable anthropological data, and during the past few decades ethnohistorians have begun to publish and analyze some of them. Also compiled for official purposes were early dictionaries of native languages, which constitute another useful set of data.

If one considers the Aztec and Inca Empires separately, the Spanish sources are not entirely equivalent. In general, the Aztec data are much better. In Mexico the Spaniards consolidated their power and established a stable colonial government within about two years, and they began to record their observations of indigenous cultures almost immediately. In contrast, the first few decades of Spanish rule in Peru were full of factional disputes, political assassinations, and civil strife among the colonists. In this atmosphere of violence hardly anyone was interested in collecting data on the Inca Empire. Aside from a few brief narrations of the conquest itself, accounts of Inca culture did not begin to appear until about twenty years after the Spaniards' arrival. During that interval, short as it was, native societies had been severely disrupted, and a great deal of information was lost.

However, the most striking difference between the Mesoamerican and Central Andean data lies in the works of native authors. In Mesoamerica native sources are both more numerous and much closer in time to the

Precolumbian world. There are accounts of the Aztec Empire written after the conquest in Spanish by Indian authors drawing on older native records (e.g., Alva Ixtlilxochitl, Alvarado Tezozomoc, Chimalpahin). We also have the codices, records set down on bark paper in the traditional Aztec picture-writing. Some of them date to the first few years of the Colonial era (e.g., Codex Mendoza, Codex Magliabecchiano, Matrícula de Tributos). Others may even be *pre-conquest* (e.g., the Borgia, Borbonicus, and Nuttall Codices). In Mexico the Aztec peoples began to speak for themselves at an early date, and they spoke relatively often.

In the Andean world native voices were fewer and later. In fact, there were only two full-blooded Indian chroniclers, Felipe Guaman Poma de Ayala and Joan de Santacruz Pachacuti, neither of whom was ethnically Inca. Both of them wrote their works some eighty years after the conquest, around 1610-15.[5] The only other figure who might be assigned to the category of 'native author', Garcilaso de la Vega, fits uncomfortably. He was born in Peru, the son of a Spanish father and an Inca mother. However, he did not set down his description of Inca culture and history until the early seventeenth century, by which time he was an old man who had lived most of his life in Spain.

All of the sources present difficulties, which we will discuss in more detail later. Here it is enough to say that the Spanish documents show varying degrees of consistency and reliability. Even the most careful writers did not fully understand Mexica or Inca culture, and they sometimes reinterpreted and Europeanized alien concepts presented to them by their informants. The works of native authors can be used to balance ethnocentric Spanish distortions, but comparative study has shown them to be full of historical inaccuracies. Some of the native chroniclers compounded the problem with confusing styles, ambiguous remarks, and internal factual inconsistency. Therefore, the ethnohistorical data must be used with great care; interpretation requires constant comparison and weighing of the evidence.

Archaeology, ethnohistory, and anthropological theory

Of course, ethnohistorical accounts are not the only kind of information at our disposal: we also have the rich archaeological records of Mesoamerica and the Central Andes. We intend to use both types of data in our analyses. If we must depend primarily on documentary sources for some questions, for others we will rely heavily on archaeological evidence and interpretations—especially in Chapter 4, where we will examine conflicting interpretations of the rise of the Aztec and Inca Empires. Our goal is to use archaeology and ethnohistory as complementary, rather than mutually exclusive, approaches to the past.

Indeed, in the past twenty-five years it has become obvious that the written records of ethnohistory and the material remains of archaeology can be profitably combined in the study of late prehistoric New World civilizations.[6] The two sets of data can serve as cross-checks on one another, with each helping to increase our understanding of the other. This statement is particularly applicable to investigations of social, political, and religious institutions, where the fragmentary documentary record has the limitations noted above and the archaeological remains are less readily interpretable than materials relating to technology or subsistence economy. By interdigitating the two kinds of evidence, we can arrive at a much fuller picture than either alone can provide.

However, the value of combining documentary accounts and archaeological evidence extends far beyond their ability to cross-check and reinforce each other in the investigation of specific aspects of Mexica and Inca society. Taken together, archaeological and ethnohistorical data can be a powerful test for evaluating anthropological theories of cultural evolution. In Kent Flannery's words:

> Most recent evolutionary studies by ethnologists are *synchronic*: they take a series of unrelated, contemporary societies on different levels of development and, by comparing them, try to imagine which institutional changes could have turned the simpler into the more complex...The ethnologists quite rightly point to the richer amounts of detail available in their contemporary societies; yet all their reconstructions amount to 'just so' stories, because there is almost no society for which time depth and rigorous proof of evolutionary causes are available.[7]

In contrast, archaeological and ethnohistorical data are both *diachronic*. When we can combine them, we can get a richly detailed view of the ways in which a single society or cultural tradition changed through time. We can then provide a comprehensive analysis of the dynamics of change—the 'rigorous proof of evolutionary causes' Flannery demands. In this way we can identify the strengths and weaknesses of competing theories on cultural evolution.

Specifically, we believe that a combination of archaeological and ethnohistorical data is the best way to begin working toward a general statement of ideology's role in cultural evolution. This problem is one of the thorniest in anthropology, and at present there is no truly satisfactory solution. Nonetheless, by reviewing a wide range of anthropological theories in the light of the Aztec and Inca case studies, we will try in Chapter 5 to show just how crucial the question is. In the end, every theory that purports to explain cultural evolution fails—almost invariably because of its inability to deal with ideology. Conversely, those current theories that are directly concerned with ideology have been unable to explain cultural evolution. If anthropological theory is to progress, we must find a new synthesis.

As we shall see (Chapter 5), in recent years several anthropologists from very different schools of thought have reached exactly the same conclusion. As a result, these scholars are paying increased attention to ideology as an active element of culture. Their numbers are few, and the Aztec and Inca data show that they have not yet gone far enough in their analyses. Nonetheless, these cultural anthropologists do at least seem to be moving toward a new synthesis. If archaeologists want to understand cultural evolution, we must do likewise. We cannot continue to treat ideology as static or passive. We must recognize that ideology can be a dynamic force, and we must seek new generalizations about its role in cultural change. While it may be too early for definitive statements, we hope that this comparative study of the Aztec and Inca Empires will be a step in the right direction.

Notes to Chapter 1

1 'Aztec' is a generic term for the late prehistoric cultures of the Valley of Mexico. The Mexica were the foremost of the Aztec peoples at the time of the Spanish Conquest.
2 Mesoamerica and the Central Andes are archaeological culture areas. They include large parts of Mexico and Peru, respectively, but their borders do not follow modern national boundaries. More precise definitions are given in Chapters 2 and 3.
3 We are speaking here only of ideas. For analytical purposes the religious and political *behaviors* of the Mexica and Inca peoples are somewhat more separable. Nonetheless, they were tightly interwoven, and any separation is to some degree artificial. In the end, the Aztec and Inca Empires can only be understood if religious and political ideas and behaviors are viewed as an integrated whole (see Chapters 4 and 5).
4 The conquistadors never referred to themselves as 'soldiers' (*soldados*). The word did exist in sixteenth-century Spanish, but it was used for men who had sold their services to professional military leaders and were bound to obey those leaders' commands. The men who toppled the Aztec and Inca Empires were taking a chance at wealth and glory, not drawing a salary, and they felt free to argue with their leaders. They called themselves 'people', 'men', 'Spaniards', 'Christians', 'horsemen', 'footmen', and 'conquerors'—'first conquerors' if they had taken part in the initial decisive battles. In their minds 'soldier' was a derogatory term combining the negative connotations of 'mercenary' and 'servant' (Lockhart 1972: 17-22).
5 Guaman Poma's (1936) copiously illustrated, 1200-page letter to the King of Spain is the closest thing we have to a Peruvian codex.
6 For example, see Menzel 1959; Rowe 1967; Murra 1962; Morris and Thompson 1970; Morris 1972, 1974; Murra and Morris 1976; Conrad 1977.
7 Flannery 1972: 404.

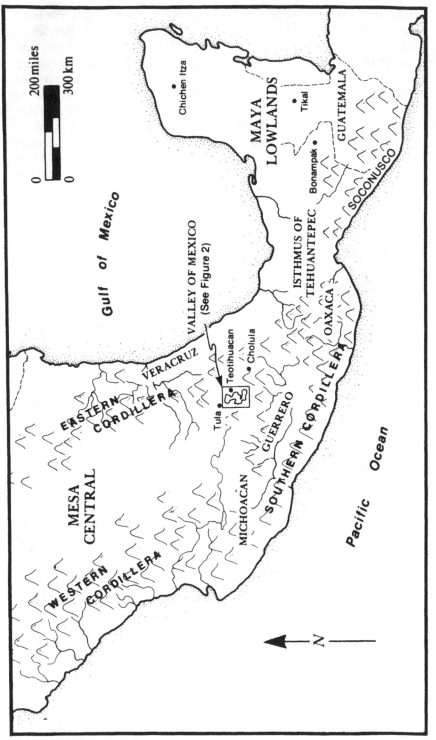

Fig. 1. Mesoamerica

2

The Aztec imperial expansion

The astonishingly rapid rise, expansion, and fall of the Aztec Empire is one of the most dramatic episodes in human history. The setting for this episode is itself suitably dramatic: the rugged highlands of Central Mexico. The dominant geographical feature of Mexico is the great 'V' of the eastern and western Mexican *cordilleras*, between which lies the *Mesa Central*, the high plateau of central and northern Mexico (Figure 1). Beyond the 'V' of the two ranges and the *Mesa*, the land drops sharply to the lush tropical lowlands of the eastern and western coasts.[1]

The central plateau itself has a complex geography, varying in altitude between 1,000 and 4,000 meters. The northern portion of the *Mesa* is covered by inhospitable deserts, traditionally the home of nomadic or semi-nomadic 'barbarians'. The southern part has been broken up by continuous volcanic activity into a series of intermontane basins. One of these southern basins, the Valley of Mexico, held a network of interconnected shallow lakes and lagoons ringed by active volcanoes (Figure 2). It was the fertile volcanic soils of this valley which supported a series of expansionistic civilizations.

The last, perhaps the greatest, of these Central Mexican expansion states was encountered by Cortés and his followers in 1519. When the Spaniards crossed the mountain ring and descended into the Valley of Mexico, they beheld the astonishing cities which formed the core of the vast Aztec Empire. So impressive was the sight of these populous lacustrine capitals that Bernal Díaz, one of Cortés's soldiers, wrote that the Spaniards had not been sure if what appeared before them was real or a hallucination.[2] At the time of the Spanish Conquest, the empire controlled by the Aztec cities sprawled across Mesoamerica from the valleys of the Central Mexican highlands to the tropical lowland coasts of Guatemala (Figure 7).

Yet this empire was dominated by the Mexica,[3] a people who had entered the Mesoamerican scene quite late as a small group despised by their neighbors as backward northern barbarians. The Mexica histories tell us that it was only in the mid-fourteenth century that they had settled on their island capital of Tenochtitlan. How was it that this

Fig. 2. The Valley of Mexico

lowly group could have risen so rapidly to power in the Valley of Mexico? What were the causes of their frenzied imperialist expansion to the lands beyond? How was it that so vast an empire, encompassing millions of people, could be so fragile and unstable that it crumbled into disarray before Cortés's few hundred men? It is these enigmas which will be explored here.

Historical background

The Aztec achievements can be understood only in terms of the ancient Mesoamerican tradition upon which the Aztecs built. While our knowledge of the Aztec Empire itself is derived from the voluminous ethnohistoric accounts of Spanish conquistadors and friars, and their Indian informants, the earlier civilizations of Middle America are largely known to us through archaeological remains. Interpretation of the archaeological record is aided by reference to the codices, the bark-paper pictographic texts of the peoples of Mexico, and by the hieroglyphic inscriptions of the Maya civilization to the east. Nonetheless, the often scanty material remains are our principal basis for reconstructing the evolution of Mesoamerican culture.

This evolution was not a steady, continuous process of gradually increasing cultural complexity. Rather, the picture revealed by the archaeological record is one of cycles of development, expansion, and collapse (Table 1). These cycles begin with the Olmec civilization of the lush tropical lowlands of the Gulf coast. The Olmec and related peoples built Mesoamerica's first complex society with many of the same economic, social, and religious elements that would recur in subsequent civilizations. After the decline of the Olmec, the focus of cultural innovation and evolution in Mesoamerica shifted to the Valley of Mexico. From about A.D. 100 to 600, Teotihuacan, Mesoamerica's first truly urban center, held sway over a vast economic empire. Indeed, Teotihuacan was only the first in a series of Valley of Mexico states which dominated extensive portions of Mesoamerica. Teotihuacan's commercial, and probably even political, influence was felt as far away as the Maya centers of the jungles of northern Guatemala.

One of the long-standing controversies among Mesoamerican archaeologists centers on the question of why the Valley of Mexico came to dominate Mesoamerica during the Teotihuacan epoch. The answers given by archaeologists to this question for the Teotihuacan expansion foreshadow the controversies that we shall discover in the Aztec case (Chapter 4, below).

The ecology of the Valley of Mexico was one factor in determining the importance of the region and major features of its sequence of expansion states. The fertile soils and lacustrine environment of the valley provided unlimited agricultural resources, as well as diverse sources of animal protein. Furthermore, William Sanders and others (see Chapter 4) have argued that the ecological *diversity* of the region necessitated exchange of products and thus fostered the rise of Teotihuacan's market economy and expansive nature.

Table 1. *Chronological framework for Central Mexican prehistory*

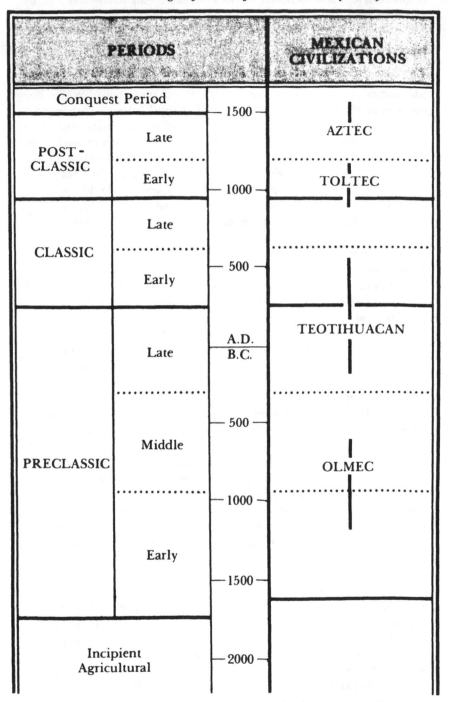

PERIODS			MEXICAN CIVILIZATIONS
Conquest Period		1500	
POST-CLASSIC	Late		AZTEC
	Early	1000	TOLTEC
CLASSIC	Late		
	Early	500	
			TEOTIHUACAN
PRECLASSIC	Late	A.D. B.C.	
		500	
	Middle		OLMEC
		1000	
	Early	1500	
Incipient Agricultural		2000	

In any case, there is no question but that Teotihuacan had a vigorous market economy. Archaeological researches there have uncovered a large market place with a restricted (state-controlled?) entrance.[4] As in Aztec times, a wealthy merchant class may have controlled local craft workshops as well as trade with distant regions. Distributions of durable goods, storage areas, and workshops have even led to the identification of a merchants' quarter.[5] The artifactual remains show that these merchants were active in obtaining products not native to the valley itself. Teotihuacan's interest in such products led to the establishment of distant outposts in Veracruz and highland Guatemala.

While these economic features were unquestionably of great importance to the Teotihuacan urban state, it is equally apparent that ideology was a vital concern of the people and a source of power for their leaders. The great center at Teotihuacan, with its massive ceremonial constructions, intricate and esoteric murals, and industries engaged in mass-production of religious objects (e.g., figurines and censers) clearly controlled an elaborate state religion. René Millon (1973, 1976) has suggested that Teotihuacan's role as a pilgrimage center was crucial in its rise to power. Beneath the site's towering Pyramid of the Sun was a cave with a spring, a geographical feature considered sacred in most Mesoamerican religions. Doris Heyden (1975) has argued that the presence of such a sacred shrine could help to explain the initiation and early development of urbanism at Teotihuacan. Later Teotihuacan representations and iconography in murals, vase paintings, and figurines demonstrate the development of warrior cults sanctioned by the state religion.[6] This evidence suggests that, as with the Aztec, the state religion may have played a major role in the more militant aspects of the spread of Teotihuacan influence.

While the processes of the rise and expansion of Teotihuacan are a source of controversy, the causes of its collapse are truly an enigma. There are indications that before A.D. 650 internal troubles had already begun to weaken the Teotihuacan state.[7] By A.D. 750 it was rapidly declining, and large portions of the capital were abandoned.[8] During the following centuries northern semi-nomadic peoples, *chichimeca*, reportedly began to move into the Valley of Mexico from more arid lands to the north and northwest.[9] The power vacuum left by the collapse of Teotihuacan allowed these less sophisticated groups to settle in the fertile lands of the northern part of the basin. Most of these intruders were probably actually Mesoamericanized agriculturalists, settlers from the archaeologically identified northern and western fringe of Teotihuacan's sphere of influence.[10] Others may have been true 'barbarians' (*teochichimeca*), nomadic or semi-nomadic hunting bands from the great deserts of the northern *Mesa Central*.[11] After A.D. 900, an amalgam of these peoples (warlike nomads, northern agriculturalists, and the remnants of the Teotihuacan populations) formed the next expansionist hegemony of Central Mexico, the 'Toltec Empire'.

At this point the principal sources of our information begin to shift from archaeology to ethnohistory:[12] many of the native histories recorded by the Spanish chroniclers open with narratives on the beginning of this 'Postclassic' epoch. Unfortunately, this shift to historical sources does *not*, as one might expect, result in a more detailed knowledge of the period. In some respects, our understanding of the first half of the Postclassic period is inferior to that of the Teotihuacan era, which has been more thoroughly researched archaeologically. Indeed, in cases where Postclassic archaeology and ethnohistory overlap, they are often contradictory. For example, the legends of the Aztec histories harkened back to a time when a marvelous Toltec people, great scholars and craftsmen, ruled over Early Postclassic Mexico from their beautiful capital of Tollan. Yet the archaeological excavations of this legendary Tollan, the ruins of Tula, have revealed a rather shoddy ceremonial center with constructions and sculptures that would have been an embarrassment to earlier Mesoamerican artisans.[13]

The discrepancies between the ethnohistorical sources themselves are even more shocking. Few dates given are in agreement, even for major events of the epoch such as the founding of Tula or the fall of that Toltec capital. Indeed, if taken at face value the various dynastic lists recorded by the native histories can be synchronized only through alignments which would have some rulers reigning for over a century and others dying twice![14] Ethnohistorians do not always agree on even the broad outlines of the major legends. Perhaps the most reported event of the Early Postclassic is the tale of the reign of the great Toltec god-king, Topiltzin Quetzalcoatl: the saga of his attempted religious reforms, his disgrace and fall from power, and, finally, his flight from the capital of Tula to a mysterious land to the east. Not only do the details of this story vary greatly between versions, but it is not even clear whether the Quetzalcoatl of this legend was among the first or very last kings of the Toltec epoch.[15]

These problems with the ethnohistorical sources have numerous and complex causes; only a few can be mentioned here. In addition to the expected ethnocentric perspective of some of the conquistadors and friars, even more serious problems arise from the regional chauvinism of native authors, informants, and codices. Each center had its own, usually self-aggrandizing, version of the history of Central Mexico. Indeed, many of the major chronicles are based upon state histories constructed under the direction of local leaders in order to justify their succession to power and glorify the history of their dynasty and their city-state.

Similarly, much of the chronological confusion and inconsistency is also due to regional factors: most ethnohistorians now believe that various year-counts were used in Central Mexico, each giving a different date notation for the same event.[16] The chronological chaos is further compounded by the calendric system used throughout Mesoamerica, the 'calendar round', in which any specific date recurred every fifty-two years.[17] Thus, a date which could correlate with the Christian calendar date of A.D. 1200 could also be interpreted as A.D. 1252 or A.D. 1148. H. B. Nicholson (1978: 324) ends a recent review of the jumbled and contradictory ethnohistoric chronologies with the conclusion that 'events' dated before A.D. 1370 should be regarded not as facts, but only as hypotheses to be tested by future research.

The greatest problem involved is the essentially mythical or allegorical nature of much Precolumbian 'history'. Because of their cyclical conception of time, Mesoamerican peoples would project events backward to create a mythical precedent in an invented or distorted account of earlier times. Conversely, their histories would often mold more recent events into the structure of earlier occurrences or revered legends. In view of these problems and other distortive factors, contemporary scholars are taking an increasingly cautious attitude toward the sources. For example, Nigel Davies, in a recent review of the ethnohistory of the Toltec period, has noted that Aztec descriptions of the Toltec state and its fabulous capital of Tollan (Tula) confused the historic Tollan with the earlier, more impressive center of Teotihuacan, as well as with a generalized mythic concept of 'Tollan', the archetypal sublime city (Davies 1977: ch. 2). Furthermore, Aztec-period leaders may have deliberately exaggerated their accounts of Tollan, since most of the dynasties of the period claimed direct or indirect descent from the prestigious Toltecs (Davies 1977: ch. 1).

While the details may be garbled, the broad outlines and central themes of Postclassic history are highlighted by the ethnohistorical sources. Fortunately, it is precisely these broad themes that interest us here. Some of the distortive factors discussed above actually illustrate one of the major themes: the Mesoamerican obsession with legitimizing power through a prestigious heritage—the elite's need to justify its rule through historical and mythical ties with the past.

The elite concern with highlighting, or even creating, an illustrious ancestry probably received special emphasis within the Toltec tribute state which ruled over the northern Basin of Mexico between about A.D. 950 and 1200. Though later histories exaggerated its extent and magnificence, the Toltec polity was probably a loose military alliance between peoples without a Mesoamerican past (barbarian *chichimeca* and semi-civilized northern agriculturalists) and peoples with deeper roots in the region (remnants of the disintegrated Teotihuacan state). The ambivalent attitude of Postclassic peoples toward their mixed ancestry is reflected in the later accounts of this period. These legends glorified the rustic, vigorous *chichimec* stock as exemplified by the hunter-warrior god-king Mixcoatl, founder of the Toltec state. Yet the histories also emphasized the civilized, skilled, and sophisticated characteristics of the

Toltecs. These cultural roots were personified in the priest-ruler Topiltzin Quetzalcoatl through his associations with older Mesoamerican peoples like the Nonoalca and the Olmeca, his connections to established southern centers like Cholula, and his evangelism for the cult of Quetzalcoatl, an ancient Mesoamerican deity.

In addition to the elite obsession with a legitimizing ancestry, the Quetzalcoatl saga also illustrates a second major theme of the Postclassic era: the struggle between the militaristic cults of war and human sacrifice and more peaceful aspects of Mesoamerican religion and culture. Scholars now agree that the peaceful nature of pre-Toltec cultures was greatly exaggerated by earlier archaeologists and historians. Nonetheless, there can be little doubt that increasing militarism and human sacrifice were, in fact, definitive characteristics of the Postclassic era. The native histories themselves show an awareness of this trend, which was allegorically illustrated in the famous struggle between the apotheosized Toltec hero Topiltzin Quetzalcoatl and his more militant opponents.[18] On a divine level, some versions tell of the temptation and deception of the priest-god Quetzalcoatl, leader of a peaceful religious cult, by the devious and bloodthirsty god Tezcatlipoca. In other versions, the conflict is represented as a more mundane power struggle between the idealistic prince Topiltzin Quetzalcoatl, advocate of peaceful policies and opponent of human sacrifice, and a more warlike faction within his Toltec state. In both cases, the forces of war and human sacrifice win out and the confrontation ends with the disgrace of Quetzalcoatl and his flight from Tula. Regardless of their precise historical correlates, the different versions of the Quetzalcoatl legend accurately portray the rapidly changing nature of Mesoamerican religion in the Postclassic period.

To judge from both ethnohistory and the sculptural representations at Tula itself, the Toltecs had inherited the elaborate pantheon of earlier Mesoamerican peoples. This pantheon included an infinite number of gods, patrons of every imaginable natural and cultural phenomenon: astral bodies, rain, war, disease, chthonic elements, temporal units, calendric cycles, etc. Yet, rather than being a straightforward one-to-one correspondence of deities with phenomena, Mesoamerican religion is exasperatingly complex; its entities are fluid, overlapping, and manifold, and its conceptual logic still defies analysis by Western minds. The most convincing generalizations about Mesoamerican religion view the pantheon as a personification of specific segments or nodes in the sacred cosmic order, the continuum of time and space itself.[19]

While they inherited this elaborate cosmology from the Teotihuacan epoch, the Postclassic peoples of Central Mexico were gradually shifting emphases, stressing certain manifold deities like Tezcatlipoca and combining other gods or aspects of gods with *chichimec* divinities and Toltec heroes.[20] Of particular interest to us here is the gradual shift in ritual presented allegorically in the Topiltzin Quetzalcoatl legend: the elaboration of cults of human sacrifice.

Human sacrifice itself is one of the most ancient aspects of Mesoamerican culture. Indeed, ritual decapitation is a widespread feature throughout the New World.[21] There is evidence for human sacrifice among Mesoamerica's earliest complex societies, and it may be present even earlier among the hunter-gatherers of the arid Tehuacan valley.[22] Millennia later (ca. 400 B.C.) sculptures in Oaxaca portray dead and mutilated captives.[23] Such human sacrifice in association with warfare had become widespread by the Classic period (A.D. 200 to 700/900). Decapitated prisoners are depicted in a Classic period mural at the Mayan lowland site of Bonampak.[24] The art of both Teotihuacan and later Tula portrays military orders.[25] In later Aztec times such warrior cults were major participants in rituals of human sacrifice and cannibalism.

In keeping with the increasing militarism of the times, Postclassic peoples intensified this tradition of human sacrifice, especially in those cults relating to warfare (Demarest ms.). Both the ethnohistorical accounts and the sculptures found at Tula itself suggest that the Postclassic militaristic cults of human sacrifice had taken their general form by the Toltec period. Toltec sculptures[26] at Tula and its distant Toltec-Maya sister city, Chichen Itza, include *tzompantli*, racks on which the skulls of sacrificed victims were displayed, and *chacmools*, reclining stone figures with a hollow basin on their stomachs to receive the hearts of sacrificial victims. Also portrayed are processions of warriors and their totemic emblems: jaguars, coyotes, and eagles (in some representations the eagles are shown devouring human hearts). The Tula sculptures indicate that cults of human sacrifice had become a major aspect of the state religion of Toltec times.

The Quetzalcoatl legend suggests that the rapid intensification of human sacrifice was somewhat alarming even to the Toltecs themselves. Once again, the sources manifest the Postclassic identity crisis: an ambivalent attitude toward warfare, sacrifice, and even the peoples' own ethnic ancestry. This ambivalence reflects the dynamic imbalance characteristic of Postclassic Mesoamerica, as military states unsuccessfully attempted to amalgamate diverse ethnic elements and shifting ideological concepts into a unified structure. The failure of these attempts can be seen in the disintegration of the Toltec hegemony at about A.D. 1200.

The small competing city-states of the post-Toltec period inherited the conflicting and unresolved Postclassic themes. New waves of *chichimec* immigrants entered the valley, merging with the remnants of the Toltecs.[27] In fact, the very term 'Toltec' shifted in meaning, thereafter signifying the older, more 'civilized' element in the Valley of Mexico. As the militarism of the city-states continually increased, so did the ideological battle. Cults of sacrifice intensified and the militant aspects of ancient deities were stressed. Some groups developed their own divine patrons, often a fusion of earlier gods with apotheosized Toltec or *chichimec* heroes.[28] Meanwhile, each center worked to legitimize its claims to power through Toltec ancestry. Such an ancestry could be obtained either through creative mythography or through marriage alliances with rulers having better established claims to Toltec descent.

This fierce ideological warfare has left its scars on the ethnohistorical record: contradictory dynastic lists, incompatible versions of historical events, and patron deities uneasily forced into the already bewildering Mesoamerican pantheon. Yet none of the competing military city-states was really able to pull together the centrifugal economic, political, and ideological forces of the Postclassic. That successful union was a destiny reserved for the least prestigious of their number, the scorned and despised Mexica Aztec.

Early Mexica society and religion

As we have seen, in the thirteenth and fourteenth centuries the Valley of Mexico had been balkanized into competing city-states and fragile alliances, each battling militarily and ideologically for the claim to be the Toltec heir. By the beginning of the fourteenth century, two loose confederations appeared to be heading toward a major confrontation. On the northwestern side of the lake system (Figure 2) the Tepanecs, with their alliance centered on the town of Azcapotzalco, were rapidly expanding in influence, despite their lack of a legitimizing quasi-Toltec ancestry. On the eastern shore of Lake Texcoco another heterogeneous group, the Acolhua, had a more established hegemony, dominated by a sequence of capitals: Coatlichan, Huexotla, and, finally, Texcoco. Amidst the growing alliances of the Tepanec and Acolhua, smaller polities fought for survival. On the southern sweetwater lakes, centers like Xochimilco and the more powerful Chalco were aided in their struggle by agricultural wealth; there, the highly productive 'floating garden' (*chinampa*) system of lake-bed agriculture was being utilized by post-Toltec times, if not earlier.[29] Another strategy was used by the center of Culhuacan, the last remnant of the original Toltec state; the Culhua dynasties traded off sons and daughters of their noble Toltec blood in order to win over threatening neighbors.[30] Across this Darwinian political landscape, an insignificant little group, the Mexica, wandered in search of a land of their own.

The origins of the Mexica remain obscure. They were probably one of the many Toltec-influenced northern groups that entered the Valley of Mexico after the fall of Tula. All of these Late Postclassic valley peoples have been called Aztecs, but specific terms (e.g., Mexica, Tepanec, Acolhua) designate particular ethnic or political groups.[31] The legendary accounts of the migrations of the small Mexica group

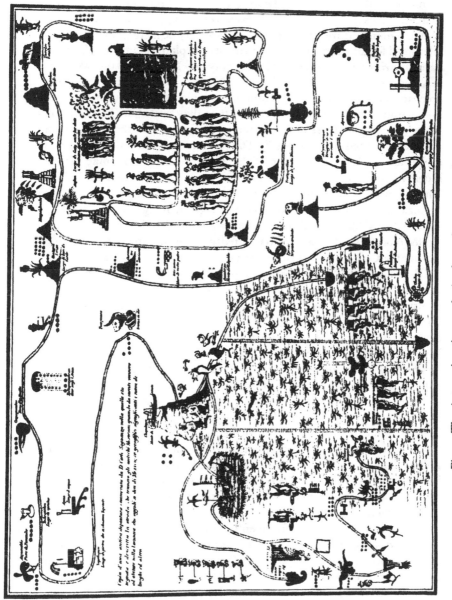

Fig. 3. The Aztec migration myth. A schematic representation from a sixteenth-century codex (the *Mapa de Sigüenza*).

Figure 3) were recounted by Sahagún and other chroniclers,[32] and the details of their wanderings have been thoroughly analyzed and debated by modern ethnohistorians.[33] Despite this careful scrutiny of numerous sources, the early history of the Mexica remains poorly understood.

While some features of the migration tale may be factual, the Mexicas' later need for a legitimizing Toltec ancestry explains many details of the native chronicles' accounts. After a stay at Tula itself, the Mexica, despised for their barbarism,[34] are said to have been driven from one area to another, invariably stopping at places with strong Toltec associations. For example, we are told that they settled at Chapultepec, there suffering a devastating defeat and diaspora at the hands of a coalition of their persecutors.[35] This event draws on Chapultepec's earlier associations as the camp of the last Toltec king, Huemac. There Huemac committed suicide in despair over the disintegration of his kingdom and the diaspora of the Toltec peoples.[36] After their defeat, the Mexica survivors are said to have been given refuge by the Culhua state.[37] As we have noted, Culhuacan was considered to be a center of Toltec blood, and the sources do pointedly emphasize that while residing among the Culhua the Mexica became 'related to them by marriage'.[38]

Obviously, the Mexica migration must be seen in the light of both the general Aztec striving for Toltec ancestry and the Mexicas' rewriting of history after their rise to power in 1428. At that time, the ruler Itzcoatl burned all earlier codices, and new historical and religious texts were drafted, versions more in keeping with the imperial ambitions of the Mexica leaders (see below, pp. 32-8).

The Mexica wanderings are reported to end with the founding of their capital, Tenochtitlan, on an uninhabited island in the western marshes of Lake Texcoco. This event occurred on a disputed date in the early to mid-fourteenth century.[39] We are told that thirteen years later the Mexica founded their sister-city to the north, Tlatelolco.[40] Again, the work of the imperial mythographers at Tenochtitlan can be suspected; archaeological excavations have discovered much earlier remains on both islands, and the evidence indicates that Tlatelolco was the older city, dating back to at least the early thirteenth century,[41] and probably much earlier.

In any case, by the mid-fourteenth century the Mexica were settled on their dual island homeland of Tenochtitlan-Tlatelolco. At this time, they became vassals of the powerful Tepanec alliance, which controlled the mainland to the west. Earlier the Mexica had occasionally served under other valley polities as mercenaries or tributaries, and, if we can believe their histories, they had gained a reputation for ferocity.[42] Continuing as part-time warriors for the Tepanecs, they were gradually drawn into the political schemes of the Tepanec tyrant, Tezozomoc, ruler of Azcapotzalco. The Mexicas' continuing acculturation and cultural evolution were undoubtedly accelerated by their participation in the

Tepanec alliance. The Tepanecs trained the Mexica warriors for their later role as military imperialists and provided a model of highly stratified society that would encourage the ambitions of the Mexicas' own developing warrior class.

It is extremely difficult to ascertain the precise nature of Mexica society prior to their sudden rise to imperial power in 1428, despite numerous descriptions in the chronicles and codices. In some instances, later chronicles unconvincingly projected back in time the political and social structure of the imperial age. In other cases, codices and histories portray the early Mexica with an almost Rousseauian nostalgia, describing them as a rustic group with a totally egalitarian social and political structure. Again, the inconsistencies may be partly the result of the Mexica imperial elite's later rewriting of history.

Yet much of the contradictory nature of the evidence on the early Mexica is due to the dynamic nature of their development; Mexica political and social institutions were probably undergoing continuous change in response to their varying fortunes and their rapid cultural evolution. Specific characterizations would only apply to a particular moment in time. However, given the near-absence of relevant archaeological data, the chronology of Mexica evolution can only be assumed on a very general level. The situation is exacerbated by accounts which confuse the features of earlier and later institutions and by fifteenth-century state propagandists' attempts to create historical precedents or allegorical justifications for the new imperial order.

Nonetheless, through a highly critical approach to the primary sources, modern scholars have been able to offer general characterizations of pre-imperial Mexica society.[43] In these discussions of early Mexica society, one particular institution, the *calpulli* (plural *calpullin*), is invariably described as the center of Mexica life.[44] The *calpulli* was the basic unit of social membership in early Mexica society, as well as the principal residential unit. In the mid-fourteenth century, there were reported to be fifteen such units in the Mexicas' newly founded capital of Tenochtitlan.[45] Members communally owned *calpulli* land, which was inalienable. However, usufruct of any given tract of land was assigned to a particular family and was passed on to heirs, provided that they continued to cultivate the plots of the communally owned lands.[46] The *calpullin* also served as organizational units for other functions: each *calpulli* ward had its own school and temple, and *calpulli* warriors often fought together as a squadron.[47]

In addition to its economic and organizational functions, the *calpulli* was some type of kinship group. Our sixteenth-century sources, the Spanish chroniclers, were somewhat perplexed as to the exact nature of the *calpullin*'s kinship structure. Alonso de Zorita discussed this problem, noting their kinship role, as well as their other functions as general neighborhoods, tribute units, and so on.[48] Furthermore, though they were unified endogamous groups, the *calpullin* apparently had internal ranking. Nineteenth-century historians such as Morgan (1877) and Bandelier (1878, 1880) argued that they were true clans, yet the internal stratification described by the sources fails to fit conventional definitions of clan structure. A widely accepted solution to this problem, first proposed by Kirchhoff (1959), is that the *calpulli* was a type of 'conical clan': a group which was interrelated, yet possessed internal stratification of a hereditary nature.[49]

While there was social and economic stratification within the Mexica *calpullin*, there were also differences between them. Some were more prestigious, wealthy, or powerful than others, and it is reported that certain *calpullin* owned more and better lands.[50] Occupational specialization, which would certainly entail differences in wealth and power, existed in some *calpullin* in imperial times and may have been present earlier.[51] Indeed, under the later imperial structure, differences between *calpullin* became extreme, but in the fourteenth century they were probably more limited.

Early Mexica leadership roles, like class differences, were far less sharply ranked than they would become in the imperial period. Most accounts portray early Mexica society as possessing considerable democratic qualities, with the *calpulli* leader being elected by the general membership of commoners (*macehualtin*) and advised by a council of elders.[52] A council of these elected leaders is said to have been responsible for major Mexica policy decisions and for the election of other officers, whose powers were sharply circumscribed. However, if such an egalitarian system ever existed, it had undergone considerable modification by the fifteenth century. It appears that by then candidates eligible for the office of *calpulli* leaders had to be members of a particular family within the *calpulli*.[53] This stipulation implies that leadership was largely hereditary, in keeping with the internally stratified nature of *calpulli* structure.

Above all, the most important characteristic of the *calpulli* was its flexibility. Its multifaceted nature allowed it to shift its functions in step with rapid changes in the society. Its fluid membership allowed for absorption and integration of new social or ethnic elements and, conversely, for easy departure of those whose duties or ambitions lay elsewhere. The internal stratification of *calpullin*, although perhaps initially limited in degree, later allowed for the formation of a class structure which cross-cut these traditional units. Yet the *calpulli* structure also left open the possibility of social mobility, a crucial feature after the Mexicas' abrupt rise to prominence in 1428 (which produced a sudden and urgent need for recruits to fill innumerable bureaucratic positions). The *calpulli*'s organizational tolerance for social mobility also proved essential to individual motivation in later times, when imperial ideology offered the promise of greater status and wealth for achievements in war and trade.

Thus in both its general flexibility and its specific characteristics, the *calpulli*, the basic social unit of Mexica society, was fortuitously 'pre-adapted' to the imperial role which would be thrust upon the Mexica. It would also form a pliable institution in the hands of the later architects of Tenochtitlan's imperial system.

By the late fourteenth century, if not earlier, another level of political structure had been superimposed over the *macehualtin* commoners and their *calpulli* leaders. There are indications that even before settling at Tenochtitlan, the Mexica had some higher level of leadership. In the migration myths, four *teomamas* (bearers of the god) were said to have interpeted the will of the Mexica patron deity (Huitzilopochtli) and relayed his orders to the people.[54] There are also references to *calpulli* war leaders.[55] Indeed, the histories indicate that some *calpulli* leaders may have risen to a position of dominance or perhaps even limited rulership.[56]

However, a formal system of monarchy was not established until about 1370, when the council of *calpulli* leaders petitioned the city-state of Culhuacan to grant them a prince of Toltec blood.[57] As we have seen, Culhuacan's foreign policy relied upon the bartering of its prestigious genealogy. That city reportedly gave the Mexica a half-Culhua prince, Acamapichtli, to be Tenochtitlan's first ruler, or *tlatoani*.[58] At about this same time, the powerful Tepanec alliance granted a ruler to Tlatelolco, Tenochtitlan's sister-city on the northern side of the Mexicas' island homeland.[59]

There are the usual contradictions in the sources, and the true story of the late fourteenth-century shift in leadership remains confused. References to the first *tlatoani*, Acamapichtli, are contradictory in terms of both his background and his status as a ruler.[60] Since the Mexica of both towns were tributaries of Azcapotzalco, the Tepanec capital, it seems most likely that the new rulers were imposed upon the Mexica by their mainland overlords.[61] Whether borrowed or imposed, this new upper stratum of leadership represented another step in the Mexicas' emulation of their more advanced neighbors.

The power of the first three Mexica *tlatoani* was limited both by the traditional authority of the *calpullin* and by the will of the Tepanec monarch; the principal duty of these early *tlatoani* was to lead the Mexica into wars fought on behalf of the Tepanec alliance. Nonetheless, the presence of a clearly defined ruler had several effects that helped to prepare the Mexica for their later imperial role. We are told that the Mexica nobility, the *pipiltin*, consisted largely of offspring of the quasi-Toltec *tlatoani* and daughters of the best families of the *calpullin*.[62] The *pipiltin* served as warriors in the Mexica armies and through polygamous marriage accelerated the development of a noble class.

Additionally, the presence of a dynastic line of Toltec ancestry (however spurious) was a necessary prerequisite for serious participation in the politics of fourteenth-century Central Mexico. With their incipient ruling class, the Mexica could begin to widen their nationalistic ambitions.

As the role of the Mexica in the Tepanec alliance grew, so did the power of this *pipiltin* class and the early *tlatoani*. Near the end of the fourteenth century, Tezozomoc, the ambitious ruler of Azcapotzalco, granted large tracts of land and a portion of tribute to the Mexica as rewards for their major victories on behalf of his Tepanec alliance.[63] This tribute benefited the *tlatoani* and his warrior elite by increasing their holdings of private property. It is also possible that some of the subjugated foreign peoples became *mayeque*, serfs paying tribute directly to Mexica knights.[64] Meanwhile, because of the Tepanec-Mexica victories, tribute began to develop into a distinct component of the Mexica economy, one directly tied to the state hierarchy and its military ambitions. In turn, the growing complexity of the economy led to an increased importance of intermediate occupational roles such as those of merchant, bureaucrat, and administrator.

Thus by the early fifteenth century, the Mexicas' role as vassals and allies of the Tepanec hegemony had led to numerous changes in Mexica political, social, and economic structure. All of these changes eroded the power of the traditional *calpullin* system while increasing the role of warfare, tribute, and the emerging warrior-noble class. Nonetheless, even in the early fifteenth century, the growing power of the *tlatoani* and *pipiltin* was constrained from both above and below: their regional ambitions fell under the shadow of Azcapotzalco, while in Tenochtitlan itself the *calpullin* still held considerable political authority and *calpullin* lands remained the principal basis of the Mexica economy. Only after the fall of Azcapotzalco could the emerging Mexica leadership fully win its internal struggle with the traditional institutions of Mexica society.

As with the evolution of its social, economic, and political institutions, the religious system of Mexica society increasingly came to resemble that of its more 'civilized' Mesoamerican neighbors. By the late fourteenth century, the Mexica shared both the gods and the rituals of other Central Mexican societies. The complex Postclassic pantheon included ancient deities of fertility and agriculture (e.g., the primordial Mesoamerican rain god, goggle-eyed Tlaloc, and Xipe Totec, patron of spring and renewal), as well as the Toltec-*chichimec* god-hero fusions (e.g., the familiar Quetzalcoatl and the cloud-serpent, Mixcoatl). Yet the principal deities were not gods in the Western sense; rather, they were divine complexes that could unfold into myriad aspects depending on specific temporal and spatial associations. For example, Tezcatlipoca (the 'smoking mirror'), who dominated Late Postclassic religion, could be associated with death, night, the night sky (and thus the stars and the moon), revelry, feasting, tricksters, magicians, the jaguar, justice, punishment, and other phenomena, depending on the specific context (festival, day of the calendar, cardinal direction, etc.).[65] Plotted on the Mesoamerican cosmological map of the calendar and the color-directions, Tezcatlipoca overlapped with or 'unfolded into' other major deities: the god Xipe was thought of as the Red Tezcatlipoca of the east, the White Tezcatlipoca of the west was one aspect of Quetzalcoatl, and so on.[66] As Postclassic peoples elaborated the ancient Mesoamerican pantheon, they also extracted their own patron gods from its infinite variety and complexity. We are told that occupations, dynasties, city-states, and even the individual Mexica *calpullin*[67] had their own divine sponsors.

In imperial times the Mexica people as a whole also had a national divinity, their militant patron god, Huitzilopochtli, the 'hummingbird on the left' or 'hummingbird of the south'. This deity was one of the few unique elements in the Mexica pantheon, since by the mid-fourteenth century they shared the religious system of their valley neighbors. Indeed, Huitzilopochtli sits rather uncomfortably in the pantheon. Later we will examine Huitzilopochtli's imperial role in his final politicized form. Here we can note that his early nature is, at best, obscure and that his role in the fourteenth century was probably quite modest.

The later imperial myths would tell how Huitzilopochtli was borne by the Mexica during their legendary migration, how he guided and advised them in their struggles, and how he finally led them to their island homeland of Tenochtitlan.[68] However, the various versions of the migration tale are so filled with contradictions that nearly a century of ethnohistorical scholarship has been unable to fathom Huitzilopochtli's true origins and early development. In some sources, the migration god of the Mexica is said to have been Mexitli or Meci, who gave his name to the Mexica.[69] Other sources claim that Meci was their tribal leader, rather than a deity.[70] But Huitziton or Huitzilopochtli is the name given this original chief in other sources.[71] In one rather shocking passage in the extremely reliable chronicle of Sahagún, an informant comments that 'he was only a common man, just a man'.[72]

Recent studies have emphasized Huitzilopochtli's synthetic, somewhat artificial nature. This ethnohistorical research indicates that he is a complex god-hero fusion, like several other Postclassic deities (e.g., Quetzalcoatl, Mixcoatl, Xolotl).[73] In most such cases, the hero followed the god, yet was somehow associated with him, perhaps taking his name. Later the achievements of the individual became confused with the myths of his divine patron. However, in the case of Huitzilopochtli, Brotherston (1974) and Davies (1973: 35-8) have argued that the man preceded the god, a possibility supported by statements not only in Sahagun, but in several other major sources.[74] Recent research by Uchmany (1979) and Zantwijk (1976, 1979) has stressed both the composite nature of the deity and his elaboration through time. The latter author argues that the composite character, mythical genealogy, and migration tales of Huitzilopochtli reflect the composite ethnicity of the Mexica themselves. Similarly, Davies (1973: 35-8; 1980: 181-3, 205) argues that the god was a fusion of an earlier tribal hero and Opochtli, a lacustrine deity of the southern valley peoples among whom the Mexica settled in the fourteenth century.

Of principal importance here is the fact that the god was a late development unique to the Mexica and of no importance to other valley peoples. In fact, Huitzilopochtli differs from most other ethnic patron deities in the strictly local nature of his following—at least prior to the Mexicas' imperial expansion. Furthermore, if the recent research is correct, he was not associated with the important sky gods like Tezcatlipoca until after his transformation in the religious 'reforms' of the early imperial period. Therefore, one may view with skepticism Huitzilopochtli's elevated role in the imperial Mexica pantheon. Imperial cosmology labeled him as one of the four principal deities of the pantheon, overlapping with major aspects of Tezcatlipoca, and often interchangeable with Tonatiuh, the sun itself. It is safe to assume that the imperial regime's later reordering of history and cosmology gave Huitzilopochtli these astonishing associations and attributes along with his imperialist exhortations and insatiable need for mass sacrifices. Such a pretentiously important godhead with boundless ambitions for his people seems hardly appropriate for the early Mexica, squatting on their muddy island in the shadow of the powerful alliances around them. It could only have been with the help of the imperial mythographers that the Mexicas' insignificant patron deity was able to elbow his way rudely into the upper pantheon.

Turning from the gods to their worship, we see that the Mexica (along with the other Late Postclassic city-states) had inherited not only the Toltecs' militarism and obsession with genealogy, but also their grisly version of Mesoamerican religious ritual. Human sacrifices were essential to the cults of most deities and to the major festivals of the calendric cycle. In keeping with the complexity of the ideology, sacrifices took a variety of forms. Depending on the sacred context of the offering, the victim could be decapitated, burned, drowned, strangled, skinned alive, thrown from a great height, slain in ritual combat, starved to death, impaled on a rack and shot full of arrows, or have his head crushed. The most common form of public sacrifice was described by a Spanish monk accompanying Cortés's troops:

> The natives of this land had very large temples...with a house of worship at the top, and close to the entrance a low stone, about knee-high, where the men or women who were to be sacrificed to their gods were thrown on their backs and of their own accord remained perfectly still. A priest then came out with a stone knife

like a lance-head but which barely cut anything, and with this knife
he opened the part where the heart is and took out the heart,
without the person who was being sacrificed uttering a word.

Then the man or woman, having been killed in this fashion, was
thrown down the steps, where the body was taken and most cruelly
torn to pieces, then roasted in clay ovens and eaten as a very tender
delicacy; and this is the way they made sacrifices to their gods.[75]

Not surprisingly, such sacrifices and ritual cannibalism appalled the
Spanish conquistadors. Yet by the Late Postclassic, they appeared to
have been an accepted and necessary part of religious ritual. Indeed,
most versions of the later Aztec mythology held that the very sun and
moon had been created by acts of divine auto-sacrifice.[76] Late Postclassic
human sacrifice must be understood in terms of the belief system and
the elaborate ritual which elevated these carnal acts into blessed offerings
to the ever-threatening gods. In most specific ceremonies of the calendric
cycle, sacrificial victims were actually god-impersonators, often costumed
as the deity being propitiated. In many rites the victim was treated, even
addressed, as if he were the very god being revered.[77] Even in the
militaristic cults of heart sacrifice, the victorious warrior would address
his captive as his son and accord him great respect, prior to offering the
foreign warrior's heart to the gods.[78] Such captured warriors were
considered the best possible sacrificial offering for most ceremonies.

The element of militarism in the sacrificial cult also leads us to suspect
that the constant struggle between Central Mexican polities influenced
the development and intensification of human sacrifice. Since pre-Toltec
times the violent competition among city-states had probably played a
major role in the elaboration of all aspects of state religion. The
Postclassic's militaristic sacrificial cults, regional patron deities, and
semi-mythical Toltec genealogies indicate that ideology was as much a
part of the power struggle as economic and military strength (cf.
Demarest 1976, ms.). In fact, as we shall see, it was the Mexicas'
ideological innovations that would ultimately give them the advantage
over their more established neighbors.

While the institution of human sacrifice was central to religion in the
fourteenth century, the *scale* of sacrifice was quite small in comparison
to the mass immolations of imperial Aztec times. Among the fledgling
Mexica, probably no more than a few hundred victims were sacrificed
yearly. Human sacrifice and ritual cannibalism would only have
occurred during the major religious rites of the sacred calendar, and
perhaps after important military victories. Among the early Mexica
most small ceremonies, household rites, or *calpullin* worship propably
were accompanied only by blood-letting and animal sacrifice. By
the early fifteenth century, the cults may have further intensified at
Tenochtitlan because of the warrior elite's initial successes in warfare,
greater access to captives, and increased interest in state-level religion

and prestige-reinforcing ritual. Nonetheless, there is no question that before the sweeping changes of 1428, neither Mexica ideology nor any other state religion in Mesoamerica had been able to cast sacrificial acts and religious cosmology into a unified imperialist cult. Only after the formulation of such a cult, under the transformed Mexica patron deity, Huitzilopochtli, would the massive slaughers of the imperial period be either useful or justifiable.

The transformational crisis

As we have seen, the Mexica had undergone considerable cultural change by the end of the fourteenth century. Under the tutelage of their more established neighbors, new social and political institutions had been added to their traditional *calpullin* structure. Their new leaders, the *tlatoani* and *pipiltin*, had led the Mexica to important victories, increasing the role of warfare and tribute in the Mexica economy and winning for themselves awards of estates in the lands they had conquered for the Tepanec alliance. By the early fifteenth century, the Mexica had risen to be almost allies, rather than mere vassals, of the Tepanec lords at Azcapotzalco. In step with the political and economic changes, Mexica religion had become more militaristic and state-oriented in nature. Their once obscure god-hero, Huitzilopochtli, had evolved into a state patron deity, although one still quite unimpressive to their valley neighbors.

Yet Tenochtitlan's rising state structure was little more than a foreshadowing of the imperial juggernaut into which it would be rapidly transformed after the fall of Azcapotzalco in 1428. Prior to that date, the Mexicas' power in valley affairs, their share of tribute, and their holdings in conquered lands were all limited by their Tepanec overlords. The existence of such limitations was made evident later by the development of an anti-Mexica faction in the early fifteenth-century court of the Tepanec ruler, Tezozomoc. Viewing the Mexica as dangerous upstarts, this group allegedly argued for their destruction.[79] These external checks on Tenochtitlan's power were paralleled by internal restraints on the power of the warrior elite: the development of elite authority was fettered by the traditional *calpullin* system, while the economic importance of warfare and tribute remained quite small in comparison to the intensive lake-bed agriculture of the *calpullin* farmers and the regional marketing activities of Tlatelolco's Mexica merchants. These external and internal curbs on the growth and centralization of Mexica power would be broken only by the series of events following the death of Tezozomoc in 1426.

From the time of his accession to the throne in the 1370s, Tezozomoc had been the tutor, adviser, and sponsor of his Mexica tributaries, using them as pawns in his grand schemes for the Tepanec alliance. The

Mexica warriors, led by their third *tlatoani*, Chimalpopoca, had aided Tezozomoc in his great war against the other major power in the valley, the Acolhua confederacy led by the prestigious city of Texcoco.[80] In 1418, the Tepanecs finally crushed this rival alliance, slaying the king of Texcoco and driving his young son, the prince Nezahualcoyotl, into exile.[81] Tezozomoc's hegemony was then unrivaled in the valley. However, unlike the later Mexica imperial rulers, Tezozomoc had taken no great pains to legitimize his power through a Toltec lineage. Furthermore, his macro-state lacked the unifying imperial cosmology that would be the inspiration for the continuing expansion of the Aztec Empire. It is not surprising, then, that upon his death in 1426 Tezozomoc's kingdom fell apart.

The events of 1426 to 1428 are confusing due to both the complexity of the intrigues that followed Tezozomoc's death and the contradictory accounts left us by the participants in the power struggle. Upon the death of the king, a war of succession broke out at Azcapotzalco, ending when a certain Maxtla seized the throne and with it control of the Tepanec alliance.[82] Shortly afterward, Chimalpopoca, the Mexica *tlatoani*, died of 'unnatural causes'. The sources disagree concerning the responsibility for Chimalpopoca's death: he was either drowned by assassins, committed suicide by hanging himself, or was murdered in Tenochtitlan itself.[83] In any case, a new *tlatoani*, Itzcoatl, succeeded to power in Tenochtitlan.[84]

The new ruler, together with his nephews Moctezuma I and Tlacaelel, led a militant faction favoring revolt against the Tepanec alliance and its new king, Maxtla. According to the Mexica histories, members of this faction argued for revolt because they considered Maxtla to be both a usurper and a tyrant; supposedly, they also objected to his insulting treatment of their polity and unreasonable demands for greater tribute.[85] However, it seems just as likely that the Mexica leaders perceived that the civil strife at Azcapotzalco had weakened the Tepanec alliance, giving them the opportunity for a daring bid for power. Itzcoatl's war faction prevailed in the debate at Tenochtitlan, and the Mexica formed an alliance with Nezahualcoyotl, the exiled prince of Texcoco, to lead a coalition of city-states in revolt against the Tepanecs.[86] Later, they were supported by the smaller center of Tacuba. This 'Triple Alliance' of Tenochtitlan-Texcoco-Tacuba defeated the Tepanecs in 1428, falling heir to Tezozomoc's realm.[87] It was this Triple Alliance which would become the Aztec Empire. Through time, the growing tribute state of the alliance would come to be dominated by the Mexica Aztecs of Tenochtitlan.

The events leading to the glorious ascendancy of the Triple Alliance have many characteristics of a military coup. Itzcoatl was a seasoned warrior who had risen to the rank of supreme commander of the Mexica armies during their long vassalage to Tezozomoc.[88] Like his faction of

noble warriors, he had everything to gain from revolt against the
Tepanecs. A victory would remove the various hindrances, internal and
external, that had limited elite power.

The mysterious circumstances surrounding the death of the Mexica
tlatoani, Chimalpopoca, also suggest a military conspiracy. In fact, in the
Anales Mexicanos it is directly stated that Itzcoatl, as leader of those
favoring revolt against the Tepanecs, sent a group of Tacuban assassins
to slay Chimalpopoca so that Itzcoatl himself and the militant faction
could seize power.[89] Another source confirms that Tacubans killed
Chimalpopoca but does not specifically accuse Itzcoatl of complicity.[90]
Most accounts report that Chimalpopoca committed suicide or that the
Tepanecs were responsible for his death.[91] However, one may suspect
that these were the official versions of the event, intended to shift blame
to the Tepanecs and provide further justification for the Mexica revolt.
The new Tepanec tyrant, Maxtla, had nothing to gain from Chimal-
popoca's death. Nigel Davies has pointed out the superior logic of the
Anales Mexicanos version:

> According to a quite different account of events, it was Chimal-
> popoca's successor, Itzcoatl, and his supporters who—disliking
> appeasement of the Tepanecs—instigated Tepanecs of Tacuba,
> basically hostile to Maxtla, to kill Chimalpopoca. This story
> certainly has a ring of truth. It is hard to see why Maxtla should
> want to take the extreme step of killing Chimalpopoca, and then
> stand idly by while a much less pliant successor was elected in his
> place.
>
> Subsequent events clearly illustrate that a version which suggests
> that Chimalpopoca was eliminated on account of his subservience
> to Maxtla—and that this was done at the behest of those who
> wanted to take a stronger line—is more likely to be accurate.[92]

Regardless of the details of Itzcoatl's rise to power, there is no question
that after the triumph of the Triple Alliance the new leaders initiated
a sweeping series of changes that transformed Mexica society. Most of
the major chronicles mention the imperial 'reforms' instituted by the
principal figures of the new order: Itzcoatl, the *tlatoani*; Moctezuma I,
his nephew and successor; and Tlacaelel, a larger-than-life figure said
to have been the *cihuacoatl* (high priest and chief adviser) of the first four
imperial rulers. It is reported that the new leaders ordered the burning
of the existing historical and religious texts.[93] Then they set about
restructuring Mexica economic, political, social, and ideological
institutions.

Modern analyses have confirmed that crucial changes in all aspects
of Mexica society can be traced to these reforms. Castillo (1972: 45, 46,
69, 70, and *passim*) and Katz (1966: 33, 34, and *passim*) have described
the economic restructuring of Mexica society that resulted from the
unequal distribution of the lands and tribute gained by conquering the
Tepanecs. López Austin (1961: 39-42) has shown that the political
system of concentration of power in a *tlatoani* and a Council of Four (all

members of the imperial family) came into existence during the reforms of Itzcoatl and his adviser, Tlacaelel. Brundage (1972: xv-xvii, 82-91) has noted the great augmentation of the power and prestige of the military warrior class after their victory in the Tepanec war. Townsend (1979) has given a new interpretation of Aztec sculpture as an imperialistic vision of the cosmos—a vision he traces to an inception in 1427. Several scholars have suggested that the rapid elevation of the god Huitzilopochtli in the early imperial period was a result of the Mexica propaganda program.[94] All of these changes were in the interest of the new leaders and the nobles. They concentrated wealth, social privilege, and political power in the hands of the ruling *tlatoani*, his warrior knights (Figure 4), and the noble *pipiltin* class. The religious reforms consolidated and legitimized these changes, forming an ideological context for the new institutions and the inspiration for the state's continued expansion.

Turning first to the restructuring of Mexica society, we see that it was hardly the complex or sophisticated process which our terms imply. The basis of wealth was land and tribute. When Itzcoatl's alliance defeated the Tepanecs, it fell heir to an empire. The lands acquired (far more extensive than all the lake-bed *chinampas* of Tenochtitlan) were not divided by the *calpulli* groups—the traditional land-holding units. Rather, the vast bulk of both the lands and tribute rights went to the *tlatoani* and his warrior elite. In their rewriting of history, the rulers justified this inequity by pointing out that the commoners had not wanted war and that only through coercion had the new regime been able to turn the Mexica against the Tepanecs. The official version of these events is propaganda in its purest form. Since the story of both the economic and the social reorganization can be read 'between the lines' of the accounts, it is worthwhile to relate this dramatic bit of state history:

> The king immediately began to prepare for war knowing that Azcapotzalco was at the point of attacking. All the people of Mexico were on the alert, though many of the common people, seeing the strength of the Tepanecs, feared that victory would be impossible.
> Many of them, filled with timidity and dread, tried to persuade the king and the great leaders to make peace, and the ruler was dismayed to see their fear. They claimed that the new king of Azcapotzalco was a merciful man and that the best course would be to carry their god, Huitzilopochtli, to Azcapotzalco and deliver him to the new ruler. Perhaps, they thought, in this way they would be pardoned. These weaklings were on the verge of offering themselves as slaves.
> Some of the leading men also thought that this was good counsel and wished to take refuge in Azcapotzalco together with their god. They went so far as to take the idol upon their shoulders and prepare to depart for Azcapotzalco.[95]

> War had been declared. The people of Mexico now knew that it could not be avoided but the common man was fearful and requested permission to leave the city. The leaders reassured the

Fig. 4. The Mexica warrior elite. Top: The various rankings of warriors shown taking captives (from the sixteenth-century *Codex Mendoza*). Bottom: A modern rendering of a Mexica warrior procession.

people, and the king himself spoke to them. 'Do not fear, my children, we will free you and no one will harm you.'

But they were doubtful, exclaiming, 'And if you do not succeed, our sovereign, what will become of us?' The king and his men replied, 'If we do not achieve what we intend, we will place ourselves in your hands, so that our flesh becomes your nourishment. In this way you will have your vengeance. You can eat us in the dirtiest of cracked dishes so that we and our flesh are totally degraded.'

'Let it be as you have said,' answered the people. 'You yourselves have delivered your sentence. We answer: if you are victorious, we will serve you and work your lands for you. We will pay tribute to you, we will build your houses and be your servants. We will give you our daughters and sisters and nieces. And when you go to war we will carry your baggage and food and your weapons upon our shoulders and we will serve you along the way to battle. In short, we will sell and subject our persons and goods to your service forever.'

The officials, hearing the answer of the common people, agreed, making the people swear that they would keep their oath. And thus it was done.[96]

The Aztec returned victorious and exulting to their city, carrying the spoils which had been taken that day. Great wealth had been acquired, for Azcapotzalco was the capital of the Tepanec empire and in the city was concentrated the wealth of the nation...[97]

The Aztec chieftains reminded the common people what they had promised. The natives of the city agreed to fulfill their promise, serving the nobles in everything.

'Lord,' said Tlacaelel to the king, 'your noble brothers and cousins, who with such bravery, courage and fearlessness have gone to war, should be rewarded. You well know that the survivors in Azcapotzalco promised us land for our crops. Let us not lose this occasion. Let us go and distribute the land among ourselves since we have won it with the strength of our arms.' The king then ordered that a count be made of the nobles who had gone to war and who had distinguished themselves in battle in order to reward them according to their merits.[98]

The largest and best fields were given to the royal government. Other lands were distributed among the nobles and a third group of fields was divided among the wards of Mexico, each ward receiving a certain amount of land to maintain the cult of its gods.[99]

The first individual to be given land was Tlacaelel, who was awarded ten pieces of property, all formerly belonging to Azcapotzalco but in different parts of the empire. All the other great warriors received two plots each. The common men who had fought in the war but had been timid and fearful and had sworn to become serfs of the nobility were not given land or anything else, except for some who had shown a certain amount of valor.[100]

Thus, imperial historians went to great pains to demonstrate the justice of the elite monopolization of land and wealth. This story that the commoners had formally 'bet' their social and economic position is, of course, implausible. Yet the very lengths to which the new order went to justify its actions underscores the sudden and radical nature of the change.

Along with these economic and social changes the new leaders elaborated and formalized the political order. In imperial decrees, Itzcoatl created the principal offices of the new government, usually combining military, religious, and political functions. A new procedure for the succession of *tlatoani* was introduced at this time, taking the choice of leader out of the hands of the *calpullin* councils and giving it to the oligarchy by establishing the so-called 'Council of Four', principal advisers of the *tlatoani* and the pool from which the next *tlatoani* had to be chosen.[101] Itzcoatl set up a hierarchy of titles and to enhance the prestige of his new nobility initiated propaganda programs in praise of his appointees:

> 'King Itzcoatl, my close relative and yours, greets you and wishes to honor you according to your merit. He wishes to give you titles and preeminence over others, as well as lands which will support you and your families.'

> Apart from giving them titles, he had stone statues carved of them in order to perpetuate their memory, and he had the historians and painters inscribe lives and deeds with fine brushes and bright colors in the books. In this way their fame would grow and magnify like the brightness of the sun throughout all the nations.[102]

Meanwhile, the ubiquitous Tlacaelel, in his role as *cihuacoatl*, reorganized civil and religious offices. It is reported in the *Codex Ramírez* that as supreme adviser to the *tlatoani* Itzcoatl and Moctezuma I he put 'in good order and harmony all of the territories. He founded as many councils as there are in Spain.'[103] He also continued his program of class structuring under Moctezuma I. This second true emperor of the Mexica issued a series of decrees formally defining the noble (*pipiltin*) and commoner (*macehualtin*) classes.[104] Privileges of dress, ownership, and education were limited to the nobles. In this new social code were such rulings as the restriction to nobles of the right to practice polygamy or live in houses of two stories.[105] The state comforted the commoner with the reminder that these decrees were established 'for the health of the entire state'.[106]

The effects of these various reforms and the unequal distribution of the Tepanec lands cannot be overestimated. Building on the fourteenth-century evolution of Mexica society, they abruptly completed and consolidated the developmental process; tribute, distributed on the basis of birthright and military achievement, now joined *chinampa* agriculture and trade as the principal economic foundations of Mexica life. The *calpullin* organizations lost much of their economic and political significance, since they were now responsible for only a tiny portion of the total Mexica landholdings and were virtually excluded from the new political structure. A cycle of increasing imperialism and class stratification was begun: the new wealth and power of the military gave them the wherewithal to support their imperialistic campaigns, which subsequently brought in more tribute—furthering their dominance. The economic and social foundations of the empire had been laid.

Yet the political, social, and economic changes resulting from Itzcoatl's coup served only to raise the Mexica abruptly to the level of Tezozomoc's macro-state. These reforms merely concluded the processes already well advanced by the beginning of the fifteenth century, completing the Mexicas' adoption of the political and economic institutions of their more advanced neighbors and allies. Though perhaps slightly better structured than earlier city-states, the new institutions of Mexica society were little different from those of the capitals of earlier military alliances. The Tepanec kingdom also had such features as a centralized political authority, a stratified class and social structure, a landed aristocracy, and a large tribute sector of the economy. Yet Tezozomoc's hegemony had never even succeeded in fully subduing the Valley of Mexico and had not survived a single succession. Also note that several structurally similar 'Triple Alliances' had preceded the Tenochtitlan-Texcoco-Tacuba union.[107] However, these had never extended beyond Central Mexico and had quickly collapsed into tiny warring polities. In contrast, the Aztec Triple Alliance poured out of the Valley of Mexico and swept across much of Mesoamerica. Rather than quickly disintegrating into diffuse centers of power, the Triple Alliance hegemony came through time to be ever more focused on a single supreme authority, the *tlatoani* of Tenochtitlan.

What was the critical difference, the competitive edge responsible for the Mexicas' phenomenal success? The answer to this question lies in an ideological transformation that assured Mexica victories and fired the continued expansion of their state.

The original contribution of the Mexica to the evolution of Mesoamerican civilization was an ideology that successfully integrated religious, economic, and social systems into an imperialistic war machine. The ideological changes which caused this integration were the work of the same handful of men (Itzcoatl, Tlacaelel, Moctezuma I, etc.) who had led the coup and instituted the other reforms. In fact, their alteration of historical and religious concepts was as much an attempt to justify their own actions and consolidate their power, as it was to insure Mexica dominance. The beginning of the ideological reformation is clearly recorded:

> The history of it was saved, but it was burned when Itzcoatl ruled in Mexico. A council of rulers of Mexico took place. They said: 'It

is not necessary for all the common people to know of the writings;
government will be defamed, and this will only spread sorcery in
the land; for it containeth many falsehoods.'[108]

Much of the rewriting of the history, as we have seen, was to justify
the elite's actions and their right to rule. Another function of the new
texts was to combat their neighbors' opinion of the Mexica as a whole.
Most of the established valley peoples probably agreed with the
Xochimilcans that 'it was a shame that men like the Mexicans, a people
of low birth and with little standing, should have prevailed...'[109] We
have already observed the mythographers' handiwork in some of the
contradictory and allegorical elements of the migration tales, with their
often transparent efforts to give the Mexica a quasi-Toltec ancestry. But
above all, the new historians and mythographers set out to alter ancient
myths and religious cosmology into an integrated cult that supported
Mexica military imperialism.

This last reform was the supreme achievement of the new order: the
elevation of Huitzilopochtli and the formulation of an imperial cult that
united the patron deity, Mexica military ambitions, and the sun into
a vision of the constant struggle between the forces of the universe. We
have seen the pre-imperial Huitzilopochtli as a late-developing and
strictly local divine patron, possibly a union of a Mexica god-hero with
a more ancient water deity of the southern lakes. In the imperial period,
in keeping with the new prominence of the Mexica themselves,
Huitzilopochtli became identified with both Tezcatlipoca and Tonatiuh,
the warrior sun[110] (Figure 5). He was now the Tezcatlipoca of the south
(the White Tezcatlipoca), the 'young' sun (the growing sun of the spring
and summer), and was also identified with the daily warrior sun,
Tonatiuh (Figure 6), who battled his way across the sky.[111] In fact,
Mexica dogma now held that Huitzilopochtli was one of the four sons
of the creator gods, the deities at the very top of the ancient Mesoamerican
pantheon.[112] This final change in the fortunes of Huitzilopochtli can be
clearly traced to the reorganization of state religion and the rewriting
of Mexica cosmology and mythology instituted by the new regime.

The new elaboration of the state cult and its combination with more
ancient beliefs had clear ramifications for the long-established cults of
warfare and human sacrifice. The imperial cosmology held that the
Mexica must relentlessly take captives in warfare and sacrifice them;
the spiritual strength of the sacrificed enemy warriors would strengthen
the sun and stave off its inevitable destruction by the forces of darkness.
Thus, it was specifically the Mexicas' sacred duty to pursue a course of
endless warfare, conquest, and sacrifice to preserve the universe from
the daily threat of annihilation. The new vision of the cosmos accelerated
the pace and scale of human sacrifices beyond all previous measure,
associating these ancient rites specifically with the Mexica state and the
imperial expansion of the Triple Alliance. In studies of Aztec imperial

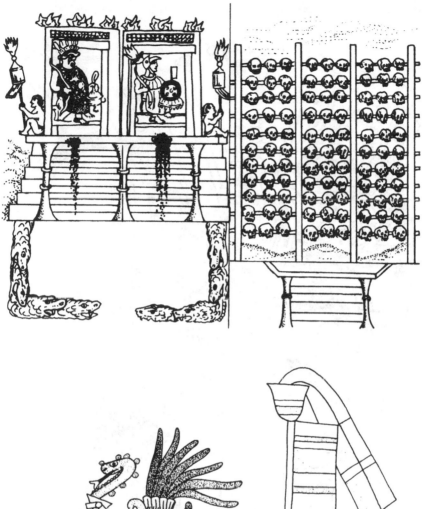

Fig. 5. Huitzilopochtli and his cult. Top: The twin 'Templo
Mayor' of Tenochtitlan with its adjacent *tzompantli* or skull rack.
Bottom: Huitzilopochtli as represented in the pre-Conquest *Codex
Borbonicus*.

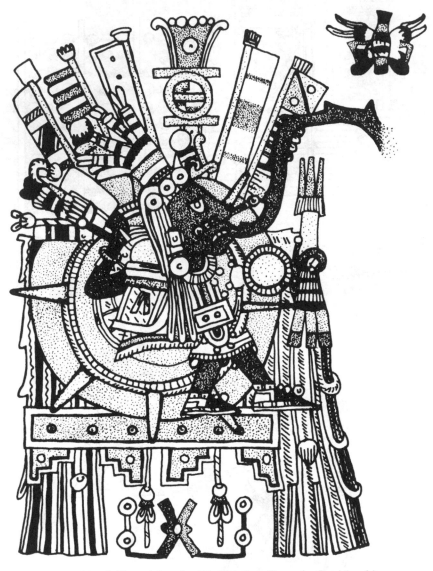

Fig. 6. Tonatiuh – the Warrior Sun (from the Precolumbian *Borgia Codex*).

religion scholars like Caso (1936, 1958) and León-Portilla (1959, 1963) have described dramatically the nature and consequences of Mexica cosmology:

> The idea that man was an indispensable collaborator of the gods, since the latter cannot subsist unless they are nourished, was clearly expressed in the sanguinary cult of Huitzilopochtli, a manifestation of the sun god.

...So it was that when the god was born he had to open combat with his brothers, the stars, and his sister, the moon; and armed with the serpent of fire he puts them to flight every day, his victory signifying a new day of life for men. When he consummates his victory, he is carried in a litter to the center of the sky by the spirits of warriors who have died in combat or on the sacrificial stone...Each day this divine combat is begun anew, but in order for the sun to triumph he must be strong and vigorous for he has to fight against the unnumbered stars of the North and the South and frighten them all off with his arrows of light. For that reason man must give nourishment to the sun. Since the sun is a god, he disdains the coarse foods of mortals and can only be kept alive by life itself, by the magic substance that is found in the blood of man, the *chalchihuatl*, 'the precious liquid', the terrible nectar with which the gods are fed.

The Aztecs, the people of Huitzilopochtli, were the chosen people of the sun. They were charged with the duty of supplying him with food. For that reason war was a form of worship and a necessary activity...[113]

Convinced that in order to avoid the final cataclysm it was necessary to fortify the sun, they undertook for themselves the mission of furnishing it with the vital energy found only in the precious liquid which keeps man alive. Sacrifice and ceremonial warfare, which was the principal manner of obtaining victims for all sacrificial rites, were their central activities and the very core of their personal, social, military, religious, and national life. This mystical vision of the cult of Huitzilopochtli transformed the Aztecs into great warriors, into 'the people of the Sun'.[114]

While some of the elements of this vision of the universe were ancient Mesoamerican beliefs, the new Mexica cosmology pulled them together, uniting them with the national needs and imperial quest of the state. Clearly, this new central role for the Mexica and their transformed patron deity was also the product of the imperial reforms. Indeed, several chronicles specifically credit the transformation of the cult of Huitzilopochtli to the ever-present high priest and chief adviser, Tlacaelel:

the most illustrious in the state was the great captain, the great warrior Tlaleltzin...It was he also who established the worship of the devil Huitzilopochtli, the god of the Mexicans.[115]

León-Portilla has concluded that this entire sacred complex might have been the work of the *cihuacoatl*: 'It was Tlacaelel who insisted on—perhaps originated—the idea that the life of the Sun, Huitzilopochtli, had to be maintained by the red and precious liquid.'[116] Even if such interpretations credit this semi-legendary figure with a little too much creativity, it is certain that the transformation of the state religion does, in fact, date to this period of ideological reform and that it coincides perfectly with the needs of the new state and its rulers. For above all, the new Huitzilopochtli was a driving force behind the imperial ambitions of the Mexica people. The *tlatoani* Itzcoatl announced the mission of their new exalted patron:

> This is also the task of our god Huitzilopochtli
> And that is why he came to us.
> He gathers, he draws to his service
> All the nations with the strength of his chest and of his head.[117]

As we have seen, the ideological manipulations were only one part of the changes instituted by the new regime. However, these religious reforms—the elevation of Huitzilopochtli and the nationalization and elaboration of the sacrificial cult—were the most innovative and crucial elements of the entire transformation. The new ideology set the Mexica apart from their neighbors and predecessors and irrevocably altered the course of Aztec history (Demarest 1976, ms.). Through an accelerated process, mass human sacrifice would reach unimaginable proportions by the late fifteenth century, with single ceremonies sometimes involving the massacre of literally thousands and even tens of thousands of captives. These rituals and the cosmology which demanded them would launch the Mexica armies on a divine quest, a quest which would result in the sprawling Aztec Empire.

Initially, it was surely not enough simply to propose such radical changes in religious doctrines. As art-historian Richard Townsend has noted:

> The mass immolation of the prisoners of war was not common practice among the other warlike peoples of the Highlands prior to the rise of Tenochtitlan, and such practices were resisted at Texcoco even after the Mexica alliance.[118]

So it was necessary to propagate the new dogma, to 'sell' the Mexica imperialist cosmology. The propaganda program of the imperial leaders would form a major portion of Aztec art and literature. Evidence of the political nature of much of Mexica art can be found in recent analyses of important Mexica sculptures. Re-examining major state monuments, Townsend (1979) concluded that the Mexica used art to promote their imperialistic view of the cosmos. He comments:

> It is quite unlikely that the Mexica were somehow compelled to an unquestioning repetition of mythological archetypes, for myths could be adapted, regenerated, or created anew according to the policies of imperial states. While a sense of divine mission surely lent impetus and inspiration to conquest, such convictions must also have been visualized and forcefully promoted by powerful rulers wishing to unite a nation in imperial endeavors.[119]

As we have seen, all of the changes were related to the rise of the Triple Alliance, the unequal distribution of Tepanec lands, and the reorganization of political power, the acts of Itzcoatl and his associates. It is, therefore, fascinating to note Townsend's comments on the inscriptions of the Sun-Stone, an important Mexica monument.

The last main element of the Sun-Stone to account for is the date-glyph 13-*Acatl*. There can be no doubt about the mythological importance of this date, for it is mentioned in at least two versions of the origin myth as the time of the present sun's creation. Yet the glyph also reoccurs in the calendar cycle to mark a more directly historical year of genesis: 1427, the year of Itzcoatl's accession to power...[120]

Previously, Henry Nicholson noted the highly integrated and standardized nature of Aztec sculptural iconography.[121] Now we can conclude that this was due, at least in part, to a tightly centralized state control of this aspect of the ideological system.

Ultimately, it was the creation and control of the religious and educational institutions which permitted the endurance of the revolutionary religious reforms. Tlacaelel and Moctezuma I were credited with the establishment of the Mexicas' highly organized educational system.[122] This system consisted of both local 'neighborhood' schools for commoners and the state-run *calmeca* schools to educate priests and young nobles. Along with such measures as the commissioning of religious art and sacred hymns,[123] the *calmecac* ensured the spread of elite dogma and the consolidation of belief. León-Portilla (1963: 3-24) has discussed the Aztec ability to distinguish between the good and evil priests and wise men, a proof of the advanced state of Aztec philosophy. But this philosophical differentiation can also be seen in a more cynical light. The people were taught to believe only the 'good' teacher as one who teaches 'the handed-down wisdom' and who gives a 'strict education'; they were advised to shun the 'false' wise man who 'has his own traditions and keeps them secretly' and thus will 'lead the people astray'.[124] Thus, only the *calmecac*-trained priest (Quetzalcoatl) would be recognized as legitimate; others would be discredited along with their 'secret traditions'. Having reworked written history and myth, the state needed to control and alter the oral literature as well. Due to the *calmecac*-trained priests' reliance on the *written* codices, the official accounts of history and cosmology quickly became the accepted versions:

> But, our lords,
> they are those who guide us;
> they govern us, they carry us on their backs and instruct us how our gods must be worshiped;
> ...those who received the title of Quetzalcoatl.
> The experts, the knowers of speeches and orations, it is their obligation...
> Those who observe the codices, those who recite them.
> Those who noisily turn the pages of the illustrated manuscripts.
> Those who have possession of the black and red ink and that which is pictured;
> they lead us, they guide us, they tell us the way.[125]

In the brave new world of Itzcoatl's reign there would be, at best, a very limited role for the independent priest and the self-proclaimed shaman.

Thus, the indoctrination through art, education, and literature consolidated the changes wrought by the many reforms of the new Mexica regime. The imperial ideology created by the elite's careful alteration of ancient myths and traditions was propagated by the state's control of monumental art, written history, and priestly instruction.

Expansion and consequent stresses

After the victory of 1428 and the subsequent transformation of the Mexica, their history becomes a tale of ceaseless conquests. Led by the Mexica warriors, the armies of the Triple Alliance marched outward, increasing with each campaign the number of centers and peoples pledging allegiance and tribute to Tenochtitlan and its Aztec allies. A comparison of the Mexicas' tiny island homeland with the extent of Moctezuma II's realm (Figure 7) shows the dramatic expansion of the empire through the conquests of Itzcoatl and the five *tlatoani* who succeeded him. Interrupted only by the great famine of 1450-4, the expansion of the Triple Alliance spread its hegemony across Mesoamerica, while Tenochtitlan rose to unquestioned dominance within the alliance itself.

The reasons for the military campaigns of the Triple Alliance were varied. Often, an alleged insult to Mexica national pride or to their god, Huitzilopochtli, would furnish the excuse for wars that had more carefully reasoned economic or political motives. Yet always beneath both Mexica patriotism and the rational goals of the state were the insatiable demands of the gods. The pantheon's need for an ever greater number of sacrificial offerings required unceasing warfare to obtain captives. The very survival of the universe depended on Mexica victories, a terrible responsibility and a powerful incentive for the imperial armies.

While Mesoamerican religions had always involved individual human sacrifices, the Mexica cosmology cast this need into a new, almost mechanistic, view of the universe. Their gods, especially the solar complex of Tonatiuh/Huitzilopochtli, required the blood and hearts of human victims to nourish them in their constant struggle with the forces of darkness and disorder. Thus, not only was the need for human sacrifice more pronounced, but there could now be no limits to its scale: the greater the number of captives offered on the sacrificial altar, the greater would be the strength (and gratitude) of the gods. Setbacks such as military defeats and famines did not diminish Mexica zeal, but rather motivated redoubled militarism. Such disasters indicated the displeasure of the gods or warned of impending doom due to their weakening. The prescription to cure such supernatural ailments was inevitably more sacrifice, requiring new victories to obtain captives.[126]

The shift in the scale of sacrifice can be seen in the many historical accounts of late fifteenth-century public rituals as well as in eyewitness

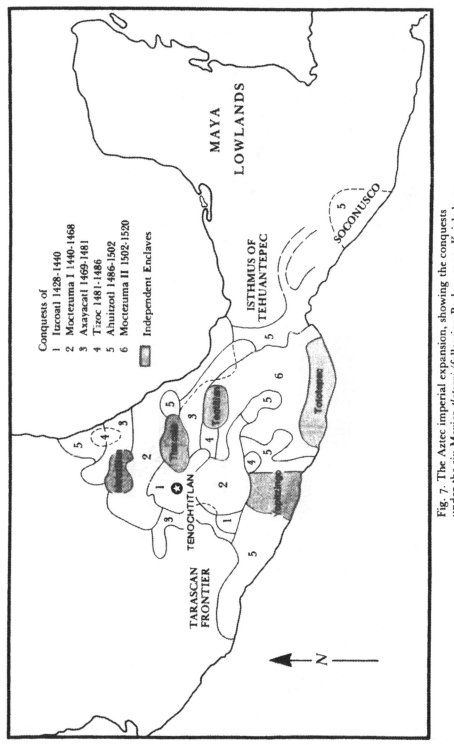

Conquests of
1 Itzcoatl 1428-1440
2 Moctezuma I 1440-1468
3 Axayacatl 1469-1481
4 Tizoc 1481-1486
5 Ahuitzotl 1486-1502
6 Moctezuma II 1502-1520
☐ Independent Enclaves

MAYA LOWLANDS

ISTHMUS OF TEHUANTEPEC

SOCONUSCO

TARASCAN FRONTIER

TENOCHTITLAN

N

Fig. 7. The Aztec imperial expansion, showing the conquests under the six Mexica *tlatoani* (following Barlow 1949, Krickeberg 1966, and Davies 1968).

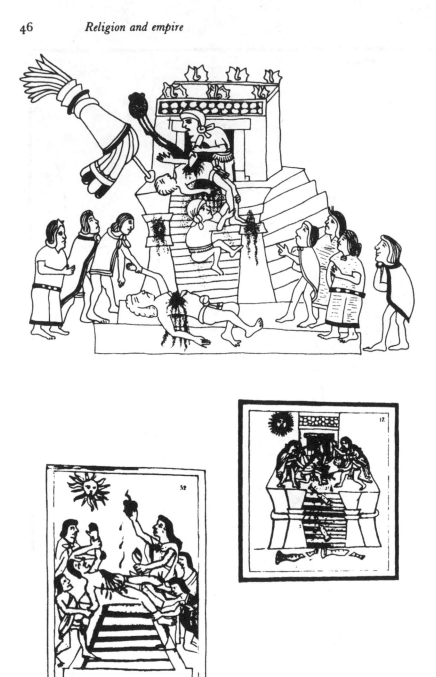

Fig. 8. Aztec human sacrifice. The heart sacrifice as shown in the sixteenth-century *Codex Magliabecchiano* (top) and *Florentine Codex* (bottom left and right).

descriptions of mass sacrifices in the early sixteenth century (Figure 8). S. F. Cook's (1946) review of the evidence on Central Mexican sacrifices estimated that an average of about 15,000 persons were sacrificed each year in Central Mexico. Most contemporary scholars believe that Cook's figures are quite conservative.[127] While human sacrifices were an integral part of every major religious festival, rituals coinciding with major imperial victories saw the most massive offerings of captives. On such occasions, thousands of captives would fall beneath the sacrificial knife.

The astonishing scale of Mexica sacrifices can be seen in the descriptions of the dedication of the Great Temple of Tenochtitlan in 1487.[128] Thousands of captives (gained in the latest victories of the great emperor Ahuitzotl) were formed into four long files running down the steps of the temple and out along the four causeways of the island city. At the top of the new temple, Ahuitzotl and the rulers of the other Triple Alliance capitals, aided by their priests, cut out the hearts of one victim after another as they mounted the temple steps. The sacrifice lasted four days and even the most conservative accounts of this even report that over ten thousand persons were sacrificed.[129] Similar mass offerings were witnessed by conquistadors and friars at the time of the Spanish Conquest. The Spaniards were horrified, not only by the mass killings, but by the cannibalistic rituals that generally accompanied them; after a sacrifice the warrior responsible for taking the captive usually sponsored a feast for friends and family in which the flesh of the victim's limbs was served in carefully prepared stews.[130]

Faced with such gruesome rituals and alien concepts, not only the Spanish friars but many modern ethnohistorians have had great difficulty in trying to analyze Aztec warfare and sacrifice objectively. Recent explanations of the Aztec state cult have spanned all extremes. One scholar (Arens 1979) has even claimed that Aztec ritual cannibalism was a myth invented by the Spanish Inquisition and biased conquistadors —an argument which ignores an overwhelming corpus of evidence drawn from hundreds of independent sources (native texts, eyewitness accounts, archaeological remains of ritual paraphernalia, portrayals in murals and sculptures, etc.). At the other extreme is a recent theory which sees the Triple Alliance as a kind of 'cannibal empire' driven by a mindless search for protein.[131] Only slightly less inaccurate is the recurrent view of the Mexica as a people enslaved by an irrational ideology, one which drove them fanatically to ignore their own political and economic well-being.[132]

More holistic interpretations of Aztec warfare and human sacrifice show that this sacred complex was a rational phenomenon, both in terms of the ideological context of Mesoamerican religious beliefs and in terms of the specific political and economic interests of the people and the state. Looking first at its ideological context, we see that the Mexica cosmology was acceptable and effective only because it drew on established religious institutions and traditional myths. Human sacrifice was a long and venerated tradition in Mesoamerica, just as it has been among many cultures in human history. The reformed imperial ideology merely altered the potential scale (and thus the consequences) of sacrifice by directly associating the strength of the astral gods with the offerings of their mortal collaborators, the Mexica. This superficially minor adjustment also served to tie the ancient sacrificial complex to the imperial ambitions of the state.

Mexica warfare and the sacrificial cult were also quite rationally integrated with all levels (collective, interest-group, and individual) of political and economic motivation. On the collective level, the 'secular' rationality of the state cult can be seen in the careful coordination of the drive for sacrificial victims with the immediate political and economic needs of the Triple Alliance peoples. Initially, at the time of the Tepanec collapse, the ideological reforms fulfilled Tenochtitlan's suddenly critical need for legitimation. The reforms of myth and history gave the state the required cultural ancestry, a Toltec heritage. More importantly, the myths of solar struggle and Huitzilopochtli gave the state a divine sanction, raising it to a level superior to its neighbors. The new cosmology conferred a sacred role on the Mexica people, giving them the national identity and collective zeal necessary for their survival and success in the greater political arena into which they had been suddenly thrust. Thus, the state cult of accelerated warfare and mass sacrifice was a timely ideological adaptation to the political environment of fifteenth-century Central Mexico. While well within the bounds of traditional Mesoamerican religious thinking, the modification of Mexica cosmology was a politically rational (indeed, astute) policy.

On the same collective level, the state cult can also be seen as economically adaptive. Though resting upon a foundation of intensive agriculture, the economies of the Central Mexican city-states also relied heavily on tribute gained through military conquests. The Mexicas' sacrificial cosmology gave them the competitive edge needed for such victories: fanaticism. The unending hunger of the gods for mass sacrifices also generated the tireless dynamism of the Mexica armies, a persistence which allowed them to wear down some of the most obstinate of their opponents. The advantage conferred by this persistence can be seen in the struggle between Tenochtitlan and Chalco, one of the Mexicas' strongest competitors for the role of heir to the legendary Toltec Empire. In campaign after campaign, the Triple Alliance battled the Chalcan hegemony. Driven by their sacrificial cult, the Mexica were invariably the aggressors in these wars, and thus the battles took their greatest toll on the Chalcan towns and lands on which they were fought. Finally, after decades of resistance, the Chalcan state was exhausted by the very persistence of its more zealous adversaries, and the Mexica economy reaped the benefits of vast new quantities of annual tribute and control over additional sources of labor.

While, as we have seen, the economic benefits of the resources acquired
through warfare were unequally distributed, they nonetheless helped
Mexica society as a whole. In her analysis of the economics of the Aztec
Empire, Frances Berdan has shown that tribute was a distinct sub-system
which together with the market and long-distance trade constituted the
Aztec economy.[133] The tribute sector can be broadly characterized as
'redistributive' in nature. Tribute supported not only the rulers,
warriors, and administrative bureaucracy, but also large-scale programs
of public works, subsistence for the urban population, and some stores
for times of famine.[134] Subjugated peoples were forced to supply labor
and materials for such projects as the construction of Tenochtitlan's
causeways, aqueducts, and dike systems.[135] The latter greatly extended
the area of reliable agriculture by creating more plots of rich drained
marsh and lake-bed lands. Thus, tribute indirectly helped to increase
even this most basic level of economic support for the Mexica population.
As the years passed, the economic role of tribute grew ever larger, since
the proportion of state employees and non-agricultural specialists greatly
increased in Tenochtitlan itself. Thus, by supplying tribute for the
nation, as well as victims for the gods, the state cult and the perpetual
warfare it demanded could be seen as economically beneficial to the
Mexica people as a whole—at least initially.

In addition to the structural coincidence of Mexica ideological,
political, and economic needs, the state's divine quest was also politically
and economically rational in the specific directions for conquest chosen
by its leaders. The *tlatoani*, in consultation with his generals, often
directed campaigns against rebellious provinces or against potentially
dangerous neighbors. This latter criterion was undoubtedly responsible
for the Mexicas' sustained attacks against the Chalca and their less
successful campaigns against the Tarascan Empire and the Tlaxcalan
kingdom; these two warlike states threatened the western and eastern
flanks of the Triple Alliance (see Figure 11). While the political and
military objectives of the state guided some campaigns, pragmatic
economic goals motivated many others. The state's foreign merchants,
the *pochteca*, doubled as spies gathering information on foreign wealth
and resources.[136] When the hunger of the gods demanded new wars, these
crusades would often be directed by the intelligence gathered by the
pochteca. It is hardly coincidental that after the famines of 1450-4 the
Triple Alliance intensified its wars against the perpetually moist and
fertile lands of the Gulf Coast. Nor is it surprising that the Mexica armies,
leaving intervening territories untouched, assaulted and conquered the
distant Guatemalan kingdom of Soconusco; this region was renowned
for its highly productive plantations of cacao, the precious chocolate
beans that were almost a currency to Mesoamerican peoples.

Thus the sacred campaigns of Huitzilopochtli were synchronized with
the political and economic needs of the Mexica nation as a whole. Yet

the rapid expansion of the empire can also be explained by the close agreement between the sacrificial cult's requirement for victims and the ambitions of specific interest groups within the state. We have already seen that the *tlatoani* and his noble warriors, the *tetecutin* class, became a landed aristocracy as a result of the early Mexica victories. These two groups continued to benefit disproportionately from the Mexica war machine. As the empire grew, they gained an ever greater share of tribute, lands, and labor. Indeed, initially small, dependent classes, the *mayeque* serfs and the *tlacotin* slave-retainers, later swelled in size to serve the needs of the growing elite.[137] Meanwhile, the lesser nobles of the *pipiltin* class also profited greatly from the military wealth of the state, since they filled the increasing number of positions in the state-supported administrative and religious bureaucracies.

The ubiquitous *pochteca*, the state-sanctioned merchants, were also among the major beneficiaries of the military expansion. The growth of the Mexica hegemony opened distant markets to their activities. These merchants cleverly multiplied their own wealth while representing the state on trading expeditions to exchange elite goods with foreign powers.[138] Mexica military might gave the *pochteca* an advantage in both their exchanges for the state and their private enterprises. One can understand that the imminent threat of the ferocious armies of Huitzilo-pochtli might discourage obstinate bargaining on the part of foreign merchants. Indeed, alleged insults or abuse of *pochteca* traders were among the most commonly cited causes for the initiation of Triple Alliance campaigns.[139] The *pochteca* class also benefited from the military expansion through special privileges conferred on them for their services to the state; as we have noted, the Triple Alliance armies often followed a path to riches that had been explored by these merchant-spies. Thus, the *pochteca* rose rapidly to a position of lesser nobility, accumulating status and power as well as wealth.

So we see that the state cult and the Mexica military expansion supported the ambitions of specific interest groups, just as they were compatible with the political and economic needs of the nation as a whole. Yet, as scholars are increasingly coming to realize, no analysis of a system is complete unless it also explains *individual* as well as collective strategy. Ultimately, most decisions are made on an individual basis, and the motivations and rationale of such decisions must also be understood. In the case of the Mexica, we again see that the state's imperialism was well integrated with the ideological, social, and economic motivations of the citizen, whether *pipiltin* noble or *macehualtin* commoner. Indeed, the state cult's ability to motivate the individual was the key to the initial success and early expansion of the Mexica imperial system.

The ideological motivations of the individual should be apparent from our earlier descriptions of the state cult. The cosmology of the daily struggle of the gods was taught to both the commoner and the noble in the well structured Mexica educational sytstem. Oral literature, monumental art, written codices, and public and private ceremonies instilled and continually reinforced belief in the divine struggle and the unceasing need for sacrificial victims (i.e., military victories). The fanaticism of the faithful was further strengthened by guarantees of immortality for those who perished in the divine quest: warriors killed in battle or on the sacrificial stone and mothers who died in childbirth (producing the next generation of crusaders) became the sacred retinue of the warrior-sun himself, accompanying him in his victorious daily march across the sky.[140]

The motivation of the individual was also secured by the more earthly incentive of social mobility, allowing each person the option of improved social, political, and economic circumstances.[141] This system of rewarding achievement inspired the maximum contribution from commoners and nobles alike. On the elite level, *pipiltin*, regardless of their hereditary status, had to prove themselves through personal prowess in war or exceptional bureaucratic or priestly abilities. Within each subdivision of Mexica society (warrior, priest, noble, merchant, etc.) a ranked hierarchy existed. Particularly during the early decades of the empire, one's position in that hierarchy was based largely on performance. The ranking was defined and reinforced by special privileges of dress, possessions, and behavior. Above all, the successful warrior, especially one of noble birth, was rewarded with tremendous economic and social advantages.[142]

This system of ranking and one's upward movement in it were integrated with the state ideology and the sacrificial cult. In many social sectors, improvements in standing were formalized by specific sacrificial rituals and cannibalistic feasts. Naturally, successful warriors who offered captives to the gods were raised in social and economic standing. Their elevation in status was commemorated by a ritual feast for their friends and relatives featuring parts of the very victim whose heart and blood they had offered to the sun and the state.[143]

More surprising is the fact that the ranking of other non-military specialists was often expressed in sacrificial terms. Among the *pochteca* merchant guilds an elaborate hierarchy of positions also existed, reflecting one's success in trading or in special services to the empire.[144] Each of these ranks was accompanied by specific privileges in dress and behavior, as well as by greater access to specific economic resources. Thus the state implicitly acknowledged that its goals were economic, as well as religious and political. The recognition of mercantile achievement was also expressed in sacrificial terms. The chronicler Sahagún detailed the ritual of the 'bathing of slaves'.[145] It involved the merchant's distribution of gifts, ritual feasting, and bathing and sacrificing of a slave. The merchant's worth was ultimately expressed by the sacrificial act which marked his step upward in the *pochteca* hierarchy. In these ways the imperial ideology permeated all aspects of Mexica society, motivating the individual and even defining his personal worth in terms of the sacrificial cult and the nourishment of the gods.

Though nobles and merchants could achieve a higher (sometimes hereditary) status, even commoners (*macehualtin*) were offered the possibility of upward mobility in the imperial system. We have already discussed the tremendous flexibility of the *calpullin* units, whose 'conical' structure allowed internal stratification. This feature was used to full advantage by the state, which offered improved standing and privileges to *macehualtin* who could prove themselves by winning captives in the military campaigns. It is no wonder that even the simple *calpullin* squadrons of the Mexica were so ferocious in battle: if successful, the freeman warrior would gain privilege in this life, and if he perished in the divine quest he would gain immortality in the next, as a warrior-companion of the sun.

So we can see that the integration of the Mexica war machine was carried down through all levels of society. The imperial expansion was driven by the Mexicas' divine task: the need to take captives for the sacrificial rituals that fed the gods and averted the destruction of the universe.

> You have been sent into warfare. War is your desert, your task. You shall give drink, nourishment, food to the Sun and to the Earth.[146]

Yet their sacred mission was not incompatible with the political and economic needs of the state as a whole—at least not in the beginning of the imperial period. Indeed, this ideology gave the Mexica the key to victory, and with victory came tribute, a major pillar of the Mexica economic system. Thus Huitzilopochtli, grateful for the bloody nourishment provided him, would in return reward the faithful:

> I will make you lords, kings of all that there is everywhere in the world; and when you have become kings you will have there innumerable, endless, and infinite vassals who will pay you tribute giving you numberless and very fine precious stones, gold, quetzal feathers, emeralds, corals, amethysts...[147]

As we have seen, the earthly spoils of the holy wars would not only fall upon the state elite, but (in differing degrees) would benefit all levels of society. The military requirements of the gods and the state also coincided with the special interests of class and occupational groups, as well as the goals of the individual; their achievements in support of the empire would be rewarded by improved economic and social circumstances.

Despite the thorough integration of Mexica cosmology with the pragmatic goals of state and citizen, most analyses of the Aztec Empire have seen it as a seriously flawed system. Leaders and individuals can only adapt to their immediate environment, short-term interests, and foreseeable future. The anthropologist and the historian benefit from both historical hindsight and a broader comparative framework. Drawing on this wider knowledge, we can see the inherent limitations and structural defects of Mexica imperialism.

Though initially the Mexicas' ideological adaptation gave them victory over their competitors and the means for imperial expansion, it does not seem to have provided them with any clear notion of what to do with the empire gained by those victories. The principal goals of the Triple Alliance wars were food for the gods and tribute for the state. Having obtained these divine and material ends, the Mexica were unprepared to face the long-term problems of governing and controlling the subjugated peoples. As the Triple Alliance hegemony grew to cover a vast portion of Mesoamerica, the limited objectives of Mexica imperialism became increasingly incompatible with the size of their realm.

Aztec imperialism can be broadly characterized as a system of conquest without consolidation. In fact, the 'Aztec Empire' was not really an 'empire' at all, at least not in the usual sense of the term. Rather, it was a loose hegemony of city-states pledging obedience and tribute to the Triple Alliance capitals.[148] After defeating the armies of a region (Figure 9), the Mexica would take hundreds or thousands of the foreign warriors as captives to be sacrificed in Tenochtitlan. Then they would install a ruler—often of the very dynasty they had just defeated—on the throne of the subjugated province. No real attempt was made to assimilate the conquered peoples, either culturally or politically. The only real change in the vanquished state would be the onerous periodic tribute payments that had to be paid to the victorious Triple Alliance. By leaving the local leadership structure intact, the Aztecs minimized their administrative problems, but they also increased the possibility of rebellion. Indeed, such insurrections, usually initiated by murdering the local Aztec tribute collectors, were common occurrences. Previously subjugated regions had to be reconquered again and again.

The loose structure of the empire and the limited immediate goals of campaigns resulted in the presence of numerous large independent enclaves within the empire[149] (see Figure 11). Mountainous regions, unyielding opponents, or areas lacking resources desirable as tribute were simply bypassed as the imperial armies swept on toward easier and richer prey. As the empire grew in size, these independent pockets became a substantial problem. Anxious to maintain their autonomy, the rulers of the enclaves encouraged insurrections in the regions of the empire that bordered them.[150] When such revolts were crushed by the Aztecs, the free states would offer asylum to rebellious leaders, who could return to trouble the empire on other occasions.

The highland kingdom of the Tlaxcalans was perhaps the most

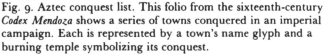

Fig. 9. Aztec conquest list. This folio from the sixteenth-century *Codex Mendoza* shows a series of towns conquered in an imperial campaign. Each is represented by a town's name glyph and a burning temple symbolizing its conquest.

troublesome of these independent realms. A warlike people, the Tlaxcalans successfully resisted the armies of the alliance for over fifty years.[151] During that time, they worked unceasingly to undermine the Aztec hegemony—conspiring, forming alliances, inciting rebellions, and harboring the enemies of the empire.[152] As we shall see, the 'Tlaxcalan problem' persisted until the last days of the Triple Alliance, exemplifying the inherent structural flaws in the Mexica imperial system.

Another threatening group, the Tarascans, also remained unconquered by the Triple Alliance. In 1478 the Mexica imperial army had invaded the Tarascan territory, which lay less than fifty miles to the west of the Valley of Mexico. The Mexica lost over twenty thousand men in this disastrous campaign.[153] The Tarascan forces were vast in number, since they controlled a large alliance of city-states.[154] More importantly, they were expert at fighting in the rugged mountain terrain of western Mexico. The Mexica never again attempted to subdue the Tarascan regions. Thus, just to the west of their own center of power, the Triple Alliance had a threatening neighbor and a total obstruction to their westward expansion. As a consequence, the empire became asymmetrical in form, its nucleus lying in Central Mexico but the region governed extending far to the south and east. Naturally, this created additional logistical problems both in administration and in staging campaigns to conquer new lands.

In addition to the Tlaxcalan enclave and the Tarascan barrier, serious logistical problems multiplied as the empire grew. Most of these difficulties were not caused merely by unconquered enemies; rather, they reflected limits to growth inherent in the very nature of Mexica imperialism. Reliance on a loosely organized tribute system became increasingly inadequate as a supplement to the growing material needs of the Central Mexican cities. Newly conquered regions became more and more distant from the capital. The outer provinces could make no substantial contribution of foodstuffs. Instead, their tribute consisted largely of elite goods such as quetzal feathers, uniforms, ceremonial costumes, decorated blankets, and other items needed by the state bureaucracy and aristocracy for prestige reinforcement and court and temple ritual.[155] However, such items did little to assuage the food shortages that plagued Central Mexico during imperial times.

The material requirements of Tenochtitlan itself had sky-rocketed as the population of the city swelled in size. Internal population growth was encouraged by the imperial ideology: the gods' demand for fresh warriors was endless. Immigration into the capital occurred on an explosive scale.[156] The growing aristocracy and state bureaucracy drew in large numbers of retainers, craftsmen, merchants, scribes, concubines, and other specialists to serve their needs. One study of early sixteenth-century Tenochtitlan (Figure 10) concluded that most of the city's population consisted of non-food-producing specialists.[157] The lake-bed gardens of the capital region could provide only a portion of the goods required to support the city. It was in response to this population boom that Tenochtitlan's leaders initiated massive land reclamation projects and raised-field construction. Since distant provinces could help little

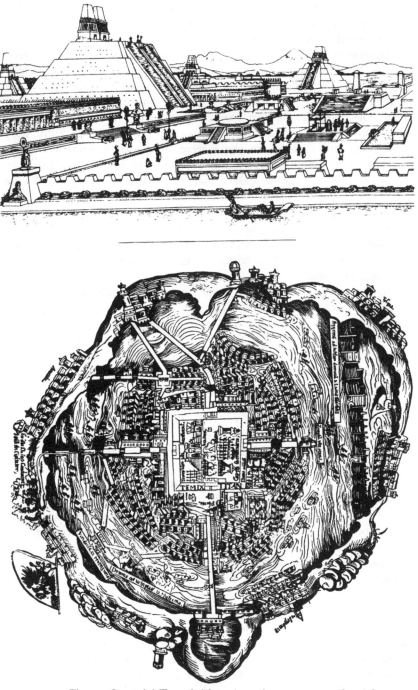

Fig. 10. Imperial Tenochtitlan. A modern reconstruction (above, after Marquina 1951) and a sixteenth-century Spanish view (bottom).

with perishable foodstuffs, the empire's central zone, especially the Central Mexican provinces, had to provide for Tenochtitlan's rapidly increasing subsistence needs. The Lake Texcoco area commoners benefited from the spoils of expansionism, since they formed the backbone of the armies of the Triple Alliance.[158] However, conquered Central Mexican provinces beyond the immediate lake area suffered greatly beneath the Alliance's ever-heavier tribute demands. Often the peoples of these regions carried a double burden, since they paid tribute both to the Triple Alliance and to their own traditional or Mexica-appointed rulers.[159] The delicate balance (later, the increasing imbalance) between population and resources led to hunger and famine in lean years, both in the central provinces and in the Aztec capitals which they supported.

In attempting to alleviate this dangerous situation in Central Mexico, the imperial rulers often adopted counterproductive measures. Tribute requirements were increased in the provinces, and this added strain often led to rebellion. Revolts were followed by Mexica invasions and reconquest. Then the insubordinate peoples would be punished with a much higher tribute quota.[160] Obviously, such higher demands would be even more difficult to meet, given the fact that Mexica reconquest usually decimated the ranks of the prime producers in the region: young adult males would perish in the futile struggles against the imperial armies, in the massacres that followed defeat, and as sacrificial victims on the altars of the Aztec capitals. Thus the provinces were being crushed beneath a cycle of imperial oppression: increases in tribute, revolt, reconquest, retribution, higher tribute, resentment, and repeated revolt.

Attempts to seek a solution to the economic ills through new conquests lost their effectiveness in the later days of the empire. All of the rich and easy prey had long since been subjugated, taxed, and retaxed by the end of the fifteenth century. Conquests of distant lands were hindered by the costs and logistical dangers of such campaigns. Imperial armies had to march through hundreds of miles of intervening regions, being supported by the provinces through which they passed. Often the imperial army had to reconquer various states before it could proceed to its original objectives.[161] Sometimes intervening areas were unconquered or were menaced by independent enclaves. These factors left the Triple Alliance troops with a highly uncertain line of advance, supply, and return. If successful, the subjugation of distant realms added little to the desperately needed subsistence support of the Aztec capitals: as we have noted, the riches the outer provinces supplied were used to reinforce the political and ideological systems of the Mexica, not to feed the growing population. As can be imagined, it was especially difficult to prevent and suppress revolts in these distant regions. In some cases the additional expense of fortified garrisons was undertaken to ensure Mexica control of fringe areas.[162]

Mexica military might was facing complex problems that force alone could not resolve. The armies of Huitzilopochtli were as ferocious as ever and were successful in achieving their ideological goals: captives were taken in large numbers (from the defeated armies of rebellious provinces or from new conquests), the gods were nourished with their blood, and the universe was preserved. Yet as an earthly economic system, Mexica imperialism was an enterprise of rapidly diminishing returns.

Meanwhile, the logistical and economic problems created by the empire's growth were paralleled by the social strains resulting from the rapid sequence of changes and transformations in Mexica society. The developing empire was a culture in a state of continuous internal upheaval. The initial reforms and transformations that followed the 1428 victory of the Mexica had not created a new society, but rather had set off a cycle of continual cultural change in response to the constant expansion of the empire. No sooner were clearly separated social strata formalized by the decrees of Itzcoatl and Moctezuma I than rapid changes in Mexica society multiplied the gradient of intervening classes. Increased social mobility arose in response to the increasing complexity of Mexica government and religion and the state's need for an ever more diverse range of occupational specialists. Yet by the last few decades of the Aztec era, the slowing growth of the empire led to restraints on social movement. Conflicts began to develop between the landed, hereditary elite and the personally successful warriors and merchants, previously the driving forces behind the imperial expansion. While such class conflicts developed, the hereditary *pipiltin* aristocracy multiplied in numbers due to their privilege of polygamy.[163] In turn, the household of each noble or bureaucrat required the services of dozens of other non-agricultural specialists to serve its needs. By the sixteenth century, the large and affluent *pipiltin* class had become a burden to the economic system that supported it.[164] The Mexica social structure had grown top-heavy through some of the very privileges originally granted as incentives to achievement.

At the root of the administrative, economic, and social instability of the empire lay the fundamental dynamics of the imperial cult itself. Although initially it gave the Mexica a driving inspiration for victory, the cult of endless war and human sacrifice was basically ill-suited to any stable political structure. It demanded constant warfare, sacrifice, and expansion, preventing any attempt to consolidate and secure the realm. While it was initially a brilliant ideological adaptation to the early fifteenth-century political and military environment, the imperial cult became a destructive burden in the late years of the empire when the Mexicas' need was for stabilization rather than expansion, for consolidation rather than conquest. Yet the wheels of the divine war machine had been set in motion and could not be stopped. The cosmology of solar struggle, the cults of mass sacrifice, and the glorification of war and the warrior were so deeply ingrained into the

Mexica way of life that no other ideological perspective could be imagined by either the people or their rulers.

Contrary to some theories, we can see that the state cult was also destructive in its effect on Central Mexican demographics. As will be discussed further below (Chapter 4), Cook (1946), Price (1978), and others (e.g., Harris 1977; Harner 1977a,b) have argued that the warfare and mass sacrifice demanded by the state religion were an adaptive response to growing population pressure in Central Mexico. Such broad theories fail to take into account the specifics of the structure of the problems of the Triple Alliance. As we have seen, the greatest population pressure was in the Aztec capitals. Yet the areas most decimated by conquest and sacrifice were the very tributaries whose foodstuffs supported the overpopulated Valley of Mexico. Thus, Aztec warfare destroyed the very subsistence support for the empire by causing the deaths of thousands of food producers.

In the late imperial period another problem was created by the increasingly maladaptive sacrificial cult. The growing obstructions to administrative, economic, and military logistics were joined by a quandary of ideological logistics: as the pace of conquests slowed and the fields of battle became more distant, it became ever more difficult to obtain the supply of victims needed by the gods. Like the other needs of Tenochtitlan, the capital's requirements for sacrificial victims were also rapidly increasing. The acceleration of the sacrificial cult was also stimulated by the disproportionate growth of the ritual needs of particular segments of Mexica society. The warriors, nobles, priests, and merchants needed sacrificial victims to participate in major calendric ceremonies and to mark their movements up the social ladder. The state itself sacrificed ever larger masses of victims; greater numbers of captives were needed for horrendous ritual displays staged to intimidate foreign leaders who were invited to witness these bloody events. Furthermore, as the late empire became swamped with difficulties in wars abroad and famines at home, the state's counterproductive response was to sacrifice even more victims.

With the pace of conquest slowed, the increased demand for sacrificial victims was met through new means. A growing class of slave-merchants developed in response to the need for both retainers and sacrificial victims.[165] This flourishing market in nourishment for the gods supplied the elite and rising classes with victims for many calendric and social rituals. Yet many major events specifically required the sacrifice of warriors *captured* in battle: only their vigor and courage could strengthen the sun. Allegedly, the so-called 'Flowery Wars' arose in response to this shortage of warriors for sacrifice. According to several chronicles, the major Central Mexican city-states agreed to meet periodically in battle so that each side might capture warriors to supply the sacrificial rituals of its gods.[166] However, some evidence indicates that accounts of

'Flowery Wars' were often merely imperial propaganda, a means of explaining to the people the empire's inability to conquer certain obstinate enemies (e.g., the Tlaxcalans) despite numerous attempts.[167] Nonetheless, it does appear that some wars of deliberately limited goals were initiated in late imperial times, both as a means of obtaining sacrificial victims and as a convenient method for training young warriors.[168]

The development of such institutions as the sacrificial slave-markets and the more problematical 'Flowery Wars' underscores the essential predicament of the late empire: the obsession with mass sacrifice was becoming increasingly maladaptive and increasingly difficult to satisfy. The slowing growth of the empire in its last decades was incompatible with the growing sacrificial requirements of the state cult. Furthermore, the crowded Aztec capitals' dependence on the provinces for subsistence support conflicted with the goals of internal wars against rebellions. Such campaigns suppressed insurrections and obtained captives for sacrifice, but often did so at the expense of the population and productive capacity of the very provinces that supported the overpopulated nucleus of the empire.

Thus the two major goals of Mexica warfare, captives for sacrifice to the gods and tribute for the support of the state, gradually came to be conflicting, rather than coinciding, objectives. The initial unity of the ideological and economic rationale for Mexica imperialism presupposed the existence of a world of limitless conquests, innumerable victims, and endless resources. Unfortunately, by the end of the fifteenth century such a boundless environment was no longer available to the armies of Huitzilopochtli.

The terminal trajectory of the Mexica state

We have seen that the problems besetting the empire at the turn of the sixteenth century had their roots in limits inherent in the imperial system from its very inception in 1428. Nonetheless, it was not until the reign of Moctezuma II, who ascended the throne in 1503, that these limits would be reached and the empire would finally confront its inevitable internal crisis. Successor of the heroic conqueror Ahuitzotl, Moctezuma II inherited not only a tradition of glorious military achievement but also its product: a far-flung, loosely organized, and totally unstable imperial hegemony. Unrivaled in the art of war, the Triple Alliance was plagued by logistical and administrative inadequacies as well as more ominous economic imbalances. A trajectory leading inevitably to crisis was generated by the accelerated urbanization of the Valley of Mexico combined with repeated destructive wars of reconquest against the very provinces which supported it. Together the empire's problems virtually cried out for solution through stabilization and consolidation rather than continued conquest and sacrifice.

Moctezuma II was the first *tlatoani* to realize the true nature of the Aztec dilemma and to attempt a policy of consolidation and stabilization. Like most leaders who inherited impossible situations, Moctezuma II would not be treated kindly by history. He would be blamed for many of the problems inherent in the Aztec system itself. Yet, by his very recognition of these flaws and his attempts to solve them, Moctezuma showed a degree of insight superior to that of his predecessors. The failure of his policies resulted more from the irreversible consequences of the imperial ideology than from Moctezuma's personal weakness. Indeed, near the end of the reign of his illustrious predecessor, Ahuitzotl, it was already apparent that the over-extended empire was entering a period of crisis.

Remembered as a great conqueror, Ahuitzotl had actually pushed the outer boundaries of the empire beyond the limits of its internal structure's ability to administer or even hold these conquests; Moctezuma II spent much of his reign reconquering Ahuitzotl's additions to the empire. Ahuitzotl may also have reached the limits of the empire's ability to stage successful campaigns. Despite his reputation as an invincible general, he suffered numerous setbacks during his prolonged campaign to conquer Oaxaca and the Isthmus of Tehuantepec region. In the face of the Aztec threat, the pugnacious Zapotec groups of Oaxaca had ceased their internal squabbles and united to block one of the Mexica campaigns.[169] In other wars in the distant Tehuantepec region logistical problems frustrated Ahuitzotl's efforts. In one campaign no captives were taken; instead they were slaughtered in the field since 'the distance from those provinces to the city of Mexico was great'.[170] In another isthmian war, the *tlatoani* called off the campaign despite the urgings of his allies to go on to conquer parts of Guatemala: 'King Ahuitzotl answered that he did not wish to go farther in part because those people had not offended him in any way and in part because his men were exhausted'.[171] Clearly, the long marches from Mexico made the imperial campaigns less effective, while the transport of booty and captives back to Tenochtitlan was also becoming extremely difficult. In fact, we are told that the leaders of some of the partner states in the 'Triple Alliance' refused to participate with the Mexica in some of these unprofitable long-distance campaigns.[172]

By the end of Ahuitzotl's reign, the diminishing returns from conquests, combined with the growing needs of the Aztec capitals, had led to periodic shortages of foodstuffs and vital goods. To help meet the food supply problems of the capital, Ahuitzotl undertook a massive hydraulic program.[173] His engineers attempted to channel the waters of a mainland spring into the Tenochtitlan area through a new aqueduct system. It was hoped that this project would augment the supply of non-saline waters on the western side of the valley's lake system. Such a controlled fresh water supply would improve yields and protect the lake-bed agricultural system from the ruinous effects of periodic droughts. Ahuitzotl's overambitious response to the city's subsistence problems ended in a disastrous flood that virtually destroyed Tenochtitlan and ruined the crops of the surrounding region.[174] There followed years of costly reconstruction made more difficult by the flood's destruction of the fields and granaries of the city. In this inauspicious atmosphere Ahuitzotl died, and in 1503 his nephew, Moctezuma II, ascended the throne.

From the very beginning, Moctezuma II shifted the imperial strategy from expansion to internal consolidation. As we have seen, internal administrative, logistical, and economic problems had already begun to restrain the centrifugal forces of the imperial cult and the search for tribute. By Moctezuma II's reign even more absolute barriers blocked expansion. To the north, Aztec conquests extended to desiccated landscapes that supported only small groups of marginal agriculturalists and nomads. To the west, Aztec expansion was restrained by the indomitable combination of mountainous terrain and the Tarascan armies. To the south, the Triple Alliance hegemony reached the Pacific, stretching tenuously across much of what is now the state of Guerrero. The wild mountain tribesmen of Guerrero could be defeated, but never subdued: each consecutive *tlatoani* had to initiate new campaigns to reconquer the region, and widespread insurrections swiftly followed the withdrawal of the imperial forces.[175] Finally, the eastern wing of the empire reached down to the Isthmus of Tehuantepec, and a thin line of defensive outposts connected it to the cacao-rich Mexica enclaves of Soconusco (Figure 11).

We have seen the Aztec predicament on this southeastern frontier. Mexica armies under Ahuitzotl and Moctezuma II fought costly and demoralizing wars trying to maintain control over the mountain valleys of Oaxaca and attempting to keep open the routes across Tehuantepec to Soconusco. While the riches of the Pacific slopes of the Soconusco province merited these efforts, additional conquests to the east would have come at great costs and for little gain. The militant highland kingdoms of Guatemala promised only stubborn resistance and few new resources. As had been seen in Ahuitzotl's earlier campaigns, the far eastern frontier was too distant either to fill the gods' constant need for captives or to help alleviate the earthly hunger of the Central Mexican peoples.

Berdan's (1975) analysis of the Aztec economic network points out an additional barrier to eastern expansion. In a complex argument she demonstrates that the Aztec tribute system was dependent on well developed markets in the conquered provinces to generate the varied goods and manufactured items required as tribute (Berdan 1975: 270-9). The rather weak development of markets in the Maya lowlands eliminated any economic incentive for conquest into these Maya lands lying to the east:

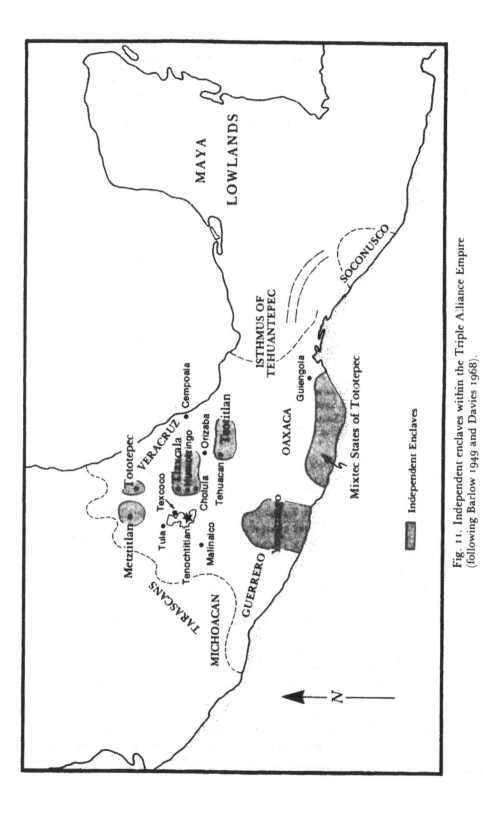

Fig. 11. Independent enclaves within the Triple Alliance Empire (following Barlow 1949 and Davies 1968).

Tribute goods were obtained by conquered populations through their market transactions or dealings with merchants. These latter networks allowed the Aztec state access to resources actually produced beyond the bounds of their conquered districts. Highly developed market systems allowed for a flow of extra-empire goods into the bounds of the empire; those goods were then demanded in tribute by the Triple Alliance. This pattern of tribute exactment would be highly adaptive in areas with an extensive market system, and patterns of both markets and tribute characterized the area included in imperial territories in 1519...[176]

In the absence of an extensive market network, and where the desired goods are non-local products, the strategies of conquest and tribute could not be effective, as they were in already-conquered districts where market networks were extensive. In fact, such desired goods would no longer even be available.
...in areas with a weakly-developed market system, foreign goods could not be obtained through conquest and tribute. In this case, the institution of foreign trade, state-controlled, would become a viable alternative strategy for gaining access to those external resources...[177]

The lowland Maya areas were characterized by a weakly-developed market system. Markets certainly did exist, yet they appear to have been highly localized and probably did not serve to integrate regions...[178]

In the lowland Maya areas, the economic context would have made conquest and the exactment of tribute an unlikely strategy for the Triple Alliance. In these areas, trading enclaves developed which remained, at least in a formal sense, neutral.[179]

Thus the Aztec tribute system's inability to absorb efficiently the dissimilar economic structure of the lowland Maya groups formed a barrier to eastern expansion that was less tangible than the Tarascan armies to the west or the forbidding deserts to the north, yet equally effective in blocking further conquests.

Having inherited such a circumscribed hegemony, Moctezuma II turned Mexica efforts toward the independent enclaves within the Triple Alliance's boundaries. These holdout groups threatened the empire's loose internal structure and routes of trade, transport, and tribute. By conquering the independent pockets and by ending the cycle of insurrections within the empire, Moctezuma II may have hoped to create a more stable and solid realm.

Unfortunately, as the new *tlatoani* would quickly learn, such a policy of consolidation did not fit the traditional pattern of Mexica warfare. The ideal Mexica war was a short campaign producing thousands of captives, rich booty, and, subsequently, a sustained flow of varied tribute goods. Such wars filled the state cult's need for victims as well as the economic desires and requirements of individuals and interest groups. Nothing could differ more from this ideal than wars of attrition against the mountain enclaves of the unconquered peoples. Indomitable and aggressive, they would not easily yield either captives or tribute. Naturally defended by topographic features, hardened by years of resisting Triple Alliance armies, and generally resource-poor, the free pockets offered little incentive for conquest and every possible obstacle to it. It was for some of these very reasons that these regions had been previously bypassed by the imperial armies as they swept on toward easier and more profitable victories.

Moctezuma's armies systematically assaulted one independent enclave after another: his campaigns besieged the northern kingdom of Metztitlan, western pockets in Michoacan, the savage mountain warriors of Yopitzingo (in what is today the state of Guerrero),[180] and numerous small resistant polities in Oaxaca and the Tehuantepec region. A series of major campaigns was also directed against the two largest and most formidable of the independent areas: the Mixtec kingdom of Tototepec and the threatening Central Mexican enclave of the Tlaxcalans and Huexotzingans.[181] Against these major foes, as well as the smaller free areas, the Mexica efforts met only limited success. For the first time since the beginning of the imperial period, the tide of battle often turned against the Triple Alliance. Apart from a few satisfying conquests in Oaxaca, the results of Moctezuma II's many campaigns were a sad mixture of pyrrhic victories, negotiated truces, and outright defeats. Indeed, even the indomitable spirit of the Aztec peoples was gradually succumbing to despair as the armies of the Alliance hammered away at these unyielding pockets of resistance. The earlier vigor of the Mexicas' bloody sacrificial victory rites is sharply contrasted by descriptions of the return of Moctezuma II's troops from some of these sixteenth-century campaigns:

> Moctezoma was notified of the death of his brothers and his nobles. He was also told how his army had been routed. When he heard this mournful news he began to weep bitterly. The tidings spread throughout the city and everyone sobbed in sadness and despair.
>
> When it was known that those who had survived the war were about to return, broken and wounded, Moctezoma comanded that they be received in a manner suiting the occasion. Their reception was a sad thing; the priests who usually wore their hair braided with colored thread appeared with unkempt hair. The old men and officials who generally showed themselves wearing feathers on the top of their heads were seen without their plumes and with the insignia of mourning. The priests who offered incense on other occasions brought no incense this time but instead brought tears and affliction. The conch shells, trumpets, flutes, and drums were mute.[182]

Meanwhile, on a completely different front, Moctezuma II had undertaken another ill-fated program of consolidation and stabilization: he attempted to centralize political power and to halt the rapid social changes that were eroding the class structure of Mexica society.

Moctezuma II's political and social reforms were compatible with both his general policy of consolidation and with his own nature, which was by most accounts aristocratic and autocratic.[183] His retrenching of the class structure was rather ruthlessly instituted early in his reign. Beginning at the top, his most sweeping (and unpopular) decrees purged the court of all counselors and leaders who were not of the highest birth.[184] Some accounts even report that he executed all of the officials of his more socially liberal predecessor, Ahuitzotl.[185] These 'reforms' were then extended downward into all levels of the administrative, military, and religious hierarchies. The upwardly mobile merchant class, cultivated and patronized by previous rulers, was now told to restrict its behavior and costume so as not to outshine its high-born superiors. Sahagún says the *pochteca* were even warned that the warrior-nobility might slay them if the merchants forgot their place.[186] The honors awarded to exceptional warriors of low birth were explicitly limited.[187] Thus, costume, insignia, and ritual privileges were tied even more closely to hereditary criteria in order to distinguish and aggrandize the nobility. All of the reforms sought to increase social distance and then freeze class structure, thus arresting the cycle of continuous internal change that had characterized the early empire.

These changes represented a radical shift in Mexica policy. As we have seen, the imperial system had always motivated and rewarded achievement through a system of controlled social mobility. Special privileges, power, wealth, and prestige had been the perquisites not only of high birth, but of achievement in state service. Warriors distinguishing themselves in battle, *pochteca* merchants excelling in state-controlled trade or diplomatic missions, and political or religious administrators of exceptional ability were all rewarded wtih promotions virtually equivalent to upward movement in the class structure itself. This system of social mobility was somewhat restrained by hereditary considerations. Yet it was capable, when combined with the force of the state ideology, of motivating the rapid expansion of the state. It was also a policy that allowed the development and reshuffling of new social and occupational categories in response to the rapidly changing needs and circumstances of the rising Triple Alliance.

In effect, whether a conscious decision or not, Moctezuma II's insistence on a rigid class structure was consistent with his military strategy of internal consolidation. By reducing the economic and social rewards for personal achievement the reforms would stabilize internal change, while removing the material aspect of the personal incentives for outward expansion. The new social order was more in keeping with the limited growth and internal reorganization that would characterize Moctezuma's reign. These new policies also represented an unconscious recognition that the tide of Mexica expansionism had crested.[188]

Moctezuma II also worked to augment his own power and to

centralize his control over the Aztec hegemony. Within Tenochtitlan itself, he reduced the duties and power of other high officials of the state. The royal adviser and high priest of Tenochtitlan, the *cihuacoatl*, became little more than an administrator of royal decrees. The role of the council of advisers was reduced by Moctezuma II to a purely formal one.[189] Elaborations of court ritual, protocol, and ceremony served to aggrandize, indeed virtually to deify, the *tlatoani*. The lavish display of the royal Mexica court was combined with an actual increase in its power and its supervision over all aspects of life in Tenochtitlan.

More importantly, the *tlatoani* of Tenochtitlan became the sole independent power in the Triple Alliance. In the early decades of the alliance of Tenochtitlan, Texcoco, and Tacuba, the ancient and prestigious royalty of Texcoco had considerable influence over the decisions and policies of the rising empire. Through the years the political and military power of Texcoco had been gradually reduced, though its cultural and economic role was still a great one.[190] In 1515, Moctezuma II put an end to any diplomatic pretense of equality among the capitals. In that year he intervened in the delicate process of selecting the next Texcocan *tlatoani*, eventually imposing his own favorite upon the throne.[191] According to Texcocan sources, this act angered and disillusioned many of their people, leading to a schism in power at Texcoco.[192] This move was consistent with Moctezuma II's tighter control over his other allies and tributaries and was a logical step toward the consolidation of the empire's loose structure. But it cost Tenochtitlan an important asset: the aggressive enthusiasm of the Texcocan allies, who had usually been major contributors to the Triple Alliance victories.

Like his military program of attacking internal enclaves, Moctezuma's new policies of social stabilization and centralization of power were probably a necessary response to the internal weaknesses and external circumscription of the Triple Alliance. Yet, like the new military policies, the social and political reforms were dismal failures. They served only to further demoralize the troubled citizenry of the alliance. His displacement of the upwardly mobile officials, warriors, and merchants of Ahuitzotl's regime caused widespread resentment among these important groups. Furthermore, the Mexica commoner and the noble of lesser birth were now faced with reduced personal incentives for vigorous participation in both the bloody wars and the civil business of the state. Meanwhile, the thinly veiled degradation of their leaders caused resentment and diminished enthusiasm among the Mexicas' allies. All of these negative reactions to the social and political programs occurred at a time when the state most desperately needed fanatical support from its people to confront economic and demographic problems and to face the arduous task of crushing the entrenched independent enclaves.

Both the shift in military strategy and the restructuring of social and political hierarchy attempted to consolidate the empire at the expense of the very dynamism that had originally created it. The political and social reforms eroded military motivation, worsening the performance of the Aztec armies in their struggle against the independent enclaves. The resentments caused by Moctezuma II's decrees, the disappointment in the Mexica military campaigns, and the periodic shortages and famines all combined to create an atmosphere of social malaise. Internal conflicts were heightened as the strain grew and as each group sought to shift the blame for the many failures.[193] The destructive emotional effect of the Triple Alliance's inability to defeat the internal kingdoms led to worsened performance in subsequent wars. This cycle of negative reinforcement accelerated rapidly as a series of major campaigns against the Tlaxcalan enclave failed to win its submission. One account of Moctezuma II's reaction to a defeat at the hands of the Tlaxcalans exemplifies the divisive effect of such military reverses:

> When the news of this defeat reached Moctezoma and when he heard that the Aztecs had taken only forty prisoners from Tlaxcala, that Texcoco had taken only twenty, and that Tacuba had only fifteen and Tlateloco five, Moctezoma rose from his seat in anger, shouting, 'What is this you say? Do you know what you are saying? Are not the Aztecs filled with shame? Since when have you lost your vigor, your strength, like weak women? Are you just learning to take up the sword and the shield, the bow and the arrow? What has happened to all the skill acquired since the founding of this renowned city? How has it been lost to the point that I stand in shame before the entire world? Why did so many courageous lords and captains, seasoned in war, go to the battlefield? Is it possible that they have forgotten how to command their squadrons in order to fight with the whole world? I can only believe that they were deliberately heedless in order to mock me.'
>
> The king then called in Cihuacoatl and his councilors, and related to them what had happened. Orders were given that those who were returning from war should not be welcomed. No conch shells or other musical instruments were to be sounded and neither men nor women were to receive them in the city. No sadness or sorrow was to be shown because of their losses and no gladness for those who had come back. Therefore, with the news of the return of the armies a strange silence spread over the entire city; not a man, a woman or priest was to be seen anywhere. When, after worshipping in the temple, the warriors went to render homage to the king, the doors were closed in their faces. They were ejected with scorn from the royal household and in shame they returned to their homes and cities.[194]

Thus the disillusionment that accompanied defeat was joined by growing internal animosities.

Even more ominous than the Mexicas' loss of confidence in themselves was the threat of potential erosion of their faith in the imperial cosmology. The state cult both demanded and promised constant victories and limitless growth. Huitzilopochtli and the pantheon required an endless supply of captured warriors to nourish them. In return they had promised invincibility to the Mexica armies and untold wealth to Tenochtitlan. The imperial ideology had led to a cycle of conquest that gathered greater momentum with each victory of the early Triple Alliance. Yet in the face of repeated rebuffs and defeats such a cycle could easily be reversed. Defeats meant fewer captives. In turn this reduced nourishment for the gods led to both their anger and their weakening, reducing the divine support for future campaigns. Without clear assurance of the total support of the gods, the zeal and confidence of the imperial armies was greatly diminished. Thus in the last decades of the Triple Alliance another cycle of negative reinforcement had been initiated, threatening the very foundation of the Aztec Empire: the sacred contract between the hungry gods and their warlike Mexica collaborators.

The weakening of the sacred bond of the sacrificial cult led inevitably to defeat, to resentments among the people, and to bitterness between the Mexica and their gods. In the face of the failure of all possible approaches to stabilization, both the warriors and their leader Moctezuma II seemed to sense the very hopelessness of the Mexica predicament:

> In this way those who returned from war entered the city, going to the temple where, instead of prayers, were long lamentations and complaints against the gods, to whom no sacrifice was offered. From the temple they went to the king's palace, where they found him sunk in despair.[196]

Such was the state of the Triple Alliance, the Aztec Empire, on the eve of the Spanish Conquest. Circumscribed by external barriers and restrained by a weak internal structure, the empire could no longer hope to maintain a policy of outward expansion. Yet Moctezuma II's programs of internal military consolidation and administrative and social stabilization had failed. The paradox which defeated Moctezuma II was that while expansion was no longer practicable, it remained the cornerstone of the Mexica ideological, social, and political systems. It was impossible to convert the Mexica imperial system to a stable state without destroying the fundamental values which held that system together. The effects of the imperial cosmology and a century of unrestrained growth were simply irreversible. Thus, Moctezuma II's attempts to prevent the empire from marching on toward disaster were doomed from the start.

With the arrival of Cortés and his conquistadors in 1519, the independent evolution of Mesoamerican civilization came abruptly to an end. New World states, weak and strong, rising and waning, were swept away by the Spanish holocaust. In the case of the Triple Alliance, it perished before the onslaught of Cortés's few hundred men. The loosely knit empire flew to pieces as tributary states rose in revolt or in actual support of the Spanish, blindly thrilled at the prospect of any force that could free them from Aztec oppression. It is significant that in the final assault on Tenochtitlan, Cortés's handful of men led an army of tens of thousands of Indian allies, most of them vengeful Tlaxcalans.[196]

It is, of course, a matter of speculation as to what the independent course of Mesoamerican cultural evolution might have been if the Spanish had not arrived. However, in the case of the Mexica state the trend seems evident. Demographic pressures, economic problems, and logistical and administrative weaknesses plagued the Aztec hegemony. Outward expansion was blocked. Attempts at internal military consolidation had only reduced, not eliminated, the pockets of resistance within the empire, and these wars of attrition had taken a terrible toll by destroying the myth of Mexica invincibility and of the total efficacy of their state cult. This ideological blow, combined with Moctezuma's counterproductive attempts to stabilize the state's internal structure, had set off a chain of events leading to defeat and despair.

As the empire's psychological state weakened, that of its enemies grew stronger. The Tlaxcalans, surrounded and besieged, fought on fanatically, inspired by their state cult of the god Camaxtli, a cult which through time functioned more and more like the Mexicas' worship of Huitzilopochtli.[197] While the Tlaxcalans brandished this ideological weapon, the Tarascan hegemony to the west grew in strength, developing utilitarian metallurgy, probably including the use of bronze.[198] With this additional advantage, the Tarascans could have become a threat to all of Mesoamerica. Meanwhile, in the wake of each Mexica disaster, defeat, or military stalemate came a series of revolts, as their oppressed tributaries would see an opportunity to take advantage of the empire's growing difficulties.[199]

Whatever the future of the Mesoamerican cultures might have been, it is clear that the era of the Triple Alliance was coming to a close. From their humble and backward beginnings the Mexica people had been launched on a truly irreversible course by the imperial reforms and the state cult. Huitzilopochtli, the state's bloodthirsty patron, had presided over one of the most extraordinary episodes in human history. Propelled by the vigor of their ideology, the armies of the Triple Alliance had swept across Mesoamerica. Yet in the end, neither the gods nor the state could adjust to the inevitable limits any polity must reach. Thus, the Mexica people were betrayed by their most fundamental beliefs. As the Spaniards arrived, the Aztec Empire was being strangled by the very forces that had created it.

Notes to Chapter 2

1 An excellent geographical survey is that of West (1964).
2 Díaz del Castillo, ch. 61, 1956: 190-1.
3 The terms Aztec and Mexica can be a source of some confusion. The word

'Aztec' was *not* used in Precolumbian times, but was popularized by nineteenth- and twentieth-century historians. It was derived from 'Aztlan', the name of the legendary first homeland of the Mexica before their migration into the Valley of Mexico. Like many unfortunate, ambiguous labels, its usage is so widespread as to render futile all attempts to replace the term or to refine its meaning. In current usage, 'Aztecs' sometimes specifically designates the ruling people of the empire, the inhabitants of the dual island capital of Tenochtitlan-Tlatelolco. However, much more commonly, 'Aztecs' is a generic label for any or all of the Nahua-speaking peoples of fourteenth- to sixteenth-century Central Mexico.

In contrast, 'Mexica' is a Precolumbian term which has a consistently narrow referent: it specifically designates the dominant ethnic group of the Aztec Triple Alliance, the people of the island capital of Tenochtitlan-Tlatelolco.

4 R. Millon 1973: 57-8, Map 18.
5 R. Millon 1976: 233-4.
6 R. Millon 1976: 239-41.
7 e.g., R. Millon 1973: 59-63; Lorenzo 1968.
8 R. Millon 1973: 59-63; Lorenzo 1968; Sanders, Parsons, and Santley 1979: 129-37.
9 cf. Jiménez Moreno 1959, 1941; Davies 1977: ch. 4.
10 Braniff 1972; J. C. Kelley 1971; E. Kelley 1978; Drummond and Muller 1972.
11 The distinctions between the various types of *chichimeca* are specifically discussed by Sahagún (bk. 10, ch. 29, 1950-69: pt. 11, pp. 170-81), who emphasizes their varying degree of sedentism and 'Mesoamericanization'. While most discussions of the *chichimeca* refer primarily to *Late* Postclassic (i.e., post-Toltec) peoples, generalizations can be assumed to characterize accurately the dynamic nature of the northern periphery of Mesoamerica in earlier times (cf. Davies 1980: ch. 4).
12 Some of the major primary sources on the Toltec climax period are: Sahagún, bk. 3, ch. 3-14, bk. 10, ch. 29, 1950-69: pt. 11, pp. 156-70; *Anales de Cuauhtitlan* 1975: 3-15; *Leyenda de los Soles* 1975; *Historia de los Mexicanos por sus Pinturas*, ch. 7-10, 1941: 215-19; Ixtlilxochitl, bk. 2, *Historia*, ch. 1-3, 1977: 7-13; Ixtlilxochitl, bk. 1, *Relaciones*, 1975: 266-91, 397-8, 418-21, 529-32; *Historia Tolteca-Chichimeca* 1947; *Origen de los Mexicanos* 1941: 260-4; *Relación de la Genealogía y Linaje* 1941: 242-4.
13 Recent archaeological excavations at Tula, Hidalgo, are described in Acosta 1940, 1944, 1956a, 1957, 1964; Diehl 1971, 1974; Cobean 1979; Matos 1974, 1976.
14 The problem of aligning Postclassic historical chronologies has been most completely reviewed by Nicholson (1978) and Davies (1980: ch. 3 and *passim*).
15 Comparison of the analyses of Jiménez Moreno (1941), Nicholson (1957), Kirchhoff (1955), Léon-Portilla (1968a), Séjourné (1965), López Austin (1973), Chadwick (1971), Willey (1976), Davies (1977), and Nicholson (1979) shows the rather extreme degree of disagreement present in reconstructions and interpretations of the Quetzalcoatl saga.
16 Until the 1940s most ethnohistorians interpreted Central Mexican dates as referring to a single calendric sequence. Studies by Jiménez Moreno (1940, 1953, 1956, 1961, 1966), Kirchhoff (1950, 1956), Caso (1951, 1953a, 1967, 1971), Nicholson (1955, 1978), and Davies (1973, 1977, 1980) have detailed the variation in regional Mexican chronologies and the presence of several, as yet incompletely correlated, chronological sequences.

17 Brief general reviews of the Central Mexican calendar and the problem of correlations can be found in Caso 1939, 1967, and 1971.

18 Important primary versions of the Quetzalcoatl legend can be found in: Sahagún, bk. 3, ch. 3-14; *Anales de Cuauhtitlan* 1975: 7-11; *Leyenda de los Soles* 1975: 123-6; *Histoyre du Mechique* 1961: ch. 10-11; *Historia de los Mexicanos por sus Pinturas*, ch. 7-8, 1941: 215-18. There are several important, but somewhat later, versions such as that in Ixtlilxochitl's *Relaciones* (1975: 269-85). See Nicholson (1957) for a complete review of both primary and secondary versions. Also see note 15 for a list of analyses and interpretations of the Quetzalcoatl legends.

19 See for example Nicholson 1971a, León-Portilla 1968b, Hunt 1977 (cf. Demarest 1981, especially pp. 71-5).

20 On the problem of these complex fusions of ancient deities and historical figures see López Austin (1973), Nicholson (1957, 1971a, 1979), Davies (1977: 55-74; 1979), Uchmany (1979), Zantwijk (1979).

21 See for example Moser 1973.

22 MacNeish 1962: 8-9.

23 This is one of several current interpretations of the 'Danzantes' sculptures of Monte Albán (cf. Coe 1962: 95-7).

24 Ruppert et al. 1955.

25 C. Millon 1973.

26 Illustrations and analyses of the Toltec sculptures of Tula and Chichen Itza can be found in Acosta 1956a, 1956b, 1956-57, 1957, 1960, 1961, 1964; Kubler 1961, 1962; Ruz Lhuiller 1945, 1962, 1971; Dutton 1955; Morris, Charlot, and Morris 1931; Covarrubias 1957; Nicholson 1971b; Tozzer 1957; Morley 1956.

27 See notes 11 and 12 above. In addition to the chronicles listed in note 12, Chimalpahin's *Relaciones Originales* (1965) and *Memorial Breve* (1958) are important sources on the confusing post-Toltec period of migrations and political and cultural realignments.

28 See note 20.

29 Armillas 1971; Parsons 1976a; Sanders, Parsons, and Santley 1979: 273-81.

30 See for example *Relación de la Genealogía y Linaje* 1941: 247.

31 See note 3. Sahagún (bk. 10, ch. 29, 1950-69: pt. 11, pp. 189-97) describes and differentiates the major ethnic groups, while the many regional chronicles (*Anales de Cuauhtitlan*, Chimalpahin, Ixtlilxochitl, *Anales de Tlatelolco*, etc.) detail the distinct but overlapping histories of the various Nahua political groups and centers.

32 See for example Sahagún, bk. 10, ch. 29, 1950-69: pt. 11, pp. 189-97; Durán, bk. 2, ch. 2-5, 1967: vol. 2, pp. 21-53; *Códice Ramírez* 1944: 24-51; *Relación de la Genealogía y Linaje* 1941: 245-50; Tezozomoc 1975: 11-100; *Historia de los Mexicanos por sus Pinturas*, ch. 9-20, 1941: 218-28; *Origen de los Mexicanos* 1941: 264-70; Ixtlilxochitl, bk. 2, *Historia*, 1977: 28-9; *Anales de Tlatelolco* 1948: 31-43. See also Cristóbal del Castillo 1908; Torquemada, bk. 2, ch. 1-10, 1975: vol. 1, pp. 113-32; Clavijero, bk. 2, 1826: vol. 1, pp. 104-16; and other early historians. Precolumbian pictorial manuscripts illustrating the Mexica migrations include the *Codex Boturini* (1944), *Codex Aubin* (1893), and the *Mapa de Sigüenza* (in Radin 1920: 12-13, Plate 12).

33 See for example Orozco y Berra (e.g., 1880: vol. 3, ch. 7, 8, pp. 131-75), Chavero (1880), and other nineteenth-century historians. Numerous syntheses and speculations are included in works by contemporary ethnohistorians, including Brundage (1972: 18-34), Davies (1973: 33-53, 1980: 172-96), Martínez Marín (1964), Zantwijk (1976), Uchmany (1978), and Bray (1978). See Martínez Marín 1976 for a recent review of the

historiography of the migration. Calnek (1978) gives insightful analyses of some of the complex problems involved in the interpretation of primary sources, including most dealing with the Mexica migration.

34 For example, Sahagún (bk. 10, ch. 29, 1950-69: pt. 11, p. 196) reports that 'they were cursed everywhere'. Scornful comments by their more established neighbors are also reported in Durán (bk. 2, ch. 3, 4, 1967: vol. 2, pp. 32, 38), Tezozomoc (1975: 46), and other sources. While the Mexica myths probably exaggerated their humble origins and rags-to-riches rise, there can be little doubt that they were one of the least prestigious Nahua groups in the fourteenth century.

35 Tezozomoc, *Crónica Mexicayotl*, 1975: 44-9; Durán, bk. 2, ch. 4, 1967: vol. 2, pp. 37-9; Sahagún, bk. 10, ch. 29, 1950-69: pt. 11, p. 196; *Relación de la Genealogía y Linaje* 1941: 248; *Historia de los Mexicanos por sus Pinturas*, ch. 12-13, 1941? 223-4; *Origen de los Mexicanos* 1941: 265.

36 e.g., *Relación de la Genealogía y Linaje* 1941: 244; *Origen de los Mexicanos* 1941: 263; *Anales de Cuauhtitlan* 1975: 15.

37 Tezozomoc, *Crónica Mexicayotl*, 1975: 48-52; Durán, bk. 2, ch. 4, 1967: vol. 2, pp. 39-41; *Historia de los Mexicanos por sus Pinturas*, ch. 16, 1941: 225.

38 Durán, bk. 2, ch. 4, 1964: 26. All the Mexica sources repeatedly stress their intermingling with the prestigious Culhuacanos. Indeed, Tezozomoc repeats and rephrases this point several times, apparently to be certain that it is not missed. He states 'the Mexicans then remained (there), taking as daughters-in-law the culhuana maidens and the culhuanos taking as their sons-in-law the young sons of the Mexica, so that they were then truly their own sons' (1975: 57). He then restates the same point a few lines later. This obsessive emphasis in Mexica state sources (in this case 'Crónica X' versions) reflects the propagandists' desire to link the Mexica to the Toltecs.

39 Most of the ethnohistorical sources placed the date of the founding of Tenochtitlan at A.D. 1325 (see Nicholson 1978: 299). Davies (1973: 198-9) presents a strong case for the date of 1345 based upon Jiménez Moreno's (1961) interpretations of varying year counts in Central Mexico. Still later dates have been cited (e.g., Brundage 1972: 34, 301).

40 *Anales de Tlatelolco* 1948: 3, 45.

41 Davies 1980: 194-5, 1973: 50-3; Espejo 1944: 522-6; Martínez del Río 1946: 148-76. Ongoing excavations in Mexico City promise to clarify the early chronology of the island.

42 For example, the Mexica were engaged as warriors on behalf of their Culhua overlords during their period of subservience to that ruler (*Anales de Tlatelolco* 1948: 40-1). Some Mexica sources claim that the Culhua granting of support and alliance to the Mexica was more due to fear of Mexica savagery than to self-interested policy (Durán, bk. 2, ch. 4, 1967: vol. 2, pp. 40-1).

43 For primary sources on the pre-imperial Mexica see note 32; for secondary sources, note 33. Unfortunately, most of both the primary material and its interpretation deals with the migration, chronology, or dynastic sequence. However, Martínez Marín (1964), Bray (1978), Castillo F. (1972: 19-46), Davies (1973), Katz (1966: 173-9 and *passim*), Caso (1954), Uchmany (1978), Zantwijk (1963, 1976), Rounds (1979) and other scholars have attempted to characterize aspects of early Mexica culture and, in some cases, to contrast pre-imperial and imperial institutions.

44 There are many excellent, if somewhat contradictory, analyses of the *calpulli*. These include Moreno 1931; Monzón 1949; Kirchhoff 1959; Caso 1963; Carrasco 1971; Katz 1966: 117-21; Zantwijk 1963, 1966, 1976; Castillo F. 1972: 72-7 and *passim*. However, extensive primary sources on

the *calpulli* are very few and all ethnohistorians rely heavily on Zorita's *Breve y Sumaria Relación* (1941), especially pp. 86-90. Important references are scattered in other sources, and Carrasco (1967) has compiled other sixteenth-century materials bearing on the *calpulli's* nature.

45 Tezozomoc, *Crónica Mexicayotl*, 1975: 74-5.
46 Zorita 1941: 86-8. The land tenure situation was apparently rather complex. See the secondary sources cited in note 44 for further discussion.
47 Sahagún (bk. 2, Appendix, 1950-69: pt. 3, pp. 179-80) describes the *calpulli* temple. Durán (bk. 2, ch. 5, 1967: vol. 2, p. 50) even states that each *calpulli* had its own patron deity worshiped in these neighborhood temples. Zorita (1941: 111-12) and Pomar (1941: 29) discuss the *calpulli* 'young men's houses' where the local youths were schooled in all matters. Castillo F. (1972: 72-3), Katz (1966: 117-21), and Carrasco (1971: 363-8) review the many other functions of the *calpulli* unit.
48 Zorita 1941: 86-90, 111-12, and *passim*.
49 Kirchhoff's proposal that *calpulli* were 'conical clans' has been embraced by some anthropologists (e.g., Sanders and Price 1968: 156; Wolf 1959: 136), but the nature of the *calpulli* and Mexica social organization were actually even more complex, as has been demonstrated by Carrasco (1971, 1976: 19-36).
50 Zorita 1941: 87; Carrasco 1971: 366.
51 Monzón 1949: 50-1.
52 See Zorita (1941: 88-90) on the election of the chief elder and on the fact that *no* decision was made without consulting the other elders of the *calpulli*.
53 Zorita 1941: 90.
54 Tezozomoc 1975: 18-19, 21; Durán, bk. 2, ch. 3, 1967: vol. 2, p. 30.
55 There are numerous references to 'capitanes' who led the migrating Mexica. E.g., *Historia de los Mexicanos por sus Pinturas*, ch. 12-13, 1941: 223-4; *Origen de los Mexicanos* 1941: 265.
56 A ruler in their mythical homeland of Aztlan named Moctezuma (Tezozomoc 1975: 15), their first migration leader, Mexi Chalchiuhtlatonac (Tezozomoc 1975: 23), and somewhat later a priest-leader Cuauhtlequetzqui (Tezozomoc 1975: 36-7), are all mentioned in the *Crónica Mexicayotl* as Migration-Period leaders. Later a Huitzilihuitl and a Tenochtzin are described by Tezozomoc (1975: 46, 60) as apparently more powerful rulers. These names appear as well in most other sources, and Huitzilihuitl and Tenocha, at least, are probably actual historical leaders of some kind. While we must suspect manipulation of these accounts by later imperial historians, it would appear that some degree of individual leadership had already arisen before the Mexicas' settlement at Tenochtitlan.
57 Actually, there are many different dates cited in the sources for the alleged accession of Acamapichtli. The full range of these dates has been detailed and analyzed by Davies (1973: 200-3).
58 The title *tlatoani* literally means 'the speaker', perhaps reminiscent of earlier periods when the holder of this office was merely one of the spokesmen for the *calpulli* elders.
59 *Anales de Tlatelolco* 1948: 46-8.
60 For example, he may have been from Coatlichan rather than Culhuacan (e.g., Tezozomoc, *Crónica Mexicayotl*, 1975: 84).
61 This tributary relationship is made absolutely clear in the *Anales de Tlatelolco* (1948: 45-7). There the first Tlatelolcan ruler (Epcouatzin or Quaquauhpitzauac) is said to have been a son of the Tepanec king, Tezozomoc, and payment of tribute both to the ruler of Tlatelolco and directly to Azcapotzalco is described.
62 *Relación de la Genealogía y Linaje* 1941: 251.

63 Clavijero, bk. 3, 1826: vol. 1, pp. 122-4. Clavijero emphasizes the social and political effects on the Mexica of their Xaltocan victories and the lands and tribute rewarded to them.

64 For recent discussions of the *mayeque* as a social class, see especially Hicks 1974, 1976; Caso 1963; Berdan 1975: 56-60; and the essays in Carrasco and Broda 1976.

65 Nicholson 1971a: 411-12, Table 3.

66 See especially Hunt 1977 for a discussion of the 'unfolding' godhead of Tezcatlipoca and other Mesoamerican divine complexes.

67 Durán, bk. 2, ch. 5, 1967: vol. 2, p. 50.

68 See note 32 for the primary sources. Durán, Tovar, and Tezozomoc (all derived from the lost 'Crónica X') are presumed to be closest to the official Mexica state version.

69 Cristóbal del Castillo 1908: 82.

70 Sahagún, bk. 10, ch. 29, 1950-69: pt. 11, p. 189. Durán, bk. 2, ch. 3, 1967: vol. 2, p. 28.

71 Cristóbal del Castillo 1908: 83; Torquemada, bk. 2, ch. 1, 1975: vol. 1, p. 113.

72 Sahagún, bk. 1, ch. 1, 1950-69: pt. 2, p. 1.

73 For recent interpretations of the composite, confusing nature of Huitzilopochtli, see Uchmany (1978, 1979), Zantwijk (1979), Davies (1973: 35-8), López Austin (1973, *passim*), Brotherston (1974), Brundage (1979: ch. 6), Carrasco (1979) and Nicholson (1971a: 425-6 and *passim*).

74 Castillo and Torquemada as cited above (note 71).

75 Aguilar 1963: 163-4. Translation by Patricia de Fuentes.

76 e.g., *Leyenda de los Soles* 1975: 119-22; Sahagún, bk. 7, ch. 2, 1950-69: pt. 8, pp. 3-8; *Historia de los Mexicanos por sus Pinturas*, ch. 7, 1941: 215-16.

77 The major sacrificial ceremonies are most completely described by Sahagún (especially in bk. 2, 1950-69: pt. 3) and in Durán's *Book of the Rites and Ceremonies and The Ancient Calendar* (bk. 1, 1967: vol. 1; English translation in Durán 1971).

78 Sahagún, bk. 2, ch. 21, 1950-69: pt. 3, pp. 52-3.

79 See for example Durán (bk. 2, ch. 8, 1967: vol. 2, pp. 69-71) and Clavijero (bk. 3, 1826: vol. 1, pp. 122-4). It is difficult to judge whether the sources were accurate here or were attempting to justify the later Mexica revolt. Nonetheless, given the growing Mexica threat, the development of Maxtla's anti-Mexica party is quite plausible.

80 The Texcocan-Tepanec war is one of the better documented events in Aztec ethnohistory. A generally reliable (but clearly biased) primary source on the war is the Texcocan chronicler Ixtlilxochitl in his various writings (especially bk. 2, 1977: 39-54; see also bk. 1, 1975: 326-42, 433-9, 536-8).

81 Nezahualcoyotl's romantic years in hiding were a favorite topic of Ixtlilxochitl, who spent the better part of five chapters of his *Historia de la Nación Chichimeca* detailing them (Ixtlilxochitl, bk. 2, 1977: 57-72).

82 Ixtlilxochitl, bk. 2, 1977: ch. 22, pp. 55-6; Tezozomoc 1975: 100-8; *Historia de los Mexicanos* 1941: 229-30; *Anales de Tlatelolco* 1948: 55; *Relación de la Genealogía y Linaje* 1941: 252; *Anales de Cuauhtitlan* 1975: 37-8. Note that all of these sources characterize Maxtla as a usurper. One of the younger sons of Tezozomoc, Maxtla was allegedly the legitimate heir only to the throne of the Tepanec vassalage of Coyoacan.

83 These particular contradictory accounts of Chimalpopoca's death are given by the *Anales Mexicanos* (1903: 50), *Anales de Tlatelolco* (1948: 55), and Durán (bk. 2, ch. 8, 1967: vol. 2, pp. 71-2), respectively. See discussion and other versions in notes 89-92 below.

84 Note that even according to Mexica sources (e.g., Durán, bk. 2, ch. 8, 1967:

vol. 2, p. 73), Itzcoatl was the illegitimate son of Acamapichtli, the first Mexica *tlatoani*, and a slave girl. This hardly makes him the most likely successor by birthright. However, Durán reports that he was elected by 'common consent' on the basis of his valor and his 'proper behavior' (Durán, bk. 2, ch. 8, 1967: vol. 2, p. 73). One may cynically note that it is odd (indeed, suspicious) that the Mexica sources are so critical of Maxtla's 'usurpation' of the Tepanec throne over his older brothers, yet so blithely dismiss any such objection to Itzcoatl's election at Tenochtitlan itself.

85 Durán (bk. 2, ch. 8, 1967: vol. 2, pp. 69-72) and Ixtlilxochitl (*Historia*, bk. 2, ch. 30, 1977: 77-8) detail the claims of the Tepanecs' unreasonable treatment of the Mexica, including insults, high tribute, and denial of access rights to water and trade routes.

86 The extent and importance of the Texcocan role varies predictably between sources. Mexica sources attribute the victory to Tlacaelel and Itzcoatl, with Nezahualcoyotl as a prestigious, but low-profile, ally (e.g., Durán, bk. 2, ch. 10, 1967: vol. 2, pp. 85-96; *Códice Ramírez*, Tovar 1944: 58-72). Naturally, Ixtlilxochitl, the Texcocan chronicler, portrays the role of the Texcocan king, Nezahualcoyotl, as critical, even crediting him with the final conquest of Azcapotzalco itself and the execution of Maxtla. See for example Ixtlilxochitl's *Historia*, in which Nezahualcoyotl leads the war against Maxtla, captures him, and sacrifices him in the main plaza of Azcapotzalco (bk. 2, ch. 28-31, 1977: 73-81).

87 Again, the relative power and influence of these three centers has been the subject of considerable debate. Despite the nominal partnership, the small center of Tacuba was clearly a minor power within the alliance. Texcoco's role was a major one, but as time went on its economic, military, and eventually political power was ever more overshadowed by Tenochtitlan. By conquest times even the Texcocan succession was manipulated by the Mexica *tlatoani* (see notes 191-2 below).

88 Itzcoatl is mentioned by Chimalpahin as a military leader and important administrator as early as 1407 (Chimalpahin 1965: 83-4), and Clavijero specifically states that he had led Mexica armies for three decades and risen to the rank of commander in chief (Clavijero, bk. 3, 1826: vol. 1, p. 144). Recall also Itzcoatl's weak hereditary claim to the throne (note 84).

89 *Anales Mexicanos* 1903: 50.

90 Chimalpahin (1965: 190-1) states that both Chimalpopoca and the ruler of Tlatelolco were murdered by assassins from Tacuba (also called Tlacopan). However, he implies that they were 'Tepanec' in affiliation.

91 Even these Mexica versions blaming the Tepanecs for Chimalpopoca's death are suspiciously contradictory. Durán (bk. 2, ch. 8, 1967: vol. 2, pp. 71-2) and Tovar (1944: 55) state that Tepanecs murdered him in his sleep in his own palace in Tenochtitlan. The *Anales de Tlatelolco* (1948: 55), Torquemada (bk. 2, ch. 20, 1975: 177), and Clavijero (bk. 3, 1826: vol. 1, pp. 139-41) describe how Chimalpopoca killed himself after being taken captive and humiliated by the Tepanecs in Azcapotzalco. The *Relación de la Genealogía y Linaje* (1941: 252) states that a broad alliance of centers conspired in the drowning of Chimalpopoca by assassins. There are many other versions.

92 Davies 1974: 61. See also Davies 1980: 307-9 and 1973: 152-8.

93 Sahagún, bk. 10, ch. 29, 1950-69: pt. 11, p. 191.

94 See especially León-Portilla (1958, 1959: 162-6, 1960), Brotherston (1974), Padden (1967: 2-13, 50-66), Demarest (1976), and Uchmany (1979: 57-9).

95 Durán, bk. 2, ch. 9. Translation by Doris Heyden and Fernando Horcasitas (Durán 1964: 52).

96 Durán, bk. 2, ch. 9. Translation by Heyden and Horcasitas (Durán 1964: 57-8).

97 Durán, bk. 2, ch. 9. Translation by Heyden and Horcasitas (Durán 1964: 59).

98 Durán, bk. 2, ch. 9. Translation by Heyden and Horcasitas (Durán 1964: 59).

99 Durán, bk. 2, ch. 9. Translation by Heyden and Horcasitas (Durán 1964: 59-60).

100 Durán, bk. 2, ch. 9. Translation by Heyden and Horcasitas (Durán 1964: 60).

101 Durán, bk. 2, ch. 11, 1967: vol. 2, p. 103.

102 Durán, bk. 2, ch. 11. Translation by Heyden and Horcasitas (Durán 1964: 70).

103 Tovar 1944: 83.

104 Durán, bk. 2, ch. 26, 1967: vol. 2, pp. 211-14.

105 Durán, bk. 2, ch. 26, 1967: vol. 2, p. 212.

106 Durán, bk. 2, ch. 26, 1967: vol. 2, p. 214.

107 These included the Toltec alliance of Tollan-Culhuacan-Otompan and the post-Toltec triple alliances of Culhuacan-Tenanyocan-Xaltocan, Azcapotzalco-Culhuacan-Acolman. See Nicholson 1978: 317-18.

108 Sahagún, bk. 10, ch. 29. Translation by C.E. Dibble and A.J.O. Anderson (Sahagún 1950-69: pt. 11, p. 191).

109 *Codex Ramírez*. Translation by Paul Radin (1920: 106).

110 The exact relationship of Huitzilopochtli and Tonatiuh probably has always been unclear precisely because of the artificial nature of the state's fusion of their mythologies (León-Portilla 1963: 161-2). Huitzilopochtli's overlapping with the all-encompassing Tezcatlipoca was inevitable given his elevation into the upper ranks of the traditional Aztec upper pantheon. Nicholson (1971a: 425-6) notes this 'fusion' of deities in Huitzilopochtli and also notes his debatable status as a solar deity in the usual sense. See also Caso 1958: 33-7.

111 See Hunt 1977 for an analysis of Huitzilopochtli as one facet of the manifold Tezcatlipoca complex.

112 *Historia de los Mexicanos por sus Pinturas* 1941: 209-10. See Caso 1958: 10; León-Portilla 1963: 33-6.

113 Caso 1958: 12-13.

114 León-Portilla 1963: 61.

115 Chimalpahin 1965: 196. Translation by Paul Radin (1920: 127).

116 León-Portilla 1963: 162.

117 Durán, bk. 2, ch. 11. Translation by Heyden and Horcasitas (Durán 1964: 69).

118 Townsend 1979: 53.

119 Townsend 1979: 49.

120 Townsend 1979: 70.

121 Nicholson 1971b: 118.

122 Durán, bk. 2, ch. 26, 1967: vol. 2, p. 213.

123 See for example Garibay 1958: 31 for a propagandist hymn deliberately combining Huitzilopochtli, the sun, and the Mexicas' militaristic mission.

124 Sahagún, cited in León-Portilla 1963: 10, 17.

125 Excerpt from a sixteenth-century manuscript edited by Sahagún (*El Libro de los Colloquios...*), as cited in León-Portilla 1963: 18-19.

126 See for example Durán's descriptions of two such setbacks (bk. 2, ch. 57, 61). Note that in both cases the state's reaction to defeat and insufficient sacrificial captives was not to regroup or consolidate, but to send out new

armies quickly to seek new conquests and captives (Durán, bk. 2, ch. 57, 61, 1967: vol. 2, pp. 436-7, 461-2).

127 See Harner's comparisons of Cook's (1946) estimates and more recent extremely high figures by Cook and Borah (Harner 1977a: 119). These latest figures are, in our opinion, far too high, ranging up to 250,000 sacrificial victims per year in Central Mexico. However, the specific estimates are unimportant; in any case, the scale of the sacrificial cult had reached a point where its social, economic, and demographic impact was tremendous (cf. Demarest ms.).

128 See Ixtlilxochitl (bk. 2, ch. 60, 1977: 157-8), Durán (bk. 2, ch. 43, 1967: vol. 2, pp. 333-41), and Torquemada (bk. 2, ch. 63, 1975: vol. 1, pp. 257-9), though these sources probably all exaggerate the scale of the event. The dedication stone of the temple provides an archaeological check on some aspects of these descriptions (see Orozco y Berra 1877; cf. Townsend 1979: 40-3).

129 Actually, Ixtlilxochitl (bk. 2, ch. 60, 1977: 157) and Durán (bk. 2, ch. 43, 1967: vol. 2, p. 340) state that 80,400 captives were sacrificed. Torquemada sets the figure precisely at 72,344 (bk. 2, ch. 63, 1975: vol. 1, p. 257). It is assumed that these sources reflect Mexica propaganda aggrandizing the event. According to Orozco and Berra's interpretation of the stone's iconography (1877: 61), as well as comparative study of the descriptions by Cook (1946: 91), a figure of about 20,000 would seem more likely.

130 The most complete and reliable descriptions of the many variations of Aztec human sacrifice and cannibalism are found in book 2 of Sahagún's *Florentine Codex* (1950-69: pt. 3).

131 The protein-search theory presented by Harner (e.g., 1977a,b) was subsequently championed and popularized by Marvin Harris (1979). We discuss it extensively in Chapter 4 below. See also Demarest ms.

132 Brundage (1975) in comparing the Aztec and Inca Empires makes such a characterization of the Mexica expansion. While we agree on the eventual stresses imposed by expansionism, the Mexicas' early successes, statecraft, and political organization have been badly underrated by Brundage. He also follows the somewhat romanticized presentation of the Inca state by late chroniclers and accepts their idealized view of the integration and symmetry of Inca political organization (cf. Moore 1958). As seen in our presentation of their histories, both conquest states shared similar structural strengths and weaknesses.

133 Berdan's (1975) analysis of the Triple Alliance economy represents a fundamental shift in thinking on the nature of Aztec economics. Following the 'substantivist' school of economic anthropology, Berdan re-evaluates the Aztec economy as an institution 'embedded' in the political, social, and ideological matrix of the society. This approach leads to a number of critical changes (followed here) in traditional views of Mexica economics. Berdan emphasizes the role of tribute in all sectors of Aztec life and the *interdependence* of tribute, market, and long-distance trade.

134 The regular redistributive functions of tribute have been summarized and documented by Berdan (1975: ch. 3). Mexica storage for famine was probably minimal, given the descriptions of the disastrous famine of the mid-fifteenth century; even official descriptions of the famine (e.g., Tezozomoc, *Crónica Mexicana*, ch. 40, 1943: 37-44; Durán, bk. 2, ch. 30, 1967: vol. 2, pp. 241-4) make Moctezuma I's redistribution of foodstuffs sound improvised, as well as insufficient.

135 See for example the conquest tribute exacted from the defeated Xochimil-

cans by Itzcoatl. They were forced to construct portions of Tenochtitlan's elaborate causeway and dike system (Durán, bk. 2, ch. 12-13, 1967: vol. 2, pp. 111-14).

136 Sahagún, bk. 2, ch. 5, 1950-69: pt. 3, pp. 21-5.

137 See Carrasco 1971; Hicks 1974, 1976; Berdan 1975: 56-65; González Torres 1976, and the various regional essays on social stratification in Carrasco and Broda 1976.

138 Berdan 1975: 178-83.

139 See for example initiations of hostilities with the Xochimilcans, Tepeacans, Coaixtlahuacans, and the peoples of the Tehuantepec region (Durán, bk. 2, ch. 12, 18, 22, 46, 1967: vol. 2, pp. 105-12, 153-62, 185-9, 357-62). Durán himself cynically notes that these alleged abuses of Mexica merchants and emissaries occur so often as to appear merely a standard justification for Mexica aggression (Durán, bk. 2, ch. 46, 1967: vol. 2, p. 357).

140 On the warriors' heavenly reward see the prayer given as chapter 3 of book 2 of the *Florentine Codex* (Sahagún 1950-69: pt. 3, pp. 11-15). On the deification of mothers who died in childbirth see Sahagún, bk. 6, ch. 29, 1950-69: pt. 3, pp. 161-5; also Sullivan 1966.

141 For discussions of social mobility through achievement, its extent and limits, see especially Carrasco (1971), Berdan (1975: 65-70 and *passim*), and also comments in most of the sources cited in note 142. In Durán's *Historia* (bk. 2, ch. 29, 1967: vol. 2, pp. 36-7) a long speech by Tlacaelel is quoted in which he specifically states that social mobility and its material rewards and privileges will be dependent upon military success regardless of an individual's birth status. Obviously, this is a presentation of the state's ideal rather than a social reality. Nonetheless, it emphasizes the early empire's use of social mobility as an incentive for militarism (cf. Sahagún, bk. 8, ch. 21, 1950-69: pt. 9, pp. 75-7; Durán, *Libro de los Ritos*..., bk. 1, ch. 6, 1967: vol. 1, pp. 67-9).

142 Durán gives several listings of some of these initial privileges (see speech cited in note 141, also bk. 2, ch. 26, and bk. 1, ch. 11, 1967: vol. 2, pp. 211-14, vol. 1, pp. 111-17). Anawalt (1977, 1981) has provided characterizations of the Mexica lords' and warriors' privileges in dress, behavior, and possessions. The noble warrior class (*tetecutin*) and their more significant material rewards in access to lands and labor were defined by Zorita (1941: 85-6) and have been debated by Carrasco (1971, 1976, 1981), Katz (1966: 32, 115-16, 123, 134-5, 173-9, 190-3), Berdan (1975: 41-2, 65-70), López Austin (1961: 59-62), Castillo F. (1972: ch. 4), Soustelle (1961: ch. 2), Offner (1981), and others. The upward social and economic mobility of the successful warrior quickly became limited by a hereditary class structure. Nonetheless, mobility within these broad class constraints was still dependent upon military prowess or state service from the level of differential privileges within the lowest *calpulli* to the selection of the next *tlatoani* from the tiny pool of eligible heirs.

143 e.g., Sahagún, bk. 2, ch. 21, 1950-69: pt. 3, pp. 46-8.

144 Sahagún (bk. 9, 1950-69: pt. 10) is the definitive source on all aspects of the merchant class, including their internal stratifications. See also Broda's insightful analysis (1976) of *pochteca* rank and ritual.

145 Sahagún, bk. 9, ch. 10-14, 1950-69: pt. 10, pp. 45-67.

146 Sahagún, bk. 6, ch. 31. Translation by C.E. Dibble and A.J.O. Anderson (Sahagún 1950-69: pt. 7, p. 171).

147 Tezozomoc 1975: 24.

148 Opinion has varied over the years regarding Tenochtitlan's dominance of the Triple Alliance. Early studies followed closely Mexica official sources

(e.g., 'Crónica X' sources: Durán, Tezozomoc, Tovar) which portray Tenochtitlan as the totally dominant power. Subsequent scholarship has drawn more heavily on Ixtlilxochitl and other non-Mexica sources which aggrandize the role of Texcoco and stress the formal partnership of the three founding centers of the alliance (Tenochtitlan, Texcoco, and Tacuba). The truth lies somewhere in between: while the role of Texcoco was initially critical, as time passed Tenochtitlan gradually came to outright dominance of the alliance. This change was due to both the rapid and massive urbanization of the Tenochtitlan zone and its booming mercantile activities, as well as deliberate Mexica expansion of its tribute base at the expense of its Triple Alliance partners (see Gibson 1971: 383-9).

149 The independent enclaves within the Mexica empire have been identified and thoroughly described by Davies (1968).

150 See for example the Tlaxcalan instigations of at least two rebellions in Orizaba (Durán, bk. 2, ch. 21, 24, 1967: vol. 2, pp. 177-83, 197-203; Torquemada, bk. 2, ch. 49, 1975: vol. 1, pp. 224-5) and their many short-lived alliances with the Huexotzingans against the Triple Alliance (e.g., Ixtlilxochitl, bk. 2, ch. 61, 1977: 111-12).

151 Note Ixtlilxochitl's comment that the Tlaxcalans and their Huexotzingan allies were perpetually in a state of war with the Mexica (bk. 2, ch. 81, 1977: 203).

152 See note 150 above; also Davies 1968.

153 Durán, bk. 2, ch. 37, 38, 1967: vol. 2, pp. 281-93.

154 Durán's *Historia* (bk. 2, ch. 37, 1967: vol. 2, p. 282) claims that the Tarascans mustered 40,000 warriors, actually outnumbering the invading Mexica army. However, keep in mind the Mexica bias of this official account of the defeat.

155 Berdan's analysis of Mexica economics indicates that foodstuffs and bulk goods were drawn only from Central Mexico, while the more distant provinces primarily supplied exotic luxury goods (e.g., Berdan 1975: 109-12, 245).

156 Calnek (1976: 288-91) argues that immigration was largely responsible for the massive urbanization of Tenochtitlan in imperial times.

157 Calnek 1972a.

158 Berdan 1975: 282-6.

159 Berdan 1975: 113-14, 287-8.

160 Berdan 1975: 246-51.

161 Durán, bk. 2, ch. 21, 1967: vol. 2, pp. 179-80. These line-of-supply problems were especially difficult in reaching and maintaining conquests in the distant Oaxaca, Tehuantepec, and Soconusco provinces far to the southeast. Tezozomoc (*Crónica Mexicana*, ch. 75, 1943: 151-2) relates how Mexica trade and tribute missions were attacked in the Tehuantepec region. Also see pp. 61-2.

162 Such garrisons were established on the menaced Tarascan frontier (Durán, bk. 2, ch. 45, 1967: vol. 2, pp. 351-5) and in the southeast provinces (e.g., Durán, bk. 2, ch. 27, 1967: vol. 2, p. 231).

163 On the privilege of polygamy see note 142.

164 The massive immigration of non-farmer specialists to Tenochtitlan in the late fifteenth century posited by Calnek (1972b, 1976) correlates closely with the growth of the elite classes (nobles, warriors, priests, and merchants) who needed their services and manufactured goods.

165 Sahagún, bk. 10, ch. 16, 1950-69: pt. 11, p. 59; see discussion in Berdan 1975: 160-1.

166 Ixtlilxochitl, bk. 2, ch. 41, 1977: 111-13; Chimalpahin, *Sexta Relación*, 1965: 157; Durán, bk. 2, ch. 28-29, 1967: vol. 2, pp. 232-8; Pomar 1941: 41-3.

167 Price (1978: 110), Davies (1974: 97-8), and Hicks (1979: 88) have all expressed this suspicion, noting the rather serious nature of Chalcan and Tlaxcalan conflicts sometimes labeled 'Flowery Wars'.

168 Hicks 1979.

169 Under the leadership of a legendary figure, Cosihuesa, the Zapotec groups united, perhaps even with the aid of their age-old enemies, the Mixtecs. This force then inflicted great casualties on the invading army of Ahuitzotl at the battle of Guiengola (Whitecotton 1977: 125-6, 130-2, 304-5). Durán (bk. 2, ch. 50, 1967: vol. 2, pp. 383-9) and other Mexica sources present this battle as a Mexica victory. However, in view of Ahuitzotl's abrupt termination of the campaign and subsequent events, it appears most likely that a negotiated truce had been arranged. (For an alternative, archaeological perspective on Guiengola, see Peterson and MacDougall 1974.)

170 Durán, bk. 2, ch. 46. Translation by Heyden and Horcasitas (Durán 1964: 203).

171 Durán, bk. 2, ch. 50. Translation by Heyden and Horcasitas (Durán 1964: 217-18).

172 Durán (bk. 2, ch. 50, 1967: vol. 2, pp. 384-5) states his doubts that the Texcocan ruler, Nezahualpilli, had participated in Ahuitzotl's Soconusco campaign and relates that the Tacuban ruler certainly declined to join the expedition. This Mexica source implies that Nezahualpilli's unmanly nature explains his refusal. The Texcocan chronicler Ixtlilxochitl (bk. 2, ch. 49, 1977: 156) admits that Nezahualpilli withdrew from the most distant final campaign, but he claims that the Texcocan lord did not wish to be in the shadow of his Mexica ally. Later, Nezahualpilli argued against Moctezuma II's continuing wars of attrition against the Tlaxcalan alliance enclaves. This time we are told that bad omens discouraged him concerning these wars (Durán, bk. 2, ch. 61, 1967: vol. 2, pp. 459-60) or that he was too obsessed with astrological studies to attend to his military duties (Ixtlilxochitl, bk. 2, ch. 72, 1977: 181). However, the unprofitable nature of these wars, as well as the increasing resentment between Triple Alliance capitals (see below), seem more likely causes of the Mexicas' allies' reluctance to support these campaigns.

173 Tezozomoc, *Crónica Mexicana*, ch. 80, 1943: 167-74; Durán, bk. 2, ch. 48, 49, 1967: vol. 2, pp. 369-81; Torquemada, bk. 2, ch. 67, 1975: vol. 1, pp. 265-6.

174 Ixtlilxochitl, bk. 2, ch. 66, 1977: 167; *Anales Mexicanos* 1903: 69; Chimalpahin 1965: 119; Durán, bk. 2, ch. 49, 1967: vol. 2, pp. 375-81; Torquemada, bk. 2, ch. 67, 1975: vol. 1, p. 266; Tezozomoc 1943: 172-4.

175 Harvey 1971.

176 Berdan 1975: 274.

177 Berdan 1975: 78-9.

178 Berdan 1975: 276-7.

179 Berdan 1975: 275.

180 Davies 1968: 157-79.

181 On the wars of Moctezuma II see especially Ixtlilxochitl, bk. 2, ch. 71-74, 1977: 179-87; Durán, bk. 2, ch. 55-60, 62, 1967: vol. 2, pp. 417-58, 463-6; Torquemada, bk. 2, ch. 69-72, 75-76, 78, 1975: vol. 1, pp. 269-79, 285-90, 293-4.

182 Durán, bk. 2, ch. 57. Translation by Heyden and Horcasitas (Durán 1964: 235).

183 Ixtlilxochitl, bk. 2, ch. 70-71, 1977: 177, 179-80; Tovar 1944: 94;
    Torquemada, bk. 2, ch. 68, 1975: vol. 1, pp. 267-8.
184 Tovar 1944: 97-8; Durán, bk. 2, ch. 53, 1967: vol. 2, pp. 403-6.
185 Durán, bk. 2, ch. 53, 1967: vol. 2, p. 407.
186 Sahagún, bk. 9, ch. 6, 1950-69: pt. 10, pp. 31-2.
187 Durán (bk. 2, ch. 53, 1967: vol. 2, p. 404) states that those who were not
    'sons of very fine ladies' could never enter into the high ranks of state
    service.
188 Note that in relation to the treatment of both warriors and merchants the
    sources repeatedly contrast Ahuitzotl with Moctezuma II. Ahuitzotl
    virtually became a symbol of social mobility to the non-noble members of
    these restrained classes of the Conquest period. For example, in book 9
    of Sahagún's *Florentine Codex* (Sahagún 1950-69: pt. 10) the privileges, titles,
    and prestige of the various merchant groups are mentioned in association
    with Ahuitzotl. In contrast Moctezuma is mentioned only in connection
    with limitations of merchant behavior (see note 186). The chroniclers, and
    perhaps the people, personified the freezing of social mobility, blaming it
    on Moctezuma II's aristocratic nature. It should be clear, however, that
    given limited wealth and bureaucratic positions, the shift was the inevitable
    result of the slowing of the Mexica expansion.
189 The roles of these offices were probably gradually diminishing throughout
    the history of the empire as power was concentrated in the *tlatoani*. This
    change is reflected in the historical chronicles which seldom mention them
    by name, after the death of the possibly legendary Tlacaelel. The now
    humble status of even the *cihuacoatl* is made clear in the *Codex Ramírez* (Tovar
    1944: 98). It is anecdotally related there that this highest adviser politely
    questioned Moctezuma II's edicts, was then sharply lectured, and quickly
    scurried away to carry out the ruler's original set of commands.
190 See note 148.
191 The more neutral chronicle of Chimalpahin (*Tercera Relación*, 1965: 121)
    asserts that the Tenocha favorite Cacama 'was installed' on the Texcocan
    throne in 1516.
192 A detailed version of the power struggle in Texcoco is given by Ixtlilxochitl
    (bk. 2, ch. 76, 1977: 190-2), who (as a Texcocoan) was clearly biased toward
    the anti-Mexica 'local rule' party. This version was expanded by
    Torquemada (bk. 2, ch. 83-86, 1975: vol. 1, pp. 303-11).
193 In the view of most chroniclers and certainly many historians, the final
    blame fell on Moctezuma II, as an insecure ruler (e.g., Brundage 1972:
    chs. 11, 12; Padden 1967: ch. 6; also most popular presentations). As our
    own version of the troubles of the Aztec state should demonstrate, the
    problems of the last decades of the empire were more the consequences of
    processes begun with the original formation of the Mexica expansion state.
    The strains created by the increasingly maladaptive nature of Mexica
    expansionism were evident in Ahuitzotl's reign, but came to a crisis stage
    in Moctezuma II's.
194 Durán, bk. 2, ch. 61. Translation by Heyden and Horcasitas (Durán 1964:
    242).
195 Durán, bk. 2, ch. 57. Translation by Heyden and Horcasitas (Durán 1964:
    235).
196 In the final campaign the central role and massive numbers of the Indian
    allies, especially the Tlaxcalans, is stressed in all versions. See especially
    Sahagún (bk. 12), Díaz del Castillo (1964, 1956). Figures in the thousands
    are given for Tlaxcalan contingents in most battles in the Spanish Conquest.

As Sahagún generalizes, the Tlaxcalans formed the bulk of Cortés's army, 'a teeming multitude, a great host' (bk. 12, ch. 22, 1950-69: pt. 13, p. 59).

197 Camaxtli, like Huitzilopochtli, was a complex hero-patron deity but, reflecting the lesser fortunes of his people, he never rose to the pretentious heights of the Mexica Huitzilopochtli. See Durán (bk. 1, ch. 7, 1967: vol. 1, pp. 71-80) on the Mexican worship of Camaxtli. Davies (1979) reviews his god-hero nature and development.

198 Porter-Weaver 1981: 471-4. It is intriguing that Durán mentions superior Tarascan weapons in his description of the Mexica defeat (bk. 2, ch. 37, 1967: vol. 2, p. 282).

199 For example, note the Mixtec reaction to a Mexica defeat by the Huexotzingans:

> When the news of these disasters became known in the land of the Mixtecs it was believed that the Aztecs would be unable to take up arms soon, and the sovereigns of Yanhuitlan and Zozola sent a challenge to Moctezoma. In addition, they obstructed the roads and killed many Aztec merchants (Durán, bk. 2, ch. 57; translation by Heyden and Horcasitas [Durán, 1964: 236]).

3
The Inca imperial expansion

We move now to the second great center of prehistoric New World civilization, the Central Andes. Archaeologists use this label to designate a section of western South America encompassing the coastal and highland zones of Peru and highland Bolivia. It is a land of striking geographical contrasts. On its western margin, along the Pacific coast, stretches a narrow desert plain that would be uninhabitable were it not transected by over forty small but fertile river valleys. Behind the coastal plain the Andes, the world's second-highest mountain range, rise to an average elevation of over three thousand meters; only the scattered intermontane valleys and basins of the highlands, or sierra, are suitable for human occupation. This dramatically inhospitable stage, coast and highlands, formed the setting for the evolution of what is variously called Peruvian, Central Andean, or Andean civilization.[1]

When Spanish conquistadors entered the Central Andes in A.D. 1532, they found the entire area, plus lands to the north and south, under the control of a single group, the Inca. From their capital of Cuzco in the southern highlands of Peru the Inca had extended their domain until their empire measured over 4,300 kilometers from end to end. Superimposed on a map of modern South America, the Inca realm would begin on the southern frontier of Colombia, stretch southward along the coast and highlands of Ecuador and Peru, sprawl across highland Bolivia to northwestern Argentina, and reach down into central Chile (Figure 12). This vast territory, which the Inca called *Tawantinsuyu*, or 'Land of the Four Quarters', was the largest empire ever formed in the native Americas, and probably the largest ever formed anywhere on a 'Bronze Age' level of technology.

Yet for all its size and splendor, Tawantinsuyu endured for only a century, and the 'mighty army' that brought it down contained merely a few hundred Spanish adventurers. This precipitous rise and fall, the how and why of the Inca expansion and collapse, are what concern us here.

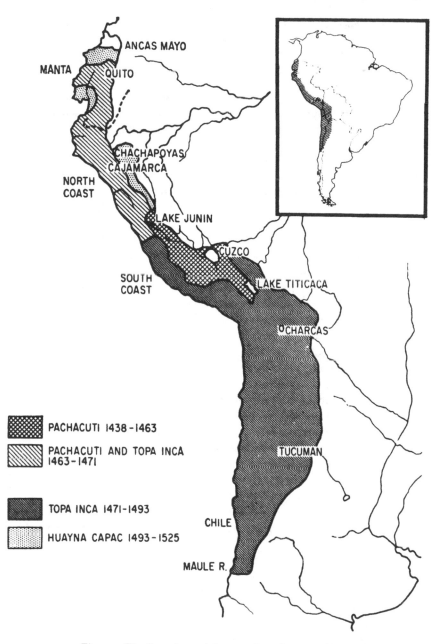

Fig. 12. The Inca imperial expansion, showing the empire's final extent and the territories conquered by individual rulers.

Historical background

In Cuzco, imperial dogma held that the entire Andean world had been in a state of savagery before the coming of the Inca Empire.[2] This claim was the most flagrant fiction. The truth of the matter is that the Inca did not establish Andean civilization; they inherited it and built upon it. Much of their spectacular but short-lived empire was based upon institutions that they shared with their competitors and precursors.

The tradition underlying Tawantinsuyu was long and complicated, and the history of Andean civilization is replete with shifts of power and prestige, with the rises and falls of individual cultures. The details of those shifts, rises, and falls are known from written accounts and archaeological research. Both sources of data have their limitations. What we might call the 'ethnohistoric threshold' occurs much later in the Andes than in Mesoamerica: the native Andean peoples never developed systems of writing, and all documentary accounts of preconquest history were compiled during the Spanish Colonial era. As a result, we have voluminous descriptions of the Inca Empire, but only scanty accounts of pre-Inca cultures. Furthermore, the latter often seem to be mythical or legendary and cannot be read as history, except in the most general sense. In the absence of reliable historical records we must depend on archaeology to illuminate pre-Inca epochs. At present the archaeological record is uneven—fairly detailed for some places, times, and topics; virtually non-existent for others—but it has provided us with a basic understanding of Andean cultural development (Table 2).

Archaeological research has shown that Peruvian civilization emerged in nascent but recognizable form some four thousand years before the Inca Empire, during Preceramic Period VI (2700-1800 B.C.).[3] Chiefdom-level organization, monumental (or 'corporate labor') architecture, and sophisticated art styles first appeared in the archaeological record at this time, but only in a few limited regions of the Central Andes (Moseley 1975b, 1978; Feldman 1980).[4] Social and cultural complexity became much more widespread in the succeeding epoch, the Initial Period (1800-1200 B.C.).

The rise of complex societies in a number of regions set the stage for the Early Horizon (1200-200 B.C.). During this era Peru was swept by the first of the three great unifying movements that punctuated its prehistory. Like later epochs of pan-Andean cultural unification, the Early Horizon is defined by the dissemination of certain distinctive iconographic art styles over much of the Peruvian area. In the specific case of the Early Horizon, stylistic diffusion began along the central and northern coasts and is generally interpreted as reflecting the spread of religious ideas.[5]

In the Early Intermediate Period (200 B.C.-A.D. 550) widespread cultural, or at least iconographic, similarity was replaced by marked

Table 2. *Chronological framework for Central Andean prehistory,*
2700 B.C.–A.D. 1532

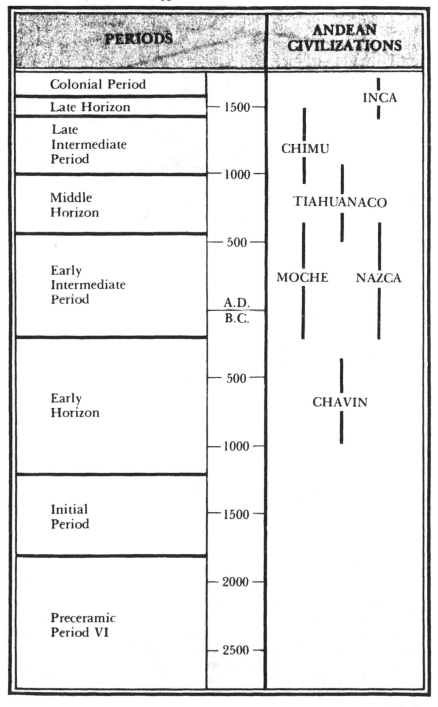

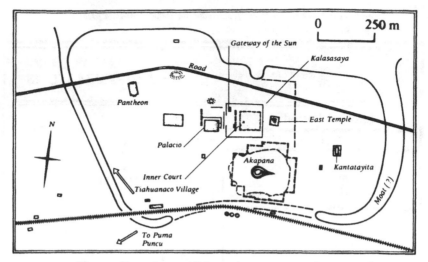

Fig. 13. Plan of some of the major monumental constructions at Tiahuanaco, Bolivia.

diversity. A number of brilliant regional states and cultures flourished during this period, including the famous 'classic' civilizations of Andean prehistory—Moche of the northern coast, Nasca of the southern coast, Recuay of the northern highlands, and so on. The Early Intermediate Period also witnessed the beginning of monumental constructions at a site that would soon come to influence much of the Andean world: Tiahuanaco in the Titicaca Basin (Figure 13).

The Middle Horizon (A.D. 550-1000), the second great epoch of cultural unification, is probably the most controversial segment of Peruvian prehistory. However, all authorities agree that the iconography which spread throughout the Central Andes during the Middle Horizon was ultimately derived from Tiahuanaco (Figure 16). Archaeologists have tended to see Tiahuanaco as a largely religious site, but it is becoming increasingly clear that Tiahuanaco must also have been a major economic and political center whose power, and perhaps imperial domination, extended across the Titicaca Basin and into adjacent parts of the southern Andes.[6] North of the Titicaca Basin the exact nature of political events remains unclear.[7] Nonetheless, regardless of the manner in which it spread, iconography related to that of Tiahuanaco reached well into northern Peru during the first half of the Middle Horizon.

In northern and central Peru the cultural 'unification' of the Middle Horizon began to break down during the latter half of the period, initiating a trend toward regionalization that continued into the Late Intermediate Period (A.D. 1000-1475). Farther to the south, in the Titicaca Basin and neighboring regions, the Tiahuanaco civilization persisted until about A.D 1200, when it collapsed for reasons that have yet to be determined.[8] Whatever the causes, the final breakdown of Tiahuanaco had repercussions throughout the greater south Peruvian area. The ensuing power vacuum gave birth to the historically known peoples of the southern sierra, who enter the archaeological record at the time of the Tiahuanaco collapse.[9] In turn, several centuries of conflicts among these southern highland cultures eventually gave rise to the last major epoch of unification in Central Andean prehistory, the Late Horizon. The unifying force of the Late Horizon was, of course, the Inca Empire (A.D. 1438-1532).[10]

This skeletal sketch can be fleshed out in any number of ways, but for our purposes Peruvian culture history can be said to have three dominant themes. The first is the cycle emphasized by the period and horizon framework: epochs of regional differentiation alternating with eras of widespread cultural similarity.

Another prominent theme is the emergence of two major demographic foci at opposite ends of the Central Andes. The principal center of agricultural production on the coast lay in the north, in the valleys from Moche to Lambayeque. Here the coastal plain is relatively low, flat, and wide; both the river valleys themselves and the inter-valley deserts were cultivated with the aid of irrigation networks. During the last several millennia of its prehistory this northern zone was the most populous region of the Central Andean coast. In contrast, the wealthiest highland districts lay at the southern end of the Central Andes, in the high, flat basin that surrounds Lake Titicaca. Today this region is known as the *altiplano*. The Inca called it the Collao and regarded it as the richest part of the Andean world. The Titicaca Basin had vast fields and pastures, huge herds of llamas, and a daily cycle of heat and frost that allowed certain foods to be naturally freeze-dried. These abundant agricultural and pastoral resources enabled the *altiplano* to support the largest populations in the sierra.[11] This economic and demographic bipolarity—north coast versus Titicaca Basin—first became apparent in the Early Intermediate Period and characterized Andean prehistory from that point on (Moseley 1978).

The last of our dominant themes is a pan-Andean religious tradition of cults of the dead—the belief that the spirits of the dead play an active and crucial role in the world of the living. In particular, such cults eventually came to manifest themselves as a tradition of formalized ancestor worship that 'formed the core of Peruvian religion'.[12] Throughout the Andean world in late prehistoric times the local kin group's ancestors were venerated as its protectors, and their bodies were treated as sacred objects. Typical expressions of these beliefs included sacrifices to the dead and the periodic repetition or recelebration of funeral rites, with renewals of grave offerings.[13]

Archaeologists are just beginning to investigate Andean ancestor worship systematically, and most of our data on the subject come from

written accounts of practices under the Inca Empire.[14] However, the
evidence at hand makes it clear that ancestor worship has great antiquity
in Peru. The archaeological data are patchy, but they provide us with
glimpses of cults of the dead at least as far back as Preceramic Period
VI.[15] Even the accounts of Inca religion themselves reveal ancestor
worship as a tradition with great depth. Inca ideology was imposed on
Tawantinsuyu less than a century before the Spanish Conquest and was
never fully integrated with local religions. In provincial areas uniquely
Incaic beliefs were easily eliminated by the Spaniards' campaign for the
'extirpation of idolatry'. In contrast, ancient and widespread religious
concepts proved to be far more durable (Kubler 1946: 396-7). Despite
the vigor with which the crusade against idolatry was prosecuted, native
rituals of ancestor worship were still being practiced throughout Peru
in the mid-1600s, over a century after the Spanish Conquest (Bandelier
1904). Indeed, in amalgamation with Christianity the veneration of the
ancestors has survived to this day (Mishkin 1946: 465; Valcárcel 1946:
474). Given this remarkable persistence, we cannot overstate the
fundamental importance of ancestor worship in Andean life.

All three of these themes—regionalism versus unification, north
coast/Titicaca Basin polarity, and ancestor worship—converge in the
epoch immediately preceding the Inca Empire, the Late Intermediate
Period (A.D. 1000-1475). The breakdown of the unifying movement or
movements of the Middle Horizon left northern and central Peru
fragmented into many small, competing polities at the beginning of the
Late Intermediate Period. Several of these small groups would eventually
grow into larger, more powerful kingdoms. In the far southern highlands
this process of fragmentation repeated itself midway through the Late
Intermediate Period, following the break-up of Tiahuanaco civilization
around A.D. 1200. The Inca themselves emerged in the aftermath of
the Tiahuanaco collapse, but throughout most of their pre-imperial
history they were a rather undistinguished society far outstripped by the
native peoples of the northern coast and the Titicaca Basin.

The largest single state of the Late Intermediate Period arose on the
northern coast. That polity was the Chimu Empire, or Kingdom of
Chimor, whose capital city was the site of Chan Chan in the Moche
Valley.[16] The city was founded about A.D. 900, and for several centuries
thereafter Chan Chan's power was strictly local. The Chimu expansion
began around 1200 and lasted until the Inca conquest of the north coast
in about 1465; at the height of their power the lords of Chan Chan
controlled the northernmost thousand kilometers of the Peruvian coast.
Fundamental Chimu institutions seem to have been similar to their
imperial Inca counterparts, and in Chimor we can glimpse dimly what
we will see much more clearly in the Inca case—the ways in which
traditional Andean beliefs and practices could be reworked and

converted into a policy of imperial expansion. In that sense the growth of Chimor might be considered the dress rehearsal for the rise of Tawantinsuyu.

There is one particularly striking parallel between the Chimu and Inca Empires: in both cases a manipulation of fundamental religious concepts helped to created pressures for territorial growth. Like the Inca, the Chimu shared in the pan-Andean tradition of ancestor worship.[17] During the imperial epoch of its history Chimor displayed a strange and spectacular manifestation of ancestor worship that would later characterize the Inca Empire—the property rights of dead kings.

Chimu rulers were believed to be of divine descent, and they owned vast amounts of personal possessions, which they held by divine right. Theft of royal property was both a religious and a civil crime, an offense so heinous that it was punished by the execution of the thief, his father, his brothers, and anyone who had harbored him.[18]

A Chimu king did not forfeit his rigidly enforced property rights when he died. Instead, those rights were guaranteed *in perpetuity* by an institution that has been designated 'split inheritance' (Conrad 1981a, 1982). By this term we mean a mode of bequeathal based on two dichotomies: state office versus personal wealth and principal versus secondary heirs. In a fully developed pattern of split inheritance one principal heir receives the governmental position, plus the attendant rights and duties, of a deceased functionary. The latter's personal possessions and sources of income are assigned to his other descendants as a corporate group. These secondary heirs are not granted actual ownership of the dead man's estate. Instead, his holdings remain his own, and his secondary heirs serve as trustees for him.

In the specific case of the Chimu royalty an emperor's principal heir was one of his sons. This son was chosen as the successor to the throne, and he assumed the rights and duties of imperial leadership upon the death of his father. However, he did not inherit at least some categories of his father's property, which were entrusted to the deceased emperor's other descendants. This corporate group of secondary heirs managed their ancestor's estate for him, using it to care for his mummy and maintain his cult. In effect, a dead king's descendants continued to serve as his court.

Archaeological evidence of Chimu split inheritance is found in Chan Chan. In the center of the capital city are ten large compounds that were the palaces of the Chimu kings (Figure 14). Inside each palace is a labyrinthine maze of doorways, corridors, courts, small administrative 'offices', and groups of storerooms that once held royal possessions (long since removed by looters and despoilers). The palaces also contain large burial platforms that served as the opulent tombs of the Chimu kings. Upon a ruler's death his mummified body was installed in one of the platforms, along with lavish funerary offerings of prestigious goods and

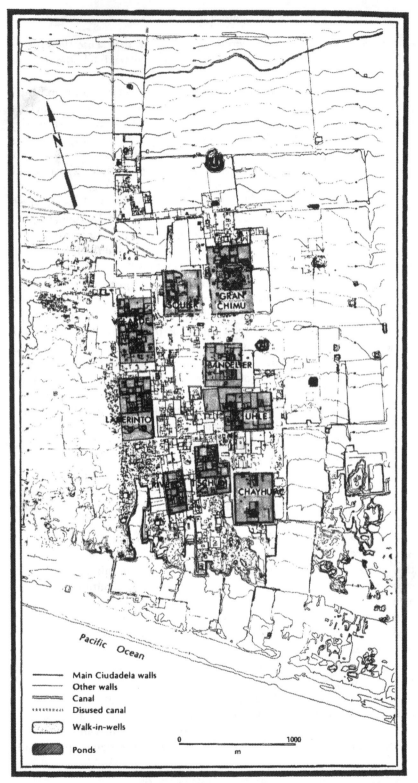

Fig. 14. Plan of central Chan Chan with the major compounds (*ciudadelas*) indicated.

sacrificed women, presumably wives and retainers of the king. Smaller platforms held several hundred of these sacrifices, while larger ones undoubtedly held thousands. Later additions to the burial platforms allowed for periodic repetitions of the royal funeral rites, complete with further offerings and sacrifices. The burial platforms were not permanently sealed, presumably so that the bodies of deceased rulers could be brought out to attend important ceremonies.

The palaces (and their burial platforms) were constructed sequentially; in imperial Chimu times each ruler erected one such structure to house himself and be the center for the management of his wealth throughout eternity. After a king's death his palace passed into the care of his secondary heirs. Some of these individuals continued to occupy and oversee the palace. Groups of retainers served the dead king and his household, just as they had done during his lifetime. Meanwhile, split inheritance forced the next ruler to build a new palace and acquire other property of his own.[19]

Another appropriate term for these practices is 'the cult of the royal mummies', for in a sense split inheritance was nothing more than a grandiose version of standard Andean manifestations of ancestor worship. The average Peruvian citizen was interred with a few simple possessions; the divine kings of Chimor retained great wealth after their deaths. Entombed in their burial platforms, they continued to own and inhabit their palaces and to be cared for by their descendants and servants. Some of their portable possessions were installed with them in their mausoleums, while others were kept in the palace storerooms. Average citizens venerated their ancestors by renewing simple burial offerings and sacrificing a few small items. A king's descendants perpetuated his worship by performing opulent ceremonies in his name and sacrificing hundreds or thousands of human beings to him. The underlying ideas and practices of ancestor worship were identical in the cases of kings and commoners, but the differences in scale of expression were vast. In the case of a lower-class Chimu citizen the material requirements of ancestor worship were meager; in the case of an imperial ruler the demands were much greater.

In the Chimu case, where we must depend on archaeological data, many details of the royal ancestor cult remain unclear. We do not yet know how fully the Chimu had developed the pattern of split inheritance by the time of the Inca conquest. For example, at present we cannot tell whether this form of bequeathal ever applied to anything other than palaces and some portable objects. However, we can say that split inheritance as it is manifested in Chan Chan was a phenomenon of empire. The Chimu did not exhibit the pattern of one king–one palace–one burial platform during their pre-imperial era, which lasted for several centuries. The two earliest palace compounds in Chan Chan each housed several generations of rulers, with imperial expansion beginning sometime during the occupation of the second palace (Conrad 1981a; Kolata 1982a; Keatinge and Conrad ms.). Hence the emergence of the royal ancestor cult in its final form was in some way correlated with the growth of empire. One link between split inheritance and militaristic expansion is fairly obvious: denied at least some categories of his predecessor's property, a new ruler would find conquests desirable as one means of accumulating his own wealth. For the moment, it is hard to say anything more on the basis of the Chimu evidence. As we shall see, the much richer documentation on Tawantinsuyu provides a more detailed picture of the specific Inca form of split inheritance. As a result, we will be able to recognize systemic relationships between the Inca cult of the royal mummies and other causes and consequences of territorial growth.

During the latter half of the Late Intermediate Period, while Chimor was vanquishing its neighbors and establishing hegemony over the northern coast, the southern highlands were divided among numerous competing polities (Figure 15). The archaeological record for the southern sierra at this time is woefully incomplete, but the largest groups seem to have been a series of peoples occupying the Titicaca Basin. These cultures—the Colla, Lupaca, Omasuyu, Pacaje, and others—emerged directly out of the collapse of Tiahuanaco civilization and were the ancestors of the modern Aymara-speaking Indians of the *altiplano*.[20]

In particular, the two most powerful of these 'Aymara kingdoms and chiefdoms'[21] were the Colla and Lupaca, who lived around the northern and western shores of the lake. Each of these kingdoms controlled a sizable sector of the Titicaca Basin. Each also maintained a string of colonies at lower elevations on both sides of the Andes in order to obtain crops that could not be grown in the *altiplano*.[22] The Colla and Lupaca seem to have maintained peaceful relations with the native peoples of the lowland valleys where they established their colonies, but they were intensely hostile to one another.

Elsewhere in the southern highlands, ethnic groups were smaller and less powerful than the Colla and Lupaca. Most of the Late Intermediate Period peoples of the southern sierra are poorly known. We cannot be certain which of them had state-level political organization; in many cases we cannot even identify them from archaeological evidence alone, at least for the time being. To what extent the Colla and Lupaca should be treated as typical or exceptional is, then, an open question. As we shall see from the Inca case, however, the ethnohistorical evidence does permit one general conclusion: there was no harmony among the heirs of Tiahuanaco. The hostile relationship between the Colla and Lupaca was completely normal for the southern highlands as a whole. Most of the native peoples were highly antagonistic toward one another.

Fig. 15. Map of the Central Andes showing the locations of late
prehistoric polities and ethnic groups mentioned in the text.

Throughout the second half of the Late Intermediate Period the
southern sierra was in a chronic state of petty war.

The Inca were born into this bitterly competitive world. Their
homeland lay to the northwest of the Titicaca Basin, in a small area
around Cuzco in the Vilcanota (upper Urubamba) river drainage basin.
In an obvious attempt to portray themselves as the rightful heirs of
Tiahuanaco, the Incas' imperial mythology would eventually trace their
origins to the Titicaca Basin.[23] Archaeology belies this claim. Even the

scanty data at hand are enough to show that the Inca were native to the Cuzco district and that their culture in its initial form developed out of local antecedents.[24]

The Inca would eventually become the master empire-builders of the Andean world. They would push the frontiers of Peruvian civilization far beyond its previous limits and alter many of its basic institutions in the process. Yet for all of their subsequent achievements, their entrance onto the Andean stage was obscure and unimpressive. In the Peruvian culture area as a whole they were eclipsed by the Chimu; closer to home, they were overshadowed by the Colla and Lupaca, and probably by several other southern highland peoples as well.

Early Inca society and religion

The early, or pre-imperial, Inca are in many ways an enigmatic and elusive people. We know them through ethnohistory and archaeology, but both sources of data have frustrating limitations. Again, all of the chronicles were written after the Spanish Conquest; there are no eyewitness descriptions of pre-imperial Inca society. All accounts of early Inca history and culture are transcriptions of oral tradition and contain a mixture of fact, myth, legend, Spanish misunderstandings of Inca culture, the personal biases of the chroniclers, and errors introduced when some authors copied earlier works carelessly (Rowe 1946: 192-7). Furthermore, the Inca leadership used history as propaganda and constantly rewrote the past to fit personal, factional, or imperial goals. When we look at early Inca society through written sources, we are confronted by all of these distortions. We also face the question of changes through time: in the volatile world of the southern highlands, Inca culture could not have remained static throughout its pre-imperial epoch. If these factors are kept in mind, it is obvious that the chronicles alone can reveal only the general outlines of early Inca society.

In theory archaeology could greatly further our understanding of the pre-imperial Inca by revealing the precise chronology of their cultural development and by serving as a means of evaluating conflicting hypotheses derived from the chronicles. The practical problem is that the archaeological data available at present are not very extensive.[25] Nonetheless, they do justify the characterization of the early Inca as a small-scale, rural society. The distribution of early Inca pottery, the Killke Series, is limited. Killke ceramics have been found only in scattered locations within the limits of Cuzco itself and at several other nearby sites (for example, Killke, Sillkinchani, Huata, Kencha-kencha, Muyumuyu, Lucre, and Kuyu). These sites are small villages, rarely measuring more than two hundred meters across, containing structures made of uncut fieldstones set in mud mortar.[26] Rowe characterizes Killke Inca architecture as 'exceedingly inconspicuous'.[27] The dead were generally buried in small, beehive-shaped tombs of rough masonry. Such tombs are usually found in caves, clefts, or rock-shelters; they contain one or more bodies and a few simple grave goods.

Drawing on the chroniclers' descriptions of Inca village life, we can characterize the probable nature of Inca culture in its earliest pre-imperial stages. Above the level of the nuclear family, the fundamental unit of Inca social organization was the *ayllu*. This word seems to have had several levels of meaning.[28] In the chronicles we find the name applied to both intra- and inter-village groupings. In general, the *ayllu* was a kin group tracing its descent from a common ancestor. Within the *ayllu* men were organized patrilineally and women matrilineally; marriage was forbidden within certain degrees of consanguinity, but the *ayllu* as a whole was endogamous. In imperial times *ayllus* were supervised by hereditary chiefs known as *curacas*, but we do not know if the original Inca headmen had hereditary positions.[29]

If the term is used in its most restrictive sense, the *ayllu* was also the basic landholding group. Each *ayllu* owned a defined parcel of land; individual families cultivated as much of this acreage as they needed for their sustenance. *Ayllu* members had a series of reciprocal obligations to one another, including the requirements that they help each other to build houses and to farm the land for their families. Members also worked together to cultivate fields for the support of the elderly, the infirm, widows, and orphans. Certain plots of ground were farmed to provide food for sacrifices to the *ayllu*'s shrines and deities. *Ayllu* leaders also had certain claims to communal labor services, but in the earliest phase of Inca history their rights may not have been very different from those of any other citizen.

In all of these duties we see a clearly expressed ideal of *ayllu* and village self-sufficiency. We can also discern the underlying structure upon which the economies of Andean states were built. *Ayllu* members were required to contribute labor time to one another and to their leaders, and the system can be viewed as a means of organizing and distributing labor time. By taking control of the mechanism, by setting itself up as the leader of a sort of super-*ayllu*, higher authority could use taxation to tap surplus labor time for state purposes. This process had been carried out by earlier Andean polities (Moseley 1975c, 1978; Recktenwald 1978), and it would be repeated by the Inca. Of course, state-controlled labor taxation, like the mutual obligations of *ayllu* members on which it was modeled, would ideally be regulated by Andean principles of reciprocity. In theory, no duty of the citizen would be unmatched by an obligation of the state.[30]

Beyond the levels of the *ayllu* and village, the original nature of Inca political organization is a particularly thorny problem. Here the available archaeological data are of little help. The evidence at hand—a series of small villages and simple burials—conveys no sense of a hierarchical settlement pattern. On the other hand, Cuzco, the logical

Table 3. *Traditional dynastic list of Inca kings.*
The reigns of the rulers from Viracocha Inca on are derived from
Cabello's (bk. 3, 1951) chronicle. All dates before 1532 should be
regarded as approximations. For further discussion see Rowe 1945.

	Dates of Reign
1. Manco Capac	
2. Sinchi Roca	
3. Lloque Yupanqui	
4. Mayta Capac	
5. Capac Yupanqui	
6. Inca Roca	
7. Yahuar Huacac	
8. Viracocha Inca	(?–1438)
9. Pachakuti	(1438–1471)
10. Topa Inca	(1471–1493)
11. Huayna Capac	(1493–1525)
12. Huascar	(1525–1532)
13. Atauhualpa	(1532–1533)

choice for a predominant site, has been so extensively modified during
the imperial Inca, Spanish Colonial, and modern eras that nothing has
been found of its Killke occupation save a few scattered refuse deposits
(Rowe 1944). These data are too scanty to permit detailed conclusions.

In the absence of relevant archaeological evidence, we must rely on
the chronicles, and they are equivocal. Like many marginal peoples who
rose to power suddenly, the Inca subsequently fabricated a glorious
history for themselves. Imperial oral tradition held that the Inca had
always been ruled by a dynasty of divine kings descended from Inti, a
solar aspect of the Incas' manifold sky god (Demarest 1981). The
standard list names thirteen rulers from the inception of the dynasty to
the Spanish Conquest (Table 3). However, imperial expansion did not
begin until the reign of the ninth king, Pachakuti, and all of the kings
before the eighth, Viracocha Inca, are nebulous figures.

The problem is not that we have no information on the reigns of the
first seven rulers. To the contrary, many of the chroniclers recorded their
exploits.[31] There is no point in recounting these deeds at length. Suffice
it to say that the accounts are a litany of names—tribes, villages, *ayllus*,
individuals, and deities are chanted through the pages. Their names are
often used interchangeably—individuals are substituted for *ayllus*,
villages for tribes, and so on. Consequently, it is often impossible to tell
what exactly is being designated. It does not seem coincidental that the
problems are most acute in chronicles written well after the Spanish
Conquest. Descriptions of the earliest Inca reigns written in the
seventeenth century (e.g., Garcilaso 1945, 1966; Guaman Poma 1936)

are full of fanciful details, contradictions, and inconsistencies; none of their specific material can be trusted. In contrast, earlier, sixteenth-century authors (e.g., Cieza 1943, 1959; Sarmiento 1942) discuss the first seven kings in vaguer and more cautious terms. We will depend heavily on these early chroniclers in our recounting of later Inca history, but even they are not much help in reconstructing events before the reign of Viracocha Inca. For these reasons, along with others discussed previously, it seems best to take a skeptical attitude toward the details of Inca history before A.D. 1400 and to leave the first seven kings in a twilight zone where fact and legend are inseparably mingled.[32]

This is not to say that the stories of the initial Inca rulers are worthless as anything other than mythology. Read with a gimlet eye, they shed their heroic overtones and emerge as symbolizing a tradition of chronic small-scale fighting. Most of the 'wars' and 'victories' of the early Inca are glorified accounts of villages' raids on one another; Sarmiento is the most explicit chronicler on this point.[33] Some episodes, such as Mayta Capac's defeat of the Alcaviza, seem to reflect nothing more than squabbles among the different *ayllus* of Cuzco.[34] The overall picture is one of a loose and rather fractious petty chiefdom.[35] The headmen of the constituent villages and *ayllus* engaged in a continuous jockeying for position but cooperated with one another in raiding villages outside the coalition. To judge from the scanty evidence available, this characterization also fits the Incas' immediate neighbors during the thirteenth and fourteenth centuries.

Given this pattern of constant minor conflicts, the *de facto* early Inca leaders were probably *sinchis*, war leaders who derived their power and prestige from personal prowess. There may have been a paramount *sinchi* of the entire coalition and lesser war leaders from each individual village and *ayllu*. Their offices seem to have been basically elective, with *sinchis* being chosen by the prominent adult male members of their communities. Positions were not necessarily permanent, and a *sinchi* who failed in war or alienated the other leading citizens of his community was certain to be deposed. However, a *sinchi* who was able to lead consistently victorious raids could use the booty to build long-lasting political support and make his office quasi-permanent. Likewise, the position was not hereditary, but there were pulls in that direction. A successful *sinchi's* sons had the advantage of learning the arts of leadership from a distinguished practitioner, and there was a tendency to choose them as *sinchis* if they showed the necessary valor.[36] In short, the ideal *sinchi* had to be bold and astute in war, adept at maintaining the support of other important men in the community (all of whom were potential challengers for his position), and able to instill the same qualities in his sons. Throughout Inca history the combined military and political skills of a *sinchi* were to remain the *sine qua non* of leadership.

If we turn now from social, economic, and political factors to pre-imperial Inca religion, we find ourselves on what can be the most treacherous ground of all. Andean concepts of divinity were highly fluid, and Inca beliefs were no exception. The Spaniards drove themselves to distraction by trying to force overlapping and interlocking ideas into neatly separated pigeonholes. The chronicler Betanzos was so confused by apparent discrepancies in the testimony he collected that he called his informants 'blind of understanding'.[37] Those modern scholars who have attempted to compartmentalize Inca beliefs have found themselves as frustrated as Betanzos. It is becoming increasingly clear that standard interpretations of Inca religion are in need of massive reanalysis. A complete re-evaluation is impossible at this point, but some of the basic principles of early Inca religion can be broadly characterized.

Nowhere are the complexities of Inca beliefs more apparent than in the case of the upper pantheon. The chroniclers tried to cast the Inca upper pantheon in a Greco-Roman mold of discrete deities, each having a simple one-to-one correspondence with an individual astronomical body or atmospheric phenomenon. Yet a recent study (Demarest 1981) has shown just how misleading such an approach may be, for the upper pantheon did not consist of 'gods' in the Western sense at all. Rather, it is best described as an overarching divine complex, a multi-faceted sky god composed of myriad individual aspects. In ceremonial contexts this divine complex was 'unfolded' into subcomplexes, or clusters of aspects—the deities of the chroniclers. However, these clusters were not fixed entities: individual aspects could be combined and permuted in an almost infinite number of ways. The precise subcomplexes into which the sky god unfolded in any given instance depended on the specific ritual context and the purpose in question. For this reason the 'gods' of the upper pantheon overlapped with and graded into one another.

The Inca celestial godhead seems to have been derived from a much earlier generalized creator/sky/weather deity of the Titicaca Basin, the so-called 'Gateway God' of Tiahuanaco (Figure 16).[38] An ancient and complex divinity of this type is readily susceptible to manipulation, and throughout their history the Inca undoubtedly reworked their upper pantheon continuously in order to meet the needs of the moment. In imperial times Inca state religion assigned special importance to three subcomplexes of the sky god: a universal creator with a variety of titles, the best known being Viracocha; the sun god Inti; and Illapa, the thunder or weather deity. Despite numerous overlaps and gradations, these three figures were sufficiently distinct (that is, emphasized in enough ritual contexts) to lead the chroniclers into their confused view of Inca divinities. However, among Andean peoples who did not become imperial powers other descendants of the Gateway God—for example, Thunapa, the supreme deity of the historic Aymara-speaking tribes of the Titicaca Basin—do not show such clearly defined subcomplexes. Hence it seems likely that in the original version of Inca religion

Fig. 16. The Monolithic Gateway (top) and 'Gateway God' (bottom center) of Tiahuanaco; for location within the site see Figure 13. The Gateway God was a precursor of the Incas' manifold high god.

Viracocha, the Sun, and Illapa were far less sharply differentiated than they eventually came to be.[39]

Underlying the upper pantheon, and inextricably linked to it, were two more fundamental religious concepts: ancestor worship and *huaca*. Ancestor worship, which we have discussed before as a pan-Andean tradition, lay at the very heart of Inca religion.[40] The ancestors were deeply revered by their descendants, and the bodies of the dead were sacred objects. One early seventeenth-century parish priest, reporting on Inca beliefs from the front lines of the war against idolatry, wrote that 'After the sacred stones, their greatest veneration is for their *mallquis*...which are the bones or mummies of their pagan progenitors'.[41] The ancestors spoke through these mummies and could answer questions in oracular fashion; one type of Inca religious practitioner was the *mallquipvillac*, 'he who speaks with the *mallquis*'.[42]

Ancestral spirits also manifested themselves in small objects with odd or unusual qualities—strangely shaped or colored stones and plants, crystals, bezoars, and so on. These portable items were kept and worshiped as family fetishes.[43] The ancestors could also appear as sparks in the fire, and they would be tossed a morsel of food to eat.[44] There is another association between the ancestors and fire: for the Inca the most solemn method of divination was by fire, and it was employed only on very serious occasions. Fire-diviners, who were greatly feared and respected, were called 'consulters of the dead'.[45]

There were a number of ritual expressions of ancestor worship in pre-imperial Inca society.[46] When an individual died, some of his scanty personal possessions were burned, and others were buried with him. Thereafter his descendants returned to his tomb at intervals to renew offerings of food, drink, and cloth.[47] The ancestors' bodies were brought out to take part in processions and other festivals (Figure 17).[48] They also received sacrifices and other ritual treatments that depended on their social and generational status.[49] An individual who neglected these rites angered his ancestors. They would then bring sickness upon the guilty party, who would have to appease them, and cure himself, by making extra sacrifices (Rowe 1946: 312-13).

Closely allied to ancestor worship was *huaca*, the great integrating concept of Inca religion. The word is a generic term for any person, place, or thing with sacred or supernatural associations; it conveys a sense of embodied holiness. In practice almost anything odd or unusual was considered to be a *huaca*. Hence the number of *huacas* in the Inca world was staggering, as is the number of references to them in the chronicles.[50] Cobo names over three hundred examples in the immediate vicinity of Cuzco, but his list includes only the principal shrines of the official state religion.[51] Lesser *huacas* of strictly local importance were beyond counting. All *huacas*, whether local or national, had oracular powers, and they were worshiped with prayers and sacrifices (Figure 18).

Huaca was linked to all the other basic elements of Inca religion, and its ties to ancestor worship are especially clear. In fact, any separation of the two concepts is largely artificial. *Villca*, a reciprocal kinship term meaning 'great-grandfather' and 'great-grandson', and by extension 'ancestor' or 'descendant', could be used as a synonym for *huaca*.[52] Many important *huacas* were explicitly identified with the ancestors; for example, some of the principal shrines around Cuzco were believed to

Fig. 17. Inca ancestor worship. This drawing by the early
seventeenth-century native Andean chronicler Felipe Guaman
Poma de Ayala shows an ancestral mummy being carried in a
procession of the dead.

Fig. 18. Inca *huaca* worship. Guaman Poma's drawing shows the emperor Topa Inca consulting with his *huacas*.

be forebears of the Inca who had turned to stone.[53] All of this evidence implies, and myriad documentary references affirm, that the bodies of the dead, their tombs, and the family fetishes were themselves *huacas*.

Not only are ancestor worship and *huaca* inseparable from one another, but they are both closely related to *ayllu* organization. Indeed, *villca*, given above as a synonym for *huaca*, was also another name for *ayllu*.[54] The ancestors defined the *ayllu*, legitimated its land tenure, and protected its members. Therefore, it is no surprise that the *ayllu's* prosperity depended on proper care of its mummies, fetishes, and other *huacas*.[55] The loss or theft of any *huaca* was a serious problem, for it weakened the *ayllu* so deprived.[56]

If the *huaca* in question was an ancestor's mummy, the *ayllu's* independence—in fact, its very existence—was gravely menaced. Hostile neighbors could bend an *ayllu* to their will by seizing this crucial *huaca*. To maintain the ancestor's worship and save themselves from ruin, the *ayllu's* members had to obey the kidnappers' commands as long as the mummy was held.[57]

The danger posed by mummy-theft reveals a central contradiction in Inca ancestor worship. On the whole, the cult of the dead was a strongly conservative force in early Inca society. It bound individuals to their kinsmen, to the *ayllu's* land, and to traditional patterns of behavior. Deviations from those patterns might anger the ancestors and bring sickness upon the individual or hardships to the *ayllu*. Yet, paradoxically, ancestor worship could also be the mechanism of change. It could and did serve as a means of upsetting the existing social and political order. Mummy-theft was a local affair, and its impact may have fallen upon a limited number of people. Nonetheless, the case of the purloined *mallquis* shows that ancestor worship could be manipulated in such a way as to affect other aspects of culture.

It is important to note that in early Inca society the economic demands of ancestor/*huaca* worship were small. When a person died, some items were burned and others buried with him, but they were few and readily replaceable. Food had to be available for sacrifices and the renewal of burial offerings, but the *ayllu* obtained what it needed by reserving patches of its cropland for the support of its ancestral mummies and other *huacas*.[58] The time spent in farming these plots and in weaving cloth for burial offerings was essentially the *ayllu's* only labor investment in its progenitors. Day-to-day tending of the *huacas* was assigned to old men no longer capable of heavy work.[59] The importance of ancestor/*huaca* worship in Inca life cannot be exaggerated, but in pre-imperial times its material costs were manageable.

Such, then, were the basic institutions of pre-imperial Inca society, and the foregoing discussion can probably stand as a fairly accurate, albeit sketchy, description of Inca culture in its original form. To be sure, that culture must have been developing continually to meet the demands and opportunities of the moment, and the Inca must have undergone numerous small changes during the first several centuries of their history. However, the present limitations of the data obscure many details of the Incas' cultural evolution, and the cumulative alteration of Inca society does not become apparent until about 1400. The changes evident at the turn of the fifteenth century reflect broader events that had been occurring throughout the southern highlands for some time.

During the fourteenth century a number of small groups in the southern sierra began to consolidate into somewhat larger and more powerful military coalitions. Prominent among these militaristic chiefdoms and kingdoms were the Quechua, who occupied the area west of Cuzco; the Chanca, who lived beyond the Quechua; and the Canchi and Cana to the south of Cuzco (Figure 15). The most powerful of all seem to have been the Colla and Lupaca of the northern Titicaca Basin, who had probably achieved the status of kingdoms at an even earlier date. As these peoples began to assert themselves, previously minor rivalries intensified. Each group sought to advance itself by maintaining alliances with some of its neighbors and hostile relationships with others. Particularly bitter enmities existed between the Quechua and Chanca and between the Colla and Lupaca (Rowe 1946: 203-4).

The Inca adapted themselves to this competitive situation; had they not, they would soon have vanished in the political and military infighting of the southern highlands. The traditional Inca practices of inter-village raiding and rule by *sinchis* had favored leaders who were both adept warriors and astute politicians, at least within the limited arena of the Cuzco region. Heightened competition now demanded rulers capable of practicing a *sinchi's* skills on a wider stage. The result was a series of changes in the nature of Inca leadership. We do not know exactly when those changes were initiated, but they had progressed far enough to become recognizable in the reign of Viracocha Inca.

Viracocha Inca, the eighth king on the dynastic list and the first to emerge from the chronicles in any kind of clearly defined form, rose to power around the beginning of the fifteenth century. The most sober account of Inca history, Sarmiento's, insists that Viracocha Inca was the first Inca ruler to attempt permanent conquests. According to Sarmiento, previous leaders had merely looted neighboring villages and then left them alone until they were worth attacking again, but Viracocha Inca actually subjugated the area around Cuzco and organized it under his control.[60] Taken literally, this version of events would make Viracocha Inca the first Inca leader who was truly a king, rather than some sort of paramount *sinchi*. However, given all of the uncertainties about earlier members of the dynasty, we prefer a more general interpretation—namely that in Viracocha Inca's time the institution of kingship was still a fairly recent development among the Inca.

The precise borders of Viracocha Inca's kingdom are unclear. Sarmiento says that it extended 'at most seven or eight leagues around Cuzco'.[61] Cieza, whose version of Inca history is only slightly less restrained than Sarmiento's, claims that the realm stretched further to the southeast, all the way to the northern margin of the Titicaca Basin.[62] Cieza specifically lists the Canchi and Cana among Viracocha Inca's southern conquests. However, it seems likely that the Cana and Canchi were Viracocha Inca's allies, rather than his subjects: during the Chanca attack of 1438 they had to be offered rewards before they came to the aid of Cuzco.[63] Balancing this evidence, we suggest that Sarmiento's description is the closest to the truth and that Viracocha Inca's domain was relatively small.[64]

Sixteenth-century sources describe how Viracocha Inca strove to increase the strength and security of his kingdom by raiding outside its borders and through adroit political maneuvering. He sought to protect the Incas' northern and western flanks through an expedient marriage to the daughter of a neighboring ruler and by maintaining an alliance with the Quechua against the Chanca.[65] In a classic double-cross he tried to turn the internal rivalries of the Titicaca Basin to Inca advantage by secretly offering to ally himself with the Colla against the Lupaca and vice versa. His intention was to provoke a war between the two groups that would weaken them both to the point where their power was at the very least neutralized, and perhaps completely broken. However, the Colla-Lupaca war ended in a decisive Lupaca victory before troops from Cuzco could intervene. Bowing to reality, Viracocha Inca abandoned his original goal and concluded an alliance with the Lupaca.[66]

The institution of Inca kingship in general and the machinations ascribed to Viracocha Inca were responses to intensified competition among the peoples of the southern highlands. However, these political and military measures did not stand alone; they were accompanied by other adjustments to changing circumstances. In particular, the Incas' adaptation to their late fourteenth-century world also had an ideological component—the creation of a national patron and celestial dynastic ancestor through manipulation of the upper pantheon.

By imperial times the Inca had come to believe that their state was under the protection of, and their rulers descended from, a divine being named Inti. The chroniclers identified Inti as the sun god, but he is more properly viewed as a cluster of solar aspects within the overarching sky god described previously. Among other things, Inti represented the conceptualization of a specific subcomplex of the sky god, the sun, as the national patron of the Inca state. This solar cluster itself could be unfolded into subcomplexes, of which three predominated: Apu-Inti ('the Lord Sun'); Churi-Inti, or Punchao ('the Child Sun', or 'Daylight'); and Inti-Guauqui ('Brother Sun'). Apu-Inti and Churi-Inti/Punchao could be separated from one another along an astronomical

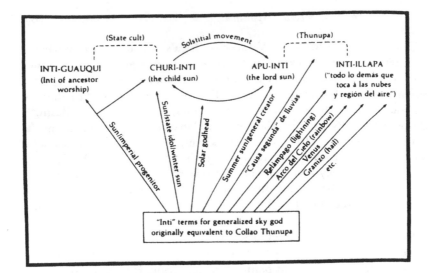

Fig. 19. The Incas' celestial high god. Top: 'Unfoldings' of the multi-faceted high god. Bottom: Guaman Poma's drawing of the emperor addressing his divine ancestor, the sun, in the feast of the summer solstice.

axis, since they were associated with the summer and winter solstices respectively. Inti-Guauqui, in contrast, unfolded from the other two solar aspects along a sociopolitical axis: he represented the sun in its specific role as the founding father of the Inca dynasty and the center of the state's official ancestor cult (Figure 19).

Depending on the ritual context in question, the sky god could be adored as a whole, the Inti complex could be venerated as a single entity, or specific solar aspects could be worshiped individually. For example, Inti could be contrasted with Viracocha, the universal creator, or the two could overlap in the Apu-Inti/summer solstice aspect of the sun. Inti-Guauqui as dynastic progenitor could be either left within or pulled out of the overall complex of Inti as protector of the state. Hence the elasticity of Inca religious concepts allowed the ideas of universal creation, national patronage, and the divine ancestry of Inca rulers to be distinguished, but not completely severed, from one another.[67]

The rise of the Inti cult must have been to some extent a conscious manipulation of religion for political purposes. Several investigators have argued that the great importance eventually attached to Inti cannot have been present in the earliest epoch of Inca history, when the subcomplexes of the manifold sky god were less sharply differentiated than they later came to be.[68] Among other things, there cannot have been a divine progenitor of the ruling dynasty in the Incas' earliest days, for that dynasty had yet to be founded; leaders were elected *sinchis*, not kings. At least in part, emphasis on Inti must have been an innovation attendant upon the development of Inca kingship.

The creation of the Inti cult obviously worked to the advantage of Inca rulers: as Garcilaso noted, the veneration of Inti meant that when the people adored their god, they were also worshiping their king.[69] An element of conscious intent behind this result is reflected in the following remarks by the Jesuit scholar Cobo, a seventeenth-century synthesizer of earlier chronicles.

> The truth is that Inca religion did not remain fixed and unchanging from the birth of the realm onward; they did not cling to the same few beliefs or worship the same few gods. At various times they were adding and discarding many notions... They were induced to make changes in [religious] matters because they began to realize that in this way they could strengthen themselves and keep the kingdom under tighter control.[70]

Of course, while the view of the sun as dynastic ancestor probably began as a fabrication, it rapidly became a matter of conviction. We do not mean to portray the Inca as hypocrites.[71] In the decades following the Spanish Conquest, when the price of worshiping their rulers could be an excruciating death, the Inca were to prove the sincerity of their faith beyond the shadow of a doubt.

If the manipulation of the upper pantheon that produced the cult of

Inti served the interests of the Inca leadership, it also benefited the Inca people as a whole. Divine patronage helped to give the Inca a sense of national identity, of being set apart from their neighbors and assigned a special place among the peoples of the earth. The institution of kingship had provided Viracocha Inca's subjects with the military and political unity they needed to maintain themselves in the increasingly competitive arena of the southern highlands. Similarly, Inti had armed the Inca with an ideological tenacity that enabled them to survive, at least for the moment.

Still, though Inti's sponsorship had furnished Viracocha Inca's kingdom with a national identity, it had not endowed the Inca with a sense of divine mission. The Inca people and their leaders may have felt themselves to be particularly blessed under heaven, but they had not yet come to see themselves as the rightful masters of the Andean world. There had been a shift of emphasis in the upper pantheon, but it had not yet fused the myriad aspects of Inca religion into the form they would eventually take: an integrated cult of imperial expansion.

In fact, the ideological shifts evident in the early fifteenth century had not given the Inca any clear advantage over their neighbors. Had there been a bookmaker in 1430 taking bets on who would control the southern sierra in the near future, he probably would have established two peoples as odds-on favorites. One top contender would have been the Lupaca, who had become the strongest group in the rich Titicaca Basin through their victory over the Colla.

The other choice would have been the Chanca. In a startling turn of events, the Chanca had completely upset the balance of power to the north and west of Cuzco. At some point during Viracocha Inca's reign they had finally defeated their traditional enemies, the Quechua, and pushed into the Quechua territory.[72] Standing at the border of Viracocha Inca's kingdom, the Chanca now began to threaten the Inca directly. Hostilities between the two peoples built steadily toward a crisis, a moment of supreme peril that would threaten the very existence of the fledgling Inca state.

The transformational crisis

The crisis broke around 1438. Intent on destroying their rivals, the Chanca invaded Inca territory. Viracocha Inca had grown old and was nearing the end of his reign; by chance or design, the Chanca had chosen to launch their attack at a time when the Inca leadership was weak (Rowe 1946: 204). The Chanca shattered the initial Inca resistance and laid siege to Cuzco. Viracocha Inca fled to the hills behind the capital, taking his son and designated successor, Inca Urcon, with him. Command of the defense of Cuzco fell to another of Viracocha Inca's sons, Cusi Inca Yupanqui.[73]

According to Inca oral history, Cusi Inca Yupanqui had one overwhelming experience as he awaited the final Chanca onslaught. In a dream or vision he beheld a supernatural figure of terrifying aspect. To Cusi Inca Yupanqui's astonishment this apparition identified itself as the Incas' sky god and addressed him warmly, calling him 'my son'. It then proceeded to reassure him that if he kept to the true religion, he was destined to be a great ruler and to conquer many nations. Thereupon the figure disappeared.[74]

With the alleged inspiration of this vision, plus the more tangible aid of allies secured by the offer of rewards,[75] Cusi Inca Yupanqui rallied Cuzco's defenders. He drove the Chanca invaders away from Cuzco and, in subsequent battles, thoroughly routed them. Thereupon he was crowned as ruler in place of his father and his brother, and he took (or was later given) the name by which he is better known, Pachakuti— 'Cataclysm', or 'He Who Remakes the World'.[76] After reconsolidating Inca control of the local area, he embarked upon the remarkable series of conquests that established the Inca Empire.[77]

Such are the outlines of the tale of Pachakuti's rise to power, which initiated the transformation of the Inca from a small and beleaguered kingdom to the master empire-builders of the Andean world. Taken together as a single episode, Pachakuti's vision, defense of Cuzco, and defeat of the Chanca are 'presented to us in the sources as the most striking event in all Inca history—the year one, as it were'.[78]

Yet if the chroniclers agree on the importance of the Chanca crisis, their accounts of that crisis and its Inca protagonists are highly inconsistent. There are sharp disagreements about Inca Urcon's character, the nature of his claim to the succession, the question of whether he ever ruled, the reasons for Viracocha Inca's and Inca Urcon's flight from Cuzco, their subsequent fates, and the precise manner in which Pachakuti gained the throne.[79] All of the controversies can be condensed into three different presentations of Pachakuti: as a noble hero motivated by civic duty; as an arrant usurper; and as the figurehead of a military coup.

> When [the leading citizens of Cuzco] learned how near the enemy was they made great sacrifices according to their custom, and decided to beg Pachacuti... to take charge of the war, looking to the safety of all. And one of the elders, speaking in the name of all, spoke with him, and he answered... that he had never aspired to assume the crown by tyranny or against the will of the people. Now that they had seen that the Inca Urco was not fitted to be Inca, let them do what was their duty for the public weal...
> [After Cuzco had been saved,] by unanimous consent of the people it was decided that the Inca Urco should nevermore enter Cuzco and that he be deprived of the fringe or crown, which should be given to Inca Pachacuti.[80]

> Made arrogant by his victory, the disobedient youth [Pachakuti] Yngayupanqui resolved upon a deed so vile that its like was never

seen or heard of by the people of that generation, either before or afterwards. Losing respect for his aged father and thinking nothing of his brothers, he snatched the royal fringe from Viracocha Ynga's head and put it on himself...[81]

This Inga Urcon was brave, but haughty and full of scorn for others. For this reason he fell into disfavor with the warriors, especially [Viracocha Inca's] legitimate sons, of whom Inga Roca was the oldest, and the valiant captains Apo Mayta and Vicaquirao. Therefore, these men decided that he should not succeed to the throne, but that they should choose one of the other brothers—the most worthy, who would treat them well and honor them, as they deserved. So they secretly fixed their eyes on the third of the legitimate sons, Cusi [Pachakuti] by name... It is said that they advised Viracocha Inga [to flee during the Chanca crisis] in order to get him out of Cuzco and give themselves an unhindered opportunity to carry out their plot and put Cusi Inga Yupangui on the throne.[82]

At this distance from the actual events we are in no position to decide which of these contradictory accounts is closest to the truth. In any case, more insights can be gained by considering the different versions together than by weighing them against one another. For if we listen to all of the voices at once, it becomes clear that we are hearing the echoes of a bitter factional debate. Five hundred and fifty years after the fact, the winners and losers are still arguing their cases in the chronicles.

What emerges from the sources is the following. In Viracocha Inca's old age his realm was not only beset from outside, but also riven by internal political factionalism. This latter state of affairs is perfectly expectable in a kingdom whose rule of succession was unclear, probably because of the relatively recent development of kingship out of leadership by *sinchis*. In late pre-imperial times the Inca ruler was supposed to bequeath his crown to his most competent son, but competence was a matter of opinion, and factional disputes were virtually guaranteed. In the specific case at hand we can identify two contending sides, an Inca Urcon 'party' that included Viracocha Inca, and a pro-Pachakuti group containing the most prominent warriors. Inca Urcon probably had the upper hand at first, since he had his father's support, but the Chanca attack reversed the situation in favor of Pachakuti's backers. Victory over the Chanca made this military faction the new leaders of the Inca state.[83] Once in power they began a vigorous rewriting of Inca history and made their view of events the officially authorized version. As losers in the dispute, Viracocha Inca, Inca Urcon, and their followers were left to keep their case alive *sub rosa* by passing it along to their descendants, who would eventually relate it to some of the chroniclers.

Having gained control of the Inca state, Pachakuti and his followers began a major program of governmental and ideological reforms. After multiple reworkings of Inca history, those reforms came to be attributed to Pachakuti himself, and they were usually treated as if he had invented them *ex nihilo*. However, there are good reasons to believe that Pachakuti's personal ingenuity has been somewhat magnified. First, Pachakuti's rise to power represented the victory of a political faction, and its ascendancy gave the Inca state not just a new king, but a whole new leadership. Undoubtedly all of these individuals were deeply involved in the program of national reorganization. However, the authorized version of Inca history eventually compressed what had been a group of leaders into the single larger-than-life figure of Pachakuti.

More importantly, the innovations associated with the growth of the Inca Empire were hardly created out of thin air. In reality, most of the reforms 'consisted of reorganizations and of projections onto a wider screen of old, deep-rooted Andean techniques'.[84] In other words, changes were produced by reworking the material at hand: traditional cultural elements shared by the Inca and many of their contemporaries.

Yet to say that the measures imposed by the Inca leadership under Pachakuti had ample precedents is not to deny that they could have far-reaching effects. In particular, one reworking of traditional cultural elements was to alter Inca society profoundly. That innovation was a form of royal ancestor cult that we have already seen foreshadowed among the Chimu, split inheritance.

Upon the death of an Inca emperor (the *Sapa Inca*, or 'Unique Inca'), the rights to govern, to wage war, and to impose taxes on the realm passed to one of his sons, who was his successor and principal heir. However, the chroniclers emphatically state that the new ruler received no material legacy from his predecessor. The deceased emperor's palaces in Cuzco and the countryside, servants, chattel, and other possessions continued to be treated as his property and were entrusted to his *panaqa*, a corporate social group containing all of his descendants in the male line except his successor.[85] These secondary heirs did not actually own the items named above. Instead, ownership remained vested in the dead king. *Panaqa* members received some of their support through their ancestor's 'generosity'—ceremonial redistribution of part of his continuing income. They derived the rest of their sustenance from the *panaqa*'s own separate holdings.[86]

The primary purposes of the *panaqa* were to serve as the dead king's court, maintain his mummy, and perpetuate his cult. *Panaqa* members performed their duties through a series of rituals so alien to European minds that the conquistadors marveled at them. The chroniclers have preserved a few of these rites in vivid detail.[87]

> [The Inca] had the law and custom that when one of their rulers died, they embalmed him and wrapped him in many fine garments. They allotted these lords all the service that they had had in life, so that their mummy-bundles might be served in death as if they were still alive.[88]

These statues [the royal mummy-bundles] were set up in the square
of Cuzco when they held their celebrations...for the devil probably
spoke to them through those statues, as they were used for this
purpose.[89]

When there was a need for water for the cultivated fields, they
usually brought out [Inca Roca's] body, richly dressed, with his
face covered, carrying it in a procession through the fields and
punas, and they were convinced that this was largely responsible
for bringing rain.[90]

It was customary for the dead rulers to visit one another, and they
held great dances and revelries. Sometimes the dead went to the
houses of the living, and sometimes the living visited them.[91]

They brought [the royal mummies], lavishly escorted, to all their
most important ceremonies. They sat them all down in the plaza
in a row, in order of seniority, and the servants who looked after
them ate and drank there. In front of the mummies they lit a fire
of a certain kind of wood that they had cut and carved until it was
very even. In the fire they burned the food they had set before the
mummies for them to eat; it was the same meal that [the *panaqa*
members] themselves ate. In front of the mummies they also placed
large vessels like pitchers, called *vilques*, made of gold and silver.
They filled these vessels with maize beer and toasted the dead with
it, after first showing it to them. The dead toasted one another, and
they drank to the living, and vice versa; this was done by their
ministers in their names. When the *vilques* were full, they poured
them over a circular stone set up as an idol in the middle of the
plaza. There was a small channel around the stone, and the beer
ran off through drains and hidden pipes... Their descendants were
continually offering [the dead rulers] large quantities of things, not
only in the frequent sacrifices they made to them of all the things
they sacrificed to their gods, but in the offerings they made for the
everyday support of the mummies, which their souls ate...[92]

If these depictions demonstrate an enormously elaborate ritual life
centered about the bodies of deceased Inca kings, they also show just
how misleading it is to impute Western notions of death to Inca minds.
A past Inca ruler was not considered 'dead' in our sense of the term
at all, as we can see from the way his *panaqa* dealt with him. A king's
descendants maintained him in state, made costly offerings and sacrifices
to him, brought him to all the major state ceremonies, talked to him,
sought his help in times of stress, ate and drank with him, and even took
him to visit his friends! In short, the *panaqas* continued to treat the
deceased rulers as if they were still alive.

This continuing 'life' was tremendously important, for it made the
royal mummies some of the holiest objects in the Inca realm. Like the
emperor actually occupying the throne, the corpses of previous rulers
were the living sons of Inti—visible links between the Inca people and
their upper pantheon, and thus the embodiment of the identity and
aspirations of the Inca state. This role was made manifest in several ways.

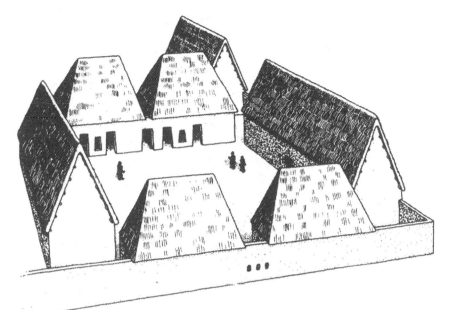

Fig. 20. Reconstruction drawing of the Coricancha, the principal temple of the Inca state religion, in Cuzco (following Gasparini and Margolies 1980: 229).

In the chief temple of the Inca state religion, the Coricancha in Cuzco (Figure 20), there were wall niches in which the bodies of past rulers were displayed along with the idols of Inti in certain festivals.[93] Furthermore, Cobo described one of the principal idols of the sun god as a golden figure in human form; this statue had a hollow stomach 'filled with a paste made of gold dust mixed with the ashes or powder of the Inca kings' hearts'.[94] In addition, a dead king could be addressed as *Illapa*, which was also the name for the thunder or weather god.[95] This subcomplex of the sky god was concerned with the meteorological phenomena that regulate agricultural production (rain, frost, hail, etc.). Hence deceased rulers were explicitly identified with both national patronage (Inti) and the fertilizing forces of nature (the sun and weather). For this reason the royal mummies were crucial *huacas* upon which the prosperity of the Inca state depended.

> Only the bodies of the kings and lords were venerated by the people as a whole, and not just by their own descendants, because they were convinced that...in heaven their souls played a great role in helping the people and looking after their needs.[96]

There can be no doubt about the sincerity of the Incas' beliefs in the continuing life of the dead kings and the supreme importance of their bodies. In the first place, those articles of faith were completely consistent with the fundamental tradition of ancestor worship. Furthermore, in the years following the Spanish Conquest the Inca gave ample proof of their piety. When the conquistadors condemned Atauhualpa, the last Inca emperor, to death, they offered him two alternatives: persist in his paganism and be burned at the stake, or convert to Christianity and be garroted. Atauhualpa chose conversion and the garrote so that his body would not be destroyed.[97] In the decades following the Conquest, the Spaniards searched diligently for the royal mummies, at first to seize their treasure and later because the religious significance of those bodies had become apparent. The Inca readily parted with treasure, but they hid the mummies for a long time and protected them at the cost of great personal suffering—including being burned alive. The Spaniards did not find the last of the dead kings until 1559, twenty-seven years after the Conquest.[98] At that time, in what can only be called a poignant display of faith, the Inca were still venerating the ashes of Viracocha Inca and Topa Inca, whose bodies had been burned some years previously. Even these pathetic relics were taken away and buried in the attempt to eradicate the imperial ancestor cult.[99]

In typical fashion, Inca oral history credited the establishment of split inheritance to Pachakuti (Rowe 1967: 60-1; Brundage 1963: 179-80). The cult of the royal dead was indeed elaborated greatly during his reign, but our previous remarks about Pachakuti's creativity are particularly appropriate in this case. When his regime came to power, some form of split inheritance already existed among the Chimu. Even if Pachakuti and his cohorts did derive split inheritance independently, without prior knowledge of the Chimu version, their 'invention' was merely a reworking of two traditional elements of Inca culture: ancestor worship and the *panaqa*.

As we mentioned earlier, the cult of the royal mummies was basically a grandiose version of standard Andean ancestor worship. In split inheritance the fundamental tenet of Inca religion was simply applied to imperial rulers on an appropriately regal scale. If the dead bodies through which the local *ayllu*'s ancestors spoke were sacred objects, the mummy-bundles containing the spiritual essences of dead rulers were to be among the holiest *huacas* in the realm. If the *ayllu*'s progenitors received small sacrifices and ritual remembrances, past kings were to be treated with all the pomp and ceremony they had enjoyed as living monarchs. If the *ayllu* supported its forebears by reserving a small portion of its fields for them, deceased emperors were to sustain themselves by keeping all of the property they had accumulated during their lifetimes. In the logic of ancestor worship split inheritance was a completely rational development.

A dead ruler's *panaqa* was the social group containing all of his descendants in the male line except the son who succeeded him. Like ancestor worship, to which it was closely related, the *panaqa* was an

Fig. 21. Plan of Cuzco with surviving traces of its imperial Inca occupation indicated. Pachakuti is said to have rebuilt the capital in the shape of a puma, with the 'fortress' of Sacsahuaman at the head and the area called Pumachupan at the tail.

institution deeply embedded in Inca culture. At heart the *panaqa* was an *ayllu* whose founder was an Inca ruler, and the *panaqas* are often called *ayllus* in the chronicles. As a specific form of the basic social unit the *panaqa* undoubtedly pre-dated Pachakuti. Several chroniclers do, in fact, call the *panaqa* a creation of earlier rulers.[100]

However, the Inca leadership of Pachakuti's reign did modify the *panaqa* system in several ways. They reorganized previously existing *panaqas*, and they may have created new ones for several early kings who were probably mythical figures.[101] More importantly, they endowed past rulers with wealth for their support. Pachakuti's regime rebuilt Cuzco (Figure 21) and repartitioned the surrounding area.[102] In the process they created individual estates for each of the previous kings and entrusted them to the corresponding *panaqas*.[103]

Clearly, then, the 'invention' of split inheritance involved nothing more than a manipulation of traditional institutions. These religious and social reforms simply ensured that when an Inca leader's turn to be worshiped as an ancestor came around, his cult would be maintained in grand style. The spiritual essence contained in his mummy would live on in splendor: he would retain everything he ever owned, and his *panaqa* would use all his wealth to glorify him. He would no longer rule the empire as a whole, but within its borders there would be a separate kingdom—his *panaqa* and his property—over which he would always reign supreme.

There was, of course, another side to the coin. What the elaborated form of mummy worship gave to previous rulers, it took away from an ascending emperor. Split inheritance left a newly enthroned emperor rich in privileges, but property-poor. Each ruler was forced to acquire his own possessions so that he might live in the royal manner, strengthen his administration by rewarding his supporters, and provide his *panaqa* with the means of perpetuating his cult.

If we ask how the new king could obtain those possessions, we are asking: What were the sources of wealth in Tawantinsuyu? The answer lies in the empire's economic basis, a system of labor taxation. Inca law required each taxpayer (able-bodied adult male head-of-household) to contribute a certain amount of labor time to the state every year. More specifically, taxpayers were required to contribute some of the surplus labor time remaining after they had satisfied the subsistence needs of their own *ayllus*. Citizens complied with these obligations by cultivating state-owned lands for the support of civil and religious authorities, constructing all public works projects, and manning the Inca armies (Figure 22). As we have noted before, this system was an extension and projection of the local *ayllu*'s economic organization. Like the duties of *ayllu* members on which it was based, state-administered labor taxation was governed by ancient Andean principles of reciprocity. During their periods of service, taxpayers had to be sustained and entertained by the beneficiary of their work, and the state fulfilled its side of the bargain by redistributing some of the produce of its lands.[104]

At least in the early years of the empire, labor taxation also supported the Inca rulers. In addition to the duties listed above, local *ayllus* were also required to contribute a certain amount of labor time to the personal service of the emperor. Directly and indirectly, this surplus labor provided the goods and service to which leaders were entitled and which constituted their wealth.

A deceased emperor and his *panaqa* continued to function as a royal court and had to be supported in an appropriate manner. Therefore, all taxes imposed by an emperor for his own benefit were covered by split inheritance and remained in effect after his death. Hence a new ruler could only accumulate his own property by increasing the imperial tax revenues—that is, by extracting more surplus labor time from the

Fig. 22. Inca labor taxation. Guaman Poma's drawing shows taxpayers carrying the produce of state-owned fields to imperial storehouses; an imperial official (center) is directing the work.

citizenry. He had two principal means of doing so. First, he could demand additional periods of service from his existing subjects, thereby increasing their tax burden. Second, he could conquer new territories, annex them to the empire as provinces, and impose taxes on their inhabitants.

However, the emperor could not levy taxes at will in his provinces, whether new or old. His own demands, like those of the state as a whole, were regulated by principles of reciprocity. He had to sustain and entertain citizens while they worked for him. Therefore, the emperor's fundamental economic need was for agricultural land whose produce could be used to fulfill his reciprocal obligations to the taxpayers. Within the context of labor taxation there was no escaping this necessity. If a ruler raised his wealth by demanding more labor from the taxpayers at hand, he needed land to support them during their additional periods of service. If he brought new subjects under his domain, he still needed land to sustain them while they worked for him.

Hence an Inca ruler's road to wealth lay in acquiring agricultural land for himself. In claiming that land equalled wealth, we are not implying that a king could 'spend' it in the modern sense. What we mean is that through reciprocity and redistribution—institutionalized generosity— land could be converted into goods, services, and political support. Without land the Inca emperor could not be 'open and generous, the culture's image of a good chief'.[105] Without land the emperor could not build a following; he could not rule, and his cult could not be sustained after his death.

Therefore, when Pachakuti's regime endowed the previous kings with riches, it did so by assigning them farmlands in the vicinity of Cuzco. At the same time certain tracts were appropriated for Pachakuti himself and set up as his own private estates.[106] Many of the chroniclers do not fully differentiate between the private holdings of individual rulers and the state-owned lands that underwrote Inca civil administration, state religion, and the army. However, there are enough references to royal estates to show that such lands existed (Murra 1980: 38-40; see below). This conclusion is confirmed by Colonial legal documents recording disputes over land tenure and water rights. In this vast body of evidence, which has only begun to be tapped, the distinctions between rulers' private holdings and 'regular' state-owned lands are crystal-clear (Rostworowski 1962, 1966). The exact amount of territory owned by any single ruler is unknown, but the total was obviously large: various sources name entire highland valleys that were the personal property of Inca sovereigns.[107] All in all, the available evidence shows that an emperor owned lands in all the provinces of his realm. At least in Tawantinsuyu's early years, these royal estates were cultivated by taxpayers as part of their labor service obligations.[108]

It is absolutely essential to note that a king's private lands were covered by split inheritance: there is no doubt that an emperor retained his lands after his death. In fact, most of the chroniclers' explicit references to royal estates are specifically concerned with the lands owned by deceased rulers.[109]

> [The dead kings] had provinces set aside for their sustenance.[110]
>
> They made a house for him [Guayna Capa] in all the provinces; they gave him women from all over the kingdom and fields [for cultivation], because they [the Inca rulers] considered it to be a point of honor not to take over or use a woman or a field or a servant or anything which had belonged to their parents; rather, in all the valleys these had to be provided...[111]
>
> They held their memory in such esteem that when one of these mighty lords died, his son took for himself nothing but the crown, for it was a law among them that the wealth and royal possessions of him who had been Inca of Cuzco were not to belong to anyone else... [The royal mummies] had their *chacaras*, which is the name they give their plantations, where they raised corn and other victuals... even though they were already dead.[112]

Since agricultural land was the ultimate source of a ruler's wealth, it is hardly surprising that split inheritance allowed them to retain their private estates. Had it not done so, the cult of the royal mummies could not have been maintained in so lavish a fashion.

Herein lies the crucial difference between Inca society before and after Pachakuti, the innovation that made his reign truly pivotal. In and of itself, the elaboration of royal mummy worship was a minor cultural change, a slight reworking of traditional Inca institutions. However, application of split inheritance to the royal estates produced a vast increase in the material demands of ancestor worship. The local *ayllu* could support all of its ancestors by reserving a small portion of its fields for them, but this inexpensive principle of 'one for all' would not do for imperial leaders. If a deceased ruler's lands were tied up in maintaining him, and if his successor could inherit none of them, then each emperor would have to obtain his own estates.

These expanded property rights of the dead were to alter Inca society irrevocably. Split inheritance would force each succeeding ruler into a constant search for new agricultural land. This much must have been obvious to the Inca leadership from the outset. What they could not have foreseen were the long-term consequences of their religious reforms.

Expansion and consequent stresses

The obvious effect of split inheritance was to reduce the supplies of land and labor available to a newly crowned Inca ruler. It is unfortunate that the chroniclers did not always clearly differentiate the king's private holdings from state-owned lands, because the distinction is significant.

State-owned lands were permanently reserved for the support of the empire's projects. However, an individual ruler's holdings were available for the purposes of the empire only while he was alive and serving as head of state (that is, while the empire's goals were *his* goals). After his death his lands and their products were entrusted to his *panaqa*. Through sacrifices and other expenditures the products of a deceased emperor's fields were to be used for the perpetual support of his mummy and his cult. Therefore, as each king died, ever greater amounts of farmland became tied up in the hands of dead men, and were thus denied to all succeeding administrations of the empire.[113]

Likewise, the cult of the royal mummies made demands on the state's labor resources. A ruler's lands had to be worked on a yearly basis. Needless to say, any labor invested in farming them was not available for other purposes. As the number of deceased kings and their private estates grew, so did the amount of labor devoted to serving the dead.

Hence the rights of dead rulers placed considerable amounts of land and labor outside a new emperor's control and left him facing the question of how to create his own agricultural estates and have them farmed. There was one obvious solution to this problem: he could conquer new territories and exploit their wealth. Since his goals were ownership of land and control of surplus labor time, the old pattern of plunder and withdrawal would no longer suffice. Instead, a ruler would have to strive for permanent annexation, for the integration of conquered regions into his realm. Accordingly, split inheritance emerges as a driving force behind the growth of the Inca Empire.

It is essential to understand at the outset that the primary economic strains resulting from the imperial ancestor cult—shortages of land and labor—affected only the king at first. Yet while the emperor felt pressures for territorial growth, he could not expand the realm unless he could persuade his subjects to march forth on his behalf. In other words, a ruler could only achieve his goals by making his problem the empire's problem, by convincing the Inca citizenry that conquest was both their right and their duty. In pursuing this task a king had three formidable allies. First, at least in the beginning, military expansion worked to the advantage of the Inca state as a whole. Even more important than these overall benefits were culturally defined rewards that motivated specific social groups and individual citizens. Finally, the growth of the Inca Empire was accompanied by an incessant campaign of explicit and implicit propaganda designed to fire its audience with a zeal for victory.

While conquests enabled a ruler to gain lands for himself, the initial expansion of the empire was also economically beneficial for the Inca people as a whole. Territorial growth brought new farmlands under the control of the Inca state, allowing its members to have both larger harvests and a wider variety of foods at their disposal. Hence the annexation of new provinces strengthened the Incas' subsistence economy:

increased agricultural production allowed the Inca to buffer themselves against crop failures in their homeland. Should the Cuzco district suffer bad harvests, produce from the provinces could help to ensure that no disastrous food shortages occurred.[114]

If militaristic expansion was advantageous for the Inca state as a collective body, Tawantinsuyu's rapid growth was more directly fostered by incentives offered to specific social groups and individual citizens. From the emperor down to the members of village *ayllus*, every level of Inca society had reasons to see constant warfare as desirable. Particularly strong motivations were provided for the state's decision-making elite, the *panaqa* nobility.

The *panaqas* as an interest group were to benefit greatly from imperial expansion. *Panaqa* members were kinsmen and descendants of Inca rulers, and they formed Tawantinsuyu's highest nobility, the 'Incas by blood'. As such their position in the Inca state was second only to that of the kings themselves. They formed the talent pool from which the empire's topmost governmental officials were drawn. Countless references in the chronicles show that the highest offices in the civil, military, and religious hierarchies were filled by close male relatives of the emperor (Rowe 1946: 257, 260, 269)—that is, by members of the *panaqas*. As Tawantinsuyu grew and the wealth poured in, the *panaqas* would profit in proportion to their status. They would eventually come to lead lives of incredible opulence and ease—so much so that one Spanish eyewitness was moved to describe them repeatedly as ridden with vice.[115] Like the emperor himself, the high nobility had a vested interest in expanding the empire in order to maintain their powers, privileges, and wealth.

Similarly, the drive for conquest was reinforced by incentives offered to *panaqa* members, lesser nobles, and commoners *as individuals*. The Inca had an elaborate system of military honors and awards.[116] Outstanding warriors among the nobility could look forward to grants of land, additional wives, servants, herds of llamas, or fine clothing, along with gold, silver, and other exotic goods that served as status symbols. While attaching great prestige to these rewards, rulers were careful to propagate the idea that the spoils of war were rightfully theirs and were only bestowed on others as signs of the emperor's favor.

Displays of martial valor were also a way for members of the upper classes to advance themselves within the state's administrative hierarchy. A noble who distinguished himself in battle could expect to be promoted to a higher governmental post. The step up in rank might also be accompanied by the conferring of special privileges, such as the right to ride in a litter, eat while sitting on a stool, or carry a parasol. As Rowe (1946: 261) notes, these activities were normally the prerogatives of the emperor, and the privileges consisted of the right to imitate one's king.

Prowess in war was also the principal avenue of social mobility in Tawantinsuyu. Commoners who fought well received small gifts from the

crown, but truly outstanding service was rewarded with a position in
the administrative hierarchy—that is, by entrance into the ranks of the
petty nobility, the class of provincial administrators known as *curacas*.

> As the route by which they had risen to such great power and
> majesty and the means by which they maintained themselves in it,
> warfare and those who waged it were so important to the Incas that
> it was the only way for their vassals to advance themselves into posts
> of honor.[117]

In other words, the soldier from the village *ayllu* who earned a reputation
as a great warrior could shed his taxpayer status and cross what was
otherwise a hereditary and impenetrable class barrier. To be sure, his
entry into the nobility was on the lowest possible level, but it was a
colossal step forward, and it also brought the hope that continuing valor
would win further promotions for himself or his descendants.

Finally, in every stratum of society the brave soldier's rewards
continued long after his death. The Inca believed that those who fought
with courage and skill would eventually occupy 'the principal place in
heaven'.[118] They would rank high among the ancestral spirits, and they
would be especially cherished by their descendants. In contrast, anyone
who had proved to be cowardly or inept in battle—even a king—could
expect nothing more than the scorn of future generations and the
shameful silence of his descendants.[119]

In all of these ways the king's quest for land was integrated with the
economic and political welfare of the state as a whole, the prosperity
of specific social groups, and the ambitions of individual citizens. Inca
leaders were quick to make certain that these lessons were not lost upon
the populace. Through a vigorous propaganda campaign everyone was
continually reminded that their king was a god, that the emperor's
interests were their interests, and that the welfare of all depended on
the prosperity of their rulers, past and present.

Some facets of this campaign could not have been more explicit. We
have already mentioned the beliefs that the spoils of war belonged to
the king and that awards and advancement were only possible through
his favor. Furthermore, sons of the Inca nobility attended a formal
program of training in Cuzco. Here, in addition to learning military
skills, they became thoroughly versed in the state religion and the
authorized version of Inca history. In later imperial times education in
Cuzco was also mandatory for certain sons of native provincial
aristocracies, namely those youths who were being groomed for important
administrative positions.[120] After several years of indoctrination the
graduates of Cuzco's schooling emerged as warriors with a cause: the
advancement of the Inca Empire and its rulers.

The same messages were conveyed in more subtle, even subconscious,
ways. Some rituals of the Inca state religion contained undertones of
implicit propaganda. In particular, certain ceremonies were accompanied

by processions of the dead kings, in which their bodies were carried past the public while their descendants sang of their divinity and their mighty exploits.[121] In a more general sense, all of the pomp and splendor surrounding the living emperor and the royal mummies was a constant reminder that these people were divine beings, crucial *huacas* who had to be treated properly if the state was to prosper.

Finally, as Cobo notes, the Incas' very successes provided a propagandistic message of the strongest sort.

> And the Incas [i.e., the rulers] justified this great burden and obligation by the idea that they were gods to the Indians, who should not fail to further the Incas' designs. This opinion was strengthened every day as the people saw the many victories that the Incas achieved over all kinds of people; and it was further strengthened by the fact that although the Incas were so few at first, they had subjugated this whole kingdom and their authority among the people was increased in no small way by the admirable order and harmony that the people saw imposed by the Incas on everything, both for the utility of the republic and for the growth of the cult of their gods. The Incas made the people listen to this sort of nonsense everyday, so the people thought the Incas were very much like gods and full of more than human wisdom.[122]

Father Cobo disagreed with the content of the Inca indoctrination program, but he readily admitted that the program itself had been highly successful.

In summary, a complicated system of benefits, incentives, rewards, and justifications meshed the emperor's desires with the interests of his subjects. Military expansionism was to provide wealth for some and economic security for all, political advancement for the state's leadership, social mobility for commoners, and an honored afterlife for deserving individuals. Furthermore, by providing the wherewithal for the proper care of the kings, living and dead, conquest would insure Tawantinsuyu of heaven's favor. The royal mummies had done what Inti alone could not do: they had given the Inca people not only a national identity, but also a sense of divine mission. The property rights of the dead kings were the final and critical element needed to fuse Inca economic, social, political, and religious institutions into an expansionistic system sanctioned by an imperial cult.

This new ideology gave the Inca a crucial advantage over their neighbors, and within a decade or so of the Chanca crisis they had prevailed in the infighting of the southern highlands. After subjugating the provinces around Cuzco, Pachakuti marched his troops into the northern Titicaca Basin and made himself master of that supremely wealthy area.[123] Armed now with religious zeal and the riches of the Collao—large populations, high agricultural productivity, and vast herds of llamas to serve as beasts of burden (Murra 1975)—the Inca armies became a juggernaut.

A detailed chronological review of Tawantinsuyu's subsequent growth is not necessary here; such accounts are available elsewhere (Rowe 1946; Brundage 1963). For our purposes it is enough to note that every Inca emperor tried to enlarge his domain; Figure 12, which is based on Rowe's (1946: 204-8) painstaking analysis of the sources, shows the territories conquered by Pachakuti (1438-71), Topa Inca (1471-93), and Huayna Capac (1493-1525). In less than a century the small highland kingdom taken over by Pachakuti became an empire spanning thirty-six degrees of latitude and measuring over 4,300 kilometers from end to end. It is possible that many of Topa Inca's southern 'conquests' were never fully integrated into the empire and that effective Inca rule was limited to Peru, Ecuador, and highland Bolivia.[124] Even so, the Inca expansion was a highly impressive achievement.

Yet the new Inca ideology was the proverbial double-edged sword. Even as it was driving Tawantinsuyu to its zenith, the cult of the royal mummies was constantly undercutting what it built. By denying the living emperor the land and labor controlled by his predecessors, the property rights of the dead forced Inca rulers to adopt a policy of continuous territorial growth. In creating unrelenting pressures for new conquests split inheritance would prove to be the fatal flaw in the Inca state. The aggressive military drive provided by the Incas' ideological system was *initially* successful in the competitive Andean world. However, the long-term consequences of the imperial ancestor cult were severe military, administrative, and economic stresses that would eventually destroy Tawantinsuyu.

Despite its initial advantages, constant expansion soon began to strain Tawantinsuyu. In the first place, military campaigns were costly, and a ruler's quest for agricultural land had to be 'financed' by the rest of the empire. The army had to be manned by citizens fulfilling labor tax obligations, and it had to be supported by the produce of state-owned lands (*not* royal estates).[125] Continual warfare required large investments of energy and resources and kept the demand for surplus production at a high level.

Figure 12 provides a clue to another problem. Andean civilization developed in coastal and highland Peru, plus highland Bolivia. The Central Andean coast and highlands are very different environments, but they do have one thing in common: both consist of open country without heavy forest cover. Central Andean military tactics, including those of the Inca, were adapted to open terrain inhabited by civilized peoples. Soldiers marched along prepared roads and were accustomed to finding stored surplus foods with which they could support themselves. Armies were drawn up in massed formations, either to fight pitched battles on level ground or to storm hilltop fortresses. Long-range weapons—slings, darts, and bolas—were intended to provide concentrated volleys, rather than supremely accurate individual shots. Much of the fighting was hand-to-hand. The Inca waged war in this manner, and they were used to opponents who did the same. In such engagements the Inca had the decisive advantages of superior numbers and organization.[126]

Yet as Figure 12 shows, Tawantinsuyu's expansion was so swift that the Inca began to run out of open, 'civilized' lands to conquer as early as the reign of Topa Inca, Pachakuti's son. However, the pressures for territorial growth continued unabated. Inca emperors began to look toward the *montaña*, the heavily vegetated eastern slopes of the Andes, and to the vast Amazonian tropical forest east of the mountains. Both Topa Inca and his successor, Huayna Capac, tried to invade the eastern forests.[127] The Inca armies had some success in the upper *montaña*, close to home, but their deeper penetrations of the forests were unmitigated disasters.

The chroniclers offered few details of these latter campaigns, as if the Inca themselves had been loath to discuss them. Of all the accounts, Sarmiento's and Cabello's are the most graphic.

> But as the forests of the *montaña* were very dense and full of thickets, [the Inca armies] could not break through them, nor did they know which direction they had to take to reach the settlements, which were well hidden in the bush... Topa Inca and his captains went into [this region], which consists of the most terrible and horrifying forests, with many rivers. There they endured immense hardships, and the men they brought from Peru suffered from the change of climate, for Peru is a cold, dry land, while the *montaña* is hot and humid. Topa Inca's troops fell sick, and many of them died. Topa Inca himself and a third of the men he had brought from Peru in order to conquer [the *montaña*] wandered for a long time, lost in the forests, unable to get out at one end or the other...[128]

> Having set out from Cuzco, [Topa Inca and his army] crossed through the other side of the cordillera, which slopes toward the Atlantic. The hardships they suffered there cannot be described. There were sudden and frightening attacks by enemies who, like unrestrained and undisciplined savages, ambushed [the Inca troops] at the worst possible moments. The enemy did not wait around to win or lose a battle. Their method of fighting was so disorderly that when the men of Cuzco wanted to attack, they could not find anyone to strike at; separately, each one on his own, the enemy vanished into the underbrush, where they could not be caught. In addition, [the Inca soldiers] were worn out by the wide and turbulent rivers that they found, the constant and vexing rains that fell upon them, the intense heat, the sweltering valleys through which they wandered, and the great hunger that they suffered. What made matters worse was not finding anyone to wage war upon...[129]

Sarmiento mentions another campaign in which five thousand nobles marched into the *montaña* and were never heard from again.[130]

It is easy to imagine the Incas' plight in the tropical forest. Wandering through dense jungles where there were no roads, unable to live off the alien land, some men deserted, while others fell sick and starving. Weakened and demoralized, the Inca armies stumbled into a kind of warfare unlike any they had ever known. There were no pitched battles to fight or fortresses to storm; superior numbers and organization counted for naught. The troops could neither maintain their formations nor mass their firepower. They could not even find the enemy, who remained hidden in the brush and sniped at them, using bows and blowguns with deadly accuracy. In their eastern campaigns the Inca paid a bitter price to learn the great lesson of military history: an attacking army advancing into an unfamiliar environment is easy prey for defenders who know the countryside and refuse to fight by the invaders' rules.

The Inca eventually abandoned their designs on the tropical forest. In later years they claimed to scorn the native peoples as stupid, naked savages, creatures so subhuman that they mated with animals.

> They also say that...these people cohabit with [monkeys]; and they say that some of them bring forth monsters...[131]

What, the Inca asked rhetorically, could possibly be gained by conquering such wretched beings? These disparaging remarks were an obvious and hollow attempt to save face. No slanderous dismissal of the enemy could bring back the thousands of men who perished in the jungle, nor could it restore the Incas' view of themselves as invincible. By creating unrelenting pressures for new agricultural lands, the cult of the royal mummies eventually drove Tawantinsuyu into disastrous military adventures.

If the initially explosive growth of the Inca Empire led its armies into wars they were ill-prepared to fight, it also posed administrative difficulties. One problem was communication. The Inca government, like any other, required information in order to make decisions and was heavily dependent on communication among the various levels of the hierarchy. For its time, Tawantinsuyu's communication network was as good as it could have been. Many of the chroniclers—above all, Cieza[132]—were impressed by the Inca road system, much of which was actually inherited from earlier polities, and by the trained relay runners who conveyed official messages along the roads, transmitting information up and down the administrative hierarchy.[133] Yet eventually even this extraordinary communication system was outstripped by the uncontrollable growth of the empire. The average speed of the runners was about fifty leagues—some 200-250 kilometers—per day.[134] Messages from the vicinity of Lima on the coast, 140 leagues from Cuzco and hardly the most distant corner of the realm, took three days to reach the Inca capital; the round trip from Cuzco to Quito in Ecuador and back took ten to twelve days. The potential problem is clear: an emperor could be forced to make urgent decisions on the basis of information that was critically incomplete or out-of-date.[135] By increasing the distances and times involved, territorial growth aggravated the dangers. In Tawantinsuyu's later days its lines of communication may have been seriously overextended.

Imperial expansion caused another kind of stress by bringing an incredibly diverse collection of peoples into the Inca domain. We do not know the total number of ethnic groups in the empire, but there were over eighty provinces, some of them containing more than one tribe, in Peru alone (Rowe 1946: 185-92). Many of these subject peoples chafed under Inca rule, and there were small-scale uprisings as early as Pachakuti's reign.[136] Later rulers were faced with larger, better coordinated revolts. Topa Inca beat down a major insurrection in the Titicaca Basin, and Huayna Capac spent several years quelling a widespread revolt in Ecuador.[137] Undoubtedly the problems of communication mentioned above furthered the cause of ethnically based provincial rebellions.

While the constant demand for territorial growth eventually subjected the empire to a variety of strains, conquest was not a ruler's only route to land (and labor) for new royal estates. There were alternative strategies, but they also led to a wider distribution of stress. For example, a king could increase his holdings by appropriating already existing farmland for himself, either by alienating the land from its original owners or by accepting it from them as a gift (Rostworowski 1962: 134, 136). The difference between confiscation and donation may have been largely a legal fiction, since the 'gifts' may well have been compulsory (Rostworowski 1962: 136). In addition, Murra (1980: 38) tentatively suggests that some royal estates may have been carved out of the regular state-owned lands. The crucial point here is that any royal holding, no matter how it was obtained, would eventually become the possession of a deceased emperor. Therefore, in all of the possibilities listed above we see the property rights of the dead taking land, plus the labor needed to work it, away from the living. The eventual results were localized imbalances between population and resources. The problem was most acute in the area around Cuzco, whose population was mushrooming with imperial success.[138] Meanwhile, more and more of the lands and labor in the capital district were being monopolized by the deceased rulers and their *panaqas*.[139]

Another way to obtain agricultural land was through reclamation projects. In Tawantinsuyu's coastal regions reclamation was accomplished by enlarging canal irrigation networks. The most famous highland projects were hillside terraces that allowed cultivation to be extended off the valley bottoms and onto the surrounding slopes (Figure 24), but irrigation was also practiced in the sierra, both in conjunction with terracing and separately.[140] Like so many other phenomena, reclamation techniques were ancient Andean practices inherited by the Inca, and every emperor from Pachakuti onward used them as a way of acquiring private estates.[141]

The problem with such projects was that they represented a major economic commitment to marginal land. They required a sizable investment of labor: taxpayers had to be provided in order to reclaim the land, after which other taxpayers had to farm it. Furthermore, once the land had been brought under cultivation, it was always susceptible to crop failure.

Highland terrace systems are a case in point. They seem to have been used mostly for growing maize,[142] a crop vital to the Inca Empire, but one that has always been at a certain disadvantage in the sierra. Throughout the highlands maize is threatened by frost, hail, and drought. It can rarely be grown above 2,700 meters in northern Peru or 3,500 meters in the south; above these points killing frosts can occur at any time of year (Murra 1960: 395). Terracing extended maize cultivation into the upper limits of the plant's altitudinal range; if the potential size of the harvest was increased, so were the chances that the crop would fail.

Frost and hail did not plague the coastal regions of Tawantinsuyu, but marginal land was still subject to crop failure. Fields reclaimed by canal construction were highly sensitive to variations in highland rainfall and runoff, from which the arid coast derives its irrigation water.

The drawbacks of reclaimed acreage and the aforementioned 'donations' of land to rulers combine to pose an intriguing question. Did Inca emperors prefer to create their estates by appropriating valley-bottom lands for themselves and giving the former owners reclaimed marginal land in return? That is, did rulers take prime acreage away from the state-owned lands or the fields of local kin groups and replace it with less desirable terrain? If so, the negative economic effects of split inheritance would have been compounded. The cult of the royal mummies placed more and more acreage under the control of deceased rulers; if the scenario given above is true, through time split inheritance would have concentrated Tawantinsuyu's most desirable agricultural land in the hands of the dead. In a direct and rather high-handed manner, the property rights of the dead would have forced other people into an increasing reliance on marginal land.[143]

In any case, there was certainly a strong indirect link between the royal ancestor cult and dependence on marginal land. By driving Tawantinsuyu's expansion, split inheritance was enlarging the empire's administrative and military requirements, increasing its need for an agricultural surplus, and forcing it to invest heavily in reclamation. The demands of uncontrollable territorial growth were fostering a potentially dangerous economic situation. Reliance on marginal land was making the empire ever more vulnerable to poor harvests caused by short- or long-term climatic deteriorations. No wonder Inca agricultural ritual reflected a profound insecurity about the success of the state's harvests, particularly the maize crop (Murra 1960).

In addition to the strains attendant upon expansion and reclamation, Tawantinsuyu was simultaneously subjected to another form of stress. At the highest levels of the administrative hierarchy there were institutionalized conflicts of interest that undermined the emperor's authority and threatened governmental stability. The source of these problems was the cult of the royal mummies and the courts of the dead kings, the *panaqas*.

As we have seen, the *panaqas* were royal *ayllus*, the relatives of the Inca rulers (living and dead). Consequently, the *panaqas* formed the empire's highest nobility and the pool from which the empire's topmost administrators were drawn. Upper-class polygyny enabled the royal *ayllus* to grow swiftly: Cabello claims that one *panaqa* alone, Topa Inca's, had about one thousand members at the time of the Spanish Conquest.[144] While this figure may be only an estimate, it does indicate that in Tawantinsuyu's later years the total membershp of the *panaqas* was considerable. This combination of high social position and large numbers gave the royal *ayllus* considerable political power. Furthermore, the power of the *panaqas* was backed by the spiritual support of the state's most prestigious leaders, the deceased kings themselves.

The royal *ayllus'* devotion to their ancestors could create severe administrative problems, for the cult of the royal mummies made strong political factionalism a built-in feature of the Inca government. In fact, Tawantinsuyu might be described as kingdoms within a kingdom. Within the borders of the empire lay a series of smaller kingdoms, each consisting of a dead ruler, his property, the members of his *panaqa*, and their possessions. In a very real sense each of these kingdoms was a sovereign state. It had its own territories and sources of support. Its ruler was viewed as a living being capable of issuing orders when he was consulted.[145] Furthermore, he was the equal of the emperor actually occupying the throne. The principal duty of the royal *ayllus* was to perpetuate the mummies and worship of past kings. Therefore, if the interests of the emperor and his predecessors clashed, each *panaqa* was expected to stand up for its royal ancestor. In other words, Tawantinsuyu's highest nobility owed its primary allegiance not to the current emperor, but to a collection of corpses.

Compounding the tensions between past and present rulers were the aspirations of the *panaqas* as collective groups and the ambitions of their individual members. The predictable result was political intrigue, and the royal *ayllus* seem to have been hotbeds of conspiracy. They meddled in the succession to the throne and plotted against the emperor.[146] Some *panaqa* members even tried to provoke provincial rebellions in the hope of benefiting from them.[147]

There was precious little the *Sapa Inca* could do to prevent all this plotting and scheming. His control of the royal *ayllus* was limited in several ways. The highest positions in the emperor's court were filled by his close male relatives. Until his sons came of age, his most important functionaries were usually chosen from a group composed of his brothers and uncles, who belonged to *panaqas* other than his own. Therefore, no matter what the ruler himself desired, his most powerful assistants had a vested interest in maintaining the rights of the *panaqas*. Furthermore, the emperor's authority could not override the rights of the royal *ayllus* because the latter had been entrusted with their duties—as well as the powers and privileges needed to carry them out—by previous rulers. Members of a *panaqa* could always justify their deeds by claiming to be working on behalf of their ancestor. In fact, given the view of past rulers as still alive and the practice of consulting their mummies, a *panaqa* could credibly assert that its actions had been directly ordered by a deceased king. By the same token, the emperor could hardly afford to weaken the *panaqa* as an institution, since his own descendants would some day be looking out for his interests.

Hence the *panaqas* had duties and ambitions that could bring them into conflict with the emperor, a degree of autonomy unparalleled elsewhere in the Inca state, and the wherewithal to be really troublesome. The royal *ayllus'* ability to act independently was a constant dilemma for the emperor, and he had to treat them very carefully. Friction between the emperor and the high nobility was a destablizing force in the Inca government, and a king who did not deal with the *panaqas* skillfully could seriously jeopardize his rule (Rostworowski 1960: 419).

In short, the cult of the royal mummies helped to drive the Inca expansion, but it also linked economic stresses, administrative problems, and political instabilities into a cyclical relationship. By placing more and more land in the hands of the dead, split inheritance forced a living ruler to seek new sources of wealth. The result was a demand for territorial growth through expansion and reclamation. Unsuccessful attempts at growth produced costly military calamities, while successful ones led to administrative and economic stresses. Further expansion and reclamation eased the strains temporarily, but exacerbated them in the long run, creating pressures for yet more territorial growth, which eventually increased the economic and administrative problems, and so on. The process could never be stopped for very long: as soon as an emperor died, his successor's need for new conquests set it off again. In the language of systems theory, split inheritance had shifted Inca society from a state of dynamic equilibrium to a 'deviation-amplifying feedback cycle'. In less exalted parlance, the property rights of the dead had trapped Tawantinsuyu in a classic vicious circle.

To be sure, in attempting to cope with its internal tensions the empire tried countermeasures other than the self-defeating policy of continuous growth. Several new social groups emerged during Tawantinsuyu's history. Two particular groups that were increasing in numbers and significance during the empire's final decades were the *yana* retainers and the *mitmaqkuna* colonists.[148] Both groups had pre-Inca antecedents, and both represented attempts to deal with certain imperial problems by modifying existing institutions.[149]

The *yana* were full-time retainers. So that they could dedicate themselves to the service of the nobility, they were removed from their traditional ethnic communities and exempted from normal taxation.[150] One of the tasks turned over to *yana* during the empire's later decades was the cultivation of royal estates and *panaqa* lands.[151] Taxpayers, who had worked on a part-time rotating basis, were replaced by agricultural retainers who in theory devoted all their time to service on royal or *panaqa* holdings. In fact, Rostworowski (1962: 133, 1966: 32) has argued that the desire for a completely secure, dependable labor force to work the estates of the nobility was responsible for the growth of the *yana*.

The *mitmaqkuna* colonists are one of the most famous of Tawantinsuyu's imperial institutions.[152] Whenever the Inca conquered a new province, they removed some of its inhabitants to other regions and replaced them with settlers from Cuzco and/or well established provinces. In part this resettlement program was a security measure designed to minimize the dangers of provincial rebellion, but some *mitmaqkuna* served an economic function. Cieza says that some colonists skilled in raising certain crops were sent to introduce those crops into areas where they had not been grown before.[153] Cieza specifically mentions *mitmaqkuna* sent to grow maize at high elevations, and Murra (1960: 400, 1980: 178) believes that one of the resettlement program's primary goals was to expand the area of state-controlled maize production.[154]

The rising importance of these two institutions, retainership and colonization, shows that in its later years Tawantinsuyu was beginning to lose hold of its traditional values. Agricultural *mitmaqkuna* undercut one long-standing ideal, for the relocation of skilled maize farmers strengthened the state-controlled sector of the economy at the expense of village self-sufficiency (Murra 1958: 36, 1980: 187-90). The *yana*, plucked from their ethnic communities and set to working permanently for the nobility, represented a disruption of the kinship basis of Andean society. To a lesser extent the same statement applies to the *mitmaqkuna*, although they were usually moved as social groups. Finally, growing reliance on full-time retainers was freeing Inca rulers from their need to be 'generous'—that is, the *yana* were enabling leaders to shed their reciprocal obligations to the taxpayers who had previously supported them. Taken together, the *yana* and *mitmaqkuna* were the first signs of fundamental changes in the relationship between state and citizen.

The Inca Empire of the early sixteenth century can be characterized as an impressive and highly ordered state, yet one increasingly pressed between internal problems and external limitations. Vast quantities of land and labor tied up in the hands of the dead, constant pressures for territorial growth, military disasters in the tropical forest, overextended lines of communication, provincial rebellions, increasing dependence on marginal land, governmental instability caused by friction between the emperor and high nobility, loss of traditional values, and a changing relationship between state and citizen—each would have been a serious difficulty in and of itself. In their combination and their interaction they were gutting Tawantinsuyu, destroying the substance beneath the glittering surface. By 1525, less than ninety years after Pachakuti's ascension, the situation had become critical.

The terminal trajectory of the Inca state

Huayna Capac, Pachakuti's grandson, spent the latter half of his reign (1493-1525) campaigning in Ecuador. He died there suddenly in 1525, the victim of a plague. His unexpected death left the succession to the throne, or at least the division of authority in the empire, in some way unclear. The years between Huayna Capac's death and the arrival of the Spaniards in 1532 were marked by a bitter power struggle between two of his sons, the half-brothers Huascar and Atauhualpa. Their quarrel and the devastating civil war it begot were the final expressions of the military, economic, and administrative stresses that destroyed the Inca Empire.

Of the protagonists in Tawantinsuyu's suicide, Atauhualpa had by far the weaker claim to the throne. In the Inca Empire the royal succession was not determined by primogeniture; instead, the emperor was supposed to bequeath his position to his most competent son by his principal wife. In later imperial times each emperor took one of his full sisters as his principal wife; Inca oral history said that Topa Inca instituted this practice of incestuous royal marriage.[155] Regardless of its precise origins, royal incest can be seen as an extreme extension of *ayllu* endogamy designed to preserve the purity and divinity of the dynastic bloodline. It was also intended to limit the number of potential claimants to the throne and to minimize conflicts over the succession (Rostworowski 1960). Once the principle of royal incest had been established, an Inca prince not born of a brother-sister marriage could not inherit the kingdom, no matter how competent he might have been.

Atauhualpa was born of one of Huayna Capac's non-incestuous secondary marriages and was not legally qualified to rule Tawantinsuyu.[156] Nonetheless, Huayna Capac looked upon him with great favor. In contrast to Huascar, who had remained in Cuzco during his father's long absence, Atauhualpa had accompanied Huayna Capac on his campaigns and distinguished himself in battle. Huayna Capac evidently rewarded Atauhualpa by making him imperial governor of Quito. However, Atauhaulpa eventually began to argue that his father had divided the empire and granted him independent sovereignty over the northern part. Since Atauhualpa's parentage made him ineligible to rule, this latter claim seems highly dubious, and Huascar was to reject it vehemently.

Whatever the truth may have been, for the first few years after Huayna Capac's death Atauhualpa controlled relatively little territory—only the northern half of Ecuador. His real strength lay in the veteran core of the army. Atauhualpa had grown up with the army; it remained in Quito with him and was fiercely loyal to him.[157] No matter what title his father had bequeathed to him, Atauhualpa was the quintessential *sinchi* (Brundage 1963: 280, 1967: 230, 234).

Unlike Atauhualpa, Huascar was born of an incestuous royal marriage: his mother was one of Huayna Capac's sisters. Huascar was therefore legally entitled to succeed Huayna Capac as emperor, or at least to be considered for the position. Huascar had probably been designated as the rightful heir to the throne during his youth, and he was crowned as emperor when the news of Huayna Capac's death reached Cuzco.[158] The newly ensconced emperor's quarrels with his insubordinate half-brother began at once.

Poor Huascar! Of the chroniclers who wrote their accounts within fifty years of the Spanish Conquest, Cieza is virtually the only one who depicts Huascar favorably, calling him 'beloved in Cuzco and throughout the kingdom...clement and pious...generous...and courageous'.[159] Nearly every other early chronicler portrays Huascar as selfish, treacherous, paranoid, and sadistic—in short, as a madman feared and hated by his subjects. His rule is usually treated as a reign of terror. Among the people said to have been tortured to death at Huascar's command are a number of his brothers and kinsmen, the leading members of his deceased father's court, and emissaries from Atauhualpa.[160]

By the time these charges were leveled, Huascar was dead and unable to defend himself. Today, more than four centuries after the fact, the chroniclers' accusations should be viewed with extreme skepticism. There is no reason to believe that Huascar was any more bloodthirsty than previous Inca emperors, all of whom were capable of treating their real or presumed enemies with great cruelty.[161] The fatal flaw of Huascar's reign, we contend, was not his character, but the compounded effects of the cult of the royal mummies. Attempting to cope with a situation that was out of control, Huascar was drawn into conflict with powerful vested interests. He clashed first with the deceased Inca rulers, and then with their *panaqas*. Early Spanish writers got their information from the Inca nobility, and the accounts of Huascar's 'tyrannies' are probably nothing more than the *panaqas'* hatred of him, fossilized in the chronicles.

Huascar inherited the Inca Empire just as its problems became

critical. Dead rulers controlled far too much of Tawantinsuyu's basic
agricultural resources, land and labor, particularly in the heavily
populated capital district. The rest of the empire was becoming overly
dependent on marginal farmland. The high nobility and disgruntled
ethnic groups were creating administrative tensions. Old values were
breaking down. Tawantinsuyu needed either new provinces or radical
social reforms. However, the empire was overextended and could no
longer expand with ease; Huayna Capac himself had been able to add
relatively little territory to the realm, and even then only at a great cost.
Furthermore, as we have seen, continued expansion would have been
a short-term and ultimately self-defeating remedy. Far-reaching reform
was the only viable solution, and Huascar chose to pursue it.

Huascar knew exactly what lay at the heart of Tawantinsuyu's
problems—the property rights of the dead. He also recognized the
fundamental reform needed to save the empire, and he tried to carry
it out. In a stunning break with the past, he proposed that the imperial
ancestor cult should be abolished.[162] Huascar,

> annoyed one day with these dead [his ancestors], said that he ought
> to order them all buried and take from them all that they had, and
> that there should not be dead men but living ones, because [the
> dead] had all that was best in the country.[163]

It is, of course, possible to view Huascar's action as an entirely selfish
attempt to remove the royal mummies because they stood between him
and wealth. However, Cieza's description of Huascar as 'generous' and
'beloved throughout the kingdom' may well be grounded in truth. In
view of all the strains that split inheritance was causing, burial of the
deceased rulers and termination of their property rights would have
benefited not just Huascar, but the empire as a whole. In many ways,
and above all economically, putting an end to split inheritance would
have been the best thing that Huascar could have done for his subjects.

Alas for Huascar, there is more to culture than economy, and his policy
was a political disaster. Huascar's assault on the royal mummies
infuriated the high nobility, both by offending their piety and by
menacing their self-interest. In the Andean religious tradition of ancestor
worship Huascar's position was the most profound heresy imaginable.
He was proposing a shocking insult to supremely important *huacas* that
linked the Inca people to their pantheon and ensured their prosperity.
The *panaqas* believed that if Huascar were allowed to carry out his
threats, they would have failed in their duty to protect their ancestors,
and the anger of the mummies would assure them of a bitter future. If
Huascar buried the dead rulers and seized their kingdoms, he would strip
the royal *ayllus* of the source of their powers and privileges. The *panaqas*
would be disenfranchised on earth and scorned in heaven.

Recognizing that Huascar's continued rule would mean the complete
overthrow of the established order, the *panaqas* began to conspire against

him (Rostworowski 1960: 425, 1962: 133-4). Openly or covertly, the high nobility threw their support to Atauhualpa in his dispute with the emperor:

> as I have said, the greater part of the chief people were with these [the dead] on account of the many vices which they had there, and they began to hate Huascar, and they say that the captains whom he sent against Atabalipa let themselves be conquered and that others deserted and passed over to him, and for this reason could Atabalipa conquer, for otherwise neither he nor his people were sufficient to vanquish a village, much less a whole kingdom...[164]

> Huascar...was lax in observing the veneration of the dead bodies of his ancestors and of the nobility that was to guard and serve these bodies; and for this reason his captains allowed themselves to be defeated by Atauhualpa and others came to Atauhualpa's side.[165]

The dead kings and the living nobility had turned against the emperor. Driven to desperation, Huascar publicly divorced himself from the social group known as the Upper Cuzco moiety, which contained the *panaqas* of the rulers from Inca Roca on, and into which both he and Atauhualpa had been born.[166]

Atauhualpa already controlled the veteran army in Ecuador; now his brother's attempt to extinguish the cult of the royal mummies had given him a political power base in Cuzco. Although Atauhualpa's non-incestuous birth was considered to be a grave spiritual handicap, in the eyes of the nobility Huascar's intentions were a far more deadly threat to the established order. With the *panaqas* behind him, Atauhualpa no longer had to confine his ambitions to the northern part of Tawantinsuyu. The entire empire could be his, if only he could eliminate Huascar. The fraternal power struggle, heretofore a verbal legal dispute, erupted into civil war.

Sarmiento says that the fighting lasted three years, which would mean that it began in 1529 or 1530.[167] The first battles were provoked by one of the empire's subject ethnic groups, the Cañari of southern Ecuador. Wishing to isolate Atauhualpa beyond a secure buffer, Huascar sent a general named Atoc northward with orders to raise an army and hold the Cañari country. Out of loyalty to Huascar, or perhaps a desire to play both ends against the middle, the Cañari invited Atauhualpa to parley and then took him prisoner. Unfortunately for themselves, they allowed him to escape. Gathering his forces, Atauhualpa defeated Atoc's army and inflicted savage reprisals on the Cañari.[168]

Ethnic diversity had always been a destabilizing force in Tawantinsuyu, and it would now contribute to the empire's downfall. From the Cañari the war spread rapidly to other groups. Both Huascar and Atauhualpa rallied various tribes and provinces to their respective causes.[169] As the half-brothers pursued this policy of exploiting ethnic divisions within the empire, the fragile unity that had been imposed on Tawantinsuyu's heterogeneous subjects distintegrated.

The military history of the civil war is recounted in numerous sources, but the literature will not be analyzed in detail here.[170] In general, Huascar's untested troops were no match for Atauhualpa's seasoned veterans:

> the men who came to [Huascar] from everywhere were innumerable, but since they were inexperienced and joined together hurriedly and without order, and since the experienced captains and soldiers defended Atauhualpa's group, the latter went forward each day and the former lost ground.[171]

Every time Huascar's forces were thrown into battle they were massacred and had to be replaced with yet more green draftees. Moving relentlessly southward, the front closed in on Cuzco. Finally, in 1532 Huascar himself took to the field to command the defense of the capital. Defeated, he was captured by Atauhualpa's men. The civil war was over, but Tawantinsuyu lay in disarray.

In one of history's most sardonic twists, it turned out that Atauhualpa had won a war and lost an empire. On his way to Cuzco to be crowned, he stopped to meet some intruders who had recently entered his realm—168 Spaniards under the leadership of Francisco Pizarro. They would prove to be the true victors in the civil war. Tawantinsuyu had been shattered, and all the Spaniards had to do was pick up the pieces.

The Spanish Conquest of Peru proceeded swiftly. On 16 November, 1532, at Cajamarca in the northern highlands, Pizarro's band captured Atauhualpa and slaughtered his entourage without losing a man. Within the next twelve months Huascar had been put to death by Atauhualpa's minions, Atauhualpa himself had been executed by the conquistadors, a puppet king named Manco Inca had been installed in his place, Pizarro's men had been bolstered by reinforcements, and Cuzco was under Spanish control. Manco Inca would rebel and besiege Cuzco in 1536, but once the siege had been lifted, Spanish domination was not to be threatened again. An Inca government in exile would survive in a remote highland region northwest of Cuzco until 1572, but it lacked the widespread support of other ethnic groups and could not seriously challenge the rapidly growing European population and its Indian allies. In the forty years after Cajamarca the Spanish colonists spent more time fighting one another than battling the remnants of the Inca state.[172]

From Pachakuti to Pizarro, from the Chanca assault on Cuzco to Atauhualpa's capture at Cajamarca, we have traversed less than a century. Within that brief time we have seen the Inca state grow from an obscure highland kingdom to the largest empire in native South America and then collapse with stunning abruptness. In searching for the links between Tawantinsuyu's rise and its fall, time and again we have come back to split inheritance, a seemingly minor manipulation of traditional ideology that profoundly altered Inca society. By creating a unified cult of imperial expansion, the worship of the royal mummies gave the Inca an advantage over their neighbors, fired the explosive growth of their empire, and drove them to their zenith. Yet the application of split inheritance to an economy based on labor taxation and the possession of agricultural land subjected the empire to strains that could not be endured forever. Paradoxically, Tawantinsuyu's rise and fall were grounded in the same phenomenon: the property rights of the dead.

In other words, at the very heart of the Inca Empire lay a combination of religious and economic factors that was inherently unstable. From its birth the empire had carried within itself the seeds of its own destruction. Pachakuti, Topa Inca, and Huayna Capac had nurtured them. Huascar and Atauhualpa had been left to reap the fatal harvest. Therein rests the tragic irony of Tawantinsuyu's brief but spectacular history: in the end the ancestors, to whom the Inca looked for protection, turned against their descendants and brought them down.

Notes to Chapter 3

1 For more detailed geographical descriptions see Tosi 1960 and Pulgar Vidal 1972.

2 This particular bit of imperial propaganda appears in nearly all of the standard sources. See for example Cieza, bk. 1, ch. 38, 1922: 126-9, 1959: 25-7; Sarmiento, ch. 8-10, 1942: 56-61; Cabello, bk. 3, ch. 9, 1951: 256-64; Garcilaso, bk. 1, ch. 15, 1945: vol. 1, pp. 40-2, 1966: 41-3; Cobo, bk. 12, ch. 1, 1890-5: vol. 3, pp. 113-14, 1979: 96-7; etc. To Andean Indians and the more perceptive early chroniclers it was a transparent lie. Cieza (bk. 1, ch. 105, 1922: 106-7, 1959: 284) relates that when he asked if the great site of Tiahuanaco had been built in the time of the Incas, his native informants laughed at him. He himself realized that the claim of pan-Andean barbarism was intended to glorify the Incas and legitimate their rule (Cieza, bk. 2, ch. 6, 1943: 51, 1959: 31).

3 All dates given in this section are conventional (uncalibrated) radiocarbon dates; for a more detailed review of Central Andean chronology see Conrad ms. Beginning with the Initial Period, the 'periods' and 'horizons' of Central Andean prehistory are defined on the basis of cultural changes in the Ica Valley of the southern Peruvian coast (Rowe 1962).

4 Moseley (1975b) argues that the early development of complex societies on the central Peruvian coast was underwritten by abundant marine resources, rather than intensive agriculture. For criticisms of this controversial idea see Wilson 1981 and Raymond 1981. Moseley and Feldman (personal communications) are reworking some details of the 'maritime foundations hypothesis' in the light of the most recent evidence but believe that the general thrust of the argument still holds.

5 Our specification of a coastal hearth for the Early ('Chavin') Horizon is based on recent syntheses by Richard Burger (1978, 1981).

6 Parsons 1968a; Ponce 1972; Browman 1978, 1980; Kolata 1982b, ms. Kolata argues that Tiahuanaco was the capital of an expanding empire, while Browman interprets the site as the focus of a vast trade and marketing network.

7 The controversy concerns the role of Huari, a smaller center with Tiahuanaco-related iconography in the south-central Peruvian highlands.

The standard interpretation holds that Huari was the capital of a large empire during the first half of the Middle Horizon (Menzel 1964; Willey 1971: 157-64; Lumbreras 1974a: 139-45, 151-77; Rowe 1976; Isbell and Schreiber 1978). For recent statements of doubts about the existence of a 'Huari Empire' see Shady and Rosas 1977; Shady and Ruiz 1979; Moseley 1978: 526-31; Donnan and Mackey 1978: 213; Conrad 1981b: 39; Kolata ms.

8 Kolata (1982b: 26, ms.) has shown that extensive tracts of ridged-field farmlands near Tiahuanaco were abandoned at the end of Tiahuanaco V. However, he suggests that this agrarian collapse may have been an effect, rather than a cause, of political disintegration (Kolata 1982b: 26). For additional data on prehistoric ridged-field agriculture in the Titicaca Basin see Parsons and Denevan 1967.

9 For the dating of the final phase of Tiahuanaco civilization (Tiahuanaco V) ca. A.D. 850-1200 see Ponce 1972: 750-1. For chronological evidence that the historically known peoples of the southern highlands first appeared around A.D. 1200 see Conrad ms.

10 The Late Horizon begins with the Inca conquest of the Ica Valley around A.D. 1476 and ends with the establishment of the first Spanish settlement in Ica (A.D. 1534). Hence the dates of the Late Horizon do not correspond exactly to the dates of the Inca Empire itself (ca. A.D. 1438-1532).

11 Murra 1975; Murra and Morris 1976; Moseley 1978; Kolata 1982b, ms. John Topic (personal communication) suggests that early descriptions of the Titicaca Basin as a land of plenty were somewhat exaggerated. Nonetheless, it is clear that the chroniclers were reporting the Incas' perception of the Collao accurately, as is evidenced by the Inca leadership's zealous attempts to gain control of that region (see note 123 below).

12 Zuidema 1973: 16.

13 Cieza, bk. 1, ch. 63, 1922: 119-20, 1959: 312; Polo 1916b: 116-19; Arriaga 1920, 1968; Avila, ch. 28, 1966: 156-7; Anonymous 1919; Hernández Príncipe 1923; Bandelier 1904.

14 For the first systematic attempt to investigate prehistoric Andean cults of the dead through archaeological research see Vreeland 1980; Vreeland and Cockburn 1980.

15 At present the burial of carefully wrapped skulls beneath a building at Asia (Engel 1963: 67-75), a Preceramic Period VI site on the south-central coast of Peru, seems to be the earliest archaeological manifestation of a cult of the dead. However, the data from earlier epochs are very sparse.

16 Our knowledge of Chimor is derived primarily from archaeological research supplemented by limited ethnohistorical sources (Cabello 1951; Calancha 1938; Means 1931: 50-65; Vargas Ugarte 1936; Carrera 1939; Rowe 1948; Rostworowski 1961; Kosok 1965). Particularly important archaeological data have been contributed by the Chan Chan–Moche Valley Project, which ran from 1969 to 1975 under the direction of Michael E. Moseley and Carol J. Mackey. For the results of this project, as well as an extensive list of references, see Moseley and Day 1982.

17 Calancha, bk. 3, ch. 2, 1938: 92; Means 1931: 61; Rowe 1948: 51.

18 Calancha, bk. 3, ch. 2, cited in Means 1931: 62 and Rowe 1948: 49-50.

19 Day 1973; Moseley 1975a; Kolata 1982a; Conrad 1980, 1981a, 1982.

20 For data on the late prehistoric archaeology of the Titicaca Basin see Tschopik 1946; Lumbreras 1974a: 200-13, 1974b; Lumbreras and Amat 1968; Hyslop 1977.

21 Lumbreras 1974a: 200.

22 For ethnohistorical evidence of these colonies see Diez de San Miguel 1964;

Murra 1964, 1968. For archaeological evidence see Lumbreras 1974a: 200-13, 1974b; Trimborn 1975, 1977; Trimborn et al. 1975. Murra believes that the maintenance of satellite settlements or colonies in different altitudinal/ecological zones was an ancient Andean economic pattern (the 'vertical archipelago'). In contrast, Browman (1980) contends that *altiplano* colonization of the lowlands was a relatively late development caused by the disintegration of earlier trade and marketing networks. Specifically, he argues that such colonies did not appear until Tiahuanaco V times (Browman 1980: 109, 117). For further discussion see Chapter 4.

23 The Incas' accounts of the creation of the world in general and of their own particular origins are heavily oriented toward the Titicaca Basin. Versions of the Inca creation myth differ in detail but invariably begin in or around Lake Titicaca. Most of them contain some mention of Tiahuanaco (e.g., Betanzos, ch. 1-2, 1924: 82-9; Cieza, bk. 2, ch. 5, 1943: 42-50, 1959: 25-30; Sarmiento, ch. 6-7, 1942: 48-55; Santacruz Pachacuti 1879: 234-40). Molina's (1913: 118-23) account specifically names Tiahuanaco as the site of the creation. Cobo (bk. 12, ch. 3, bk. 13, ch. 2, 1890-5: vol. 3, pp. 121-7, 308-12, 1979: 103-7) compiled several versions, including a copy of Molina's, that place the creation at Tiahuanaco.

Imperial mythology held that the founders of the Inca dynasty eventually emerged from a cave in the hill of Tambotoco at Pacaritambo, 30 km. south of Cuzco (Betanzos, ch. 3-5, 1924: 90-9; Cieza, bk. 2, ch. 6, 1943: 50-6, 1959: 30-3; Sarmiento, ch. 11, 1942: 61-4; Molina 1913: 120; Morúa, bk. 1, ch. 2-3, 1922-5: vol. 4, pp. 7-11; Guaman Poma 1936: 280-7; Garcilaso, bk. 1, ch. 15, 18, 1945: vol. 1, pp. 39-42, 45-7, 1966: 40-3, 47-9; Cobo, bk. 12, ch. 3, 1890-5: vol. 3, pp. 121-7, 1979: 103-7). Several of the chroniclers recorded multiple versions of the tale. Molina, Morúa, Guaman Poma, Garcilaso, and Cobo each list one or more variants in which the dynastic founders came to Pacaritambo from the Titicaca Basin, either after a period of wandering (most accounts) or directly via an underground passage (Molina, copied by Cobo). Guaman Poma and Garcilaso both mention versions in which the founders of the Inca dynasty came from Tiahuanaco itself.

24 Rowe 1956; Rivera Dorado 1971a,b, 1972, 1973; Lumbreras 1974a: 174, 214-15.

25 We are speaking here only of the pre-imperial epoch. There have been a number of recent surveys and excavations of imperial Inca sites. See for example Murra 1962; Morris and Thompson 1970; Morris 1972, 1974; Kendall 1974, 1979; Alcina 1976; Alcina et al. 1976; Conrad 1977; Gasparini and Margolies 1980.

26 For the original descriptions of Killke ceramics and architecture see Rowe 1944. For more recent descriptions of Killke ceramics see Rivera Dorado 1971a,b, 1972, 1973. For 'Killke-related' materials in the Urubamba Valley northwest of Cuzco see Kendall 1976. The latter indicate that the early Inca were one of a series of small, culturally related groups in the Urubamba basin.

27 Rowe 1944: 61.

28 González Holguín 1608: bk. 1, p. 32.

29 Garcilaso, bk. 4, ch. 8, 1945: vol. 1, p. 195, 1966: 206; Cobo, bk. 12, ch. 25-26, 1890-5: vol. 3, pp. 235-6, 239, 1979: 200-1, 204-5; Rowe 1946: 252-5; Brundage 1967: 34-5; Zuidema 1973: 17-20. As in the case of the *calpulli* (see Chapter 2), social evolutionists at the turn of the century regarded the *ayllu* as a typical matrilineal clan (e.g., Bandelier 1910). Rowe's analysis demolished this interpretation.

30 Behind this cursory sketch of *ayllu* economy and its implications lie a vast
number of documentary references; for a complete explication see Murra's
(1980) classic analysis of Inca economic organization.

31 Brundage (1963) has provided a handy compilation of these accounts.

32 This position is intermediate between those of Rowe (1967), who sees the
first four rulers as mythical personages, and Zuidema (1962, 1964, 1977d),
who feels that the entire list has more to do with Inca cosmology and social
structure than with actual history. For a critique of Zuidema's (1964) early
analyses see Hammel 1965.

33 Especially Sarmiento, ch. 24, 1942: 92-3.

34 This legendary event is probably the most vivid clue to the nature of early
Inca 'conquests'. While sixteenth-century chroniclers treat the defeat of
the Alcaviza as a significant Inca victory, they describe it as little more than
a series of street brawls. Cieza (bk. 2, ch. 33, 1943: 178-80, 1959: 197-8)
says that the incident started when an Alcaviza boy jostled an Inca woman
in the street, insulted her, and broke her water jar. Sarmiento's (ch. 17,
1942: 78-80) and Cabello's (bk. 3, ch. 12, 1951: 284-6) versions are even
more remarkable: they report that the fighting occurred during Mayta
Capac's youth and was caused by his penchant for bullying his Alcaviza
playmates. Cobo's (bk. 12, ch. 7, 1890-5: vol. 3, pp. 138-9, 1979: 118-19)
later account is similar to those of Sarmiento and Cabello, although other
seventeenth-century writers tend to portray Mayta Capac as a great ruler
with wide-ranging conquests (e.g., Guaman Poma 1936: 98-9; Garcilaso,
bk. 3, ch. 1-9, 1945: vol. 1, pp. 130-47, 1966: 137-54).

35 We use this term loosely. At present there is no way to give a precise cultural
evolutionary classification of Inca society in its nascent form. Several recent
analyses (Katz 1972, Schaedel 1978) have tried to show that the Inca passed
through all of the classic cultural evolutionary stages from tribe through
empire and to specify the exact points of transition. We do not think that
the available evidence permits such fine distinctions, nor do we believe that
Inca history necessarily recapitulated all of the classic stages of cultural
evolution. In general, the Inca picture is one of gradual and limited change
followed by rapid and massive social transformation (see Chapters 4 and
5).

36 For early leadership by *sinchis* see Sarmiento, ch. 8, 1942: 56-7; Anonymous
1920: 106-7; Rostworowski 1960: 419; Brundage 1963: 119-22. Note also
the name of the legendary second Inca ruler, Sinchi Roca. The word itself
means 'strong, courageous' (Santo Tomás 1951: 223, 263; González
Holguín 1608: bk. 1, p. 74, bk. 2, pp. 161, 325; Sarmiento, ch. 8, 1942:
56).

37 Betanzos, ch. 11, 1924: 140.

38 The Gateway God is named for his most famous depiction, which appears
on the 'Monolithic Gateway', or 'Gateway of the Sun', at Tiahuanaco.
This carved stone monument dates to Tiahuanaco IV (Classic Tiahuanaco)
times, ca. A.D. 450-850.

39 These interpretations, which are only summarized here, are based on
myriad documentary references. For a more extensive analysis of the Inca
sky god complex and its antecedents see Demarest 1981.

40 Zuidema 1973; Rowe 1946: 252, 297; Brundage 1967: 34-5.

41 Arriaga, ch. 2, 1920: 25, 1968: 27.

42 Arriaga, ch. 3, 1920: 32, 1968: 33.

43 Arriaga, 1920, 1968; Rowe 1946: 297.

44 Calancha, bk. 2, ch. 12, 1938: 89; Brundage 1967: 35.

45 Cobo, bk. 13, ch. 35, 1890-5: vol. 4, pp. 142-4; Molina 1913: 129-30; Rowe 1946: 299, 302-3.

46 Bandelier 1904; Rowe 1946: 286, 298; Zuidema 1973.

47 Cobo, bk. 14, ch. 19, 1890-5: vol. 4, pp. 236-8; Bandelier 1904; Rowe 1946: 199, 223-4.

48 Pizarro 1844: 264, 1921: 251-2; Guaman Poma 1936: 256-7; Rowe 1946: 298; Brundage 1967: 50.

49 Polo 1916a: 7-10, 1916b: 116-19; Cobo, bk. 13, ch. 10, 1890-5: vol. 3, pp. 338-43; Hernández Príncipe 1923; Rowe 1946: 252; Zuidema 1973.

50 For early summaries in the form of instruction manuals for Spanish priests charged with the extirpation of idolatry see Albornoz (Duviols 1967) and Arriaga (1920, 1968). For modern summaries see Rowe (1946: 295-7) and Brundage (1963: 46-52, 1967: 144-55).

51 Cobo, bk. 13, ch. 13-16, 1980-5: vol. 4, pp. 9-47; Zuidema 1964; Rowe 1979. These particular *huacas* were conceived of as lying on forty imaginary lines (*ceques*) radiating from the Coricancha, the principal temple of the Inca state religion. Cobo's list (the *Relación de los Ceques*) is central to Zuidema's controversial interpretations of Inca social structure and history.

52 González Holguín 1608: bk. 2, p. 330; Zuidema 1973: 19.

53 Sarmiento, ch. 13, 1942: 70; Cobo, bk. 13, ch. 13-16, 1890-5: vol. 4, pp. 9-47; etc.

54 Santo Tomás 1951: 143, 173, 232.

55 Arriaga, ch. 5, 15, 1920: 49-55, 137-44, 1968: 46-52, 117-23; Cobo, bk. 13, ch. 10, 1890-5: vol. 3, p. 342; Rowe 1946: 298; Brundage 1967: 35, 149.

56 Anonymous 1919: 184; Brundage 1967: 145. In imperial times important *huacas* from conquered provinces were held as hostages in Cuzco to ensure the good behavior of the Incas' subjects (Cieza, bk. 2, ch. 29, 1943: 161-4, 1959: 190-3; Polo 1940: 154; Molina 1913: 136-7, 151-3; Cobo, bk. 13, ch. 1, 1890-5: vol. 3, p. 300; Rowe 1967: 63).

57 Anonymous 1848: 448; Rowe 1946: 252. Romero (1916: 463-4) attributes the Anonymous Letter of 1571 (Anonymous 1848) to Juan Polo de Ondegardo.

In regard to the importance of mummies, it is also interesting to note Guaman Poma's (1936: 187, 190, 302-3, 307) description of the Inca punishment for what he considered the most heinous crimes (treason, theft, adultery, incest, etc.). According to Guaman Poma, the criminal was not simply executed: his body was left to be destroyed by wild beasts.

58 Arriaga, ch. 4, 1920: 43-5, 1968: 42-3; Avila, ch. 19, 1966: 110-11; Cobo, bk. 13, ch. 10, 1890-5: vol. 3, p. 339; Murra 1958: 32, 1980: 34.

59 Polo 1916b: 114-15; Rowe 1946: 299; Murra 1980: 34.

60 Sarmiento, ch. 24-25, 1942: 91-6; cf. note 34.

61 Sarmiento, ch. 25, 1942: 95.

62 Cieza, bk. 2, ch. 42, 1943: 209-13, 1959: 217-19.

63 Polo 1916b: 54, 1917a: 46.

64 See also the limited archaeological evidence cited in note 26.

65 For Viracocha Inca's marriage to a high-ranking woman from Anta see Cieza, bk. 2, ch. 38, 1943: 195, 1959: 209; Sarmiento, ch. 24, 1942: 92; Cabello, bk. 3, ch. 14, 1951: 297-8. Rowe (1946: 204) discusses the political expediency of this marriage. Cieza (bk. 2, ch. 34, 1943: 184-5, 1959: 201) relates that Capac Yupanqui established the alliance between the Incas and the Quechuas; Rowe (1946: 203-4) suggests that such an alliance was in effect during Viracocha Inca's reign. Regardless of the exact historical

details, the implication is one of continual political maneuvering on the part of the nascent Inca state.

66 Cieza, bk. 2, ch. 41-43, 1943: 205-15, 1959: 215-21.

67 Cobo, bk. 13, ch. 4-5, 1890-5: vol. 3, pp. 320-7; Molina 1913: 126-7, 150; Zuidema 1977a; etc. Again, for a detailed analysis and an extensive list of references see Demarest 1981.

68 Pease 1973; Duviols 1976; Zuidema 1977a; Demarest 1981. Pease refers to a 'solarization' of Inca ideology in general.

69 Garcilaso, bk. 6, ch. 20, 1945: vol. 2, pp. 46-7, 1966: 356.

70 Cobo, bk. 13, ch. 1, 1890-5: vol. 3, p. 302. Cobo's bias against the content of Inca beliefs did not prevent him from having perceptive insights into the political effects of Inca state religion.

71 Indeed, the view of Inti as dynastic progenitor was readily acceptable because it was completely compatible with existing beliefs. The building-blocks of the Inti cult—elements of myth, ritual, and symbolism—had been around for a long time (Demarest 1981).

72 Sarmiento, ch. 25, 1942: 95; Cabello, bk. 3, ch. 14, 1951: 298. Cieza (bk. 2, ch. 37, 1943: 192-3, 1959: 207) places this event in the later part of Yahuar Huacac's reign. In either case, the Chanca defeat of the Quechua apparently occurred during the early part of the fifteenth century (Rowe 1946: 204).

73 Betanzos, ch. 6, 1924: 100-5; Cieza, bk. 2, ch. 44-45, 1943: 216-22, 1959: 222-7; Sarmiento, ch. 25-26, 1942: 94-8; Cabello, bk. 3, ch. 14, 1951: 299.

74 This episode is undoubtedly a piece of imperial propaganda, an after the fact fabrication designed to give Pachakuti's rise to power a divine sanction. The chroniclers who relate this story identify the vision figure differently. Molina (1913: 127-8), Cobo (bk. 12, ch. 12, 1890-5: vol. 3, pp. 157-8, 1979: 133-4), and Casas (ch. 250, 1909: 656) claim that the apparition was the sun. Sarmiento (ch. 27, 1942: 99-100) says only that it was 'like the sun'. Polo (1940: 153) and Acosta (bk. 6, ch. 21, 1894: vol. 2, pp. 204-5) identify the figure as Viracocha, the creator. Betanzos (ch. 8, 11, 1924: 114-15, 141) offers two versions: in the first the apparition is Viracocha, and in the second Cusi Inca Yupanqui reasons that it must have been the sun. These seeming contradictions have been reconciled by the identification of Viracocha and the sun as two aspects of a manifold sky god (Demarest 1981).

75 Cieza, bk. 2, ch. 45, 1943: 220, 1959: 225; Polo 1916b: 54, 1917a: 46.

76 Sarmiento, ch. 29, 1942: 105; González Holguín 1608: bk. 1, pp. 267-8, bk. 2, p. 156; Rowe 1946: 204.

77 Betanzos, ch. 8-10, 17, 1924: 112-38, 190-1; Cieza, bk. 2, ch. 45-47, 1943: 221-9, 1959: 226-31; Sarmiento, ch. 27-29, 34-35, 1942: 99-105, 112-15; Cabello, bk. 3, ch. 15-16, 1951: 303-20.

78 Brundage 1963: 95.

79 The versions of Betanzos (ch. 6, 8-9, 17, 1924: 105, 113, 118-29, 191-7) and Cieza (bk. 2, ch. 43-46, 1943: 214-25, 1959: 220-9) depict Pachakuti favorably; Cieza's is the most pro-Pachakuti and is probably closest to the version taught in the official state schools. In contrast, Sarmiento's (ch. 24-29, 32-33, 1942: 93-105, 110-12) and Cabello's (bk. 3, ch. 14, 1951: 296-303) accounts portray Pachakuti in a negative light.

We should also mention the generally discredited version of Garcilaso (bk. 4, ch. 21-24, bk. 5, ch. 17-20, 1945: vol. 1, pp. 217-24, 258-68, 1966: 230-7, 276-87), in which the entire episode is moved back one generation. Viracocha Inca becomes the heroic prince who saves Cuzco when his father, Yahuar Huacac, loses his nerve. Cobo's (bk. 12, ch. 10, 1890-5: vol. 3, pp. 147-51, 1979: 126-9) account is copied from Garcilaso.

80 Cieza, bk. 2, ch. 45-46, 1943: 220, 223. Translation by Harriet de Onis (Cieza 1959: 225, 227); interpolations added.

81 Cabello, bk. 3, ch. 14, 1951: 301.

82 Sarmiento, ch. 25-26, 1942: 95, 98.

83 In fact, it is possible to interpret all three versions of Pachakuti's ascent as differing presentations of a military coup, distinguished mainly by the descriptions of the conspiracy's scope. According to this view, Cabello (note 81) says that Pachakuti seized power on his own, Sarmiento (note 82) depicts him as acting in concert with other military leaders, and Cieza (note 80) states that the coup had widespread popular support.

84 Murra 1958: 31.

85 Sancho, ch. 17, 1917: 159, 1962: 92; Cieza, bk. 2, ch. 11, 61, 1943: 77-8, 284, 1959: 188-9, 247; Pizarro 1844: 238-9, 1921: 202-3; Castro and Ortega Morejón 1936: 237-9; Acosta, bk. 6, ch. 20, 1894: vol. 2, pp. 201-2; Cobo, bk. 12, ch. 4, 36, 1890-5: vol. 3, pp. 131-2, 290, 1979: 111, 248. We should note that many details of the *panaqa* system are controversial. Most notably, Zuidema's (1964, etc.) interpretations are very different from our own.

86 Anonymous 1848: 466-8; Rostworowski 1962, 1966.

87 Pizarro 1844: 239-40, 264, 1921: 203-5, 251-2; Polo 1916b: 123-5; Santillán, no. 29, 1879: 34; Cobo, bk. 12, ch. 9, bk. 13, ch. 10, 1890-5: vol. 3, pp. 146-7, 339-40, 1979: 125.

88 Pizarro 1844: 238, 1921: 202.

89 Cieza, bk. 2, ch. 11, 1943: 77. Translation by Harriet de Onis (Cieza 1959: 189); interpolation added.

90 Cobo, bk. 12, ch. 9, 1890-5: vol. 3, p. 147. Translation by Roland Hamilton (Cobo 1979: 125); interpolation added.

91 Pizarro 1844: 239, 1921: 203. See also Cobo, bk. 13, ch. 10, 1890-5: vol. 3, p. 340.

92 Cobo, bk. 13, ch. 10, 1890-5: vol. 3, pp. 339-41. See also Pizarro (1844: 264, 1921: 251-2), from whom Cobo copied this account.

93 Cobo, bk. 13, ch. 10, 1890-5: vol. 3, p. 339. See also Santacruz Pachacuti 1879: 286-7.

94 Cobo, bk. 13, ch. 5, 1890-5: vol. 3, p. 325. Cobo claims that this idol was eventually captured by the Spaniards. However, he himself never saw it, and the story may be apocryphal. Even so, it is a perfect symbol of the identification of the royal mummies with Inti.

95 Cieza, bk. 2, ch. 30, 1943: 169, 1959: 183; Guaman Poma 1936: 287, 288, 377. Guaman Poma (1936: 288) makes an explicit distinction between the royal mummies, which were called *Illapa*, and all other corpses, which were called *aya*. However, Albornoz says that the members of any Inca kin group referred to the mummy of its founder as *Illapa* (Duviols 1967: 19). The implication of this statement—that the royal mummy cult was an upward projection and elaboration of traditional Inca practices and institutions—is completely consistent with our interpretations (see below).

96 Cobo, bk. 13, ch. 10, 1890-5: vol. 3, pp. 342-3.

97 Pizarro 1844: 246-7, 1921: 218-19. See also Sancho, ch. 1, 1917: 17-19, 1962: 18-19; Jérez 1853: 344-5. These are all eyewitness accounts. Atauhualpa's body was, as promised, given a Christian burial, but later it was secretly disinterred and removed by his followers.

98 Polo 1916b: 97; Acosta, bk. 5, ch. 6, 1894: vol. 2, pp. 23-4; Cobo, bk. 12, ch. 4, 11, 17, 1890-5: vol. 3, pp. 132, 155, 190-1, 1979: 112, 132, 161-2. The hunt for the royal mummies was completed under Polo's personal supervision.

99 Sarmiento, ch. 54, 1942: 153; Acosta, bk. 6, ch. 20; 1894: vol. 2, p. 202; Cobo, bk. 12, ch. 11, 1890-5: vol. 3, p. 155, 1979: 132.
100 Sarmiento, ch. 14, 19, 1942: 74-5, 83; Acosta, bk. 6, ch. 20, 1894: vol. 2, pp. 201-2. Acosta ascribes the invention of the *panaqa* to Inca Roca; Sarmiento says that it originated with Manco Capac but that the system was reorganized by Inca Roca.
101 Betanzos, ch. 17, 1924: 195-7; Sarmiento, ch. 19, 34, 37, 1942: 83, 112, 141; Rowe 1967: 60-1. While Sarmiento treats the *panaqa* system as a previously existing institution (see note 100), he credits its final form to Pachakuti.
102 Betanzos, ch. 11-13, 16, 1924: 139-62, 178-86; Sarmiento, ch. 30-32, 1942: 106-10.
103 Betanzos, ch. 17, 1924: 195-7; Sarmiento, ch. 30, 32, 1942: 106, 110; Rowe 1967: 60-1; Murra 1980: 38-9.
104 Again, for a detailed analysis of Inca economic organization and an extensive list of references see Murra (1980). For an earlier analysis of Inca labor taxation see Rowe (1946: 265-9).
105 Murra 1958: 35-6.
106 Betanzos, ch. 17, 1924: 195-7; Sarmiento, ch. 32, 1942: 110.
107 For the ownership of entire valleys in the imperial heartland by Inca rulers see Sarmiento, ch. 32, 1942: 100; Rostworowski 1962: 136. The precise division among royal estates, regular state-owned lands, and the lands retained by local groups varied from province to province (Polo 1916b: 58, 1940: 133-4; Acosta, bk. 6, ch. 15, 1894: vol. 2, pp. 185-7; Cobo, bk. 12, ch. 28, 1890-5: vol. 3, pp. 246-7, 1979: 211). For description of the division in the Chincha Valley of the southern Peruvian coast see Castro and Ortega Morejón 1936: 244-5. Unfortunately, this source is highly equivocal. Ambiguities in the wording, uncertainties about the units of measurement employed, and variations in the productivity of land leave the account open to multiple interpretations and render any attempt at quantification extremely dubious (cf. Moore 1958: 35-8). When these factors are added to unspecified inter-provincial differences, it is obviously impossible to calculate the amount of land owned by any single ruler.

    From a motivational standpoint, however, the question is less important than it may seem. An Inca emperor was legally entitled (and economically required) to own lands in all the provinces of his empire but could not obtain them through inheritance. Therefore, he felt the need to create his own estates by whatever means were open to him (see below).
108 Castro and Ortega Morejón 1936: 237-9, 244-5; Ortiz de Zúñiga 1967: 25-6; Rowe 1967: 61. It is worth emphasizing that the first two references are both early *provincial* sources: Castro and Ortega Morejón (1558) on the Chincha Valley and Ortiz de Zúñiga (1562) on the Huánuco region of the north-central Peruvian highlands.
109 For example, Pizarro 1844: 238, 1921: 202; Sancho, ch. 17, 1917: 159, 1962: 92; Cieza, bk. 2, ch. 11, 61, 1943: 77-8, 284, 1959: 188-9, 247; Castro and Ortega Morejón 1936: 239; Santillán, no. 29, 1879: 34; Polo 1916b: 123, 1917b: 134-6; Acosta, bk. 5, ch. 6, 1894: vol. 2, p. 24. The ownership of land by corpses must have struck the early chroniclers as utterly bizarre, and their emphasis on this particular aspect of royal land tenure is unsurprising.
110 Pizarro 1844: 238, 1921: 202.
111 Castro and Ortega Morejón 1936: 239. Translation and interpolation by John H. Rowe (1967: 68). Again, this is an early provincial source (see note 108).

112 Cieza, bk. 2, ch. 11, 1943: 77-8. Translation by Harriet de Onis (Cieza 1959: 188-9); interpolation added.

113 Pizarro 1844: 238-9, 1921: 202-3; Cobo, bk. 13, ch. 10, 1890-5: vol. 3, pp. 338-41; Rostworowski 1960: 418.

114 For further discussion of Inca conquests as an 'energy averaging mechanism' (Isbell 1978) and the underlying concept of verticality (Murra 1972) see Chapter 4.

115 Pizarro 1844: 239, 240, 276-8, 1921: 203, 206, 273-7.

116 Cobo, bk. 14, ch. 9, 1890-5: vol. 4, pp. 192-3; Bram 1941: 65-75; Rowe 1946: 260-1, 279-80.

117 Cobo, bk. 14, ch. 9, 1890-5: vol. 4, p. 192.

118 Cobo, bk. 14, ch. 9, 1890-5: vol. 4, p. 192.

119 Cieza, bk. 2, ch. 11, 46, 1943: 76-7, 225, 1959: 188, 228-9.

120 Cieza, bk. 1, ch. 89, 92, bk. 2, ch. 14, 1922: 289, 195, 1943: 91, 1959: 129, 148, 157-8; Segovia 1943: 33; Garcilaso, bk. 4, ch. 19, 1945: vol. 1, p. 214, 1966: 226-7; Morúa, bk. 3, ch. 4, 1922-5: vol. 4, pp. 123-4. In the edition cited, Segovia's account is attributed to Molina of Santiago. For its authorship by Segovia see Porras Barrenechea's (1943: 91-2) epilogue in the same volume.

121 Sarmiento, ch. 31, 1942: 108; Cobo, bk. 12, ch. 2, 1890-5: vol. 3, pp. 119-20, 1979: 101.

122 Cobo, bk. 12, ch. 35, 1890-5: vol. 3, pp. 281-2. Translation by Roland Hamilton (Cobo 1979: 241-2); interpolation added.

123 Cieza, bk. 2, ch. 52, 1943: 245-8, 1959: 231-4; Sarmiento, ch. 37, 1942: 116-19; Cabello, bk. 3, ch. 15, 1951: 306-7; Cobo, bk. 12, ch. 13, 1890-5: vol. 3, pp. 162-7, 1979: 138-41; Rowe 1944: 58-9; Murra and Morris 1976: 275. Despite all of their disagreements on other matters, the early chroniclers are unanimous in stating that the northern Titicaca Basin was the first major target of the Inca expansion.

124 The Inca occupation of the South Andean culture area is a complex problem, and we cannot treat it fully here. For sixteenth-century discussions of Topa Inca's conquests in southern Bolivia, Chile, and northwest Argentina see Cieza, bk. 2, ch. 60, 1943: 279-80, 1959: 244; Sarmiento, ch. 50, 1942: 145-6; Polo 1917b: 116; Cabello, bk. 3, ch. 18, 1951: 336-7. All of these accounts are very brief and sketchy. Longer, more detailed narrations did not appear until the seventeenth century (Garcilaso, bk. 7, ch. 18-20, 1945: vol. 2, pp. 128-33, 1966: 445-50; Cobo, bk. 12, ch. 14, 1890-5: vol. 3, pp. 171-3, 1979: 145-7; see also Santacruz Pachacuti 1879: 292). Once Topa Inca's conquests have been cited, Chile and Argentina virtually disappear from the standard Peruvian sources, except in the context of Huayna Capac's inspection of his empire at the beginning of his reign (Cieza, bk. 2, ch. 62, 1943: 287-9, 1959: 249-50; Sarmiento, ch. 59, 1942: 156-7; Garcilaso, bk. 9, ch. 4, 1945: vol. 2, p. 224, 1966: 549; Cobo, bk. 12, ch. 16, 1890-5: vol. 3, p. 179, 1979: 153). Even then, only Cieza and Sarmiento say that Huayna Capac himself actually visited Chile, and only Cobo mentions northwest Argentina, implying that Huayna Capac did not go there. Cabello (bk. 3, ch. 21, 1951: 362) omits both areas from the emperor's itinerary. Inca and Inca-related archaeological materials do indeed occur in Chile and northwest Argentina (the literature is extensive; see Willey 1971: 242-3 for a somewhat outdated but still useful summary), and ongoing archaeological research promises to clarify the nature of the Inca presence in those areas.

125 For detailed descriptions and analyses of Inca militarism, including the manning and provisioning of the army, see Cobo, bk. 14, ch. 9, 1890-5: vol. 4, pp. 192-8; Bram 1941; and Rowe 1946: 274-82.

126 See note 125.
127 Cieza, bk. 2, ch. 60, 64, 1943: 280, 295-6, 1959: 244-5, 251; Sarmiento, ch. 41, 49-50, 1942: 128, 143-6; Cabello, bk. 3, ch. 18, 1951: 334-5; Garcilaso, bk. 7, ch. 13-14, 17, 1945: vol. 2, pp. 117-21, 125-7, 1966: 434-8, 442-4; Santacruz Pachacuti 1879: 289-91; Cobo, bk. 12, ch. 14, 1890-5: vol. 3, p. 168, 1979: 142.
128 Sarmiento, ch. 49, 1942: 144.
129 Cabello, bk. 3, ch. 18, 1951: 334.
130 Sarmiento, ch. 41, 1942: 128. Sarmiento's precise figure is, of course, highly dubious. What matters is the implication of heavy losses in the tropical forest campaigns.
131 Cieza, bk. 1, ch. 95, 1922: 301-3, 1959: 256-8. Quotation translated by Harriet de Onis (Cieza 1959: 257); interpolation added.
132 Cieza, bk. 1, 1922, 1959.
133 Cieza, bk. 2, ch. 21, 1943: 124-7, 1959: 139-40; Rowe 1946: 231-2.
134 Cobo, bk. 12, ch. 32, 1890-5: vol. 3, pp. 268-9, 1979: 230; Rowe 1946: 231-2. Means (1931: 334) lists various chroniclers' estimates of the runners' speed.
135 See Trigger 1978 for a general discussion of communication problems as limiting factors in the growth of preindustrial states.
136 Sarmiento, ch. 39, 41, 1942: 124, 127-8.
137 For the Titicaca Basin revolt: Cieza, bk. 2, ch. 53-55, 1943: 251-7, 1959: 235-9; Sarmiento, ch. 49-50, 1942: 145; Cabello, bk. 3, ch. 18, 1951: 335-6; Cobo, bk. 12, ch. 14, 1890-5: vol. 3, pp. 168-9, 1979: 143.
   Huayna Capac's long campaigns in Ecuador combined the suppression of revolts with new conquests. The only true Ecuadorian rebels were subject peoples who had been conquered and integrated into the Inca Empire by Topa Inca and who tried to free themselves from Inca domination during Huayna Capac's reign. Unfortunately, the chroniclers' accounts of Huayna Capac's wars in Ecuador do not always clearly differentiate true rebels, peoples whom Topa Inca defeated in battle but did not integrate into his empire, and Huayna Capac's new conquests (Cieza, bk. 2, ch. 64-67, 1943: 295-308, 1959: 46-50, 251-2, 332-4; Sarmiento, ch. 59-62, 1942: 157-64; Cabello, bk. 3, ch. 21-23, 1951: 362-86; Cobo, bk. 12, ch. 16-17, 1890-5: vol. 3, pp. 180-7, 1979: 153-9). However, Cieza (bk. 2, ch. 61, 1943: 282) states that at the beginning of Huayna Capac's reign 'there were those who plotted to recover their past liberty and throw off the rule of the Incas...' (translation by Harriet de Onis [Cieza 1959: 246]). Both Sarmiento (ch. 59-60, 1942: 157) and Cabello (bk. 3, ch. 21, 23, 1951: 365, 368, 383) specifically mention rebels in Ecuador.
138 For early Spanish estimates of Cuzco's population see Sancho, ch. 17, 1917: 158, 1962: 91; Ruiz de Arce 1933: 368; Segovia 1943: 33 (cf. note 120). For a modern analysis of these and other documentary sources on Cuzco and its environs, along with the archaeological evidence, see Rowe 1967. Ruiz de Arce says that there were about 4,000 residences in Cuzco proper; Sancho and Segovia estimate the total settlement of the capital district at over 100,000 buildings, including storehouses, and about 200,000 people respectively. As Rowe (1967: 60-1, 66-7) indicates, these estimates are impressionistic and of dubious value. He declines to offer a precise population figure but does conclude that the capital district was heavily built up and densely settled.
   As in the case of Aztec Tenochtitlan, much of imperial Cuzco's population growth can be attributed to immigration. Virtually all of this immigration was compulsory. Among the peoples resettled in the capital

district were the most important native provincial nobles, who were required to maintain residences near Cuzco and live in them for part of each year (Sancho, ch. 17, 1917: 155, 158, 1962: 88, 91; Ruiz de Arce 1933: 368; Segovia 1943: 33); those sons of the native provincial nobilities who were attending the state-run schools (see note 120), provincial groups brought in to serve their native lords (Cieza, bk. 1, ch. 93, 1922: 296-7); certain skilled artisans (Cieza, bk. 2, ch. 58, 1943: 269, 1959: 328); and the growing class of retainers attached to the Inca elite (see notes 148-151 below).

139 See the sources cited in note 113.

140 For example, Sarmiento, ch. 19, 1942: 82; Cobo, bk. 14, ch. 8, 1890-5: vol. 4, pp. 188-9; Rowe 1946: 210-11; Murra 1960: 395-6; Rostworowski 1962: 135-6; Kendall 1974, 1979.

141 For Pachakuti's use of reclamation techniques in creating his private estates see Sarmiento, ch. 30, 1942: 106. For evidence of land reclamation in pre-Inca times see Kosok 1965; Lumbreras 1974a; Moseley 1977; Recktenwald 1978; or any recent summary of Peruvian archaeology.

142 Pizarro 1844: 291-2, 1921: 305; Garcilaso, bk. 5, ch. 1, 1945: vol. 1, p. 226, 1966: 241-2; Murra 1960.

143 This argument is obviously speculative—in modern bureaucratic parlance, a 'worst case scenario'. Its applicability to provincial regions is at present a moot point. It probably does hold for the area around Cuzco, where land shortages did occur in later imperial times (see note 113 for sources). The right to own land in the sacred capital district was an important royal privilege, and Inca emperors evidently took whatever steps were necessary to create their own estates around Cuzco (compare note 154 below).

Again, the key point is that one must consider the culturally defined values placed on different categories of land and questions of property rights, not just the total acreage under cultivation. As motivational factors in Inca imperialism, the former outweighed the latter. It was perfectly possible for Inca rulers to perceive shortages, or for some of their subjects to experience real deprivation, even when there was ample land to support the empire's population (compare note 107).

144 Cabello, bk. 3, ch. 31, 1951: 464. Corroboration of the royal *ayllus'* large size is provided by the fact that there were still 567 *panaqa* members alive in 1603—that is, after a period of about seventy-five years in which the upper nobility had been ravaged by its own civil war, the Conquest, subsequent Inca uprisings, the civil wars of the Spanish colonists, and European diseases (Garcilaso, bk. 9, ch. 40, 1945: vol. 2, pp. 296-7, 1966: 625-6; Rowe 1946: 257).

145 Pizarro 1844: 239, 1921: 203; Cobo, bk. 13, ch. 10, 1890-5: vol. 3, p. 340.

146 Sarmiento, ch. 55-57, 1942: 153-5; Cabello, bk. 3, ch. 20, 25, 1951: 358-60, 396-7; Cobo, bk. 12, ch. 16, 1890-5: vol. 3, pp. 178-9, 1979: 152.

147 Sarmiento, ch. 51, 1942: 147-8; Cabello, bk. 3, ch. 19, 1951: 346-7.

148 Rowe 1946: 268-70; Rostworowski 1966; Murra 1966, 1980: ch. 8.

149 Rowe 1948: 47; Murra 1966, 1968, 1972.

150 Rowe 1946: 268; Rostworowski 1966; Murra 1966, 1980: 163-72.

151 Cieza, bk. 2, ch. 18, 1943: 118, 1959: 164-5; Morúa, bk. 3, ch. 12, 1922-5: vol. 4, p. 146; Rostworowski 1962, 1966; Murra 1980: 39-40, 168-9. Probably the change to cultivation by *yana* was still in progress at the time of the Spanish Conquest. Agricultural *yana* seem to have been the norm in the area around Cuzco, but provincial practices may have varied. Cieza makes a distinction between the capital district and provinces, but does not provide specific details on the latter. Ortiz de Zúñiga (1967: 25-6) implies

that royal estates in Huánuco were farmed by taxpayers. For Chincha, Castro and Ortega Morejón (1936: 39, 44) seem to suggest that royal estates were cultivated by taxpayers but that the work was overseen by *yana*; however, other interpretations of this account are possible.

152 Cieza, bk. 2, ch. 17, 22, 1943: 106-7, 127-34, 1959: 59-63, 160-1; Sarmiento, ch. 39, 1942: 124-5; Cobo, bk. 12, ch. 23, 1890-5: vol. 3, pp. 222-7, 1979: 189-93; Rowe 1946: 269-70; Murra 1980: 173-81.

153 Cieza, bk. 2, ch. 17, 22, 1943: 106-7, 131-3, 1959: 61-2, 160-1.

154 Rostworowski (1962: 134) suggests that another goal was the removal of native social groups from the heavily populated Cuzco district so that their lands could be freed for the creation of new royal estates.

155 Sarmiento, ch. 43, 1942: 132; Cobo, bk. 12, ch. 14, 1890-5: vol. 3, pp. 167-8, 1979: 142.

156 Cieza, bk. 2, ch. 62, 69, 1943: 289, 314, 1959: 78, 251; Sarmiento, ch. 60, 1942: 158; Cobo, bk. 12, ch. 17, 18, 1890-5: vol. 3, pp. 189-90, 192, 1979: 161, 163.

157 Cieza, bk. 2, ch. 62, 68-70, 1943: 289, 311-18, 1959: 52-3, 78-81, 251; Sarmiento, ch. 60, 1942: 158; Cobo, bk. 12, ch. 18, 1890-5: vol. 3, pp. 192-4, 1979: 163-4; Rowe 1946: 208-9.

158 Cieza, bk. 2, ch. 70, 1943: 316-18, 1959: 79-81; Sarmiento, ch. 60, 63, 1942: 158, 166; Cabello, bk. 3, ch. 21, 24, 1951: 363-4, 394-5.

The problem of Huayna Capac's heirs is extraordinarily complicated, and there may have been another legitimate claimant named Ninan Cuyoche who died in the same epidemic that killed the emperor. Some of the confusion undoubtedly arose after the Spanish Conquest, when the different factions involved in the Inca civil war tried to justify their actions to the chroniclers.

The basic problem seems to be that Huayna Capac married at least two of his sisters, Cusi Rimay (Mama Cusirimay) and Rahua Occllo (Araua Ocllo). According to Sarmiento (ch. 60, 62-63, 1942: 158, 164-6), Cusi Rimay was Huayna Capac's first principal wife (*coya*), but she bore him no sons. Huayna Capac then married Rahua Occllo, by whom he had Huascar. On his deathbed Huayna Capac decided that the question of who would succeed him, Ninan Cuyoche or Huascar, should be decided by divination; augury predicted bad futures for both candidates. Ninan Cuyoche was chosen as ruler, but he died before the news reached him, and Huascar inherited the kingdom. Cabello's (bk. 3, ch. 21, 24, 1951: 363-4, 394) version is similar to Sarmiento's, but not identical. According to Cabello, Huascar's mother was not the *coya* at the time of his birth, but Huayna Capac had no sons by Cusi Rimay, and Huascar was universally regarded as the legitimate heir. On his deathbed Huayna Capac changed his mind and chose Ninan Cuyoche, but the latter died within a few days, and the kingdom reverted to Huascar. Cobo (bk. 12, ch. 17, 1890-5: vol. 3, pp. 189-90, 1979: 161) claimed that Ninan Cuyoche was in fact Huayna Capac's only son by Cusi Rimay, and therefore the legitimate heir, but that he died while his father was still ruling. Brundage (1963: 245-6, 372) summarizes other variants of the tale.

In any event, it is clear that Huascar was born of an incestuous marriage, while Atauhualpa was not. Accordingly, Atauhualpa did not have a legitimate claim to the throne.

159 Cieza, bk. 2, ch. 69, 1943: 315. Translation by Harriet de Onis (Cieza 1959: 79).

160 Sarmiento, ch. 63, 1942: 167; Cabello, bk. 3, ch. 24-25, 26, 1951: 395-8, 406-16.

161 For numerous examples see the accounts of Pachakuti's, Topa Inca's, and
    Huayna Capac's reigns in Cieza (1943, 1959), Sarmiento (1942), Cabello
    (1951), and Cobo (1890-5: vol. 3, 1979).
162 Pizarro, 1844: 240, 1921: 205-6. Cobo (bk. 13, ch. 10, 1890-5: vol. 3,
    p. 340) copies Pizarro here.
163 Pizarro 1844: 240. Translation and interpolation by John H. Rowe (1967:
    68).

   Frank Salomon (personal communication) has suggested that this
   incident is suspect because Pizarro may be following a Western tradition
   of historical narrative traceable to classical authors like Thucydides. In
   this tradition the account of a war begins with a speech, fabricated by the
   writer, in which one of the leaders involved sets forth the causes of the war
   and states his position.

   This suggestion has some merit, but it does not really affect our argument.
   Pizarro's format may or may not follow classical conventions, but it seems
   most likely that he was reporting the substance of his informants' testimony
   accurately. If he was trying to explain the Inca civil war in European terms,
   we doubt that he would have invented a cause so alien to Western minds—
   the ownership of vast amounts of property by corpses. Regardless of the
   form of Huascar's 'cause of the war' speech, its *content* is purely Andean.

   As to the less important question of whether Huascar actually made such
   a speech, there is obviously no way to tell. Perhaps he did state his position
   in a single frustrated outburst; perhaps he formulated his policy over a
   period of time and expressed it through a series of speeches and actions.
   Perhaps what Pizarro reported was only the *panaqas'* perception of the
   emperor's position, and not necessarily the workings of Huascar's mind.
   It makes no difference. The outcome would have been the same in any case.

164 Pizarro 1844: 240. Translation and interpolations by Philip A. Means
    (Pizarro 1921: 206).
165 Cobo, bk. 12, ch. 18, 1890-5: vol. 3, p. 195. Translation by Roland
    Hamilton (Cobo 1979: 166).
166 Sarmiento, ch. 63, 1942: 167-8.
167 Sarmiento, ch. 69, 1942: 184.
168 Cieza, bk. 2, ch. 71-73, 1943: 319-28, 1959: 81-7; Sarmiento, ch. 63, 1942:
    168-9; Cabello, bk. 3, ch. 28, 1951: 427-36.
169 Cieza, bk. 2, ch. 73, 1943: 325-6, 1959: 85; Cabello, bk. 3, ch. 27-29, 1951:
    417-46.
170 See Brundage (1963, 1967) for composite accounts of the civil war's
    campaigns.
171 Cobo, bk. 12, ch. 18, 1890-5: vol. 3, p. 195. Translation by Roland
    Hamilton (Cobo 1979: 165-6); interpolation added.
172 Prescott 1847 (or any of the numerous modern editions); Hemming 1970;
    Lockhart 1972; etc.

4
Precolumbian imperialism: theories and evidence

We have accompanied the Aztec and Inca on the journeys that transformed them from small and marginal societies to great imperial powers, and eventually to nations in ruins. Along the way we have seen many beliefs and practices that lie far outside our own experience: massive human sacrifice to feed the sun and forestall the end of the world, cannibalism, kings who claimed to be sons of the sun, mandatory incest in royal marriages, and a dividing line between life and death so blurred that living people conversed and partied with the dead. These phenomena are so alien to the Western mind that many of the sixteenth-century Spaniards who first encountered them could only shake their heads and conclude that the Aztec and Inca peoples had been led astray by the devil.

Initial bewilderment gave rise to serious inquiries, and the Aztec and Inca have attracted attention for so long that we have learned a great deal about the nature and development of their cultures. Yet in some ways the question of 'Why?' remains as mystifying as it was in the days of Cortés and Pizarro. The processes involved in the two imperial expansions are extremely complex and have defied convincing explanation. Indeed, questions of causality have been so intractable that scholars cannot even agree as to whether the Aztec and Inca cases should be seen as highly similar or totally different.

One could take the view that there are some superficial parallels between the Aztec and Inca developments, but that the two imperial expansions were fundamentally incomparable. By citing detailed differences in economy, social organization, political structure, and religion, it could be argued that the Triple Alliance and Tawantinsuyu were the products of unique historical developments (cf. Brundage 1975).

Yet from the viewpoints of archaeology and anthropology, structural similarities can be seen in the histories of the two empires. Our presentations of Aztec and Inca history in the previous chapters have been organized so as to highlight these parallels in the development and demise of Aztec and Inca imperialism. The specific details of these historical similarities demonstrate the truly multicausal nature of cultural evolution in Mesoamerica and the Andean world.

The ideological adaptations of the Mexica and Inca states

As we have seen, both polities began as small, backward chiefdoms amidst more powerful and prestigious states and alliances. The threatened status of the early Mexica and Inca peoples resulted in their increasing emphasis on warfare. In political development this militarization was manifested in the elaboration of the offices of *tlatoani* and *sinchi* and in the gradual augmentation of their power at the expense of the traditional sociopolitical units such as the *calpulli*, *ayllu*, and tribal councils composed of kin-group leaders. At least in the Aztec case, late fourteenth-century intensifications of agricultural and mercantile activities were other responses to the insecurity of the early Mexica predicament. As we have seen, both the Mexica and the Inca leaders also worked to preserve their fledgling states through manipulation of alliances. The Inca extended their sphere of influence through meddling in the internal politics of neighboring regions like the Titicaca Basin. The Mexica initially hitched themselves to the rising star of the Tepanec Empire, while forming alliances by marriage with the more prestigious Acolhua polities and the neo-Toltec bluebloods of Culhuacan.

These Mexica and Inca military, economic, and political responses to the dangers and challenges of their political environments were accompanied by shifts, revisions, and realignments of religious institutions and concepts. We have seen various elements involved in these ideological reforms. Patron solar/sky/warfare deities, Huitzilopochtli and Inti, were elaborated from specific aspects of more inclusive and ancient manifold sky gods. These divine patrons became nationalistic symbols, and the dogma and ritual of their cults exhorted the people toward war and conquest. The militaristic state deities also justified and sanctioned the aggressive policies of the two expansionist states.

Even more important than the nationalization and militarization of the upper pantheon were the modifications of ancient Mesoamerican and Andean religious institutions. The Mexica elevated the cult of human sacrifice to an unprecedented scale by tying the sacrificial cult to Huitzilopochtli, Tonatiuh (the 'warrior sun'), and the cosmology of the sun's battle against darkness. Combined with the general imperialistic tenor of Mexica religious dogma, the sacrificial cult became a driving force motivating and legitimating the expansionistic policies of the new Mexica leadership. Similarly, Inca elaboration of the royal ancestor cult—with its crucial extension of the property rights of dead kings—created an institutionalized imbalance in the Inca dynastic system: it virtually required expansionistic policies on the part of each heir to the throne. Split inheritance assured the militarism of the Inca state's rulers, while the dogma of Inti gave those rulers the justification and propaganda they needed to carry out imperialist policies.

We are convinced that these ideological elements were the cutting edge of Mexica and Inca imperialism. It was principally these religious concepts which distinguished the early Mexica and Inca states from their competitors in Central Mexico and the Andean highlands. The reworkings and manipulations of religious institutions were primarily motivated by the self-interest of leaders: warriors like Tlacaelel attempted to institutionalize and aggrandize their militaristic profession through the dogma of Huitzilopochtli, while Inca rulers like Pachakuti glorified their own heritage and assured their eternal wealth and comfort through the Inti cult and property rights of the dead. However, regardless of the motives of the new leaders, the fact is that these ideological changes were highly 'adaptive' for their societies as a whole.

To explain this point further, we must first stress that in this context 'adaptation' refers broadly to a society's ability to survive and prosper in a competitive environment. Here the concept of 'environment' clearly includes social and cultural 'superorganic' surroundings, as well as the physical and ecological setting. Ultimately, the adaptive value of cultural changes is measured in terms of the overall benefit to the society as a system—in a sense, the 'reproductive success' of that society or the body of ideas and strategies that constitute its culture.[1] In the specific case at hand, we contend that the Mexica and Inca ideological reforms of the early fifteenth century were highly successful adaptive responses to the natural and cultural environments of Central Mexico in the Late Postclassic and the southern Peruvian highlands in the Late Intermediate Period.

In presenting this model of an 'ideological adaptation' by the Mexica and Inca, we must take care not to propose yet another monocausal explanation—in this case substituting religion for demographic pressure, climatic change, or other phenomena commonly cited as possible 'prime movers' in the dynamics of Precolumbian imperialism. The complexity and intermingling of cause and effect in the Aztec and Inca expansions negate all single-factor explanations, which are about as convincing as the Colonial Spaniards' devil. Review of each artificial 'category' of cultural components ('ideological', 'political', 'economic', etc.) demonstrates the multifaceted nature of Mexica and Inca imperialism. Furthermore, we feel strongly that analyses of culture change should *explicitly* describe the interplay among various elements, rather than merely give lip service to a vaguely defined 'multicausality'. Therefore, let us begin to expand our model of ideological adaptation by examining the environmental and demographic factors involved in the expansion of Mesoamerican and Central Andean states. An assessment of these ecological factors should reveal the strengths and weaknesses of current theories on Precolumbian imperialism, while guiding us to a more complex and realistic understanding of these parallel episodes in human cultural evolution.

Environmental factors

During the past two decades cultural materialism, in one form or another, has been the dominant theoretical approach in New World archaeology. Accordingly, environmental and ecological factors involved in state formation and expansion have been much discussed and explored. As we shall see, some of the ecological explanations of Precolumbian imperialism have been rather simple-minded deterministic theories which assume environmental pressures to be the *only* major causal forces involved in cultural evolution.

Other, more sophisticated ecological analyses have treated environmental characteristics not as determining elements, but as a source of 'selective pressures' favoring the growth of ever-larger political units in Central Mexico and the Central Andes. These studies do not claim that environmental factors *caused* cultural change. Instead, they argue that certain environmental characteristics *promoted the success* of cultural groups who developed more intensive agricultural techniques, more complex social and political institutions, and control of more diversified territories—regardless of the reasons for which such cultural changes were undertaken. Scholars who hold this view seek to identify the environmental selective forces that operated on New World societies from before the development of agriculture to the time of the Conquest and that favored the rise of the Aztec and Inca Empires.

Agricultural potential

One factor to be considered is the extraordinary agricultural potential of the Valley of Mexico and the southern Peruvian highlands. The Basin of Mexico, with its rich volcanic soils and internal lake system, provided a subsistence base capable of supporting several successive expansionist states. During the Aztec period this agricultural potential was fully utilized by the state-directed extension of lake-bed (*chinampa*) agriculture (Figure 23). Similarly, the rich highland valleys of the greater south Peruvian area had provided the subsistence base for a sequence of states. Yet, again, it was only in the final imperial period that the productivity of these regions was most fully exploited through Inca expansion of these valleys' terrace systems (Figure 24).[2]

However, as comparison with other fertile regions will show, agricultural potential alone *allows*, but does not demand, the evolution of complex polities. Furthermore, the initial immediate environments of the Mexica and Inca, the western marshes of Lake Texcoco and the hilly district around the small valley of Cuzco, show no advantages over the other sub-regions of the Valley of Mexico and the Central Andes. Indeed, in Central Mexico the sweetwater marshes of Lake Xochimilco and Lake Chalco show far greater potential for *chinampa* agriculture than the semi-saline swamps of western Lake Texcoco. It was only *after* significant

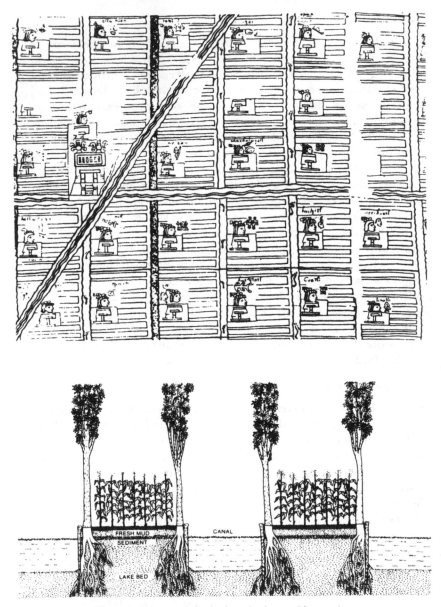

Fig. 23. *Chinampa* lake-bed agriculture. Above: A sixteenth-century Aztec map of Tenochtitlan's *chinampa* plots and canals. Below: A cross-section diagram of *chinampa* plots and canals (following Coe 1964).

Fig. 24. Imperial Inca agricultural terracing at Pisac in the Vilcanota (upper Urubamba) Valley.

military and political successes that the Mexica had the wealth, labor, and resources necessary to create large, fertile, fresh-water *chinampa* zones out of the saline western marshes of Lake Texcoco. In fact, recent ethnohistorical and ecological studies[3] have noted that the Mexica homeland, if assessed only on its agricultural potential, would have been an unlikely candidate for super-state formation:

> unlike nearly every other Late Postclassic urban center in the Valley of Mexico, Tenochtitlan lacked a productive agricultural zone of any significance in its immediate environs.[4]

In the Central Andean highlands, the Titicaca Basin, homeland of the Aymara-speaking peoples, was a richer environment than the Incas' restricted valley. The Titicaca region had vast flatlands for crop raising and pasturage, along with the resources of the lake itself. So if agricultural potential had been the prime determinant of the dominant powers of late Precolumbian times, the Collao peoples of the Titicaca region or the peoples of Chalco or Xochimilco in the Mexican case would have constructed the dominant imperial hegemony—not the Inca in their little valley or the Mexica in their saline swamps.

Nonetheless, once the greater Valley of Mexico was under the control of the Aztecs' Triple Alliance, their further successes were clearly bankrolled by the riches of that region, just as the earlier hegemony of Teotihuacan had rested upon the valley's potential. In the Inca case, the rich Titicaca Basin was an early and deliberate target of Inca military strategy.[5] Once its wealth was incorporated into Tawantinsuyu, the young empire's further expansion became feasible, despite the obstacle of the Chimu super-state on the north coast. The fact that the areas of greatest agricultural potential were not in the initial Mexica and Inca homelands, but were conquered early, suggests that the environmental factors involved in the two expansions were neither simple nor obvious.

Clearly a complex interplay of political, economic, and ideological factors was of greater significance than any environmental advantages in the initiation of the Mexica and Inca expansions. Only conquest of the entire Central Mexican and Central Andean regions gave the respective states the impressive agricultural support described in the Conquest-period chronicles. The integration of these complex subsistence systems occurred only *after* the imperial juggernauts were in motion. Both the Central Andean hillside terraces and the Mexican lake-bed or drained fields were largely created by Inca and Mexica state policy. For example, recent extensive archaeological surveys in Central Mexico[6] have left no doubt that the vast Aztec *chinampas* were largely a consequence, not a cause, of Late Postclassic expansionism.

> Regardless of the possibility of some small-scale chinampa cultivation in earlier times, Armillas' surveys, and our own, clearly demonstrate that there was a rapid, planned, massive colonization of the lakebed during the fifteenth century.[7]

Furthermore, the new archaeological evidence and recent ethnohistorical studies both point—once again—to the critical period of the Mexica ideological and political transformations as the time when this state-directed agricultural intensification was undertaken.

> All indications point to the reigns of Itzcoatl (A.D. 1426-1440) and Moctechuzoma Ilhjiamina [Moctezuma I] (A.D. 1440-1467) as the principal period during which large-scale conquest, land reclamation, and chinampa construction were initiated and carried out.[8]

Environmental diversity

Environmental diversity may have been more important than agricultural potential in initiating expansionism. Some scholars have argued that where there are many different microenvironments, producing different crops and possessing localized raw materials, it is advantageous for polities to control as much territory as possible—ensuring a balanced diet, access to necessary resources, protection against crop failures, and so on. Thus, environmental diversity is seen as a stimulus to the development of state-level organization and as a continuing pressure for later growth of states, leading eventually to vast macro-states such as the Aztec and Inca.

Specific variants of this general theory have been proposed for both

Mesoamerica and the Andes. For Mesoamerica William Sanders and others (e.g., Sanders 1956; Sanders and Price 1968) have put forth the theory of interregional 'economic symbiosis'. Stimulated by the environmental diversity of the Central Mexican basins and highlands, 'symbiosis', as defined by Sanders and Price, involves 'the economic interdependence of social and physical population units in a given region to the advantage of all'.[9] Given the complicated mosaic of microenvironments and the highly localized distributions of important raw materials in Central Mexico, Sanders and Price (1968: 188-93) argue that the most efficient means of meeting community needs was through organized trade based on part- or full-time community specialization combined with a market economy.

Precisely such a system of specialized communities linked by a network of periodic markets was (and still is today) characteristic of most of Mesoamerica. In Central Mexico itself these symbiotic networks allowed communities in the rich lakeside bottom lands to specialize in intensive agricultural pursuits (irrigation and drainage systems, *chinampa* gardens, multi-cropping, etc.). Communities in drier or less fertile zones supplemented their less intensive farming techniques (e.g., 'slash and burn' agriculture, rainfall and runoff systems) with specialized craft industries, or with control over localized resources. In Central Mexico such unevenly distributed resources included deposits of obsidian (volcanic glass) or other useful stone materials, fine clay deposits, salt flats, wood forests, stands of the multi-purpose maguey cactus, and so on (Figure 25).

Sanders and Price go on to point out that networks of specialized communities linked into trade and market systems

> are difficult to maintain except when the communities are part of some larger sociopolitical structure such as a regional state. Wholly aside from the need of a peaceful and stable political climate for the successful establishment of such economic patterns, the traditional market encounters of people from different communities would tend to produce a feeling of community interests and social identification that should act as a subtle integrative factor.[10]

In other words, environmental diversity promotes not just specialization, interdependence, and markets, but also state formation, as well as the development of even larger political units. 'Symbiosis' brings direct economic benefits—and in Sanders' and Price's opinion, a sense of national unity—to polities that can incorporate larger and more diverse territories under their control.

We agree that 'economic symbiosis' was a subtle pressure favoring larger polities, but we hasten to add that it cannot be regarded as a *determining* factor in the case of Aztec expansion. There are other potentially 'symbiotic' regions in Mesoamerica, all of them characterized by environmental diversity and localized distribution of raw materials.

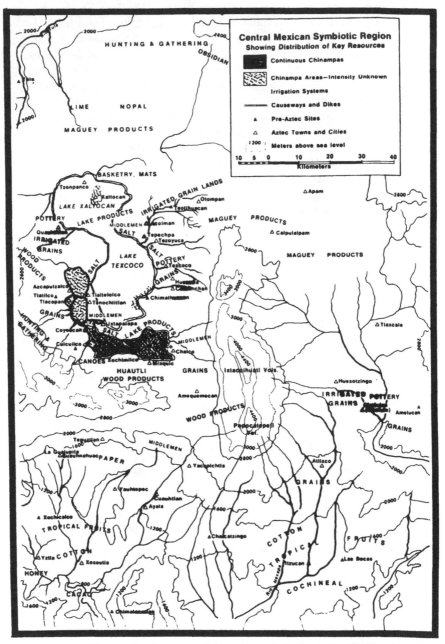

Fig. 25. Environmental diversity and the irregular distribution of
resources in Central Mexico.

Indeed, adjacent and symbiotic highland-lowland regions are typical of Mesoamerica and include such closely interactive pairings as Highland Chiapas/Gulf Coastal Tabasco, Highland Guatemala/Pacific Coastal Guatemala, Highland Guatemala/Peten, and so on. Yet these regions, where similar selective pressures would have operated, did *not* give rise to imperialism, or, in some cases, even to true state formation. Furthermore, environmental diversity only operates as a broad general stimulus toward the growth of states: it was never intended by Sanders and Price to explain the particular factors involved in the Mexica success.

We should note that Sanders (1956), Sanders and Price (1968), and others[11] propose a model of cultural evolution that also invokes population pressure and the intensive agricultural systems which arose in response to such pressure (e.g., irrigation, *chinampa* farming) to explain macro-state development in Central Mexico. We shall return to the question of demography later. For the moment, we can conclude that in Central Mexico environmental diversity and the accompanying symbiosis do appear to have exerted a subtle but constant influence on the growth of states.

Turning to the Andean data, we find that both the strengths and the limitations of environmental diversity as an explanatory factor are even clearer in the Inca case. Like Mesoamerica, the Andean world is a highly complicated ecological mosaic. Local microenvironments are shaped by a number of variables, but one of the chief determinants is elevation. In the Andes, climate varies with altitude, and different food plants grow at different elevations; in general, a wider variety of crops can be grown at lower altitudes than at higher ones (Figure 26). Furthermore, within any given region, climatic fluctuations influence the agricultural productivity of all microenvironments, but different altitudinal zones are affected in different ways. Conditions causing poor harvests at one elevation may produce bumper crops at another. Hence, in order to obtain a balanced diet and protect themselves against crop failure, members of an Andean farming community find it desirable to maintain fields at different levels.

The most marked altitudinal zonation occurs in the southern sierra, the highest part of the Central Andes. For this reason the prehistoric inhabitants of the region developed the economic institution that John Murra (1972) calls 'vertical control'. Southern highland communities tried to exploit a maximum number of microenvironments by maintaining satellite settlements at different elevations. Since these settlements were separated from one another by uninhabited areas and/or lands belonging to other groups, a community's territory resembled a chain of islands running up and down the slopes of the Andes—a 'vertical archipelago', as it were.[12]

William Isbell (1978) has argued that the 'verticality' of the Andean

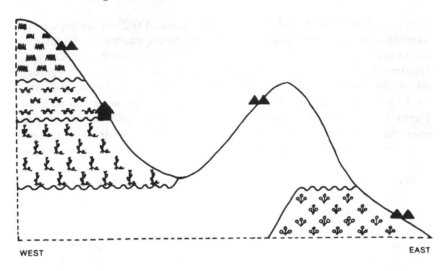

WEST   EAST

  Pasture Zone

  Tuber Zone

  Maize - Bean - Squash Zone

  Coca and Fruit Zone

  Main Community

  Satellite Settlements

Fig. 26. Schematic diagram of a 'vertical archipelago'. Note the altitudinal separation of different land-use zones and the satellite settlements that allow the community to exploit all of the different zones (following Brush 1977: 12).

environment is a selective factor favoring large-scale polities with centralized authority. The more ecological zones an Andean state controls, the better it can buffer itself against environmental perturbations and variable harvests. Even in bad years, some of its regions will yield excellent crops, and their surplus foodstuffs can be redistributed to areas suffering hard times. In years when overall production is high, large surpluses can be stored against future needs. Hence if the state has enough territory within its borders, it can be virtually certain that it will always have enough food to support its population and its projects. Isbell concludes that by giving the Inca access to a wide variety of environmental zones, conquest served as an 'energy averaging mechanism' helping to ensure the economic welfare of the state as a whole.

However, as Isbell (1981) has stated, the fact that verticality gave large-scale polities certain economic advantages does not mean that environmental diversity *caused* Tawantinsuyu's expansion. Vertical control could be maintained without military conquest and annexation. During the Late Intermediate Period the Colla and Lupaca kingdoms of the Titicaca Basin had extensive vertical archipelagoes with lowland colonies as far as forty to fifty days' travel from the *altiplano*.[13] Yet neither the Colla nor the Lupaca dominated large, continuous tracts of lowland territory. Instead, political control was limited to the zones actually occupied and exploited by colonists. A single small valley might contain colonies established by several *altiplano* kingdoms and an indigenous population, with each party acting independently of the others. Each group had jurisdiction within its own defined territory but no control over its neighbors. Clearly, in the Andes verticality did not demand imperial expansion.

Likewise, it should be obvious that while access to multiple environmental zones could benefit an Andean kingdom, vertical control *per se* did not confer decisive military advantages on a polity. After all, during the Late Intermediate Period the Colla and Lupaca maintained extensive archipelagoes, while the Inca, their conquerors, had none. We might also point out that in the Sanders and Price model, environmental diversity supposedly makes state-level organization and a market economy 'functionally related'. However, in the highly variegated *Andean* world, both state and macro-state levels of organization were achieved without a market economy. The rise of empire simply produced an intensification of traditional patterns of reciprocity and redistribution.

It is exciting to note that recent archaeological projects have begun to obtain data for testing some of the proposed ecological explanations of the rise of states and macro-states. In southern Peru, northern Chile, and eastern Bolivia surveys and excavations[14] have identified several settlements which may well have been outposts in the kind of 'vertical archipelago system' that Murra originally defined on the basis of documentary sources. These lower-lying sites are obviously linked to archaeological cultures of the Titicaca Basin. However, all of the settlements in question date to periods long *after* the time of initial state formation in the *altiplano*.[15] In fact, a number of the sites that have actually been excavated may have been founded after the Inca conquest of the Titicaca Basin.[16] Hence the role of verticality in state development remains obscure.

In Mesoamerica a recent series of archaeological surveys and settlement pattern studies has provided the first detailed picture of the settlement patterns and subsistence systems of the Valley of Mexico.[17] This new evidence throws doubt on the economic symbiosis model for the pre-Aztec evolution of Central Mexico, since earlier settlement locations do not fit the predicted pattern of ecological diversity.

> In Sanders' original formulation, however, the purpose was to explain how centralized political systems emerged in earlier times. It was seen as a mechanical process brought about by the need for exchange. The very divergent settlement system from earlier times, particularly during the First Intermediate Period [1150 B.C.-A.D. 100], when the first stages of political centralization were achieved, weakens considerably the explanatory value of this model. For example, not only was virtually all of the First Intermediate population distributed in a narrow band along the lower-middle piedmont, but much of it was in a dozen or so communities.[18]

The economic symbiosis model fits the Late Postclassic Aztec evidence somewhat better, since settlement locations during that period were found to be more ecologically diversified, and thus closer to the model's predictions.[19]

In overview, the archaeological evidence indicates that environmental characteristics served only as enabling factors or general selective forces in the formation of Central Mexican and Central Andean macro-states. Both regions were productive enough to support empires, but agricultural potential can hardly be said to require or cause imperialism. The regions of greatest productivity were targets rather than original centers of imperialism. Furthermore, surveys and dating of Inca terraces and Aztec drainage/*chinampa* systems now show that political, military, and ideological institutions were more the causes than the consequences of the most dramatic agricultural advances. Similarly, the archaeological data indicate that although environmental diversity played a role in the growth of economically variegated macro-states, it was clearly not the primary factor in their origins. Again, some peoples who already enjoyed the advantages conferred by symbiosis and verticality failed to become imperial powers, while the Mexica and Inca gained those benefits only after they had begun their successful campaigns of conquest.

Thus any attempt to explain the rise of the Aztec and Inca Empires solely in terms of environmental characteristics is bound to fail. The actual causal relationships among ecology, human settlement, agricultural regimes, and social institutions were considerably more complex. Features such as agricultural potential and environmental diversity set broad guidelines favoring macro-state development, but they were not determining elements.

Demographic factors

Demographic determinism

If the environmental factors discussed above are identifiable only as enabling or selective forces favoring expansion states, another proposed material determinant—population pressure—is far less convincing as an independent causal factor in Precolumbian expansionism. Yet the very simplicity of some population pressure theories (as well as their topical reflection of current world problems) has given them a certain degree of popularity. Since the publication of Malthus's *Essay on the Principle of Population* in 1798,[20] demographic pressure has been repeatedly named as a prime mover in history. Some of the most heated recent controversies on the role of demography have involved Aztec and Inca expansionism.

S. F. Cook offered one of the earlier theories on demographic factors favoring expansionism. Cook (1946) compared a population estimate of two million people for Central Mexico in the Late Postclassic Period with ethnohistorical evidence on mortality rates caused by Aztec human sacrifice, cannibalism, and warfare. Cook's quite conservative estimate was that over fifteen thousand victims were sacrificed annually in Central Mexico, while tens of thousands more died during warfare waged to obtain such sacrificial captives. He argued that the demographic impact of the warfare/sacrifice complex would have helped to alleviate population pressure in Late Postclassic Central Mexico—increasing the mortality rate by twenty-five per cent. According to Cook's theory, warfare and human sacrifice were adaptive responses (conscious or unconscious) to overpopulation and strain on the food supply; the policy of militarism itself could be traced to overpopulation.

Like most of the demographic arguments, Cook's apparently reasonable correlation and conclusion do not survive close scrutiny of the ethnohistorical evidence on Late Postclassic economics, population distribution, and militarism. Frances Berdan in her analysis of Aztec-period economics points out a critical flaw in Cook's theory:

> Cook...suggests that the practice of human sacrifice may have relieved some of this population pressure, but this is questionable. If human sacrifice were used as a population control measure (conscious or not), it could not have been too effective. The problem was undoubtedly less one of total population, than of the distribution of the population. Increasing human sacrifices tended to depopulate outlying provincial areas more than the dense urban areas; it reduced the number of producers while changing little the population structure of the urban consumers.[21]

The fact that the casualties of warfare and sacrifice were predominantly young adult males is also difficult to reconcile with Cook's theory. As they were major food producers, the depletion of their ranks would have exacerbated, not alleviated, food shortages. Furthermore, as Marvin Harris has noted:

> the 25 percent rise in death rates refers only to males and could be easily matched by a 25 percent rise in the birth rate. If the Aztecs were systematically intent upon cutting back on the rate of population growth, they would have concentrated on sacrificing maidens instead of men.[22]

The same objections can be raised to arguments seeing Andean Late Intermediate Period militarism and Inca expansionism as adaptive responses to population pressure and food shortages. Most of the people killed in Inca wars were also able-bodied adult males. Inca soldiers were taxpayers fulfilling one type of labor obligation; their enemies were also potential taxpayers. In other words, the victims of war were taken from the agricultural labor force that farmed state-owned lands and supported the empire. These same men, with the aid of their families, worked their local *ayllus'* fields. Killing able-bodied adult males served only to reduce the ranks of the food-producers. However, their deaths would have had little effect on the birth rate, since polygyny (linked to social rank) was allowed in Inca (and Aztec) society. Again, the unpleasant but inescapable biological fact is that if wars were fought to reduce population pressure, their primary victims should be women of child-bearing age, followed by children and the elderly. Read as a program for population control, the casualty lists of the Aztec and Inca campaigns make no sense at all.

Other, more complex, theories have been proposed as links between demography and warfare. Some scholars have argued that a variety of economic factors, each of them ultimately dependent on population pressure, caused the Aztec and Inca expansions. Arguments of this type treat warfare as a response to demographic pressure in the sense that conquests are viewed as a means of acquiring the resources needed to support an oversized and growing population.

Allison Paulsen (1976, 1981) has proposed one such model to account for the rise of the Inca Empire. Basing her interpretation on archaeological data from coastal Ecuador, Paulsen hypothesizes that between about A.D. 1000 and 1400 the Andean climate was moister than it is at present. Wetter conditions allowed marginal land to be reclaimed for cultivation; more land meant more food and, inevitably, increased populations. Beginning around 1400, Paulsen's model continues, the climate became dryer, and at least some of the reclaimed marginal land could no longer be farmed. Populations were now too large for their subsistence bases; the result was competition for land. The Inca prevailed in the fighting and expanded in search of farmland to support themselves. Tawantin-suyu's growth was, then, a response to climatic change and demographic pressure.

While Inca conquests did have the goal of acquiring farmland, there are a number of flaws in Paulsen's argument. First, the postulated shift to dryer conditions is an inference from cultural evidence. It is not supported by paleo-environmental data, and climatic change remains unproven.[23] Furthermore, if Paulsen's scenario is correct, competition among the peoples of the southern highlands should have been slight prior to 1400. However, the data at hand suggest that the southern sierra was a highly competitive arena even under the supposedly favorable climatic regime of 1000-1400. If arid conditions made large amounts of marginal land uncultivatable after 1400, why does there, in fact, seem to have been a great increase in the amount of reclaimed land around Cuzco during imperial Inca times? If expansion was a response to population pressure, why didn't the Inca slaughter or drive off the indigenous inhabitants of a conquered territory and usurp the entire region for themselves? Instead, victories brought more people into the Inca realm; conquests might well have compounded demographic problems.

Finally, there is the recurrent problem of the incompleteness of the analysis: who exactly was feeling the alleged stresses? Why was military expansion the solution chosen to alleviate these problems? And, above all, why were the *Inca* able to expand and conquer their neighbors? Paulsen's proposal, like many other ecologically oriented theories, discusses broad trends in cultural evolution but fails to address one of the major questions which interest us here: why were the Inca and the Mexica the peoples able to respond most successfully to such pressures? However, in the case of Paulsen's specific theory, there is the more immediate objection that there is simply no evidence for any of the alleged causal factors (climatic change, desiccation, alternations in periods of militarism, etc.) and no reason to think that the Inca brand of imperialism would have alleviated the problems even if they had existed.

Similar direct flaws in evidence and logic invalidate a parallel theory proposed to explain the Mexica imperial complex of warfare and human sacrifice. Michael Harner (1977a,b) has proposed one of the most extreme, and ill-conceived, arguments on the determinants of Aztec expansionism. Unfortunately, it has become widely influential through the proselytizing efforts of Marvin Harris (1977, 1979). Harner's argument rests upon extraordinarily high population estimates for Aztec-period Central Mexico. These estimates have been rejected by most Mesoamericanists, since they are much higher than the figures indicated by the past two decades of combined archaeological survey and ethnohistorical research.[24] Having adopted the dubious figure of twenty-five million for the population of Central Mexico, Harner then observes that such a population would strain available resources, particularly the protein supply. Harner concludes from this train of thought that the Aztecs resorted to a program of militarism, human sacrifice, and cannibalism in order to supply their protein needs through the consumption of human flesh. In other words, a mindless search for meat was the driving force behind Aztec expansionism.

The problems and flaws in this theory are so legion that only a few need be mentioned here. We refer the reader to several detailed reviews (including some by embarrassed fellow materialists) rejecting Harner's hypothesis.[25] To begin with, as noted above, the population estimates he cites are, by all accounts, exaggerated. Hence the hypothesized protein deficiency simply did not exist. Barbara Price and other Mesoamericanists

> question the entire hypothesis of the existence of widespread protein deficiency in the Basin of Mexico...[26]

> There is no concrete evidence that the bulk of the population of Central Mexico—the lower classes—were any more protein deprived than the lower classes of the same area today, or than the lower classes of other known paleotechnic empires, where the domestic sources of protein in the system were available only at an economic and bioenergetic cost that precluded regular distribution on any but a sumptuary basis. Harner nonetheless argues, in evolutionary terms, that the human sacrifice/cannibalism complex is selected for (that is, is maintained in the system), on the basis of its ability to assuage chronic protein shortages. No independent evidence of such shortages can be demonstrated.[27]

Furthermore, Harner's ethnocentric assumption that *meat* protein is essential to the human system contradicts established nutritional studies.[28] In particular, the typical Mexican diet of maize, beans, squash, and supplementary cultigens like chili and amaranth has been shown to supply the amino acids essential to proper nutrition.[29] Harner (1977a: 127) and Harris (1979: 339) argue that famines would have upset the scheduling of this balanced dietary regime. However, such famines, in every documented Mesoamerican example, resulted in shortages in basic staples like maize and beans—shortages whose immediate effect was far more devastating than undersupplies of meat protein.

> In the face of absolute shortages of basic staples—shortages that in stratified society always have disproportionate impact upon the poor (Wrigley 1969)—it frankly makes no sense to talk about protein deficiencies. A doctor does not treat varicose veins when a leg is broken.[30]

Even if Harner's fictional parameters for population and nutrition had existed, the Aztec warfare/sacrifice/cannibalism complex would not have have been a necessary or successful response to protein deficiency. To begin with, actual calculations of the energy cost versus caloric yield prove conclusively that Aztec cannibalism was distinctly non-economic. Even using generous estimates of the 'nutritional value' of captives, Stanley Garn (1979) has demonstrated that Aztec cannibalism would have resulted in an actual net *loss* in caloric value. Indeed, cannibalism in general has been shown to be perhaps the least efficient means of obtaining protein.[31] Furthermore, even a cursory review of the chroniclers' descriptions of the Aztec markets shows that endless sources of protein were available for purchase by those who could afford them. Sahagún lists turkey, rabbit, duck, crane, goose, quail, opossum, turkey and duck eggs, shrimp, fish, shellfish, turtles, eel, cayman, fish roe, water fly larvae, algae cakes, and hundreds of other protein sources as available daily in the great market of Tlatelolco.[32] Only those people at the absolute bottom of the socioeconomic scale would be unable to obtain any of these nutriments. Yet this poorest element of the population did *not* participate, to any significant degree, in rituals of sacrifice and cannibalism. Indeed, as detailed in Chapter 2, participation in Mexica sacrifice and cannibalism was closely linked to social position and prestige. Thus, those people who most often participated in cannibalism were the best-fed ('least protein-deficient') members of society, while the allegedly meat-starved masses were virtually unaffected.

Once made aware of this great hole in the argument, Marvin Harris shifted the theory a bit so as to portray cannibalism as a way for leaders to motivate the more affluent and powerful classes.

> If an occasional finger or toe was all anyone could expect, the system would probably not have worked. But if the meat was supplied in concentrated packages to the nobility, soldiers, and their retainers, and if the supply was synchronized to compensate for deficits in the agricultural cycle, the payoff for Moctezuma and the ruling class might have been sufficient to stave off political collapse.[33]

Unfortunately, at this point Harris seems to have forgotten that it was precisely these important interest groups who could purchase or receive as tribute all the protein they needed.

Finally, recall our earlier description of how the taking of captives affected one's lot in Mexica society. Even commoners who distinguished themselves by taking captives were rewarded with increased prestige and, often, with improved socioeconomic circumstances. Such lasting rewards resulted in substantial improvements in the lifestyle and diet of the warrior and his family. This incentive surely provided a more powerful material motivation than any single cannibalistic ceremony of ritual consumption.

Clearly, specific theories such as Harner's meat-hunt model and Paulsen's climatic determinism are laden with problems of both logic and evidence. As will be discussed in the next chapter, these cultural materialist theories share a number of general theoretical problems, including the confusion of presumed 'function' with proven 'origin', tautologous or circular reasoning, and internal contradictions in logic and methodology. In particular, the ethnohistorical and archaeological evidence has shown that the Aztec and Inca population pressure theories are not convincing explanations for Precolumbian imperialism. In addition to the errors cited above, these models possess some common oversights. For one thing, in conquered regions resources come encumbered with the people who live atop them. Since the Aztec and Inca did not choose to massacre or drive away the populations of conquered provinces, territorial growth did not necessarily relieve the demands placed on the resources of the two empires. The Aztecs often invested large quantities of basic foodstuffs in military campaigns to suppress rebellions in provinces that provided only exotic goods for use as status symbols. The result was a net *loss* of energy and subsistence resources. Similarly, because the Inca exploited conquered regions through labor taxation, and because labor taxation entailed reciprocal obligations on the part of the state, some provinces were economic liabilities rather than assets, at least initially.[34] There is another reason to doubt that the Inca expansion was driven by resource shortages resulting from demographic stress: among the most important resources sought through conquest were the conquered peoples themselves. Tawantinsuyu's incorporation of new peoples swelled the taxable population whose labor supported the growing ranks of the upper classes and the dead.

Demographic pressure

It is less easy to dismiss some of the general demographic principles which many archaeologists assume to affect cultural evolution. One influential demographic theory, resting uneasily upon the concept of inevitable population increase, is the model proposed by Ester Boserup (1965). Boserup begins with the hypothesis that population growth is the primary independent variable in cultural evolution. Agricultural intensification is seen to result from, rather than to allow, population increase. Assuming the primacy of the 'economic base', in this case subsistence technology, some cultural materialists contend that increasingly complex social, political, and religious institutions would then be generated by more labor-intensive agricultural systems. Thus, population growth is assumed to be the prime mover stimulating agricultural intensification, which in turn underlies the increasing complexity of society.

Like environmental diversity, Boserup's principle is assumed to be a general pressure guiding all steps in cultural evolution. Presumably, it would lead eventually (and inevitably?) to macro-states like the Aztec and Inca. Several scholars have applied this model to Mesoamerica and the Andes. As discussed earlier, Sanders, Parsons, Price, and other archaeologists working in Central Mexico have combined Boserup's principle with the 'economic symbiosis' factor to explain the cultural evolution of Mesoamerican civilization. Other scholars (e.g., M. Cohen 1977, 1978, 1981) have applied the theory to the development of Andean civilization.

Many objections have been raised to the assumption that population pressure orthogenetically and inevitably guides cultural evolution. We refer the reader to a corpus of recent articles rejecting this principle, in terms of both logic and cross-cultural evidence.[35] Their principal objection is a rather cogent one: there is simply no reason to *assume* that populations naturally tend to increase to the point of demographic stress. By making such an assumption and combining it with the dogma that subsistence strategy determines all other aspects of culture, anthropologists have been able to force the data, somewhat uncomfortably, into the required mold. However, archaeologists like Blanton, Cowgill, Brumfiel, and Flannery have argued that there is no actual evidence for population pressure *prior* to periods of state formation in New World prehistory.[36] Indeed, their archaeological evidence indicates that major periods of population growth and population pressure were usually a result of earlier sociopolitical evolution.

For example, after meticulous statistical analyses of the archaeological evidence on the period of initial state formation in the Valley of Mexico (the 'Terminal Formative' period, ca. 250 B.C.-A.D. 100) Brumfiel has concluded:

> that population pressure in the Valley of Mexico was brought about by changes in the sociopolitical sphere rather than in the material conditions of existence. Terminal Formative population pressure should be regarded as an effect, rather than a cause, of the evolution of the state.[37]

In the Postclassic, population density was greater than in these earlier periods, but this same causal order is found in the archaeological evidence. Indeed, as even advocates of Boserup's model admit, their own recent demographic estimates (under 250,000 persons in the *pre-Aztec* Valley of Mexico) offer little comfort to those seeing population pressure as the major force in the early evolution of Mesoamerican civilization.[38]

As Cowgill (1979) has suggested, in later periods (such as the imperial epochs) overpopulation is more often the result, rather than the cause, of militaristic and expansionistic policies. Cowgill makes analogies with Chinese states which encouraged population growth, even to the point of strain on resources, so as to increase the number of potential warriors and taxable citizenry. Both the Mexica and the Inca followed precisely this kind of policy—undoubtedly for the very same reasons. The Inca state explicitly favored population increases and rewarded the fathers of large families.[39] In the Aztec case the state religion spared no expense in promoting population growth. Women who died in childbirth were actually deified as the *mociuaquetzque* goddesses, to whom small shrines were erected in all parts of Tenochtitlan.[40] An entire chapter of Sahagún's *Florentine Codex* is devoted to a description of the military honors and martial symbolism of the funeral rites of these martyred mothers.[41] Also described there is the deceased mothers' ascent into heaven to become the companions of the warrior-sun in its daily march across the sky.

And these little women who thus had died in childbirth, those said to have become *mociuaquetzque*, when they died, they said, became goddesses.[42]

When this sun had already advanced along its course, then the women arrayed themselves, armed themselves as for war, took the shields, the devices. Then they rose up; they came ascending to meet the noonday sun there. There the eagle-ocelot warriors, those who had died in war, delivered the sun into the hands of the women... And the women then began; they carried, they brought down the sun...And as they bore it, they also went giving cries for it, they were gladdening it, they went gladdening it with war cries.[43]

The *mociuaquetzque's* sacred status as war heroes allowed the state to encourage, indeed to glorify, the role of mothers as producers of the Mexica armies.

Thus, Aztec and Inca demographic strategy was actually circular in its effect. Warfare tended to reduce the food-producing segments of the Aztec and Inca population, undercutting the subsistence economy. Yet imperial policy also promoted population increases by encouraging parents to have many children who could grow up to be soldiers and taxpayers.

In looking specifically at the imperial period, we should pay close attention to the nature of demographic pressure and resultant stress. The problem was really one of the distribution of people, not their total numbers. In both empires the most heavily settled regions were the capital districts—the Valley of Mexico and the area around Cuzco. Those segments of the capital populations that were actually increasing—the native nobility, administrators brought in from outlying areas, full-time craft or market specialists, retainer and slave classes, and so on—were growing *because* of imperial successes. Overpopulation was localized; where it existed, it was a result, as much as a cause, of expansion. As Calnek has thoroughly documented, the population explosion in Aztec Tenochtitlan was largely caused by the immigration of vast numbers of non-agricultural specialists into the city, including non-Mexica craftsmen and laborers.[44]

Likewise, some resource shortages connected with demographic pressure were also consequences of expansion. A good example is the Aztec famine of 1500. Some seventy years of imperial growth and centralization had swollen Tenochtitlan's population to the point where there were periodic food shortages. In an attempt to improve the local subsistence economy, the *tlatoani* Ahuitzotl tried to construct a new aqueduct system on the western side of Lake Texcoco. The result of his efforts was a catastrophic flood that destroyed local crops and produced several years of famine.[45] Again, the problem seems to be more one of population distribution than of total size, and imperial responses were generally counterproductive.

Despite these objections to monocausal theories of demographic determinism, it is clear that population problems did play a part in New World cultural evolution. By *late* Precolumbian times, localized population pressure had begun to affect specific political developments. While probably largely a result of state policies, population growth also affected the states in question, accelerating the pace and scale of their military struggles. This feedback cycle between militarism and population growth helped to generate the political competition to which the Mexica and Inca *ideological* adaptations responded. Thus, without assuming that demographic trends are the sole independent variable in cultural evolution, it is possible to integrate demography into a multicausal perspective on Precolumbian expansionism.

Yet, even if one assumes that factors such as environmental potential, environmental diversity, and population pressure provided some general trends favoring expansionism, it still leaves open the more specific question of the reasons for the phenomenal success of the *Mexica* and *Inca* states. The failure of specific theories like Cook's, Paulsen's, and Harner's shows that there is no *unique* correlation between the forces they identify (or imagine) and the success of Inca and Mexica imperialism. To address this more focused question, we must examine the exact nature of the cultural adaptations of these peoples, the particular level of society at which the relevant decisions were made, the stresses to which such decisions responded, and the benefits accrued through such adaptations to distinct individuals and classes, as well as to the society as a whole. Only by reviewing these details of the rise of Aztec and Inca imperialism is it possible to discover the links between general evolutionary principles and the known historical development of these peoples.

The economic and political rationale of Precolumbian imperialism

The environmental and demographic factors reviewed above are primarily concerned with the balance between the availability and distribution of resources and the consuming population. However, models which attempt to account for Tawantinsuyu and the Triple Alliance solely in terms of *general* economic stresses are at best inadequate, and at worst completely misleading. Archaeological theorizing about causality in cultural evolution tends to slip into a metaphor of society as a single organism. In this implicit line of reasoning, adaptation occurs because a society responds to circumstances by acting as a single body with one unified mind. Every member has the same goals; decisions and actions reflect some sort of collective will. Some of the specific theories discussed above share this largely unconscious assumption.

Yet as anthropologists and social planners have come to realize, such a view is totally unrealistic. Most individuals are not omniscient, objective social scientists whose criterion for action is the greatest good for the greatest number. Human beings usually hold personal, family, small-group, or class interests above the needs of society as a whole. Even in the smallest and most egalitarian societies individual desires and actions are often at cross-purposes with one another. The discrepancy between individual or interest-group strategies and a society-wide perspective has been amply demonstrated by such problems as the failure of birth control programs in many Third World countries. A country may be suffering from severe overpopulation, but if parental self-esteem or family agricultural goals are predicated upon a couple having many children, the birth rate will not go down.[46]

The potential for conflicts between individual, group, and national wants and needs means that we cannot simply describe state formation, imperial expansion, or any other cultural process in terms of external pressures on the group as a whole. We must also show the advantages of such changes on the precise level at which the relevant decisions were made.[47] In addition to demonstrating that a particular change was adaptive for society as a whole, a convincing causal argument must explain the motivations of individuals, classes, and interest groups—especially leadership groups. When unity of purpose exists, it is underlain by a multiplicity of motives that must be explicitly identified if culture change is to be understood.

As we have seen in our specific accounts of the Triple Alliance and Tawantinsuyu, the expansionistic policies of the two empires were economically *motivated* (again, not determined) by benefits at nearly every level of society. As collective bodies the Inca and Mexica peoples gained greater wealth in the sense of broader and stronger economic foundations. In the Aztec case the tribute system became a major component of the national economy, increasing the flow of resources into Tenochtitlan. The other subsystems of the Aztec economy, market exchange and long-distance trade, also benefited, since they were interdependent with the tribute system. Moreover, the early phases of the imperial expansion opened wider markets and trade contacts. For the Inca, the basis of both the local and the national sectors of the economy was ownership of agricultural land. Conquests brought the Inca not only more acreage, but also farmlands in a wider variety of environmental zones. As we noted in our discussion of verticality, expansion improved the subsistence base of the Inca people as a whole.

While these collective benefits may have been perceived by the Aztec and Inca leadership, they were hardly the sole motivation for the actions of the rulers or the powerful interest groups that formed the decision-making structure. As we have seen, both rulers and upper classes benefited directly from the young states' shifts to imperial policies. Conquests brought the Aztec leadership wealth in the form of land and tribute; Inca rulers obtained wealth in the form of land and the labor needed to work it. Redistribution of the goods and services gained through military victories enabled the ruling members of both empires to convert their wealth into political support.

These advantages have more real explanatory value than any collective economic profit, since they accrued to the people in power—that is, to those individuals who were in a position to make and enforce decisions. However, the rulers obviously could not have expanded their domains by themselves. Imperial growth would not have occurred had there not been perceivable advantages for other individuals and interest groups. Their participation in the states' goals—usually synonymous with the rulers' goals—was inspired by a broader distribution of the economic benefits of expansion. Members of every level of Aztec and Inca society, from the *tetecutin* and *panaqa* nobilities down to commoners, could look forward to sharing in the wealth provided by conquests.

It is important to understand that most of the incentives offered to less powerful individuals and interest groups were created by the leadership. Again, the spoils of war belong to the rulers. Advances in social, political, and economic status were granted to other individuals as rewards for distinguished service in battle or the administrative hierarchy. As we have noted previously, this kind of redistribution was necessary to ensure the ruler's popularity and power, as well as to create an image of generosity and benevolence for the state structure itself.

The highly political nature of the distribution of imperial wealth reminds us of the artificiality of causal categories such as 'economics', 'politics', and 'religion'. Qualitatively and quantitatively, the economic redistribution of the booty gained from conquests followed the lines of the political structure, a structure whose legitimation and justification were as much religious as political. We must, therefore, turn to these other 'causal categories'—in reality, overlapping cultural subsystems—in order to provide a holistic explanation of the Aztec and Inca expansions.

The inseparability of the political and economic stimuli for expansion is most readily apparent in the state's control and manipulation of the wealth acquired by conquest. As we have seen, in both the Aztec and Inca cases the material benefits of imperialism were distributed along the lines of a social and political hierarchy. In turn, the booty helped to reinforce that hierarchy. In each empire, much of the newly gained wealth was given to administrators, priests, and warriors—that is, to people who earned their rewards through full- or part-time service on behalf of the state and its rulers. Conquest allowed leaders to build political support through patronage.

The Aztec *tlatoani*'s generals, warriors, and priests were all supported by tribute, which flowed from its source to its recipients through the ruler. The Inca emperor's patronage structure even survived the ruler himself: the *panaqa* was charged with maintaining the deceased ruler's patronage network of reciprocity and redistribution. In this way, the ruler could go on being 'open and generous' for all eternity. In both cases, economic dependency on a ruler's generosity assured his personal political well-being through the loyalty of his followers and agents. Among the Inca loyalty remained so fierce that civil war pitted the living emperor against the patronage structures of past rulers, some of whom had been dead for a century or more. Upper-class polygyny and the expansions themselves led to the proliferation of the administrative bureaucracy of the empire. The continuing growth of the patronage structures required increasing supplies of wealth so that state and ruler could keep up their largesse and hence maintain political support of the nobility and administrative hierarchy. The demands of political patronage added yet another powerful stimulus for expansion and conquest—especially for the Inca, since each ruler had to build his own patronage network from scratch.

Even beyond the patronage structure itself, more widespread programs of redistribution—'institutionalized generosity'—generated political support and loyalty among commoners. Until the rigid, elitist reforms of Moctezuma II, booty from warfare and the increased social and economic prestige granted to victorious fighters provided strong incentives to Mexica warriors, regardless of their class. These political and economic rewards, along with the possibility of limited social mobility, reinforced the ideological motivations and the prestigious symbols (in costume, sumptuary rights, etc.) promised to successful warriors. In Inca oral history the traditional contrasting characterizations of Huayna Capac as a friend of the poor and Huascar as stingy underscore the importance of the patronage structure. If the *Sapa Inca*, regardless of the circumstances, could not generously support his administrative structure or could not meet the reciprocal obligations owed to taxpayers, he faced the threat of disloyalty, civil strife, and the loss of his state-supported eternal pension plan, his *panaqa*. It is also important to note that redistribution generally occurred in ritual or political contexts rather than as simple rewards of subsistence goods. Above all, the importance of the resources acquired through conquest was not merely their collective or individual benefits *but the fact that those benefits were channeled through the state.*

Political and social mobility was utterly dependent upon military expansion. By increasing their wealth as a whole, the two macro-states were able to elevate ever larger numbers of Mexica and Inca individuals to positions of power and privilege. Shifts of social and economic position occurred throughout the two societies during their expansions. In every case, upward mobility was linked to service on behalf of the state and contributions toward its imperialist goals.

Even at the very highest level of society, the royal court, a certain degree of flexibility in the laws of succession assured that military prowess would be the quality most heavily weighed in the selection of a ruler. In imperial times, the Aztec *tlatoani* was selected from the royal family by agreement among a limited oligarchy, dominated by the top advisers of the realm, the Council of Four—sometimes acting with the advice of the rulers of the other two Triple Alliance capitals.[48] It is clear from the choices made that either a brother, son, or nephew could succeed to rule—the deciding factor being the candidate's perceived competence as a military leader. An Inca ruler's successor was supposed to be his 'most competent' son by his principal wife.[49] We can see how competence was defined from the fact that princes of the royal court received extensive training in the use of arms and were taught that reckless courage in battle was the *sine qua non* of leadership. Above all else, the Aztec *tlatoani* was expected to be a victorious general, while Tawantin-suyu's emperor had to be like the *sinchis*, the fierce war leaders of Inca tradition. This cultivation of aggressiveness in their leaders was yet another element driving the Aztec and Inca peoples outward in a constant militant march—even long after expansionist policies had become detrimental to their well-being.

As we have seen, political mobility among the upper classes was just as closely tied to military achievements or other efforts on behalf of expansionist policies. Members of the Aztec *pipiltin* class were noble by birth, but could attain the more prestigious position of *tetecutin* knights through exceptional prowess in battle. The highly prized economic and political power accompanying *tetecutin* rank helped to assure that Mexica society would maintain its militaristic tone. Likewise, members of the Inca *panaqa* nobility earned promotions and rewards for distinguishing themselves in war and had a vested interest in keeping the drive for conquests alive.

At lower levels, the social mobility of intermediate classes was also used as a means of motivating imperialism. We have seen that in the Aztec Empire both administrative hierarchies and the *pochteca* guilds were internally ranked, these rankings having important religious, as well as economic, significance. In each case, one's position in the occupational hierarchies depended directly upon service to the state. Similarly, members of the Inca *curaca* class, or petty nobility, could move upward in the administrative hierarchy through personal courage and/or skilled leadership of their taxpayer troops in battle, as well as exceptional performance of their political duties. Martial valor could even enable a commoner to step up into the lower ranks of the administrative hierarchy. As with the Aztec, promotion from taxpayer to *curaca* could occur, carrying an individual across what was otherwise a hereditary and impenetrable class barrier.

Hence the results of Aztec and Inca conquests can be summarized as a series of economic and social benefits flowing downward along lines of political power. Through interlocking sets of economic, social, political, and religious incentives the two states were able to motivate their subjects by making militarism something that seemed to be in everybody's best interests. Incessant propaganda campaigns strove to convince every Mexica and Inca citizen—from childhood on—that he or she stood to gain from conquest, that the state's victories would be his or her victories. No wonder both peoples believed that 'fighting was the natural and proper occupation of any able-bodied man'.[50]

A comparative appraisal of Mexica and Inca expansionism

Looking over the theories and the evidence on the development of Aztec and Inca imperialism, we can assert that the interweaving of environmental, economic, social, political, and religious factors could not be more complex. All the elements of this network of causality are indispensable. Above all, the development of these societies must be understood not by viewing the cultures as unified, single-minded, ecologically intuitive organisms, but rather through the analysis of all levels of decisions and adaptations. Furthermore, these adaptations must be understood in terms of cultural and political environments, as well as the physical environment. Finally, we must ask how the interplay of causal forces changed through time. That is, we must confront the collapse of the Aztec and Inca Empires, as well as their rise. We have tried to present such holistic analyses in the preceding chapters. Our conclusions can be summarized by reviewing four key themes: external pressures and selective forces, internal transformations, ideological adaptations, and the limitations of adaptive responses.

External pressures and selective forces

Both the Mexica and Inca peoples first appeared in the context of a power vacuum left by the breakdown of earlier civilizations—the Toltec Empire of Central Mexico and the Tiahuanaco civilization of the Titicaca Basin. While both of these cultural entities are still poorly understood, it is clear that their collapses in the later part of the twelfth century produced the balkanized political situations that characterized their respective culture areas for the next several hundred years. During the thirteenth and fourteenth centuries Central Mexico and the southern Peruvian highlands were fragmented among many small states and chiefdoms, each competing militarily and politically for the right to be the heir of the Toltecs or Tiahuanaco.

In part these conflicts reflected long-term environmental pressures acting on the late Precolumbian peoples of Central Mexico and the southern sierra. Foremost among these pressures was environmental diversity, along with the concomitant principles of economic symbiosis in Mesoamerica and verticality in the Andes. Both of these principles conferred the advantage of a more productive and reliable subsistence base on any polity able to control access to multiple ecological niches.

Perhaps coupled with this 'diversity factor' were some localized population pressures leading to competition for resources in certain regions. Responses to demographic problems—agricultural intensification and increased interregional exchange—further heightened the importance of symbiosis/verticality and the benefits accruing to states able to establish dominion over varied environmental zones.

Nonetheless, we have seen that environmental and demographic factors alone are insufficient explanations for late Precolumbian imperialism. Political factors were equally vital considerations. Regardless of general pressures or the adaptive (or maladaptive) nature of warfare for society as a whole, the leadership classes would *not* have undertaken expansionist policies had they not been in their own best interest. Success in war brought direct benefits to the leadership groups of Mesoamerican and Andean societies. Even if victory did not lead to permanent conquest, it produced booty that increased the power and prestige of leaders. By distributing the spoils of war to his followers, a successful military leader could build a patronage network to serve as his power base. Of course, maintenance of this patronage network would require a continuing flow of loot from new victories. Otherwise, a leader would soon be surpassed by a more adept rival, either within his own society or from another group. So, in late prehistoric times Mesoamerican and Andean rulers had strong vested interests in pursuing militaristic policies.

In short, no single factor explains the intensely antagonistic atmosphere of Central Mexico and the southern Peruvian highlands in the centuries immediately preceding the Spanish Conquest. Instead, competition among local states and chiefdoms was the result of interrelated and inseparable historical, environmental, demographic, and political forces. The bellicosity they produced built toward a staggering crescendo in the fierce struggles of the fourteenth and early fifteenth centuries. These struggles formed the setting, the political environment of the early Mexica and Inca. It was to this cultural environment that the Aztec and Inca societies adapted through their internal transformations.

Internal transformations

As we have seen, the internal transformations of Mexica and Inca society began during the pre-imperial epochs of their histories, when the institution of hereditary rulership developed through the increasing permanence of what had been the temporary office of elected war leader. Concomitantly, the authority of traditional kin group leaders began to be undercut. This process of centralization of power and incipient social stratification was a successful adaptive response to the environmental-demographic-political pressures made manifest in the threats posed by the larger and stronger societies surrounding the early Mexica and Inca.

The continuing operation of those same pressures eventually triggered the two parallel transformational crises—the Mexicas' overthrow of the Tepanecs and the Incas' defeat of the Chanca. In both cases victory brought power to a small corps of military leaders who set about restructuring their societies by intensifying existing developmental trends. Each transformational crisis was followed by a series of reforms enacted by the new leadership. The effects of these changes were further centralization of authority in the office of *tlatoani* or *Sapa Inca*, the institutionalization of patronage networks through greater social stratification, consolidation of a hereditary nobility, increasingly unequal distribution of wealth, and continuing drives for new conquests to support the system.

Again, these cultural changes were adaptive responses to the natural and social environments of fifteenth-century Mexico and Peru, in that the initial expansions brought benefits to the Mexica and Inca peoples as a whole. Yet these collective benefits were an unintended by-product of the shift to empire. The cause of the imperial reforms, at least in the sense of the *conscious* reasons for which they were undertaken, lies in the fact that they served the ambitions of the new rulers. Moreover, the institution and maintenance of an imperial system demanded that the new leadership offer something to their followers in return for their support—that is, the creation of economic and social incentives for warriors, administrators, merchants, and commoners. In the most practical sense, expansionism succeeded because leaders were able to create wants and aspirations in every interest group and individual—and then to satisfy those desires through conquest.

However, as we have argued, the most critical measures enacted by the new leaders were religious reforms. Economic and political changes merely enabled the Mexica and Inca to compete with their neighbors on a roughly equal footing. Neither society rose to mastery until the sanctions and drives generated by a reformed state religion gave it a decisive advantage. This process of ideological adaptation gave the Mexica and Inca states the competitive superiority which transformed them into empires.

Ideological adaptations

As we have seen, the ideological adaptations of the Mexica and Inca peoples were of two main types: manipulations of the upper pantheons and reworkings of ancient, basic institutions. Subsumed within these broader categories were a number of specific changes in ritual and belief. Some of these shifts, innovations, and borrowings may have been unconscious or unintentional, but it is clear that many of the reforms were consciously directed toward the goals of leadership groups.

Manipulations of the upper pantheons began in pre-imperial times with the crystallization of patron deities, the Mexicas' Huitzilopochtli and the Incas' Inti, out of fluid, manifold sky gods. The Mexica and

Inca inherited long-standing traditions of multi-aspected deities based on the movements and transformations of astronomical phenomena. Both peoples came to place their greatest emphasis on the solar associations of the ancient divine complexes and eventually to isolate one solarized aspect as a national symbol and dynastic ancestor.[51]

As has been seen in Chapters 2 and 3, the actual mechanics of these parallel pantheon shifts were somewhat different in the two cases. To a large degree the Mexica began as outsiders to the Mesoamerican cultural tradition, and Huitzilopochtli seems to have arisen through the fusion of a tribal deity/culture hero with the divine complex of Central Mexican civilization. In contrast, the Inca began as marginal members of Andean civilization, but members nonetheless. Their elevation of Inti seems to have been strictly a matter of manipulating existing elements of the traditional southern highland sky god. Hence the Mexica pantheon shift may involve a historical complexity greater than that of Inca religious developments. Still, despite these differences in historical origins, the result was the same in terms of political and economic adaptation.

Huitzilopochtli and Inti ultimately became imperial patrons, intensifying the 'solarization' of Aztec and Inca religion. This emphasis on solar aspects of the divine complexes is hardly surprising. Even in pre-imperial times, when the Mexica and Inca were small-scale societies, the sun was naturally important to them as the source of agricultural life and growth. The transition to empire brought demands for the increased production of a mobile, storable food surplus—especially maize—to support the state and its projects. Agricultural intensification centered upon the all-important staple crop, maize. Hence the great elaboration of ritual related to corn and the sun in imperial Mexica and Inca religion was economically logical.

However, had religious reforms stopped with the creation of solar patron deities, the ideological adaptations of the Mexica and Inca would have been of purely local significance. In and of themselves, Huitzilopochtli and Inti did not have economic and political ramifications that permitted or required these societies' rampant expansions. Rather, the most crucial ideological elements in the transitions to empire were reworkings of fundamental religious institutions—the warfare/sacrifice complex in Mexico and ancestor worship in Peru.

We have seen how the Mexica combined Huitzilopochtli, the sun, and their own military ambitions with an ancient vision of constant struggle among the forces of the universe, making the daily struggle of the sun not only parallel to, but actually dependent upon, continuing Mexica militarism and human sacrifices. Only through endless warfare, conquest, and sacrifice could the Mexica save the universe from the daily threat of annihilation. Likewise, we have seen how the Inca aggrandized the fundamental Andean tradition of ancestor worship through their cult of the royal dead. As the sons of Inti and the corporeal manifestations of Illapa, the thunder and weather 'god', the bodies of the dead kings became the tangible links between the Inca people and their pantheon. To preserve those links and ensure their own prosperity, the Inca had to maintain the 'living' corpses of their rulers in splendor for all eternity. Each ruler's property rights were assured in perpetuity by split inheritance.

Taken together, these pantheon shifts and manipulations of basic institutions had multiple consequences. First, they necessitated imperial expansion in ideological terms. The supernatural forces upon whom society's welfare—in fact, mankind's very existence—depended had to be supported in proper fashion. The Mexicas' gods demanded daily rations of human blood, and the Incas' living dead demanded perpetual income. Only continual conquest could supply these paramount necessities.

Yet ironically the 'ideological' need for expansion cannot be understood as simply ideological. In each case the reformed state religion had economic and political side-effects that maintained steady pressures for conquest. The Aztec economy and political patronage networks became increasingly dependent on the tribute that could be provided only by military victories, while each succeeding Inca emperor through his conquests had to provide for a patronage structure that would be comparable or superior to that of preceding rulers. Both empires needed a constant flow of goods and services through their patronage networks, so that the view of the state and its rulers as 'open and generous' could be maintained. Furthermore, individuals and groups in both societies were motivated by economic, social, and ideological rewards obtained through patronage. On the individual level, ferocity in combat earned a warrior not only a highly honored position in the afterlife, but upward mobility as measured in deliberately emphasized terms: e.g., sumptuary perquisites, greater access to property or labor, additional wives, and more prestigious roles in public and cult ceremonies.

Finally, both state religions provided ample justifications for imperialism, and legitimation of the state policies. In their own eyes, the Mexica and the Inca had the right to conquer. The Inca dynasty had a divine ancestry, and Inti was an evangelistic father/sponsor: witness the oft-repeated Inca claim that the goal of their campaigns was to spread the true religion and their grafting of sun worship onto the myriad local beliefs of their subjects. As for the Mexica, how could the sanctions for their expansion have been stronger? Without their victories the universe would perish. Both nations saw themselves as people with a mission: conquest was not merely their right, but their sacred duty.

All told, the ideological reforms carried out by the Mexica and Inca military leaders who came to power through the Tepanec and Chanca crises were nothing short of revolutionary. The new state religions achieved something that all previous cultural changes had not accomplished—the integration of economic, social, political, and religious factors into unified cults of imperial expansion. By institutionalizing virtually fanatical drives for conquest, the reformed state religions transformed Mexica and Inca society into the most dynamic and ferocious war machines in New World prehistory. The all-pervasive militarism of their cultures gave the Mexica and Inca the decisive advantage over their neighbors and propelled them outward as irresistible forces. In turn, their expansions were favored by environmental selective forces. Access to the products of varied ecological zones, to land and labor for agricultural intensification, made both societies stronger and richer than any potential competitor. Conquest poured wealth into the hands of Mexica and Inca leaders. As the rulers channeled some of their newly won riches downward through their patronage networks, a wide spectrum of Mexica and Inca society shared in the economic, social, and political benefits. Both peoples flourished because of their supremely successful ideological adaptations to their natural and social environments.

The limitations of adaptive response

However, the successes of the Mexica and Inca ideological adaptations were short-lived. No one can predict what would have happened if European invaders had not truncated the independent evolution of Mesoamerican and Central Andean cultures, but in their final decades the Aztec and Inca Empires were obviously deeply troubled. The Mexica were a people divided against themselves; many had even come to resent their *tlatoani*, Moctezuma II. If the Triple Alliance seemed poised on the brink of internal strife, Tawantinsuyu had taken the terrible plunge into civil war. After several years of self-inflicted devastation, the Inca faced the task of rebuilding their shattered empire before it could be seized by someone else. As we know, they never got the chance.

The fate of the Aztec and Inca Empires shows that adaptive value has a temporal component: there can be a tremendous difference between the short term and the long run. The problems that beset the Mexica and Inca in the early sixteenth century were unforeseen long-term consequences of the reforms instituted by the first imperial regimes. In the first place, military expansion simply could not go on for ever. As the Aztec and Inca armies found themselves fighting farther and farther from their capitals, logistical difficulties arose. Overextended, vulnerable lines of supply and unfamiliar terrain (to which traditional tactics were ill suited) swelled the costs of long-distance campaigns while decreasing the rewards. In the mountainous Tarascan homeland of western Mexico and the Amazonian jungle east of the Andes the imperial armies suffered appalling losses and came away with nothing. The Mexica and Inca were running out of suitable peoples to conquer, and warfare was becoming a matter of diminishing economic returns.

The dwindling cost/benefit ratio of imperialism was aggravated by the shifting demographic patterns discussed in previous sections. The results were localized imbalances between population and resources, especially in the capital districts, with their rising concentrations of hereditary nobles and non-food-producing specialists. As we have seen, attempts to correct these imbalances were counterproductive. Continued expansionism served only to intensify existing strains. In established provinces, increasing tax burdens and ethnic tensions between rulers and ruled combined to create smoldering resentments that regularly ignited into rebellions. Such uprisings were beaten down in campaigns that further decreased local agricultural work forces, making future tribute or tax payments even harder to meet. Likewise, agricultural intensification in the capital districts and established provinces eventually became a self-defeating measure. As the demands for surplus production grew, increasing reliance on marginal land actually served to decrease the security of the imperial subsistence economies by heightening the risk of crop failure. This problem is evidenced by Ahuitzotl's disastrous aqueduct extension and Polo's testimony that in many regions of Tawantinsuyu crops failed three years out of five.[52]

As if all of these difficulties were not bad enough in and of themselves, they also created ideological problems. Military setbacks eroded both peoples' sense of invincibility, undermining their self-confidence, their trust in the imperial order, and their motivation. Mexica cosmology held that the destruction of the universe was inevitable: the forces of darkness could be held in check for a time, but they would prevail in the end. The Aztec Empire's travails began to be seen as evidence that the end of the world might be at hand. By the eve of the Conquest resignation, pessimism, and despair were widespread. Meanwhile, among the Inca the rise of the *yana* and *mitmaqkuna* started to weaken fundamental values. The *mitmaqkuna* colonists undercut the old Inca ideal of village self-sufficiency, while the *yana* retainers signalled the disruption—and potential termination—of the traditional reciprocal obligations between rulers and ruled. These new trends threatened not just provincial subjects, but ethnically Inca citizens themselves.

In both cases economic, demographic, political, and ideological problems combined to produce an atmosphere of social malaise. The net result was the emergence of class conflicts in the Triple Alliance and Tawantinsuyu. However, while overt class conflict eventually became a characteristic shared by Mexica and Inca society, the patterns of antagonism were different. Among the Mexica, the growing demands of the hereditary landed elite led to reductions in the material incentives and rewards previously offered to successful warriors, merchants, and administrators of lower birth. Class resentments arose between the high nobility and the upwardly mobile segments of the population—the 'middle classes', as it were. Still, the more overtly expressed conflict between the Mexica and conquered ethnic groups represented a greater physical threat—at least at the time of the Conquest.

In contrast, class conflicts among the Inca were confined to the uppermost strata of society, yet were far more pronounced. As the pace of conquest slowed, the emperor's need for land and labor began to clash with the monopolization of those resources by past rulers. In the process his interests ran counter to those of the *panaqa* nobility. The *panaqas* derived their power from and owed their primary allegiance to the mummies of their founding ancestors, the deceased Inca kings. In other words, class conflict aligned the living ruler against a collection of corpses and their descendants.

Whether or not the commoners played a role in this struggle is a moot point. In retrospect we can see that the emperor's interests coincided with those of lower-class taxpayers. Both the king and his subjects could have benefited from burial of the royal mummies and disenfranchisement of the *panaqas*. The *Sapa Inca* would have gained easier access to land and labor, and the average citizen might have seen a reduction of his tax obligations. We do not know whether this theoretical alliance of the living ruler and the lower classes against the dead kings and the *panaqas* ever existed in fact. The only hint that it might have is Cieza's description of Huascar as 'generous' and 'beloved throughout the kingdom'. However, the evidence is equivocal. As we have noted, Cieza is unique among the early chroniclers in his favorable treatment of Huascar. On the one hand, Huascar lost the civil war, and the overwhelmingly negative accounts of his relationships with his subjects may simply reflect the fact that most descriptions of his character were provided by his enemies. On the other hand, claims that Huascar was universally despised may be an indication that when the lines were drawn, even the commoners chose their traditional ideology over the logic of economic reform.

Most of the troubles assailing the Aztec and Inca Empires in their final years can be traced to one fundamental problem: the contradiction between the demands of state religion and economic, social, and political needs. In late imperial times the Triple Alliance and Tawantinsuyu desperately needed major internal reorganizations. Necessary measures included an end to costly military campaigns in distant regions, easing of tribute and tax burdens on established provinces, decreased reliance on marginal agricultural land, and reductions in the numbers and privileges of the hereditary upper nobility—in short, social and economic restructuring to redress the growing imbalances between population and resources. All of these reforms required policies of *stabilization*, a shift in political priorities from expansion to consolidation.

Yet Mexica and Inca state religion decreed that warfare and conquest go on for ever. Huitzilopochtli still needed the blood of sacrificial victims, lest the universe perish. Indeed, the Mexicas' woes were evidence that the sun was undernourished, and the demand for blood was greater than ever. The living corpses of past rulers—the crucial links between the Inca people and their pantheon—still required eternal sustenance, and the current emperor continued to face the problem of providing his own support. Everything else was crying out for stabilization, but imperial ideology commanded that there be *no* stabilization.

No matter how one tried to resolve this contradiction, the state religion prevailed. In fact, there were only two basic approaches, and both were doomed to failure. Moctezuma II attempted to alleviate the Aztec Empire's troubles by instituting a series of social, political, and economic reforms while leaving the now maladaptive cult of warfare and sacrifice intact. His program managed to alienate virtually the entire Mexica citizenry without doing anything to relieve the fundamental problem. Huascar chose to attack the Inca Empire's central flaw directly by threatening to abolish the royal ancestor cult. In so doing he menaced the rights and privileges of the upper nobility, united the *panaqas* against himself, and precipitated the civil war. No matter which way a ruler turned, his efforts were frustrated by powerful vested interests.

Nonetheless, we must not suppose that state religion remained inviolate only because of the political and economic concerns of individuals and interest groups. Imperial ideology could not be significantly changed without violating deeply held values and beliefs. Events of the early Colonial era reveal the awesome strength of those values and beliefs. After the Conquest many Mesoamericans persisted in ancient rituals even though such practices led to execution by the Spanish Inquisition. During the Spaniards' twenty-seven-year hunt for the Inca royal mummies *panaqa* members gave up their wealth and endured excruciating tortures—including being burned alive—to protect their ancestors' bodies from discovery. People who will impoverish themselves and die hideous deaths to honor their gods or hide a sacred corpse may well be acting in what they see as their own best interests. However, they are clearly not calculating self-interest in purely material terms. They have decided that in the final analysis their own best interests lie in preserving the sacred order that defines and justifies their existence.

So in the end it turns out that religious beliefs and values not only allowed the rise of Tawantinsuyu and the Triple Alliance, but also triggered their fall. In essence, the initial success of the Mexica and Inca ideological adaptations made them irreversible. They were maintained after they had become detrimental to individuals, interest groups, and society as a whole—in a word, maladaptive. These facts argue that, far from being epiphenomenal, religion plays just as fundamental a role in the rise and fall of civilizations as do the economic and political institutions of societies.

Looking at Aztec and Inca imperialism in this holistic perspective, we begin to understand the complexity of the interplay among environmental, economic, social, political, and ideological elements. Indeed, for the Aztec and Inca the analysis of events, institutions, and processes blurs the very distinctions usually drawn between categories of cultural phenomena. Nonetheless, conscious manipulations of state religion, ritual, and cosmology can safely be termed ideological factors.[53] It was precisely these ideological adaptations that initiated the rapid feedback cycles which transformed the Mexica and Inca into imperial powers. Yet the initial success and eventual failure of these adaptations were ultimately measured in political and economic terms. These terms were broadly guided by environment and ecology, but they were more directly affected by the inner workings of society. Hence the nature-culture cycle defies any simplistic assignment of priorities. The rise and fall of the Aztec and Inca Empires can only be understood as a truly multicausal process.

Notes to Chapter 4

1 Compare to similar concepts of adaptation in the writings of Leslie White (1959), Julian Steward (1955), Sahlins and Service (1960), and other theorists whose work is discussed further in Chapter 5.

2 The best archaeological data on agricultural terracing in the southern Peruvian highlands have been provided by Ann Kendall's (1974, 1976, 1979) surveys and excavations in the Cusichaca district of the Urubamba Valley, 87 km. northwest of Cuzco. Kendall's work shows that in imperial Inca times local terracing and irrigation systems were greatly enlarged and expanded in a 'vast maize producing development scheme' (Kendall 1979: 154). For Inca terraces in the Titicaca Basin see Cordero Miranda 1971; Kolata 1982b, ms. Kolata's data indicate that the indigenous form of agricultural intensification in the Titicaca Basin was the construction of ridged-field farmlands and that extensive tracts of ridged fields near the lake were abandoned at the end of Tiahuanaco V times, ca. A.D. 1200. Hillside terracing was a new development introduced by the Incas after about 1450, and it produced a significant increase in the amount of land under cultivation.

3 See for example Parsons 1976b and Calnek 1972a,b for discussions and reviews of the new evidence on the nature and development of the *chinampa* systems.

4 Parsons 1976b: 235.

5 Again, the earliest and most reliable chroniclers all state that the Titicaca Basin was the *first* major target of the Inca expansion. See Chapter 3, note 123.

6 Sanders, Parsons, and Santley 1979; Wolf 1976; Armillas 1971; Blanton 1972a, b; R. Millon 1973; Parsons 1971, 1974, 1976a, b; Sanders et al. 1970; Tolstoy 1975; Tolstoy and Paradis 1970; Tolstoy et al. 1977; Palerm 1973.

7 Sanders, Parsons, and Santley 1979: 281.

8 Parsons 1976b: 236; see also the ethnohistorical evidence concerning the major *chinampa* constructions given by Calnek 1972a,b, 1973.

9 Sanders and Price 1968: 188.

10 Sanders and Price 1968: 189.
11 e.g., Logan and Sanders 1976; Sanders, Parsons, and Logan 1976; Sanders, Parsons, and Santley 1979; Parsons 1976a.
12 For a more detailed presentation of the vertical archipelago model see Murra 1972. The concept of verticality is much discussed in Andean studies today; see for example Earls 1976, Brush 1977, or the papers compiled in Flores Ochoa 1978. Murra originally proposed vertical control as a pan-Andean economic pattern; subsequent analyses have shown that the model probably does not fit all Central Andean regions (cf. Rostworowski 1977), but it certainly seems to hold for the southern highlands. However, for an argument that the 'vertical archipelago' was a late prehistoric development in the Titicaca Basin, rather than an ancient institution, see Browman 1980. For a structuralist reinterpretation of verticality see Duviols 1973, 1979.
13 Murra 1964, 1968, 1975.
14 Lumbreras 1974a: 207-10, 1974b; Trimborn 1975, 1977; Trimborn et al. 1975; Browman 1978, 1980; Kolata 1982b, ms.
15 Browman 1978, 1980. In fact, Browman argues that such colonies did not appear until Tiahuanaco V times (ca. A.D. 850-1200) and that they reflect the beginning of the *breakdown* of the Tiahuanaco state.
16 Trimborn 1975, 1977; Trimborn et al. 1975.
17 See sources cited in note 6.
18 Sanders, Parsons, and Santley 1979: 402.
19 Sanders, Parsons, and Santley 1979: 402.
20 Malthus (1926) argued that food supply can only increase arithmetically, while population can increase geometrically. Therefore, unless the birth rate is controlled, any improvement in subsistence brought about by technological advances will lead to—and be rapidly surpassed by—population growth.
21 Berdan 1975: 304.
22 Harris 1977: 107.
23 The Holocene climatic history of the Central Andes is poorly known. Paulsen's evidence for desiccation is the abandonment of prehistoric wells on the Santa Elena Peninsula of coastal Ecuador. However, the dating of the wells is questionable. Furthermore, Conrad (1981a: 7, 1981b: 38) has suggested that the abandonment of the wells was caused not by decreasing rainfall, but by lowering of the water table due to tectonic uplift, a phenomenon that has been well documented for the Peruvian coast (Richardson 1973, 1974, 1981; Moseley 1975b: 46; Feldman 1977: 15). More recently, and completely independently, Ferdon (1981) has made the same argument in much greater detail.
24 See for example Sanders, Parsons, and Santley 1979; Parsons 1976a; Sanders 1970, 1972, 1976; Calnek 1970, 1972b; cf. Price 1978 for a critical assessment of Harner's figures and ecological evidence.
25 e.g., Price 1978; Sahlins 1978; Ortiz de Montellano 1978; Garn 1979; Castile 1980; cf. Demarest ms.
26 Price 1978: 101.
27 Price 1978: 102.
28 The most recent results of many nutritional studies among both hunter-gatherers and Third World communities have disproved the myth that protein deficiencies in general, and meat protein deficiency in particular, are the predominant cause of human nutritional problems. See for example Chagnon and Hames 1979, Beckerman 1979, Sahlins 1978, and Waterlow and Payne 1975. For surveys and articles on the protein deficiency

controversy see the volumes edited by Steele and Bourne (1975), Olson (1975), and Allyne et al. (1977). See Diener, Moore, and Mutaw 1980 for a comprehensive review of the current evidence on nutrition and indications that the protein obsession of both cultural materialists and earlier nutritionists can be attributed to ethnocentrism (and perhaps even Western commercial interests).

29 Pimentel et al. 1975: 756; Pike and Brown 1967: 43.

30 Price 1978: 101.

31 See for example Garn and Block 1970. Note also that Garn's (1979) calculations assumed, for the sake of argument, that most of the captives' edible flesh was consumed. We know from descriptions of sacrifice that it was not.

32 Sahagún, bk. 10, ch. 22, 24, 1950-69: pt. 11, pp. 80, 85.

33 Harris 1977: 110.

34 Rowe 1946: 274. Cieza (bk. 2, ch. 18, 1943: 108, 1959: 162) speaks of a province or provinces so poor that the inhabitants were ordered to pay their taxes by collecting lice until Inca development projects brought them to the point where they could bear normal taxation. The tale itself seems apocryphal, but it does reflect the fact that some provinces required a considerable investment of imperial resources before they became economic assets. Also, as in the Aztec case, several chroniclers mention Inca provinces that provided only sumptuary goods and services (Sancho, ch. 16, 1917: 147, 1962: 85; Sarmiento, ch. 49, 1942: 143; Cobo, bk. 12, ch. 33, 1890-5: vol. 3, p. 273, 1979: 234).

35 e.g., Cowgill 1975a,b; Lee 1972; Sheffer 1971; Beshers 1967; Nardi 1981; Polgar 1972. See also Chapter 5, note 16.

36 Blanton 1975, 1980; Cowgill 1975a,b, 1979; Brumfiel 1976; Flannery 1976: 225-7.

37 Brumfiel 1976: 248.

38 Sanders, Parsons, and Santley 1979: 378; see Chapter 5, pp. 193-4.

39 Guaman Poma 1936: 188-9.

40 Sahagún, bk. 2, ch. 19, 1950-69: pt. 3, p. 37.

41 Sahagún, bk. 6, ch. 29, 1950-69: pt. 7, pp. 161-5 is devoted to a description of the *mociuaquetzque* rituals and funerary worship.

42 Sahagún, bk. 6, ch. 29. Translation by C.E. Dibble and A.J.O. Anderson (Sahagún 1950-69: pt. 7, p. 164).

43 Sahagún, bk. 6, ch. 29. Translation by C.E. Dibble and A.J.O. Anderson (Sahagún 1950-69: pt. 7, p. 163).

44 See Calnek 1976: 288-90 for a concise review of the ethnohistorical sources demonstrating that immigration, rather than local population increase, was responsible for the rapid urbanization of Tenochtitlan-Tlatelolco. See also Calnek 1972a,b, 1973, and Parsons 1976b. For data on Cuzco and its environs see Chapter 3, note 138.

45 Durán, bk. 2, ch. 49, 1967: vol. 2, pp. 375-81; Chimalpahin, *Séptima Relación*, 1965: 226-7; Ixtlilxochitl, *Historia*, ch. 66, 1977: 167; Torquemada, bk. 2, ch. 47, 1975: vol. 1, pp. 219-22.

46 See note 35 above and note 16 of Chapter 5 for sources on the individual and familial nature of population strategy.

47 cf. Cowgill 1975a,b; Kohl 1981: 109-10. See also the discussion and notes on Marxist approaches in Chapter 5. One of the strengths of such approaches is their awareness of the divergent interests of different subsectors of a society.

48 Even within one version (Durán's) of the state's 'Crónica X' there are numerous contradictions concerning the details of the electoral process. In

some cases, as in the election of Ahuitzotl, a rather broad participation is (undoubtedly fallaciously) implied (Durán, bk. 2, ch. 4, 1967: vol. 2, pp. 37-45). In other cases, as with Tizoc's and Moctezuma I's election, according to Durán not even the other Triple Alliance rulers were consulted ('Nezahualcoyotl *heard* of the election of Moteczoma'—Durán, bk. 2, ch. 15, 1964: 87). But in any case only close male relatives of the previous *tlatoani* were chosen, and all were good warriors. Note especially Durán's (bk. 2, ch. 52) description of why Moctezuma II was selected among the eligible relatives to be the *tlatoani*:

> After Cihuacoatl, the son of Tlacaelel, had spoken and some discussion had followed, Moteczoma, son of King Axayacatl [nephew of the previous *tlatoani*, Ahuitzotl] was chosen. There was no opposition to this choice for he was a mature man, pious, virtuous, generous and of an invincible spirit. He was blessed with all the virtues that can be found in a good ruler and his decisions had always been correct, especially in matters of war. In the latter he had performed feats which showed remarkable bravery (translation by Doris Heyden and Fernando Horcasitas [Durán 1964: 220]).

49 The chroniclers' accounts of any specific case of succession to the Inca throne vary widely; see for example the discussions of the cases of Pachakuti and Huascar in Chapter 3 (pp. 110-12, 134-5) and the sources cited in Chapter 3, notes 79-82, 158. Nonetheless, it is clear that primogeniture was not an Inca custom and that competence and 'legitimacy' (being born to the ruler and his principal wife, or *coya*) were the qualities that mattered in the selection of a new king. For a more detailed analysis of succession to the Inca throne see Rostworowski 1960.

50 Rowe 1946: 274.

51 See Demarest 1981 for exposition of such shifts in the Inca pantheon and comparison to similar changes in Aztec religion.

52 Polo 1916b: 156, 1940: 168. Polo did not specify which crops failed, but Murra (1960: 396) believes he was referring to maize.

53 See Chapter 1, pp. 4-5 for a discussion of our specific application of the term 'ideology' and the inseparability of ideology from religion in analyses of Precolumbian states.

5
Ideology and cultural evolution

In our discussion of the Mexica and Inca peoples we have been moving from specific considerations to more general ones, from the highly concrete to the more abstract. Through individual examinations of the Triple Alliance and Tawantinsuyu we have tried to elucidate each state's unique historical trajectory. We have also argued that, despite the differences in detail, the two empires developed in the same way, through a similar progression from adaptation to maladaptation. Now it is time to move to the most abstract level of analysis and ask about the most general implications of everything that has gone before. That is, what do Mexica and Inca history—and the crucial role of religious ideology in late Precolumbian imperialism—tell us about the nature of cultural evolution?

In the previous chapter we have criticized some of the current explanations of the nature and causes of Aztec and Inca expansionism and have offered, in what we hope were jargon-free terms, our own alternative reconstructions. In so doing we have deliberately skirted the broader theoretical controversies underlying the conflicting reconstructions of these two dramatic episodes in human cultural evolution. Yet the views of the anthropologists and archaeologists cited above were informed by more general anthropological theories, overarching intellectual frameworks that guided their research and interpretations. It follows that to understand these alternative hypotheses fully one must be aware of the theoretical premises underlying them. In turn, the reconstructions of Aztec and Inca history we have offered can be used to examine not only the specific hypotheses on Precolumbian imperialism, but also the general theories of cultural evolution that have guided them. Such evaluations necessarily involve difficult and controversial problems in contemporary anthropology. We are not so rash as to claim that we can resolve these questions completely. Nonetheless, we believe that discussion of the problems can lead us to new insights into the role of religious ideology and institutions in cultural evolution and the nature of the evolutionary process itself.

Since the beginnings of anthropology as a social science, scholars have struggled with the question of the role of beliefs in cultural and historical development. Yet in many ways ideology remains poorly understood as an element in culture change. The various general theories and approaches to cultural evolution—some of them quite successful in dealing with a large range of phenomena—have had great difficulty in integrating religion into dynamic models. It has either been viewed as a conservative and stabilizing component of culture whose function is to reinforce the status quo, or it has been dismissed completely as epiphenomenal—as a mere by-product or mental reflection of the true causal forces in cultural evolution (invariably, *economic* forces).

This latter approach of simply denying any independent causal role to religious ideology characterized many of the specific materialist or ecological interpretations criticized in Chapter 4. As we have seen, there are numerous errors in both the supposed 'facts' and the logic of these reconstructions of Aztec and Inca expansionism. Indeed, the flaws in these interpretations point out some basic fallacies in cultural materialist theory itself.

The demographic machine

Among the least convincing materialist models are those which rely directly upon population pressure and its effects as prime movers in late Precolumbian imperialism. Yet most of the interpretations of Aztec and Inca expansionism have at their core a population pressure model. Paulsen hypothesized that desiccation created a demographic strain on limited resources and motivated Inca militarism in a search for food.[1] Cook viewed Aztec militarism as a means of reducing population to mitigate stress on resources.[2] Harner and Harris, in perhaps the most simplistic reconstruction yet proposed, hypothesized that overpopulation led to protein deficiency, which was alleviated through the Mexicas' cannibalistic expansionism.[3] As we have noted, the more complex theories of Sanders, Price, and others deserve separate consideration as ecological models.[4] However, in the end they also rest upon the fallacious assumption of the inevitability of population growth. In its actual application by cultural materialists, the principle of inevitable population growth takes the form of a tautologous assertion about human nature.

> We strongly favor the position that population growth is a general phenomenon and that human reproductive behavior generally is unlike that of most other species only in its tendency towards sustained growth. The validity of these positions cannot be argued philosophically, they must be supported by empirical data, and the data are overwhelmingly in favor of population growth as a universal phenomenon. Very simply, if this was not the case we would still be Australopithecines living in South Africa. It is undoubtedly true that the growth rates prior to the Industrial Revolution were much slower (primarily due to a much higher

infant mortality), but the fact is that there has been a steady increase in the human population since Paleolithic times.[5]

This tautology is built on an error that any philosophy student could identify: the mistaking of correlation for causality. 'Empirical' demonstration that two variables (in this case increasing cultural complexity and population growth) are highly correlated does not tell us which of them, if either, is the *independent* variable. It makes *no* statement about the direction of causality.

Few anthropologists would deny that cultural evolution—in the sense of increasing cultural complexity through time—has occurred. It is universally recognized that this process has involved numerous highly correlated factors such as greater social segmentation and differentiation, stratification, centralization of authority, agricultural intensification, and the proliferation of formal political, military, and religious institutions. Population growth is also one of the many factors that constitute the evolutionary process. However, this simple statement tells us nothing about which of these elements was primary—chronologically *or* causally. One could just as easily assert that social stratification (or any other factor) is the 'prime mover' behind human history because it is also highly correlated with population increase, specialization, centralization, and the other characteristics that together define what anthropologists call 'cultural evolution'. Contrary to the cultural materialist tautology, a determinant role for population pressure can be verified only if demographic stress is shown to both *precede* and *cause* increases in cultural complexity. In the previous chapters we have reviewed and analyzed the archaeological, ethnohistorical, and ethnographic evidence demonstrating that in Central Mexico and the Andes population pressures were not only late and highly localized, but also more a result than a cause of state formation and expansion.

Despite cultural materialists' frequent assertions that they alone are following a truly 'empirical' course (e.g., Paulsen 1981; Harris 1979: 5-46; Sanders, Parsons, and Santley 1979: 364), sometimes they seem to be unresponsive to the implications of actual empirical tests of their models.[6] One recent regional survey, the Valley of Mexico Project, is one of the most impressive and ambitious archaeological projects ever undertaken.[7] Sanders and his colleagues set out to test Boserup's population pressure model and the auxiliary hypotheses that responses to demographic stress would be hydraulic agriculture and economic symbiosis, which in turn would require more complex and centralized political and economic institutions.[8] After years of work, the empirical results of the survey were quite surprising to many Mesoamerican archaeologists.

During the crucial periods of pre-imperial state evolution, only scattered local irrigation or terracing systems were constructed.[9] These systems were on a scale hardly requiring organization and planning beyond the community level.[10] As detailed in Chapter 4, the massive lake-bed (*chinampa*) agricultural system of the southern Valley of Mexico was found to be almost entirely a fifteenth-century phenomenon, a by-product rather than a cause of the new imperial order (Parsons 1976b; Sanders, Parsons, and Santley 1979: 281). Furthermore, settlement patterns did not demonstrate economic symbiosis during the critical periods of state formation: in each of those periods sites were virtually confined to a single environmental zone.[11] Finally, and most surprisingly, the population estimates inferred from the archaeological evidence were unexpectedly low for the pre-imperial period.

> Our estimate of the carrying capacity of the same area, plus the chinampa zone in the lakes, with intensive agriculture, is 1,250,000 people. Our various estimates for the population in 1519 were 800,000 (derived primarily from the archaeological data with documentary estimates added in for the large cities like Tenochtitlan, Texcoco, Tlacopan, and others), and 900,000 to 1,100,000 (from documentary sources alone). This means the population had reached from 65-88% of carrying capacity with intensive agriculture.
> Considering these raw figures and particularly considering the fact that the pre-Late Horizon population of the Basin never exceeded 250,000, the theory that population pressure produced sociopolitical evolution would seem to be of very doubtful utility.[12]

Note that these population estimates are considerably lower than the archaeologists' expectations prior to the completion of the survey (Sanders 1970, 1976; Sanders and Price 1968: 175). Nonetheless, only one of the directors of the archaeological team, Richard Blanton (1976b: 179-80), accepted the results as a negation of the population pressure hypothesis. Other project members (Sanders, Parsons, and Santley 1979) proposed complex reconstructions of carrying capacity and land use in order to hold to most aspects of their original propositions.

> In fact, if we take into consideration all the variables that limited agricultural expansion during the First Intermediate [1150 B.C. to A.D. 300], and apply Boserup's ideas as to how the process of intensification operates, then the model does provide a powerful explanatory framework for at least the early stage of cultural evolution in the Basin.[13]

In our view, their subsequent analysis avoids some of the obvious implications of their own findings. In any case, it still leaves us without any convincing evidence of demographic pressure as a causal factor leading to the *later* Aztec-period (Late Horizon) expansion. The acrid debate over the project's results, and over the conclusions of similar projects elsewhere in Mesoamerica,[14] reinforces the impression that the population pressure model is not really a hypothesis to be tested, but rather is an unassailable and tautologous guiding principle.

These doubts concerning the empiricism of cultural materialism are magnified when one realizes that the notion of a universal and 'natural' human tendency toward population growth was already easily testable against the data of contemporary ethnography. Demographic studies of hundreds of contemporary societies have thoroughly disproven the notion that population growth to the point of ecological stress is in any way 'natural' to the human race (for example, Lee 1972; Rappaport 1971; Wagley 1973; Cowgill 1975a,b). Contrary to the claims of Sanders et al. cited above, the actual empirical data show that human societies are not 'unique' and aberrant in their population dynamics. Rather, like all other species, humans tend to maintain populations far below the level of ecological stress. Indeed, recent cross-cultural surveys of demographic patterns indicate that fertility regulation and population control, rather than continuous growth, are the factors common to human societies:

> we know that people in all cultures and epochs have regulated fertility. In fact, there are many data to suggest that fertility regulation is a virtually universal phenomenon.[15]

Freed of the *a priori* assumption that population growth is inherent in 'human nature', contemporary demographers have largely shifted their attention to detailing and analyzing the vast array of cultural methods and reasons for population control.[16]

Given the existence of this historical and ethnographic corpus on the realities of human demography and references to these data by perceptive contemporary archaeologists (e.g., Cowgill 1975a,b; Blanton 1975, 1980; Flannery 1976: 225-7, 1977; Brumfiel 1976), one wonders why the cultural materialists cling so doggedly to a logically and empirically disproven premise. The answer lies not only in differing perceptions of the data, but in the mystical philosophy of cultural materialism itself—a doctrine that, unfortunately, has dominated archaeological interpretation for the last two decades.

Faulty mechanics

The single most prominent and influential spokesman for the cultural materialist approach is Marvin Harris, whose work also provides the most explicit presentation of the underlying theory. Harris, through a highly selective and sometimes distortive reading of earlier thinkers—most notably Karl Marx, Lewis Henry Morgan, Leslie White, and Julian Steward—has constructed what he purports to be the first and only 'science of culture' (Harris 1979). However, what he has actually preached in numerous books and articles is a reductionist and monocausal version of cultural ecology.

> I believe that the analogue of the Darwinian strategy in the realm of sociocultural phenomena is the principle of techno-environmental

and techno-economic determinism. This principle holds that similar technologies applied to similar environments tend to produce similar arrangements of labor in production and distribution, and that these in turn call forth similar kinds of social groupings, which justify and coordinate their activities by means of similar systems of values and beliefs. Translated into research strategy, the principle of techno-environmental, techno-economic determinism assigns priority to the study of material conditions of sociocultural life, much as the principle of natural selection assigns priority to the study of differential reproductive success.[17]

This theory holds that a culture's technology and subsistence system (its 'infrastructure') interacts with the environment and generates all of the other, secondary aspects of society (e.g., social, political, and religious values and institutions). The process of cultural evolution can be reduced to the development of more adaptive and efficient subsistence systems, which in turn require and generate more complex 'structures' and 'superstructures' of economic, social, political, and religious institutions. The process is given direction by recurrent demographic strains and intercultural competition, which select for the more economically efficient or ecologically adaptive traits or systems. Hence, Harris presents human history as a series of mechanical responses to ecological stress, intercultural competition, and (most commonly) protein deficiencies, all of which are ultimately caused by the species' inability to control its own growth.[18]

In actual application, Harris's science of culture takes the form of a disconnected series of essays 'explaining' the hidden economic rationality of such bizarre and apparently irrational religious institutions as the sacred cow of India, Islamic prohibitions on pork, or Aztec sacrifice and cannibalism.[19] The appeal of his writing to popular audiences can be attributed to the natural desire of the Western reader to have the difficult, alien concepts of other cultures explained in 'rational' (i.e., Western) terms, as responses to the most basic and common human needs.

However, as we have seen with the Aztec sacrificial cult, specific cultural institutions are the products of long historical traditions, external cultural and ecological pressures, individual political ambitions, class economic interests, and so on. Harris's solutions to such cultural 'riddles' as Aztec cannibalism ignore all of these factors by positing more direct economic causes: in the Aztec case, population pressure caused protein shortages, which in turn necessitated cannibalism. Unfortunately, massive ethnohistorical and archaeological evidence demonstrates that there were neither population pressure nor protein shortages prior to the acceleration of the sacrificial cult. Furthermore, as explained in Chapters 2 and 4, Aztec sacrifice would only have exacerbated shortages had they existed.

In each case, Harris's solution to a specific 'riddle' of cultural behavior has met with voluminous and angry responses by scholars actually familiar with the primary data on the culture under study—data usually ignored by Harris and his disciples.[20] For each 'riddle', evidence already existed showing the specific historical reasons for the development of particular institutions. In all three of the cases mentioned above (Islamic pork taboos, Hindu cow worship, and the Aztec central cult), more meticulous research has identified complex but parallel chains of causality: during situations of intercultural conflict powerful interest groups effected changes in specific religious institutions—changes that were in their own immediate political and economic interests and yet were consistent with older religious traditions.[21] Any 'adaptive' advantages to the society as a whole were both inadvertent and short-term, with the changes proving to be highly maladaptive in the long run. Furthermore, any general adaptive advantages were ones of political unification, legitimization of the social order, and ideological motivation —not direct improvements in subsistence strategy.

In Chapters 2 and 3 we demonstrated such a chain of causality for the Aztec sacrificial cult and Inca royal ancestor worship; in Chapter 4 we analyzed the development of these traits in a historical and evolutionary context. We gave the highest priority to establishing the *chronological order* of events and *historically documenting* the reconstruction using primary ethnohistorical and archaeological sources. Similarly, other scholars have accounted for the sacred cow of India and Islamic pig taboos by presenting well documented and highly detailed *historical* reconstructions. These anthropologists have explained the origins of seemingly irrational religious institutions by proving that particular chronological sequences of events took place and then relating those events to complex political and economic forces.[22] They have *not* been content to offer purely hypothetical reconstructions whose 'proof' lies in the argument that certain religious beliefs and practices would have been ecologically adaptive.

In contrast, many cultural materialists and cultural ecologists (see below, pp. 201-5) mistake synchronic analysis of an institution's supposed 'adaptive value' for historical analysis of its origins. In the specific case of the Aztec, Harner and Harris argue that since cannibalism would have alleviated alleged protein shortages, its origins or development can be explained as a response to such shortages (without reference to any ethnohistorical evidence concerning the origins). Likewise, Paulsen and Cook, without any specific historical or archaeological data, argue that warfare would have relieved imagined Inca- and Aztec-period resource shortages. Therefore, they reason that the *cause* of militarism and expansionism can be presumed to be population pressure and ecological stress. Diener et al. (1978) have pointed out the logical flaws in such reasoning.

> A specific fallacious form of explanation which has plagued functional-ecological investigation in anthropology, as it plagued classical functionalism before it, involves the improper accounting

for historical origins by reference to observed or assumed functions. The explanation of origins in terms of functions is formally invalid because it involves an affirmation of the consequent; a conclusion concerning the origin of a trait can validly be derived from an observation of the functions of that trait if and only if that trait is the only possible trait which can satisfy the functional imperative specified. This is never the case with social and cultural systems, for we can always imagine functional alternatives which might meet the needs described.[23]

For example, intensification of guinea pig or turkey breeding, emphasis on certain protein-rich crops, or simply population control would have been more efficient responses to the imagined Aztec and Inca resource shortages. Imperialism did not relieve any of the shortages that can actually be demonstrated—it caused them in the first place!

In general, cultural materialism consistently confuses hypotheses of ecological utility with the historical documentation of origins. Accordingly, cultural materialists try to substitute synchronic functional explanations of institutions for the actual historical research needed to identify and describe the development of cultural traits. In so doing, cultural materialism runs a continual risk of mistaking real or presumed effects for underlying causes. As Diener et al. have concluded, 'this objection to functional-ecological arguments for origins is insurmountable'.[24]

We have taken some pains in the previous chapters to avoid yet another error inherent in functional-ecological explanations: the organic metaphor, the assumption that society, individuals, and diverse interest groups all mysteriously move together as an organic unity toward ecologically adaptive behavior. Instead, Aztec and Inca history and archaeology (as well as the South Asian and Near Eastern cases mentioned above) show that individual, small-group, and class interests can be held above the well-being of society as a whole. If self-interested groups are in positions of sufficient power, they can initiate and maintain long-term patterns of behavior that propel society along a devastatingly maladaptive path—even to the point of the total collapse of the system.

World archaeology is littered with the remains of extinct civilizations driven to the point of systemic collapse by such maladaptive behavior— behavior that can only be explained by reference to the dominance of individual, small-group, or class interests during critical periods of cultural evolution. The inability of most cultural materialist models to deal with maladaptation is yet another fundamental flaw.

> History is built on the failure of social forms as much as on their success. If social forms fail, it is because they have laws of their own whose purpose is other than making optimal use of their techno-environments.[25]

The Aztec and Inca ideological 'adaptations' cannot be understood without reference to such *internal* factors ('laws of their own'). The modifications of religious institutions were 'adaptive' changes in that they initially fulfilled the needs of interest groups (in both cases military elites) powerful enough to institute them. They were also adaptive in that they assured the *short-term* success of the Inca and Aztec societies in their military struggles with the peoples around them. Yet even on this society-wide level military success itself can be explained only in terms of the 'internal' (non-ecological) workings of the societies. The fanatical militarism of the Mexica and Inca resulted from class, small-group, and individual economic and political interests, combined with the unique advantage in battle given by ideological necessity: without victory in combat the Aztec sun would perish and the Inca ruler/gods, living and dead, could not be maintained. So the short-term success and the long-term failure of these cancerous states cannot be understood without reference to the various *motivational* factors that affected every level of society (individual, subgroup, class, and whole) and provide the key to both the 'adaptive' and 'maladaptive' aspects of the system.

The ghost in the machine

Cultural materialists' failure to explain maladaptations and their inability to present logically consistent and historically verifiable explanations can be traced to their explicit refusal to admit motivational and ideological factors as significant variables in culture change. The philosophers of cultural materialism divide all anthropological data into *emic* and *etic* observations.[26] Emic data concern the point of view of the native informant, of the individual in the culture under study. The etic perspective is the point of view of the observing anthropologist who is aware of the 'real' forces at work (naturally, technoeconomic forces) in the function and development of the society. Orthodox cultural materialists, such as Marvin Harris, argue that cultural evolution can be understood only by strict adherence to the etic perspective. Regardless of the motivational, ideological, or mental factors that mystify the culture under study, the materialist scientist claims to be able to determine—externally and objectively—the ecological constraints and responses that are the 'real' forces guiding the functioning of that society's institutions and its change through time.

Thus, such elements as shared belief patterns, psychological factors, individual perceptions, class interests, and all aspects of motivation should be admitted by the analyst only as curious by-products of the etically observable constraints of the culture's ecology. Preferably, state the cultural materialists, they should be purged from scientific analyses.

> In my opinion, free will and moral choice have had virtually no significant effect upon the direction taken thus far by evolving systems of social life.[27]

A principal goal of cultural materialism is to eliminate such emic factors from evolutionary explanations and to generate a purely etic 'culture-free science of culture'.[28] Anthropologists who admit the independent importance of ideological, mental, or motivational factors are condemned and castigated as being 'obscurantists' or 'eclecticists'—'subjectivists' whose analyses are contaminated by their confusion of the etic forces of reality with the emic mental mirages of the cultures under study.

Having purged his own analyses of such muddled thinking, Marvin Harris offers us a vision of cultural evolution as an ecological machine driven toward higher levels of complexity by relentless population growth and resultant ecological stress.

> In the past, irresistible reproductive pressures arising from the lack of safe and effective means of contraception led recurrently to the intensification of production. Such intensification has always led to environmental depletion, which in general results in new systems of production—each with a characteristic form of institutionalized violence, drudgery, exploitation, or cruelty. Thus, reproductive pressure, intensification, and environmental depletion would appear to provide the key for understanding the evolution of family organization, property relations, political economy, and religious beliefs, including dietary preferences and food taboos.[29]

We have seen how in individual applications this doctrine is consistently unsuccessful. Yet its failure is not merely a quirk of specific instances, but a product of its most basic premises: the emic/etic distinction and demographic determinism.[30] As we have shown, cultural adaptations cannot be explained without reference to human beliefs and motivations. The impossibility of eliminating emic considerations from explanation (even at a distant general level) is proven by the fundamental contradiction found in the very engine of culture materialism—the demographic drive.

For years cultural materialists could simply assert dogmatically that human populations tend to grow beyond their resource bases. They have been increasingly threatened by the mounting ethnographic evidence that population control is the rule, not the exception. It is now overwhelmingly obvious that humans, like other species, normally maintain population levels well below environmental carrying capacity and that when growth to the point of ecological stress does occur, it is something to be explained rather than assumed. In order to preserve the principle of demographic determinism some materialists and cultural ecologists have resorted to tautologies like the confusion of correlation and cause expounded by Sanders et al. (see above, p. 193). Finally, even the foremost philosopher of cultural materialism has admitted that a new justification of the dogma must be presented.

> It has lately been established that pre-state populations generally stop growing when they reach as little as one-third of the maximum carrying capacity of their techno-environmental situation (Lee and

DeVore 1968, Casteel 1972). As we shall see, this has been interpreted by structural Marxists and others as a refutation of the importance of Malthusian forces. Yet no such interpretation is warranted until the nature of the restraints on population growth has been clarified.[31]

To justify clinging to a version of demographic determinism, Harris then offers a surprising argument:

> slow rates of population growth were achieved only at great psycho-biological costs through infanticide, abuse, and neglect.[32]

> Before the development of the state, infanticide, body-trauma abortion, and other malign forms of population control predisposed cultures which were in other respects adjusted to their habitats to increase production in order to reduce the wastage of infants, girls, and mothers. In other words, because prehistoric cultures kept their numbers in line with what they could afford by killing or neglecting their own children, they were vulnerable to the lure of innovations that seemed likely to allow more children to live. Thus, Malthus was correct in his surmise that population pressure exerted an enormous influence on the structure of pre-state societies.[33]

As an aside we can note that this reconstruction ignores the nearly universal use of non-traumatic forms of birth control such as post-partum taboos, celibate sectors of society, homosexuality, coitus interruptus, periodic abstinence, lactational amenorrhea, and so on.[34] But as a cultural materialist explanation it contains a more fundamental flaw: it is *emic*! It replaces the myth of 'natural' population growth with the idea that the human *desire* to avoid the 'psycho-biological' trauma of 'malign forms of population control' has driven the search for more complex and productive subsistence systems. When pressed, the culture-free science of culture must preserve demographic determinism by inventing a universal human *psychological* trait— the abhorrence of birth control. In the end, the priest/mechanics of cultural materialism must invoke a 'mentalist' phantasm to energize their demographic machine.[35]

The static functionalist tradition

In the final analysis the failure of cultural materialism can be traced to its roots in a long tradition of static approaches to culture. This tradition includes functionalism, structural-functionalism, and the equilibrium-maintenance models at the heart of much cultural ecology. Here it is impossible to do justice to these diverse theories by detailing their theoretical premises and the problems in their logic or application. However, we can focus on one shared flaw in these approaches that renders them useless as general strategies for analyzing the evolution of culture and the role of ideology in evolution. This common shortcoming is their fundamentally *synchronic* nature—their inability to explain change.

Functionalism is an approach whose origins are usually attributed to

Bronislaw Malinowski.[36] It assumes that elements of cultural and social institutions function to serve the basic biological and psychological needs of the individuals in a society. Since these basic needs are fulfilled through cooperation, political and social institutions exist for the *purpose* of ensuring the success of cooperative efforts. Structural-functionalism is a related theoretical approach most explicitly presented by the British social anthropologist A.R. Radcliffe-Brown.[37] Like Malinowski's functionalism, structural-functionalism explains social traits and institutions in terms of their functions. However, their overall purpose is seen as maintenance of the social structure rather than the fulfillment of basic individual needs. As Radcliffe-Brown summarized his theory of culture, it

> implies that a social system...has a certain kind of unity, which we may speak of as a functional unity. We may define it as a condition in which all parts of the social system work together with a sufficient degree of harmony or internal consistency, i.e. without producing persistent conflicts which can neither be resolved nor regulated.[38]

Some of the difficulties with this approach should be apparent in view of our Aztec and Inca analyses, as well as the preceding theoretical discussions. It clearly involves the discredited metaphor of society as a unified 'organism', as Radcliffe-Brown himself admitted.

> In using the terms morphology and physiology, I may seem to be returning to the analogy between society and organism... But analogies, properly used, are important aids to scientific thinking...[39]

However, as we have seen, society does not consist of harmoniously coordinated somatic organs, but rather of individuals, families, and subgroups whose goals are not necessarily identical and whose interests may not be concordant with the 'adaptive' or 'functional' needs of the total social system. Furthermore, the inequitable distribution of power in complex societies often leads to the dominance of individual, small-group, or class interests, even if they are maladaptive for society as a whole—a situation we have observed in the late Aztec and Inca Empires. This discordant reality differs sharply from the hypothetical idea that social institutions or individual cultural traits exist because they fulfill basic *common* needs (as Malinowski's functionalism would tell us), or because they maintain the social structure's 'harmony', 'internal consistency', and 'functional unity' (as structural-functionalism holds), or even because they are 'ecologically adaptive' (as the cultural materialists argue). Thus, the fallacy of the 'organic metaphor' shared by functionalism, structural-functionalism, and the materialists' cultural ecology also entails the corollary flaw of its inability to explain 'maladaptation' or the collapse of civilizations.

Upon scrutiny, we see that these versions of functionalism are not only unable to explain the collapse of civilizations, but incapable of dealing with change at all. As was shown in the specific case of cultural materialism (see pp. 197-8), all functionalist approaches rely on the 'improper accounting for historical origins by reference to observed or assumed functions'.[40] The actual reconstruction of human history reveals the diverse aspirations, motivations, and needs of individuals, who sometimes cooperate and sometimes pursue more limited interests. These 'emic' and often disharmonic factors drive cultural evolution as much as the need for functional unity or ecological adaptation. By ignoring such realities functionalist theories only describe the allegedly rational nature of the system at one point in time, and then must assume (or concoct) a history teleologically guided to this functionally balanced state.

It must be conceded that many of the pioneering functionalists, unlike their cultural materialist heirs, were at least willing to deal with religion and ideology as principal aspects of social integration. Most of the functionalists' analyses of religion built upon the original conception of the French sociologist Émile Durkheim, who interpreted religious behavior as symbolic reinforcement of social communion and cooperation—in a sense, the worship of society itself (Durkheim 1915). The more significant functionalist studies of ideology explored the 'function' of specific institutions or beliefs in relieving anxiety, reducing intra-societal conflict, and enforcing social conformity. For example, Malinowski argued that magic relieved anxiety about the uncontrollable elements of life,[41] functionalist studies of witchcraft accusations stressed their role in dramatizing and transforming individual or group conflicts and tensions,[42] and one influential study interpreted statistical correlations as evidence that active high gods 'function' to enforce moral codes in complex societies.[43]

Some of these functionalist studies of religious ideology have been useful in elucidating the integration of specific religious institutions and beliefs with other aspects of the social system. They did not merely dismiss religion as an inevitable reflection of social structure (as did some structural-functionalists) or as a mystical disguise for elements of subsistence strategy (*à la* Marvin Harris). Nonetheless, functionalist approaches to ideology could not address the central question of interest here, the role of ideology in cultural evolution. Due to its static nature, the functionalist model was inappropriate for the analysis of such diachronic problems.

As we (above, pp. 197-8) and many other critics[44] have noted, cultural materialism and most other forms of cultural ecology are, conceptually, only variations on the classical functionalist theme. The only difference is that 'environmental adaptation', a balance between population and resources, replaces Malinowski's 'cooperation for basic human needs' or Radcliffe-Brown's 'maintenance of social structure' as the principle defining and determining the functions of a group's traits and institutions. In cultural materialist models culture is designed to preserve the balance between a society and its environmental context, and changes can only be generated by external pressures which upset that balance. Culture itself is passive and, in the absence of external pressures, remains static. The neo-functionalism (cf. Orlove 1980) of most varieties of cultural ecology has all of the limitations of classical functionalism, including the confusion of assumed functions with historical origins, the organic metaphor, and the inability to deal with sustained internal conflict, maladaptation, or social collapse. The cultural materialist version has the additional flaw of a pretense of diachronic analysis. As we have seen, in this kind of analysis culture can be made to move in an evolutionary sense only by bolting a misfiring demographic engine to the static functionalist chassis.

However, by avoiding the pretensions of cultural materialism, some neo-functionalist equilibrium models of cultural ecology (like functionalist studies before them) can provide insights into the nature of social systems. For example, they can be used to evaluate actual cultural behavior in terms of the projected ideal ecological 'functioning' of a society. In the past decade, some versions of cultural ecology have borrowed sophisticated concepts from biology and cybernetics, particularly systems theory and feedback models.

So-called 'systems theory' is an approach to modeling that focuses on the organizational workings of the phenomenon under study—be it an organism, ecosystem, or a society in its environmental context. This approach describes and analyzes systems according to the way their components are interrelated by using multi-directional models of causality such as deviation-amplifying (positive) and deviation-dampening (negative) feedback, 'linearization', segregation, and so on (for more complete introductions to systems modeling in anthropology see for example Flannery 1972; Rappaport 1971; Plog 1975). As has been shown in both ethnography and archaeology,[45] such systems models of cultural adaptation can be used to generate specific hypotheses on the structure of social institutions, societies' short-term responses to ecological stress, and the incremental effect of initially minor changes in cultural systems.

Yet it should be remembered that systems approaches do not in and of themselves constitute a single specific 'theory' of culture. As a recent conference on 'system theories' concluded, the popular term

> 'general systems theory' is slightly misleading. There is no single systems theory; there are many ways to examine the dynamic relationships among parts and the implications of these relationships for the whole.[46]

To achieve an understanding of cultural evolution, the bundle of concepts and techniques now used for systems and feedback models must be informed by some higher-level theory, and any specific systems model is no better than the theory used to select its variables and define its structure. If functionalism, cultural materialism, or equilibrium-maintenance versions of cultural ecology are chosen as the guiding theories, then the resulting models cannot accurately explain culture *change*. Despite more complex and more explicit presentations, such systems models still treat culture as passive and essentially static, since they explain change only as a response to external threats to a society's state of social harmony or ecological equilibrium. Consciously instituted change, initiated by the actions of individuals, subgroups, or classes, cannot be incorporated into functionalist or neo-functionalist models.

Nor are massive social transformations like those of the Aztec and Inca compatible with this perspective on cultural evolution.[47] As we have seen with the Precolumbian empires, such transformations do occur, and they are often driven by *consciously instituted* adaptations motivated by identifiable individual, small-group, and class interests. Therefore, no matter how sophisticated the modeling methods employed, it is not enough to provide functional evaluations of a society's cultural elements, including religious beliefs and practices. Analyses of cultural evolution must also account for the historical origins of traits and institutions in the complex interplay between human will and cultural adaptation.

Ideology, free will, and the search for an evolutionary approach

Our analyses of the rapid transformations, expansions, and collapses of the Mexica and Inca states demonstrate that theories of cultural evolution must address some very tricky problems of anthropology and philosophy—problems that archaeologists have been reluctant to face. Ideology and belief systems were shown to be fundamental to the most dynamic aspects of the Mexica and Inca societies. Politically motivated changes in these belief systems created the new ideologies that in turn became both the keys to success and the sources of instability in Aztec and Inca imperialism. Furthermore, the ideological changes restructured the economic systems so that expansion became advantageous for important interest groups and inescapable as state policy. Thus the histories of these Precolumbian empires prove that ideology, however difficult it may be to deal with archaeologically, must be included as a principal variable in analyses of culture change.

A second 'lesson' of Precolumbian imperialism touches upon the even more treacherous problem of 'free will' versus necessity in human history. Anthropologists are able to skirt the unresolvable philosophical questions surrounding this issue. However, we must confront the fact that the only reconstructions of culture change able to survive scrutiny are ones which consider the motivations and actions of individuals and interest groups. It follows that human volition must be incorporated into any convincing general theory on cultural evolution. The inclusion of human desires, ambitions, and motivations in models of culture change does not spell the 'emic' catastrophe predicted by the cultural materialists. Indeed, the systematic study of the structural similarities in human behavior must have—and always has had—a central place in anthropology. Unfortunately, theories concerned with general cultural evolution and theories about human motivations, group interests, or belief patterns have been almost mutually exclusive.

The particular history of American anthropology and archaeology helps to explain this disjunction between evolutionism and theories concerned with human beliefs or conflicting intra-societal interests and desires. The revival of American anthropology's interest in general theories of cultural evolution was led by Leslie White and Julian Steward, both of whose evolutionary theories were dominated by a concern with cultural ecology. White's evolutionism, perhaps the more influential version, was primarily concerned with discovering the 'laws' of cultural development.[48] White's laws were derived from his view of human history as a competition between energy systems. For example, his 'Law of Cultural Dominance' stated:

> that cultural system which more effectively exploits the energy resources of a given environment will tend to spread in that environment at the expense of less effective systems.[49]

Such principles, the building blocks of White's theory, are clearly deterministic. Drawing on his own reading of Marx, White held that religion and ideology were 'epiphenomenal' factors in evolution. In his view ideology was a by-product of technology and economy, and he could not have been more explicit about the technoeconomic determinism of his approach.

> The technological factor is the basic one; all others are dependent upon it. Furthermore, the technological factor determines, in a general way at least, the form and content of the social, philosophic, and sentimental sectors.[50]

> We set forth a theory of technological determination of cultural systems. Social systems and ideologies were seen as functions of technological systems.[51]

> The philosophy, or ideological component, of every culture thus far is made up of naturalistic and supernaturalistic elements. The role of each in any given situation is determined by the underlying technology.[52]

We should also note that White's laws contain the failings of cultural ecological and cultural materialist theories that too literally impose biological analogies on human social systems—the foremost of these analogies being what we have called the 'organic fallacy'.

Steward's 'multilineal' version of evolutionism was less reductionist, since he placed a far greater emphasis on a society's total 'cultural core'. He defined this term to mean 'the constellation of features which are most closely related to subsistence activities and economic arrangements'.[53] Steward was willing to allow social, political, and religious elements into the core if they were obviously tightly linked to economic features. In the final analysis, however, Steward left no doubt that he too considered environmental adaptations by societies' technology and subsistence systems to be the primary determinants of culture *change*.

> Cultures do, of course, tend to perpetuate themselves, and change may be slow... But over the millennia cultures in different environments have changed tremendously, and these changes are basically traceable to new adaptations required by changing technology and productive arrangements.[54]

Thus, while White and Steward took the crucial step of reintroducing the study of macroevolution to American anthropology, they also led their followers down the path of technological determinism and biological reductionism.[55] In ethnography cultural ecologists like Harris and Vayda combined White's and Steward's concepts with neo-functionalist interpretations of specific institutions to produce the cultural materialist tradition criticized above. In archaeology the revival of theoretical concerns in the early 1960s began as an explicit preaching of White's ideas. Lewis Binford's (1962) seminal article 'Archaeology as Anthropology' applied White's concepts to the interpretation of artifacts, while later theoretical syntheses of the New Archaeology merely restated White's neo-evolutionism in the updated jargon of systems modeling (e.g., Watson, LeBlanc, and Redman 1971).

While the study of cultural evolution was revived in a form that denied any causal role for volition or ideology, other anthropological schools did analyze human belief systems, psychology, and motivation—but without any concern for cultural evolution. Cognitivism, psychological anthropology, and other explicitly 'emic' approaches to culture have directly studied the nature of human motivation, cognitive categories, and ideological systems. However, while the works of these schools have contributed to a synchronic understanding of culture, they have usually not been interested in questions of cultural evolution.

There has long been the potential for evolutionary studies utilizing religious ideology and volition, but it has never been realized. A good example of these unfulfilled possibilities can be found in the pioneering studies of Max Weber. In his classic work Weber (1930) argued that the origins of capitalism could not be separated from the rise of Protestantism, whose beliefs and values *motivated* the participants in the economic transformation and provided the very dynamics of change. Had Weber gone on to produce a general theory comparable to that of Marx and Engels, he might have founded a tradition of anthropological debate on the role of ideology in cultural evolution. Unfortunately, he died prematurely, without distilling a set of unifying arguments from his individual case studies of Protestantism and other religions. It should be noted that Weber's writings did generate considerations of values and ideology across a broad range of studies in history and sociology. However, to date his work has had no lasting effect on evolutionary theorists in American anthropology and archaeology.[56]

As matters stand, the most influential of the current theories dealing with ideology is undoubtedly structuralism. Claude Lévi-Strauss and his disciples see the patterns reflected in myth, ritual, and social structure as surface reflections of the underlying cognitive structures of the universal human consciousness—i.e., the way the human mind thinks. Structuralists argue that any society's distinctive ideas and their cultural expressions are logically unfolding transformations of a few basic binary oppositions that underlie all human thought (life:death, male:female, self:others, and so on). Using these basic concepts to generate complicated analyses, structuralist anthropologists have given us some fascinating insights into specific cultures' cognitive categories, myths, or social and political institutions. However, the convoluted reasoning of structuralism raises problems of both logic and verification, and its results tend to be highly controversial.[57]

In any case, this currently popular method of studying belief systems seems to have little relevance to general theories of cultural evolution. In its pure form structuralism is concerned with the universal processes of human thought and does not seek causal explanations of cultural differences, let alone of culture change. Some anthropologists claim that their proposed structuralist transformations of one set of cognitive structures into another can also be applied as chronological models of shifts in social structures or institutions (e.g., Friedman 1974, 1975; Godelier 1978c; Meillassoux 1972). Yet even those who believe that structuralism can be applied to historical and evolutionary problems must derive the *dynamic* aspects of their analyses from other, truly diachronic theoretical approaches such as Marxism (see below, pp. 212-15).

On other fronts, some anthropologists have made important breakthroughs in studying specific aspects of ideology's role in culture change. For example, Anthony Wallace's studies (e.g., 1956, 1966, 1970) of religious revitalization movements demonstrated that in specific situations religion can be a powerful agent affecting political change and cultural realignment. Nonetheless, such contributions have focused on particular diachronic problems without clearly drawing general conclusions for the study of cultural evolution. In any case, evolutionists and archaeologists remained unaware of the broader implications of these works and retained a non-ideological, determinist, and materialist slant in their own approaches.

We can conclude that the history of anthropology has led to a lamentable dismemberment of the body of concepts needed for holistic study of cultural evolution. Theories that meaningfully address culture change and cultural evolution in American anthropology and archaeology have been deterministic and/or functionalist in their logic and have treated ideology and human volition as dependent or epiphenomenal variables. Meanwhile, theories and specific analyses of cultures that have addressed the perplexities of religious ideology, cognition, and will have generally been limited in focus and synchronic in structure—in other words, unconcerned with the problems of general cultural evolution.

Admittedly the state of the art is perhaps less dismal than we have portrayed it. In both anthropology and archaeology there have been grumblings of dissatisfaction with the simplistic biological and ecological thinking that dominates evolutionary studies. In American archaeology scholars such as Kent Flannery and Gordon Willey have challenged their colleagues to look beyond technoeconomic reductionism.

> How do ideas, or ideologies, articulate with other cultural systems? This is a complex question, and archaeologists, in their study of the rise and growth of civilizations, have been hesitant to address it... Still, if thinking human beings are the generators, as well as the carriers, of culture it seems highly probable that, from very early on, ideas provided controls for and gave distinctive forms to the materialist base and to culture, and that these ideas then took on a kind of existence of their own, influencing, as well as being influenced by, other cultural systems. If this is so, then it is of interest and importance to try to see how ideas were interrelated with other parts of culture and how they helped direct the trajectories of cultural and civilizational growth.[58]

> Archaeologists must cease to regard art, religion and ideology as mere 'epiphenomena' without causal significance...such 'epiphenomena'...lie at the heart of society's environmental and interpersonal regulation, and as such cannot be omitted from any comprehensive ecological analysis...[59]

Meanwhile, cultural ecologists, systems theorists, and others have begun to question deterministic models of cultural evolution which offer no role for human choice, group interest, or class action (see for example Orlove 1980; Rodin et al. 1978; Diener 1980; Rappaport 1978a).

No satisfactory answer, in the form of a coherent, complete theory, can yet be provided for these challenges or the questions raised by our own analyses of the evolution of Mexica and Inca society. There are, however, the beginnings of a response in a number of recent works on cultural evolution. Surprisingly, some of these glimmerings of hope have arisen from an old theoretical tradition usually considered the very bastion of technoeconomic determinism: Marxism!

Marxism comes of age

Marxism, from its very inception as a political and historical doctrine, has seemed ambivalent about the question posed above. Marx's theory was diachronic, historical, and eventually influenced by the early version of cultural evolutionism formulated by Lewis Henry Morgan (1877). However, the strongest formative influence on Marx's thought was the dialectical philosophy of Hegel, who believed that any idea ('thesis') automatically evokes an opposing idea ('antithesis'). This contradiction is resolved by a third idea, or 'synthesis', which then becomes a new thesis and brings forth its own antithesis, leading to a new synthesis, and so on up the line. Drawing on Hegelian philosophy, Marx proposed a theory of human progress in which dialectical conflicts in individual actions, 'class consciousness', and other *volitional* elements formed the most dynamic (indeed, violent) aspect of historical development.

Yet, unlike Hegel, Marx believed in the '*economic* interpretation of history', and many aspects of his theory have a strongly deterministic tone. In some readings of Marx, a society's economic base is said to determine the nature of its political and ideological institutions. Furthermore, 'orthodox' interpretations of Marx hold that in its evolution any given cultural tradition passes through specific developmental stages as man's technology leads to the mastery of nature, producing successive transformations of the economic system.

In essence, then, the writings of Marx and his co-author Friedrich Engels were inherently ambiguous about the relative emphasis to be placed on motivation or choice and on technoeconomic determinism. This ambiguity has dominated subsequent applications of Marxist ideas to history and anthropology. The confusion lies in varying interpretations of Marx's concepts concerning the economy. Marxist theory defines a 'social formation' as consisting of an *infrastructure* (the 'forces of production' and corresponding 'relations of production') and an associated *superstructure* of social, political, and ideological elements and institutions. The very definitions of these concepts and their causal linkages to one another are a source of controversy that has divided contemporary Marxists into bitterly opposed camps.[60]

Many 'orthodox' Marxists see technology and subsistence systems, the forces of production, as *determining* the nature of the 'relations of production'. The latter include all those elements of society involved in 'material production and reproduction'—access to resources, distribution of the products, economic stratification, and so on. Many Marxists go further to insist that the economic base or 'infrastructure' determines the nature of most elements in the 'superstructure' of social and political institutions and ideologies. Thus, the forces of production generate the relations of production, which together as the society's economic infrastructure determine the corresponding superstructure of politics, ideology, etc.[61] Clearly environment and technology dominate this interpretation of history, and such versions of Marxist theory can be little different from cultural materialism. Technoeconomic determinists cite those statements of Marx which support such a reductionist view of human history.

> In the social production of their existence, men inevitably enter into definite relations, which are independent of their will, namely relations of production appropriate to a given state in the development of their material forces of production. The totality of these relations of production constitutes the economic structure of society, the real foundation, on which arises a legal and political superstructure and to which correspond definite forms of social consciousness. The mode of production of material life conditions the general process of social, political and intellectual life. It is not the consciousness of men that determines their existence, but their social existence that determines their consciousness...changes in the economic foundation lead sooner or later to the transformation of the whole immense superstructure. In studying such transformations it is always necessary to distinguish between the material transformation of the economic conditions of production, which can be determined with the precision of natural science, and the legal, political, religious, artistic or philosophic—in short, ideological forms in which men become conscious of this conflict and fight it out. Just as one does not judge an individual by what he thinks about himself, so one cannot judge such a period of transformation by its consciousness, but, on the contrary, this consciousness must be explained from the contradictions of material life...[62]

Emphasis on these aspects of Marx's writings guides one to a technoeconomic theory of history. For decades many Marxist writings in the Soviet Union and Europe have propounded this view that technology determines economy and economy determines all other aspects of society. In particular, religious ideology is dismissed as a mystified reflection or sacred justification of the existing economic system (and its inequities)—beliefs and values are little more than 'the echoes of this life process'.[63] This school of Marxist thought has produced mechanical interpretations of history in which developing human technology drags all other aspects of society through a rigid succession of predetermined stages dominated by specific modes of production ('slavery', 'feudalism', 'capitalism', and so on).[64]

In view of our previous discussion and the Aztec and Inca cases, this version of Marxism is clearly untenable. We have demonstrated that ideology can be an independent variable transforming the economic system itself, rather than merely legitimizing the traditional order. The 'stages' as a sequence of 'modes of production' have no meaning in the Precolumbian world, to which concepts like 'slavery' and 'feudalism' can be applied only in the vaguest sense, with no chronological order or explanatory force. There are also logical objections. For example, the driving element, technology, seems to exist simply as a given. Neither the level of technology in any specific society nor the reasons for successive technological changes are explained. Like the 'population pressures' of the cultural materialists, technology and the 'forces of production' are mystically existent and teleologically dynamic in many applications of orthodox Marxism.

Unfortunately, it is this mechanistic variant of Marxism—denounced by less doctrinaire contemporary Marxists—that has had the greatest impact on American anthropology and world archaeology. In American anthropology, Steward, White, and other evolutionists were influenced by the deterministic aspects of Marx. Marvin Harris and others have granted Marx the dubious distinction of being the founder of cultural materialism. In archaeology V. Gordon Childe (1936, 1954, 1957, etc.) repeatedly applied a technologically dominated version of Marxism in his influential syntheses of Old World culture history. Karl Wittfogel (1957) reworked some of Marx's concepts to argue that the development of irrigation technology led to the rise of early Asiatic states and determined their despotic form. This offshoot of mechanical Marxism sent archaeologists scurrying across the deserts of Mesopotamia, Mexico, and Peru seeking to explain the rise of the state by finding early canal sytems. While Wittfogel's 'hydraulic theory' has been disproven by archaeological research in most regions,[65] there are still a few archaeologists clinging to fragments of the hypothesis.[66] Rigid, explicitly deterministic versions of Marxism are still influential in American archaeology, as is indicated by two recent textbooks (Smith 1976; Patterson 1981).

Though the mechanical variant of Marxism has been the most influential in archaeology and cultural materialism, it represents only one extreme in the range of Marxist interpretations. Disagreement over the meaning of basic concepts like 'mode of production' and 'relations of production', along with varying emphases on the causes and role of 'social consciousness', the dialectic of class struggle, and other volitional elements, have generated a great variety of Marxist approaches. Some of them were merely strident political statements, some were deterministic theories of history, and others were more complex approaches to historical development. However, recent research in ethnography and archaeology, as well as theoretical debate, has rendered technoeconomic determinism less plausible as an explanation of social change. Reflecting this shift, contemporary versions of Marxist anthropology have begun to place a greater emphasis on the role of non-technological factors such as political action and ideology in human history.

The most intriguing of these new Marxist approaches, 'structural-Marxism', combines Lévi-Strauss's structuralist approach to kinship with Marx's historical theory. As we mentioned above (p. 208), one of structuralism's goals is to explain how one kinship structure can be logically transformed into another. However, while structuralism in its pure form analyzes the structural similarities and derivations of kinship systems, it does not attempt to provide a historically ordered explanation of their transformations. As some Marxists have noted, structuralism *per se* is an essentially synchronic theory.

> The structuralist can generate a system of transformations, but he cannot explain how they are to be distributed, which forms can or cannot occur and the limiting conditions of their existence.[87]

But by combining structuralist transformations of kinship systems with a historical direction and causal explanation provided by Marxist analyses of economic development, structural-Marxists seek to create a holistic, economically grounded, and diachronic approach to the evolution of social systems.

> The 'concrete factors' which are exterior to the structuralist analysis are an essential component of the Marxist analysis.[68]

> By determining the real relationship between forces and relations of production as well as understanding the internal structure of the latter, we can hope to go a long way towards explaining the distribution and development of social formations.[69]

From our perspective the fascinating aspect of structural-Marxism is that it is an attempt to incorporate ideology into the oldest *economic* theory of history. This realization of the role of ideology rests on structural-Marxists' understanding that the economic base is itself defined by, 'embedded in', and inseparable from the totality of society. Recall that in Marxist theory the all-important economic base, or infrastructure, consisted of the forces of production and the corresponding 'relations of production'. The latter were limited by many orthodox Marxists to those aspects of social organization directly associated with material production (division of labor, control of resources, ownership, etc.). Yet some structural-Marxists recognize that such 'relations of production' are themselves inseparable from ideas and institutional factors that would traditionally be called 'social', 'political', or 'ideological' elements of the 'superstructure'.[70]

For example, Maurice Godelier has argued that in ancient Greece political concepts and institutions functioned to determine the division of labor, access to resources, distribution of wealth, and so on. In other words, politics functioned as the 'relations of production' and were therefore part of the infrastructure.

> In conclusion, the economy of a Greek city during the Classical period was a coherent whole, even in its contradictions. For us the source both of this coherence and these contradictions was the same and was to be found in the fact that political relations functioned as relations of production giving this system its original form and structure as a totality.[71]

This willingness to allow nominally 'superstructural' elements into the economic base has brought harsh criticism from more orthodox Marxists and cultural materialists, who accuse the structural-Marxists of being 'soft-core Marxists' (Harris 1979: 229), or of not being Marxists at all (e.g., Tagányi 1978).

Of particular interest to us is some structural-Marxists' inclusion of religious ideology as a critical factor in economics, and, therefore, in the dynamics of their economic theory of history. For example, Friedman's interpretation (1975) of the evolution of the Kachin state in southeast Asia asserts that the ideology of ancestor worship defined the levels of status and prestige in society.[72] In turn, the varying ideological prestige of groups and individuals defined their political and economic stratification as well. Furthermore, Friedman argues that changes in these ideological elements were central to the transformation of Kachin society and its shift to a highly stratified state system. Thus religious ideology, usually considered an element of the 'superstructure', can actually *dominate* the nature of relations in the economic 'infrastructure' and the dynamics of historical change.

> A change in dominance can be explained only by taking the whole social formation into account, for if we restrict ourselves to the infrastructural level alone, we exclude the possibility that a formerly super-structural element will become part of the relations of production, a phenomenon which characterizes the great majority of historical transformations.[73]

In an example closer to home, Godelier argues that Inca ideology was actually an inseparable part of the 'relations of production' in the economic base of Inca society.[74] He stresses the Incas' identification of their king with the sun and thus the ideological reinforcement of the ruler's absolute political and economic control of society.

> But, in this context, we see that religious ideology is not merely the superficial, phantasmic reflection of social relations. It is an element internal to the social relations of production; it functions as one of the internal components of the politico-economic relation of exploitation between the peasantry and an aristocracy holding State power. This belief in the Inca's supernatural abilities, a belief shared by the dominated peasantry and the dominant class alike, was not merely a legitimising ideology, after the fact, for the relations of production; it was a part of the internal armature of these relations of production.[75]

The most sophisticated structural-Marxist theories are at least attempting to achieve a more holistic approach to historical causality. Escaping the technoeconomic straitjacket, Friedman, Godelier, and some other contemporary Marxists include religion, politics, and other motivational and ideological factors in their historical interpretations. They explicitly reject any form of 'vulgar materialism' in which technology, ecology, or demography are seen as 'prime movers'.

> If we are to transcend the false determinism that claims to be able to explain a society in terms of one of its parts, systematically doing away with the problem of history, we must aim at a complete theory of structural transformation...[76]

While most Marxists reject the possibility of a general theory of cultural evolution, these recent breakthroughs in Marxist-historical theory parallel cultural evolutionists' increasing interest in multicausal approaches and the role of ideology (see below, pp. 221-4). Indeed, in both their strengths and weaknesses recent structural-Marxist analyses exemplify the current state of the search for a theoretical approach to religion's role in cultural change.

Dynamic ideologies: beyond legitimation

It is encouraging to see the structural-Marxists' shift toward holistic studies. However, comparison to the Aztec and Inca cases (see below) indicates that they have not gone far enough toward reintegrating ideology into models of culture change. The restraints seem to be imposed by several of Marx's original concepts. For example, Godelier retains the rule that 'base determines superstructure' by allowing the infrastructural 'relations of production' to include all the elements of religion, kinship, and politics that affect the economic system (e.g., Godelier 1977, 1978a,b,c).[77] Similarly, Bloch (1978) explicates the importance of kinship ideology in Merina economics by distinguishing between the aspects of ideology accepted to be functioning elements of the political economy and what he considers pure ideology. The latter is defined as 'the system of ideas...separated from the reality of life' and dismissed as 'pseudo-reality'.[78] Again, the traditional economic orientation of Marxism is retained by redefining the *causally* active aspects of ideology to be elements of economic relations. Thus, even the writings of those contemporary Marxists most interested in holistic approaches (e.g., Godelier, Friedman, Terray, Bloch) show certain *a priori* limits in their evaluation of ideology. In this sense, some aspects of the original works of Marx and Engels may have themselves become 'fetters on the development of the mode of analysis'!

It is the structural-Marxists' assumptions about the *legitimating* role of ideology that show the most constraining effect of some traditional Marxist tenets. Ever since Marx and Engels' analyses of capitalist societies, Marxist approaches have always stressed the legitimating role of ideology, particularly in its most institutionalized forms such as state religion and public ritual. In general, there is an essential truth to this perspective. It does appear that a primary 'function' of ideology in stratified societies is to justify the existing order, including the unequal distribution of power and property. Yet review of the Aztec and Inca cases shows, on both empirical and logical grounds, that the dynamics of culture change cannot be understood if legitimation is held to be the *only* effect of ideological systems.

We should first note how widespread (in practice if not in theory) is the doctrine that ideology serves only to legitimate the existing order. In Marxist analyses this tenet is explicit in the assertion that ideology either justifies the 'relations of production' or is merely their phantasmic reflection. In other materialist studies or 'atheoretical' descriptions a similar interpretation is usually implicit. Even recent attempts to define the state have incorporated such interpretations of ideology in their lists of necessary traits:

> (6) The population shows a degree of social stratification so that emergent social classes (rulers and ruled) can be distinguished.

> (7) A common ideology exists, on which the legitimacy of the ruling stratum (the rulers) is based.[79]

Likewise, recent cross-cultural surveys of early states have concluded that ideology served this limited purpose.

> State ideologies, as our sample data attest, were obviously designed for the justification and perpetuation of the early state and of the basic division of the society into two main strata or emergent classes.

> The most important element in the legitimation of the state and the eventual establishment of its ideology was the belief in the supernatural qualities of the sovereign.[80]

> Everywhere a basic myth of the society concerned...which legitimized the position of its leader, chief or sovereign, was found...This seems to suggest that, generally speaking, the role of the state ideology is one of legitimizing, explaining, or justifying...We are inclined to believe, however, that ideological activities have no more than a secondary influence upon the formation of the early state...[81]

Turning specifically to current analyses of the Aztec and Inca states, we find that scholars holding a wide range of theoretical perspectives share this restricted interpretation of the purpose of ideology. For example, in an article suitably entitled 'The Legitimation of the Aztec State' Kurtz concludes that in such 'inchoate' (non-centralized) polities 'the state obtains religious justification for the social order' through ideology.[82] Kurtz also stresses the role of the state mythology in legitimating the power of the *tlatoani* and nobles and the effectiveness of the sacrificial cult as a tool of intimidation, 'state directed terror'. Similarly, Bray argues that Aztec state religion 'was calculated to legitimise the highly stratified social system', while mass human sacrifice was used for 'political intimidation'.[83]

For the Inca, legitimization of authority is also seen as the primary effect of religion and ideology,[84] although recent analyses have begun to realize that something more was involved. For example, Schaedel argues that Inca state religion 'to some extent legitimized hierarchical levels of differentiation',[85] but he also notes the *active* role of ideology in the 'cognitive integration' of economic and political networks. Furthermore, though Schaedel stresses the economic and political rationality of the state religion, he seems puzzled by its 'anti-economic' mass sacrifices of animals, food, and goods in rituals of 'extravagant consumption'. Perhaps because of the overwhelmingly religious 'tone' of the Inca state, Godelier (1977, 1978a) also expresses some uneasiness with an interpretation of Inca religion as merely legitimating authority 'after the fact' (see the quotation on p. 214). He has gone beyond Schaedel in stressing the importance of religious legitimation in integrating Inca society. Godelier focuses on the myth of the ruler's descent from the sun and its role in actively motivating, as well as legitimating, the relations of production through the aggrandizement of the Inca dynasty.

All of these analyses are correct in seeing legitimation as a primary effect (both intentional and unintentional) of religious ideology. As our own analyses in the preceding chapters have emphasized, Kurtz, Bray, and Schaedel are correct in viewing the imperial ideologies as conscious products designed to legitimate the authority and further the interests of the military elites who came to power through the transformational crises. The 'ideological adaptations' sanctioned the new orders, including the more militaristic tenor of state policy and the highly stratified and inequitable 'relations of production'. The new state religions were also intended to justify these upstart conquest states in the eyes of their more established neighbors. Furthermore, as each empire's stratification and institutional order grew more complex, ideology also became more complicated through conscious and unconscious responses to new needs for legitimation. For example, Broda (1976) has shown how growing stratification within *pochteca* guilds was reified and justified by new ceremonies and mythology.[86] Murra (1960) has shown that changes in Inca ritual were designed to legitimate the increasing state emphasis on corn (rather than tuber) agriculture. Demarest (1981: 43-9, 71-5) has hypothesized that even more fundamental changes in the upper pantheon sanctioned these new agricultural concerns.

Godelier (1977, 1978a) is also correct in stressing the active aspect of religious legitimation. As he argues, the sanctions of state religion played an active role in integrating and mobilizing the state's social, political, and economic institutions. In both the Aztec and Inca cases the effects of religious ideology went beyond merely justifying the militaristic and self-interested policies of the elite. The reformed state cults also *motivated* society while legitimizing the social order, since they generated the active participation of all classes.

Note, however, that while Godelier has gone somewhat beyond the usual Marxist interpretations, he does not really go beyond a legitimizing role for ideology: he merely emphasizes its *active* aspect more than other Marxists. Godelier speaks *only* of the state cult of the sun god, Inti, and its effects on the social relations of production. Yet as we have seen in Chapters 3 and 4, the elaboration of the royal cult of the dead, and particularly the eternal property rights of deceased rulers, were far more crucial in generating the needs, structure, and expansionism of the Inca state. The same can be said for the Mexica elite's (perhaps inadvertent) creation of an open-ended demand for captured warriors through changes in the sacrificial cult. The cults of Inti and Huitzilopochtli legitimized imperialism, but the elevation and transformation of the Inca cult of the dead and the Aztec sacrificial cult actually *necessitated* expansionism by creating dynamic imbalances in these two societies. These imbalances did not merely justify conquest for economic gain. Rather, they demanded expansionism in response to the Aztec sacrificial cult's need for warriors' blood and the Inca ancestor cults' strain on land and resources.

This verifiable reality goes far beyond the usual *a priori* theoretical perspective on the role of religious ideology. In these two cases, ideology did not just legitimate the social order, as most scholars have argued, or legitimate and motivate social relations, as Godelier has posited. Religious reforms actually helped to generate and form the political, economic, and social order. Thus, ideology was a key factor in the historical formation of the Aztec and Inca 'relations of production'. In fact, ideology was the most dynamic aspect of these relations, driving expansionism through legitimation and evangelism, but more importantly through the creation of concrete (and eventually staggering) economic imbalances.

Ultimately, the inadequacy of analyses that limit ideology's role to legitimation can usually be traced to exactly the same cause, regardless of the underlying theoretical position. When cultural materialists, cultural ecologists, or Marxists discuss religious ideology, they often slip inadvertently into functionalist interpretations. Then they mistake their hypotheses about ideology's *functions* for actual verifiable reconstructions of *history*. A recent statement of the template for development exemplifies this kind of reasoning, in which a set of synchronic functionalist interpretations of religious ideology is transmuted into a diachronic sequence by imposing a predetermined chronological and causal order on events.

> In more generally applicable terms the state develops a theology to support its authority system giving it a legitimacy that is omnipotent and supernatural. As the power and authority of the leader is increased, through the increased demands placed on his office by his people, so too are the religious and symbolic meanings and beliefs which enhance and explain his power to others inside his society and beyond. What was previously a set of beliefs

> concerned with fertility of land and people, of rectitude sanctioned
> and defended by the people, the ancestors, and the spirits of a
> locality, now becomes state religion whose avowed purpose is to
> provide sanctions for the legitimacy of the ruler, his duties to his
> people and they to him, and for his capacity to contact and intercede
> with the supernatural for their benefit.[87]

Without any actual historical evidence for doing so, the anthropologist
has assumed a causal order that denies religion a major role in cultural
dynamics. Beliefs and values are simply dragged along by unfolding
economic and political processes.

Analyses of the legitimating purpose of Aztec and Inca religion follow
this tradition of imposing a predetermined historical order on functional
interpretations. For example, after discussing Mexica state religion from
a purely synchronic perspective, Kurtz (1978) reaches the following
conclusions:

> It was suggested that the Aztec state represented an inchoate
> incorporative state (Cohen 1969), that is one which has not usurped
> the power of local centers of potential autonomy within its national
> territory and thus, is not very legitimate. One way for a state to
> overcome inchoatcy is to acquire legitimacy, or the support of the
> polity, as quickly as possible...

> At the core of this process is the establishment of authority based
> upon law, for the state requires and obtains validation to pursue
> legitimacy from legal institutions and codified laws. In addition,
> the state obtains religious justification for the social order, values,
> and ideology it is trying to develop from state affiliated religious
> institutions and personnel.[88]

This reconstruction, like nearly every other treatment of Aztec and Inca
ideology, incorrectly shifts from functionalist to historical explanations.
The 'inchoate nature' of the Aztec state is introduced as a given, and
the ideology is assumed to have arisen in some unspecified manner, but
definitely after the fact, to carry out its legitimating 'function'.

The real order of historical events requires a less neatly unidirectional
interpretation of the causal interplay among institutions. While legitimation was the major intended function of the new state religion, it was
far from the only actual *effect*. As we demonstrated in Chapter 2,
modifications of Mexica state religion helped both to generate the Aztec
Empire itself and to give it a *decentralized* form. Aztec expansionism was
driven by both the desire for tribute for the economic system and the
demand for captives for the sacrificial cult. These demands were most
easily met by a far-flung, loosely knit imperialism. The fact that such
an 'inchoate' structure virtually assured constant rebellions was not only
acceptable, but actually desirable: rebellions and their military
suppression furnished the captives desperately needed by the state cult
to stave off the sun's demise (and viewed more cynically, to maintain
the ideological order of the entire imperial system). In other words, the

'inchoate' nature of the Aztec Empire was not merely justified by Mexica beliefs and values—it was largely a *result* of that ideology.

Clearly we must go beyond mere 'legitimation' in analyzing the role of ideology in cultural evolution. For example, if one tries to maintain the structure of a Marxist analysis and still arrive at valid conclusions, then ideology and economics must be examined together without any confusion of 'function' and effect, and without any preconceived notions as to where ultimate causality lies. If such a flexible perspective is taken, a modified structural-Marxist approach could be applied to the Inca and Aztec cases. It would differ little in substance from the conclusions given in Chapter 4—though it would be restructured by a Marxist analytical framework and translated into the appropriate jargon. Yet some of the results of such a 'Marxist' analysis, one which would not *impose* a model of unidirectional causality, could be truly surprising.

For example, Marxist analyses generally seek to discover the internal contradictions in a society that lead to stress, inter-class tension, and eventually to social revolution (and thence to the ascent of a new 'social formation'). In the Aztec and Inca cases, the internal contradictions in the relations of production included not only exploitative economic and political relations, but the tremendous exacerbation of these inequities by imbalances resulting from the sacrificial cult and property rights of the dead. In the Aztec case, Moctezuma II failed to stabilize the ideologically driven expansion and the contradictions it generated. As a result, at the time of the Conquest the Aztec Empire was torn by inter-class tensions, growing economic pressures, and ceaseless regional revolts. Ultimate social crisis was inevitable, given the Mexicas' inability to escape the ideology of expansionism.

In the Inca case, the tensions generated by contradictions within the expansionist social order actually reached the point of crisis before the Spanish Conquest. The Inca civil war itself can be seen as a kind of class struggle. Huascar and his supporters were well aware of the direct and indirect strains placed upon the society by the control of too much of the nation's rich agricultural lands ('the means of production') by an 'exploitative, parasitic class'—the dead! Huascar's own actions may have been motivated by self-interest, given his frustrated need for land to establish his own ancestor cult. Yet regardless of his motives, Huascar's response to these stresses pitted him and his followers against the vested interest of society's most privileged class, the dead rulers and the powerful *panaqa* cults that administered their lands. Seen from this perspective, Huascar's shocking proposal to eliminate the royal ancestor cult was nothing less than a call for agrarian reform and social revolution, as is echoed in the very tone of the rhetoric attributed to him:

> [Huascar] said that he ought to order them [the mummies] all buried and take from them all that they had, and that there should

not be dead men but living ones, because [the dead] had all that was best in the country.[89]

Thus, the accurate application of a Marxist model to the Aztec and Inca cases requires interpretations unanticipated by orthodox Marxists—including class struggle between the living and the dead![90] When viewed in a *historical* perspective, the interrelations between religious, political, and economic elements and institutions can be structured by a Marxist framework, but they *cannot* be assigned any *a priori* order of causality (cf. Demarest ms.). For the Aztec and Inca, the admission of a critical and dynamic role for ideology can be avoided only by completely ignoring large portions of the society's religious system and their effects on culture change. Precisely this error—ignoring the broader evolutionary effects of Aztec sacrifice and Inca ancestor worship—has characterized both Marxist and non-Marxist approaches to these Precolumbian empires.

For both the Aztec and Inca, the development of the state apparatus and economic order was tightly and inextricably interwoven with the development of the imperial ideology. As was indicated in Chapter 4, causal interrelationships were exceedingly complex; when they can be sorted out at all, they can only be revealed by detailed *historical* research. Such research indicates a crucial role for religion as it interacted with other forces in the development of Precolumbian imperialism. Ideology was manipulated to legitimize power, but in turn religious reforms greatly influenced the nature of the developing state political and economic systems. Initially, religion was a key element in the dynamics of Aztec and Inca expansionism; later, it became an inescapable maladaptive force in the dynamics of imperial collapse. Recent evidence indicates that in the historical trajectories of other states and civilizations ideology has also played such a truly causal role (e.g., Freidel 1981, Conrad 1982).

Ideology and cultural evolution: toward a holistic approach

Despite our many criticisms, we are encouraged by the positive aspects of recent studies of ideology and culture change. Across a wide range of theoretical schools, archaeologists and ethnohistorians, the anthropologists most interested in large-scale cultural change, are attempting to grapple with the difficult task of finding a coherent approach to the role of ideology in cultural evolution. Unfortunately, their analyses, while seeking holism, have usually found only functionalism. It has been difficult for many anthropologists to see beyond ideology's legitimating function to its broader effects on the actual dynamics of cultural evolution. Nonetheless, their efforts have shown the way toward more holistic studies, as well as some of the pitfalls to be avoided.

In this regard, it is fascinating to note how closely current trends in

Marxist interpretations parallel those in cultural ecology, systems theory, and other theoretical approaches. We have seen that the recent work of the structural-Marxists decries mechanical materialism and seeks to incorporate volition, motivation, and ideology—in other words, social consciousness—into models of historical change. Along with some other contemporary Marxist anthropologists, the structural-Marxists argue that by ignoring these factors mechanical materialist approaches have become a kind of behaviorism in which culture exists merely to justify, rather than also to direct, human action. They explicitly reject any approach which relegates beliefs to a passive role and dismisses the force of independent human volition—including Marxist concepts of 'praxis', theory-in-action, and social consciousness.[91]

Many contemporary Marxists eschew general theories of evolution, seeing purely historical analysis as their goal (e.g., Legros 1977; Mendelson 1979). It is surprising, then, that their shift toward volitional, cultural interpretations so closely parallels shifts in anthropological evolutionism. For example, in cultural ecology, perhaps for entirely different reasons, a similar dissatisfaction with determinism has spread through the field during the past decade. In a recent review of ecological anthropology Orlove (1980) has charted this trend. As he notes, recent processual approaches have included 'actor-based models' that stress human variability and decision-making strategies. Note that considerations of decision-making return us to a concern with human motivations, volition, and beliefs, which in their collective expression *are* ideology. As Orlove concludes, this trend must inevitably guide cultural ecology away from deterministic or equilibrium models and closer to the holistic perspective we seek.

> The incorporation of decision-making models as mechanisms of change has led to a greater emphasis on social organization and culture. Social and cultural systems influence the goals which actors have, the distribution of resources which they use, and the constraints under which they operate... As this work progresses, materialist and idealist approaches in anthropology are likely to find more common ground through a more thorough interpretation of culture and ideology as systems which mediate between actors and environments through the construction of behavioral alternatives.[92]

Paralleling this trend in cultural ecology are new concerns in 'systems theory' approaches, which most often model culture-environment interaction. A recent conference on systems theory failed to develop any coherent approach to human volition and ideology. Yet most of the participants stated that the incorporation of such factors and the escape from mechanical materialism were a major goal of current studies in this field. They agreed that systems applications must avoid

> the assumption that human systems are bound by mechanistic links so that an event must evoke a unique response. Such models...

reduce human behavior to determinate output and ignore the variability of social behavior.[93]

They also came to several other conclusions closely paralleling the lessons of Aztec and Inca history that we reviewed in Chapter 4:

> we recognized the conceptual and operational difficulties of modeling situationally plastic human action... To apply 'system' characteristics to individual actors is an ecological fallacy.

> While the attribution of purpose to social systems is fallacious, the failure to attribute goals to individuals and corporate groups is also in error. Social systems analysis must encompass the dynamics of uneven distributions of beliefs, abilities, knowledge, and resources among people, as well as the genuinely differing goals among individuals and the corporate groups they form.[94]

Indeed, one of the pioneers of cultural ecology and systems modeling in anthropology, Roy Rappaport (1978a,b), is now actively attempting to incorporate human volition and beliefs into systems models, not only of adaptation, but of *mal*adaptation as well. As he argues, systems models must acknowledge that 'organisms are, and in their nature must be, more coherent than social systems...'.[95] Thus, as we have argued, it is necessary to avoid the 'organic fallacy' and to account for the varying motivations of individuals and interest groups. Rappaport emphasizes the factor of systemic 'usurpation' in human ecological systems:

> it becomes increasingly possible for ancient and complex systems, particularly ecological systems, to be disrupted by ever smaller groups with ever more narrowly defined interests...the short-run interests of a few powerful men or institutions come to prevail...[96]

In the Aztec and Inca cases, we have seen precisely this kind of divergence from the concept of unified, organic 'adaptiveness'. As critics have noted (e.g., Whyte 1978) and Rappaport (1978b) himself admits, systems models that incorporate volition, ideology, and maladaptation still face many problems of both logic and application—primarily because of the essentially homeostatic orientation of the cybernetic reasoning that still lies beneath most systems models. Nonetheless, they have begun to evaluate human social behavior in its full spectrum of manifestations, including class interests, irrationality, and the kind of ideologically and politically reinforced 'negative feedback cycles' that drove the Inca and Aztec Empires to ruin.

Thus, systems theorists, cultural ecologists, Marxists, and neo-evolutionists are all struggling toward holistic models of cultural dynamics. One reason for this consensus is that such models, even in their present flawed state, can more easily explain the sudden and radical culture changes that have actually characterized much of human history. The rapid transformations, cancerous expansions, and swift disintegrations of the Precolumbian empires were only particularly dramatic examples of phenomena all too common in human history. Archaeologists have uncovered the fossil remains of dozens of such 'exploding' social systems in the New World alone. Models of materialist determinism or ecological equilibrium are unable to account for such transformations, radical shifts, and maladaptations. No form of determinism can explain these phenomena precisely because they are largely the products of human will, class interests, and ideological imperatives— volitional elements whose importance is denied by deterministic theories. So the recent interest in 'quantum evolution' in both biological and cultural evolutionary theory has encouraged social scientists to seek explanations of such irregularities in culture process.[97] Despite differing theoretical orientations, anthropologists and archaeologists have been led back to conscious human action (and its motivation in class interest, ideology, and belief) in the search for the source of such salient irregularities in historical development.

While we consider this return to cultural holism a positive development in social science, it nonetheless brings us back to some of the oldest and nastiest philosophical questions. 'Rationality versus irrationality', 'free will versus necessity', and other paradoxes that anthropologists have tried to ignore must once again raise their ugly heads. The cultural ecologist, faced again with age-old questions, is also confronted by the identity crises that accompany them.

> We are led to a yet more radical question. If civilization with its maladaptive regulatory hierarchies and misguiding ideologies is an inevitable outcome of culture, and culture in turn an inevitable outcome of the human level and type of intelligence, and if human intelligence is capable of violating adaptive logic, we may ask if human intelligence is in the long run adaptive, or if it is merely an evolutionary anomaly bound finally to be destroyed by its own contradictions or the contradictions of its cultural products.[98]

Though these concerns and fears are real ones, the return of volition to anthropological thinking can also be viewed in a positive light. As Ronald Cohen (1981), Rappaport (1978a), and Whitebook (1976) have all recently observed, it can reanimate the discipline by giving it the possibility of meaning and utility through the application of theory. For while deterministic and materialist theories may have avoided the philosophical problems of free will and consciousness, they did so by essentially denying free will. Yet if human behavior is mechanically determined by external and ecological processes, then it follows as a rather discomforting corollary that social science cannot serve to redirect history or help us to avoid previous errors. So, in a sense, the return to models including volition and ideology in cultural evolution rescues us from deterministic fatalism. We can once again logically entertain the possibility of a social role for the social scientist. In response to this escape from determinism, those few anthropologists interested in volition and ideology (whether Marxists, cultural ecologists, or neo-evolutionists) have sounded a call for such an active role for the discipline.

> Insofar as the subject matter of the social sciences does indeed consist of subjects who are capable of self-consciousness, the theory does not stand on one side and the field of investigation on the other; but to the degree theory becomes part of the self-understanding of the subjects, it also becomes a moment of its own field of investigation. In short theory, as Marx put it, can become a material force.[99]

> Conscious reason has entered into evolutionary processes for better or worse. It cannot be ignored and should, obviously, be put to the task of ameliorating adaptive difficulties... We must, therefore, investigate the possibilities for developing theories of action which, although based upon incomplete knowledge, will permit us to participate in systems without destroying them and ourselves along with them.[100]

> Evolutionary theory is a viable and productive means for building a platform, both scientific and visionary, from which to see realistically into our past and our future. We are not going inevitably anywhere; we have the power to create some of our future and to understand where we have come from, where we are now and why, and where we may try to go.[101]

Unfortunately, the majority of archaeologists have remained unaware of these recent important shifts in the thinking of the most perceptive anthropological theorists. Many archaeologists continue to work toward the goal of erecting neat, deterministic theories with invariable 'laws' and little or no role for mankind's most problematic, but also most human, aspect: ideology. If we are to redirect archaeology toward holistic studies, we must make ideology itself a more comprehensible object of study—rather than an unpredictable element, and thus an obstruction to evolutionary theory (as many archaeologists now view it). To do so we must try to discover generalizations (*not* 'laws') about the nature of ideology and its dynamic effects, and our only hope of deriving such generalizations lies in archaeological and ethnohistorical research on ideology's role in the development of ancient social systems. Here we have offered an analysis of the dynamics of two such systems, the expanding Aztec and Inca Empires. Similar studies of other culture-historical trajectories must be undertaken if we are to achieve a broader comparative perspective on ideology in cultural evolution.

Undertaking such studies in archaeology will be a difficult task. But in accepting this challenge we can reanimate the field with a positive motivation. For, as the anthropological theorists cited above have realized, if ideology affected past developments, it follows that contemporary ideologies and their anthropological re-education can alter our own direction and, perhaps, help us to avoid some of the disasters that seem to lie ahead. In view of the state of research, these activist aspirations may be just as unrealistic as they were over a century ago, when archaeology began to take form as a social science. But at least the original goal itself has been returned to us: the hope that our study of the past may, in some small measure, help to guide us into the future.

Notes to Chapter 5

1 See Chapter 4, pp. 166-7.
2 See Chapter 4, pp. 165-6.
3 See Chapter 4, pp. 167-9.
4 See Chapter 4, pp. 158-61; 170-1.
5 Sanders, Parsons, and Santley 1979: 364.
6 Or they are unable to provide any real empirical data. See the critique of Paulsen's theory in Chapter 4, pp. 166-7.
7 For summaries of the nature and results of these projects see especially Wolf 1976; Sanders, Parsons, and Santley 1979; Parsons 1968b, 1971, 1974; Sanders 1970, 1972; Blanton 1972a,b.
8 For presentation of the hypothesis to be tested see Logan and Sanders 1976, and also Sanders 1956, 1968, 1972; Sanders, Parsons, and Santley 1979: ch. 1.
9 Sanders, Parsons, and Santley 1979: 252-81, 385-92; Sanders and Santley 1977; Sanders et al. 1970; Armillas, Palerm, and Wolf 1956; Nichols 1982.
10 This point seems to be overlooked in most of the sources cited above. As Adams (1965, 1966; Adams and Nissen 1972) has demonstrated in Mesopotamia, only complex, regionally regulated irrigation systems necessitate state control. None of the pre-fifteenth-century canal and irrigation systems so far discovered in the Valley of Mexico would have required more than local cooperation (on the village or even extended family level).
11 See Chapter 4, pp. 155-8, 163-4.
12 Sanders, Parsons, and Santley 1979: 378.
13 Sanders, Parsons, and Santley 1979: 378.
14 See for example Santley 1980; Sanders and Santley 1978; Blanton 1980, 1976b,c; Kowalewski 1980; Flannery 1977.
15 Nardi 1981: 31.
16 Nardi 1981; Devereux 1967; Lee 1972; Beshers 1967; Mamdani 1974; Carr-Saunders 1922; Langer 1974; Wrigley 1969; Himes 1963; Polgar 1971, 1972, 1975.
17 Harris 1968: 4.
18 See especially Harris 1979: 77-114 for a brief recapitulation of the cultural materialist history of mankind.
19 See for example Harris's recent popular collections of essays on materialist 'solutions' to cultural riddles: *Cows, Pigs, Wars, and Witches: The Riddles of Culture* (1974b), *Cannibals and Kings: The Origins of Cultures* 1977).
20 e.g., Simoons 1979; Azzi 1974; Ortiz de Montellano 1978; Price 1978; Sahlins 1973, 1978; Castile 1980; Diener, Nonini, and Robkin 1978, 1980; Diener and Robkin 1978; Diener, Moore, and Mutaw 1980.
21 See note 20.
22 See especially Simoons 1973, 1979; Simoons and Simoons 1968; Diener, Nonini, and Robkin 1978, 1980; Diener and Robkin 1978; Azzi 1974.
23 Diener, Nonini, and Robkin 1978: 223. See also Gilman 1981: 3.
24 Diener, Nonini, and Robkin 1978: 223.
25 Friedman 1974: 466.
26 See Harris 1979: ch. 2 or Harris 1968: ch. 20 for an explicit presentation

of the theory that the 'emic' and 'etic' perspectives can be segregated. For denouncements of the evils of 'emics' see Harris 1974c as well as introductions and scattered comments in Harris's popular works (1974b, 1977), in his materialist textbook (1980: 115-16), or his critical history of anthropological theory (1968).

27 Harris 1977: xii.

28 Harris 1964: 17, 1979; see note 26 for further references.

29 Harris 1977: xi.

30 See Paul and Rabinow 1976, Fisher and Werner 1978, and especially Oakes 1981 for discussions of the logical and operational problems inherent in the emic/etic distinction. As these authors point out, each of Harris's materialist 'solutions' to cultural riddles contains within it a shift from 'etic' to 'emic' levels like the one exposed here concerning demographic drives (pp. 200-1).

31 Harris 1979: 69.

32 Harris 1979: 69.

33 Harris 1979: 68-9.

34 cf. sources cited in note 16.

35 For other critiques of 'emic' fallacies within Harris's 'etic' solutions to cultural riddles see Oakes 1981; Diener, Nonini, and Robkin 1978, 1980; Diener, Moore, and Mutaw 1980; Paul and Rabinow 1976; Diener and Robkin 1978.

36 For example see Malinowski 1927, 1929, 1935, and especially 1922: ch. 1, 1939, 1944, 1945, 1948 for his classic functional analyses of cultural institutions.

37 For this version of functionalism see especially Radcliffe-Brown 1935, 1946, 1949, 1952, 1957. Note the widespread influence of Radcliffe-Brown's theories as a major perspective in related fields such as sociology (via Talcott Parsons' writings and teaching).

38 Radcliffe-Brown 1952: 181.

39 Radcliffe-Brown 1952: 195.

40 Diener, Nonini, and Robkin 1978: 223.

41 Malinowski 1948.

42 e.g., Fortune 1932; Evans-Pritchard 1937, 1956; Middleton and Winter 1963.

43 Swanson 1960.

44 e.g., Paul and Rabinow 1976; Orlove 1980; Friedman 1974; Diener and Robkin 1978; Diener, Nonini, and Robkin 1978; Gilman 1981; Kohl 1981: 97-101.

45 e.g., Rappaport 1967, 1971; Flannery 1972; Blanton 1976b; Plog 1975; Vayda 1976, Vayda and McCay 1975.

46 Rodin, Michaelson, and Britan 1978: 749. See also Kohl 1981: 94-5.

47 There is currently a growing interest in quantum evolution and relatively rapid transformations of biological species or cultural systems. The assumption of relatively gradual rates of change and cybernetic modeling of the nature of change have been challenged from various quarters. In the theory of biological evolution 'punctuated equilibrium' models are gaining credence, paralleled by anthropologists' interest in structuralist and Marxist models (among others) of system transformations. See for example Eldredge 1976, 1979; Eldredge and Gould 1972; Gould and Eldredge 1977; Dodson 1975; Woodcock and Davies 1978 on the quantum revolution in biology. See Diener 1980 for a review of similar thinking in anthropology. Note the relationship of this shift to the trend discussed below on volitional elements in anthropological theory.

48 Sahlins and Service (1960) have most explicitly reworked and presented White's theories of macro-evolution.

49 Kaplan 1960: 75.

50 White 1959: 19.

51 White 1959: 273.

52 White 1959: 23.

53 Steward 1955: 37. Steward spent much time in his theoretical writings disagreeing with White's general evolutionism and stressing non-ecological factors in evolution. Nonetheless, the general direction of his work is revealed by its applications in ecological models, his support of such deterministic theories as Wittfogel's (see below), and his effect on archaeology. Indeed, despite Steward's inclusion of non-technoeconomic elements in the 'culture core', he can be seen as perhaps the primary source of the dominance of cultural materialist theory in archaeology for the past two decades.

54 Steward 1955: 37.

55 This may seem a bit harsh, especially to Steward, who was well aware of the non-ecological elements in cultural evolution. Nonetheless, it does accurately describe the *effect* of their work and the basic theoretical slant that created that effect (see note 53).

56 This statement is particularly true of American archaeology, where Weber's influence on recent theoretical developments has been virtually nil.

57 Structuralism is one of the most popular theoretical approaches in social anthropology today, and we can hardly provide a full review of its concepts, methods, and literature here. For discussions of basic principles see Lévi-Strauss (1963, 1966) or Leach (1976); for the cultural materialist critique of structuralism see Harris (1968: ch. 18, 1979: ch. 7). For an unconvincing argument that 'pure' structuralism is the only kind of historical analysis possible see Leach (1977).

The strengths and limitations of structuralism for our purposes are evident in the largest single body of structuralist writings on the New World empires, R. Tom Zuidema's analyses of Inca society. Zuidema (1958, 1962, 1964) originally tried to apply Lévi-Strauss's (1969) concept of 'generalized exchange' to Inca social organization but later decided that the concept was invalid. He now believes that he has found the organizing principle of Inca religion, astrology, calendrics, ritual, myth, and kinship in a cosmological descent model of a male line and a female line, both descending in four generations from a male founder (Zuidema 1973, 1977a,b,c,d; Zuidema and Quispe 1968; Zuidema and Urton 1976). Zuidema has provided some invaluable insights into Andean ideology, but his arguments are extremely complicated, and his conclusions tend to be highly controversial. Furthermore, the avowed goal of his analyses is to discover the basic cognitive structures shared by *all* native Andean societies, pre- and post-Conquest alike (Zuidema and Quispe 1968: 25). This search for pan-Andean similarities seeks to strip away, rather than explain, synchronic differences and diachronic changes in Andean cultures. Therefore, it runs counter to our attempt to find the *unique* factors responsible for the transformations of Inca society.

58 Willey 1976: 205.

59 Flannery 1972: 400.

60 Inevitably, our own discussion of Marxism and structural-Marxism must fail to satisfy many proponents of these contradictory interpretations, particularly given both our brevity and our rejection of 'orthodox' versions

of Marxism. Note that the controversies and debates among Marxists usually center around the exact definitions of critical terms such as 'mode of production', 'relations of production', 'social formation', etc. For our purposes here we do not think it is necessary to give a full review of the terminological debate, which appears to be unresolvable, at least within the context of Marx's own writings. As Legros, Hunderfund, and Shapiro (1979) have recently shown, the ambiguity of the terminology can be traced to Marx's original works.

61 Again, note that there are many alternative definitions of these terms; here we are simplifying for the sake of brevity. For example, compare Legros 1977, Friedman 1974, and Godelier 1978c. Also see note 60.

62 Marx, *Contribution to the Critique of Political Economy*, 1971: 20-1.

63 Marx and Engels in Bottomore 1956: 75.

64 The works of Marx which were most influential in anthropology were the *Contribution* cited above in note 62, *Pre-Capitalist Economic Formations* (1965), *Capital* (1975), and Engels's *The Origin of the Family, Private Property, and the State* (1972).

65 Adams 1965, 1966, 1969; Adams and Nissen 1972; Moseley 1975b; R. Millon 1973.

66 Recent attempts to document irrigation works in the Valley of Mexico (e.g. Armillas, Palerm, and Wolf 1956; Sanders 1965, 1972; Sanders, Parsons, and Santley 1979; Sanders and Santley 1977; Wolf 1976) are, of themselves, an important contribution to our knowledge of the prehistory of the region. Yet their findings often have been assumed to correspond to the causal order of Wittfogel's hydraulic theory. As discussed above (pp. 155-7, 193-4), neither the chronological placement nor the scale of these runoff and canal systems argues for a determinative role for irrigation before the fifteenth century. See Blanton 1976c, 1980; Flannery 1977, for critiques of this Mexican research and note 65 for evidence from other regions refuting Wittfogel's theory.

67 Friedman 1974: 453.

68 Friedman 1974: 455.

69 Friedman 1974: 456. For more complete expositions of structural-Marxist theory see Bloch 1975; Godelier 1977, 1973; Friedman and Rowlands 1978; Meillassoux 1972; and, most concisely, Friedman 1974 and Godelier 1978c, who draw a sharp distinction between structural-Marxism and deterministic materialism.

70 Again, terminology is quite controversial, and even the more 'liberal' contemporary Marxist thinkers disagree over the content, role, and breadth of these concepts. See notes 60 and 61 above.

71 Godelier 1978b: 27.

72 Note that Friedman (1975) integrates a Marxist interpretation of techno-economic development with a structuralist interpretation of the transformation of Kachin social structure via the development of conical clans. Ideology provides both the mechanism and justification for this shift to a stratified social and political structure.

73 Friedman 1975: 198.

74 Godelier 1978a, 1977: ch. 2.

75 Godelier 1978a: 8-10; see also Godelier 1977: ch. 2. Compare to Demarest 1981 for a detailed exposition of Inca solar worship and the interplay between doctrine, economics, and political legitimation in Inca state religion.

76 Friedman 1975: 198.

77 cf. Friedman 1974.

78 Bloch 1978: 336.
79 Claessen and Skalnik 1978a: 21.
80 Skalnik 1978: 606.
81 Claessen and Skalnik 1978b: 628.
82 Kurtz 1978: 185.
83 Bray 1978: 392.
84 e.g., Katz 1972: 291-3, 198-9.
85 Schaedel 1978: 312.
86 See Chapter 2, pp. 51-2.
87 R. Cohen 1978: 64-5.
88 Kurtz 1978: 185.
89 Pizarro 1844: 240. Translation by John H. Rowe (1967: 68), interpolations (except [the dead]) added. See Chapter 3, note 163 for a discussion of this quotation.
90 Even if put in less dramatic terms, the determination of property distribution by the concept of property rights of the dead unquestionably generated inequities in land distribution that eventually helped to trigger the civil war. Given the motivations attributed to Huascar, the characterization of the civil war as a class struggle over land can be justified. While Huascar was for most purposes a member of the ruling class, in this case the conflict was between the landed classes (the dead, the *panaqas*, and their supporters) and those who perceived themselves as having insufficient land—including Huascar. Atauhualpa apparently took advantage of this struggle to further his own personal interests.
91 e.g. Diener 1980; Diener, Moore, and Mutaw 1980; Diener, Nonini, and Robkin 1980; Godelier 1978c; Friedman 1974; Whitebook 1976; Mendelson 1979; Legros 1977; Kohl 1981; see above, pp. 213-15.
92 Orlove 1980: 262.
93 Rodin, Michaelson, and Britan 1978: 751.
94 Rodin, Michaelson, and Britan 1978: 751.
95 Rappaport 1978a: 53.
96 Rappaport 1978a: 63.
97 See note 47 on the current interest in rapid transformations in both biology and anthropology. See also Colin Renfrew's (1978, 1979) attempts to apply catastrophe theory to archaeology. However, catastrophe theory does not seem capable of dealing with ideology, volition, motivation, and their expressions in conscious action. Therefore, in our opinion Renfrew's applications of catastrophe theory provide only graphic representations, but not real *explanations*, of rapid, massive social transformations.
98 Rappaport 1978a: 67.
99 Whitebook 1976: 185.
100 Rappaport 1978a: 68.
101 R. Cohen 1981: 208.

BIBLIOGRAPHY

Acosta, Jorge R.
  1940 Exploraciones en Tula, Hidalgo, 1940. *Revista Mexicana de Estudios Antropológicos*, vol. 4, pp. 172-194.
  1944 La tercera temporada de exploraciones en Tula, Hidalgo, 1942. *Revista Mexicana de Estudios Antropológicos*, vol. 6, pp. 125-164.
  1956a El enigma de los chacmooles de Tula. In *Estudios Antropológicos Publicados en Homenaje al Doctor Manuel Gamio*, pp. 159-170. Mexico: Sociedad Mexicana de Antropología.
  1956b Resumen de los informes de las exploraciones arqueológicas en Tula, Hidalgo, durante las VI, VII, y VIII temporadas, 1946-1950. *Anales del Instituto Nacional de Antropología e Historia*, vol. 8, pp. 37-115.
  1956-57 Interpretación de algunos de los datos obtenidos en Tula relativos a la época tolteca. *Revista Mexicana de Estudios Antropológicos*, vol. 14, pp. 75-110.
  1957 Resumen de los informes de las exploraciones arqueológicas en Tula, Hidalgo, durante las IX y X temporadas, 1953-54. *Anales del Instituto Nacional de Antropología e Historia*, vol. 9, pp. 119-169.
  1960 Las exploraciones en Tula, Hidalgo, durante la XI temporada, 1955. *Anales del Instituto Nacional de Antropología e Historia*, vol. 11, pp. 39-72.
  1961 La doceava temporada de exploraciones en Tula, Hidalgo. *Anales del Instituto Nacional de Antropología e Historia*, vol. 13, pp. 29-58.
  1964 La décimotercera temporada de exploraciones en Tula, Hidalgo. *Anales del Instituto Nacional de Antropología e Historia*, vol. 16, pp. 45-76.
Acosta, Joseph de
  1894 *Historia Natural y Moral de las Indias* (1590). 2 vols. Madrid: Ramon Anglés.
Adams, Robert McC.
  1965 *Land Behind Baghdad: A History of Settlement on the Diyala Plains*. Chicago: University of Chicago Press.
  1966 *The Evolution of Urban Society*. Chicago: Aldine.
  1969 The study of ancient Mesopotamian settlement patterns and the problem of urban origins. *Sumer*, vol. 25, pp. 111-124.
Adams, Robert McC., and Hans J. Nissen
  1972 *The Uruk Countryside: The Natural Settling of Urban Societies*. Chicago: University of Chicago Press.
Aguilar, Francisco de
  1963 The chronicle of Fray Francisco de Aguilar. In *The Conquistadors: First-Person Accounts of the Conquest of Mexico*, edited by P. de Fuentes, pp. 134-164. New York: Orion Press.

Albornoz, Cristóbal de
(See Duviols 1967)
Alcina Franch, José
1976 *Arqueología de Chinchero, 1: La Arquitectura.* Memorias de la Misión Científica Española en Hispanoamérica, no. 2. Madrid: Ministerio de Asuntos Exteriores.
Alcina Franch, José, Miguel Rivera, and others
1976 *Arqueología de Chinchero, 2: Cerámica y Otros Materiales.* Memorias de la Misión Científica Española en Hispanoamérica, no. 3. Madrid: Ministerio de Asuntos Exteriores.
Allyne, Gao, R. Hay, D. Picon, J. Stanfield, and R. Whitehead
1977 *Protein-Calorie Malnutrition.* London: E. Arnold.
Anales de Cuauhtitlan
1975 Anales de Cuauhtitlan. In *Códice Chimalpopoca,* translated by P. Feliciano Velázquez, pp. 3-118. Mexico: Instituto de Investigaciones Históricas.
Anales de Tlatelolco
1948 *Anales de Tlatelolco.* Edited by Heinrich Berlin. Mexico: Antigua Librería Robredo.
Anales Mexicanos
1903 Anales Mexicanos, México-Azcapotzalco (1426-1589). *Anales del Museo Nacional de México,* época 1, vol. 7, pp. 49-74.
Anawalt, Patricia R.
1977 What price Aztec pageantry? *Archaeology,* vol. 30, pp. 226-233.
1980 Costume and control: Aztec sumptuary laws. *Archaeology,* vol. 33, no. 1, pp. 33-43.
1981 *Indian Clothing Before Cortés: Mesoamerican Costumes from the Codices.* Norman: University of Oklahoma Press.
Anonymous
1848 *Copia de Carta que Según una Nota se Hallaba en el Archivo General de Indias ... y se Impugna la Opinión del Padre Fr. Bartolomé de las Casas* (1571). Colección de Documentos Inéditos para la Historia de España, compiled by Miguel Salvá and Pedro Sainz de Baranda, vol. 13, pp. 425-469. Madrid: Imprenta de la Viuda de Calera.
1919 Idolatrías de los indios Huachos y Yauyos (1613). *Revista Histórica,* vol. 6, pp. 180-197. Lima.
1920 *Informaciones del Virrey Toledo, Verificados en Jauja, Cuzco, Guamanga, y Yucay* (1570-72). Colección de Libros y Documentos Referentes a la Historia del Perú, edited by Horacio H. Urteaga, 2nd series, vol. 3, pp. 103-144. Lima: Sanmartí.
Arens, William
1979 *The Man-Eating Myth: Anthropology and Anthropophagy.* New York: Oxford University Press.
Armillas, Pedro
1971 Gardens in swamps. *Science,* vol. 174, pp. 653-661.
Armillas, Pedro, Ángel Palerm, and Eric R. Wolf
1956 A small irrigation system in the Valley of Teotihuacan. *American Antiquity,* vol. 21, pp. 396-399.
Arriaga, Pablo Joseph de
1920 *La Extirpación de la Idolatría en el Perú* (1621). Colección de Libros y Documentos Referentes a la Historia del Perú, edited by Horacio H. Urteaga and Carlos A. Romero, 2nd series, vol. 1. Lima: Sanmartí.
1968 *The Extirpation of Idolatry in Peru* (1621). Translated and edited by L. Clark Keating. Lexington: University of Kentucky Press.

Avila, Francisco de
1966 *Dioses y Hombres de Huarochirí* (ca. 1598). Fuentes e Investigaciones para la Historia del Perú, Textos Críticos, no. 1. Lima: Instituto de Estudios Peruanos.
Azzi, Corry
1974 Comment on Harris. *Current Anthropology*, vol. 15, pp. 317-321.
Bandelier, Adolph F.
1878 On the distribution and tenure of lands and the customs with respect to inheritance among the ancient Mexicans. *11th Annual Report of the Trustees of the Peabody Museum of American Archaeology and Ethnology*, vol. 2, pp. 385-448. Cambridge: Harvard University.
1880 On the social organization and mode of government of the ancient Mexicans. *12th Annual Report of the Trustees of the Peabody Museum of American Archaeology and Ethnology*, vol. 2, pp. 557-699. Cambridge: Harvard University.
1904 On the relative antiquity of ancient Peruvian burials. *Bulletin of the American Museum of Natural History*, vol. 20, pp. 217-226.
1910 *The Islands of Titicaca and Koati*. New York: The Hispanic Society of America.
Barlow, Robert H.
1949 *The Extent of the Empire of the Culhua Mexica*. Ibero-Americana, no. 28. Berkeley: University of California Press.
Beckerman, Stephen
1979 The abundance of protein in Amazonia: a reply to Gross. *American Anthropologist*, vol. 81, pp. 533-560.
Berdan, Frances
1975 Trade, Tribute, and Market in the Aztec Empire. Ph.D. dissertation, Department of Anthropology, University of Texas, Austin.
1976 La organización del tributo en el imperio Azteca. *Estudios de Cultura Náhuatl*, vol. 12, pp. 185-196.
1977 Distributive mechanisms in the Aztec economy. In *Peasant Livelihood: Studies in Economic Anthropology and Cultural Ecology*, edited by R. Halperin and J. Dow, pp. 91-101. New York: St Martin's Press.
1978 Tres formas de intercambio en la economía Azteca. In *Economía, Política e Ideología en el México Prehispánico*, edited by P. Carrasco and J. Broda, pp. 77-94. Mexico: Centro de Investigaciones Superiores.
Bernal, Ignacio
1957 Huitzilopochtli vivo. *Cuadernos Americanos*, vol. 16, pp. 127-152. Mexico.
Beshers, James M.
1967 *Population Processes in Social Systems*. New York: The Free Press.
Betanzos, Juan Diez de
1924 *Suma y Narración de los Incas* (1551). Colección de Libros y Documentos Referentes a la Historia del Perú, edited by Horacio H. Urteaga, 2nd series, vol. 8, pp. 75-208. Lima: Sanmartí.
Binford, Lewis R.
1962 Archaeology as anthropology. *American Antiquity*, vol. 28, pp. 217-225.
Blanton, Richard E.
1972a *Prehispanic Settlement Patterns of the Ixtapalapa Peninsula Region, Mexico*. Occasional Papers in Anthropology, no. 6. University Park, PA: Department of Anthropology, The Pennsylvania State University.
1972b Prehispanic adaptation in the Ixtapalapa region, Mexico. *Science*, vol. 175, pp. 1317-1326.
1975 The cybernetic analysis of human population growth. In *Population Studies in Archaeology and Biological Anthropology: A Symposium*, edited by A.

C. Swedlund, pp. 116-126. Society for American Archaeology Memoirs, no. 30.

1976a Anthropological studies of cities. *Annual Review of Anthropology*, vol. 5, pp. 249-264.

1976b The role of symbiosis in adaptation and sociocultural change in the Valley of Mexico. In *The Valley of Mexico*, edited by E. R. Wolf, pp. 181-202. Albuquerque: University of New Mexico Press.

1976c Comment on Sanders, Parsons, and Logan. In *The Valley of Mexico*, edited by E. R. Wolf, pp. 179-180. Albuquerque: University of New Mexico Press.

1978 *Monte Albán: Settlement Patterns at the Ancient Zapotec Capital*. New York: Academic Press.

1980 Cultural ecology reconsidered. *American Antiquity*, vol. 45, pp. 145-151.

Bloch, Maurice

1978 The disconnection between power and rank as a process: an outline of the development of kingdoms in central Madagascar. In *The Evolution of Social Systems*, edited by J. Friedman and M. J. Rowlands, pp. 303-340. London: Duckworth.

Bloch, Maurice (editor)

1975 *Marxist Analysis and Social Anthropology*. London: Malaby Press.

Borah, Woodrow, and Sherburne F. Cook

1963 *The Aboriginal Population of Central Mexico on the Eve of the Spanish Conquest*. Ibero-Americana, vol. 45. Berkeley: University of California Press.

Boserup, Ester

1965 *The Conditions of Agricultural Growth*. Chicago: Aldine.

Bottomore, T. B.

1956 *Marx's Social Theory*. London: Watts.

Bram, Joseph

1941 *An Analysis of Inca Militarism*. American Ethnological Society Monographs, no. 4.

Braniff, Beatriz

1972 Secuencias arqueológicas en Guanajuato y la Cuenca de México: intento de correlación. *XI Mesa Redonda Sobre Problemas Antropológicos de México y Centro América*, vol. 2, pp. 273-323. Mexico: Sociedad Mexicana de Antropología.

Bray, Warwick

1978 Civilizing the Aztecs. In *The Evolution of Social Systems*, edited by J. Friedman and M. J. Rowlands, pp. 373-398. London: Duckworth.

Broda, Johanna

1976 Los estamentos en el ceremonial Mexica. In *Estratificación Social en la Mesoamérica Prehispánica*, edited by P. Carrasco and J. Broda, pp. 37-66. Mexico: Centro de Investigaciones Superiores.

1978 El tributo en trajes guerreros y la estructura del sistema tributario Mexica. In *Economía, Política e Ideología en el México Prehispánico*, edited by P. Carrasco and J. Broda, pp. 175-194. Mexico: Centro de Investigaciones Superiores.

Brotherston, Gordon

1974 Huitzilopochtli and what was made of him. In *Mesoamerican Archaeology: New Approaches*, edited by N. Hammond, pp. 155-166. London: Duckworth.

Browman, David L.

1978 Toward the development of the Tiahuanaco (Tiwanaku) state. In *Advances in Andean Archaeology*, edited by D. L. Browman, pp. 327-349. The Hague: Mouton.

1980 Tiwanaku expansion and altiplano economic patterns. *Estudios Arqueológicos*, no. 5, pp. 107-120. Antofagasta: Universidad de Chile.

Brumfiel, Elizabeth M.
1976 Regional growth in the eastern Valley of Mexico: a test of the 'population pressure' hypothesis. In *The Early Mesoamerican Village*, edited by K. V. Flannery, pp. 234-249. New York: Academic Press.

Brundage, Burr C.
1963 *Empire of the Inca*. Norman: University of Oklahoma Press.
1967 *Lords of Cuzco: A History and Description of the Inca People in Their Final Days*. Norman: University of Oklahoma Press.
1972 *A Rain of Darts: The Mexica Aztecs*. Austin: University of Texas Press.
1975 *Two Earths, Two Heavens: An Essay Contrasting the Aztecs and the Incas*. Albuquerque: University of New Mexico Press.
1979 *The Fifth Sun: Aztec Gods, Aztec World*. Austin: University of Texas Press.

Brush, Stephen B.
1977 *Mountain, Field, and Family: The Economy and Human Ecology of an Andean Valley*. Philadelphia: University of Pennsylvania Press.

Burger, Richard L.
1978 The Occupation of Chavin, Ancash, in the Initial Period and Early Horizon. Ph.D. dissertation, Department of Anthropology, University of California, Berkeley.
1981 The radiocarbon evidence for the temporal priority of Chavín de Huantar. *American Antiquity*, vol. 46, pp. 592-602.

Cabello Valboa, Miguel
1951 *Miscelánea Antártica* (1586). Lima: Instituto de Etnologia, Universidad Nacional Mayor de San Marcos.

Calancha, Antonio de la
1938 Corónica moralizada del Orden de San Agustín en el Perú (1638). In *Los Cronistas de Convento*, edited by Pedro M. Benvenutto Murietta, Guillermo Lohmann Villena, and José de la Riva Agüero, pp. 15-140. Biblioteca de Cultura Peruana, 1st series, no. 4. Paris: Desclée, de Brouwer.

Calnek, Edward E.
1970 The population of Tenochtitlan in 1519. Paper presented at the 69th Annual Meeting of the American Anthropological Association, San Diego, CA.
1972a Settlement pattern and chinampa agriculture at Tenochtitlan. *American Antiquity*, vol. 37, pp. 104-115.
1972b The organization of urban food supply systems: the case of Tenochtitlan. *Atti del 40 Congresso Internazionale degli Americanisti*, vol. 4, p. 97. Rome.
1973 The localization of the sixteenth-century map called the Maguey Plan. *American Antiquity*, vol. 38, pp. 190-195.
1976 The internal structure of Tenochtitlan. In *The Valley of Mexico*, edited by E. R. Wolf, pp. 287-302. Albuquerque: University of New Mexico Press.
1978 The analysis of prehispanic Central Mexican historical texts. *Estudios de Cultura Náhuatl*, vol. 13, pp. 239-266.

Carrasco, Pedro
1967 Relaciones sobre la organización social indígena en el siglo XVI. *Estudios de Cultura Náhuatl*, vol. 7, pp. 119-153.
1971 Social organization of ancient Mexico. In *Handbook of Middle American Indians*, vol. 10, edited by R. Wauchope, G. Ekholm, and I. Bernal, pp. 349-375. Austin: University of Texas Press.
1976 Los linajes nobles del México antiguo. In *Estratificación Social en la Mesoamérica Prehispánica*, edited by P. Carrasco and J. Broda, pp. 19-36. Mexico: Centro de Investigaciones Superiores.
1978 La economía del México prehispánico. In *Economía, Política e Ideología en el México Prehispánico*, edited by P. Carrasco and J. Broda, pp. 15-76. Mexico: Centro de Investigaciones Superiores.

1979 Las bases sociales del politeismo Mexicano: los dioses tutelares. *Actes du 42e Congrès International des Américanistes*, vol. 6, pp. 11-17. Paris.
1981 Comment on Offner. *American Antiquity*, vol. 46, pp. 62-68.

Carrasco, Pedro, and Johanna Broda (editors)
1976 *Estratificación Social en la Mesoamérica Prehispánica.* Mexico: Centro de Investigaciones Superiores.
1978 *Economía, Política e Ideología en el México Prehispánico.* Mexico: Centro de Investigaciones Superiores.

Carrera, Fernando de la
1939 *Arte de la Lengua Yunga* (1644). Edited by Radamés A. Altieri. Publicación Especial, no. 3. Tucumán, Argentina: Instituto de Antropología, Universidad Nacional de Tucumán.

Carr-Saunders, A. M.
1922 *The Population Problem: A Study in Human Evolution.* Oxford: Clarendon Press.

Casas, Bartolomé de las
1909 *Apologética Historia de las Indias* (1561-66). Historiadores de Indias, edited by M. Serrano y Sanz, vol. 1. Nueva Biblioteca de Autores Españoles, vol. 13. Madrid: Bailly-Bailliére e Hijos.

Caso, Alfonso
1927 *El Teocalli de la Guerra Sagrada.* Mexico: Talleres Gráficos de la Nación.
1936 *La Religión de los Aztecas.* Mexico: Enciclopedia Ilustrada Mexicana.
1939 La correlación de los años azteca y cristiana. *Revista Mexicana de Estudios Antropológicos*, vol. 3, pp. 11-45.
1945 *La Religión de los Aztecas.* Mexico: Secretaría de Educación Pública.
1951 Base para la sincronología mixteca y cristiana. *Memoria del Colegio Nacional*, vol. 6, pp. 49-66.
1953a Calendarios de los Totonacos y Huastecos. *Revista Mexicana de Estudios Antropológicos*, vol. 13, pp. 337-350.
1953b *El Pueblo del Sol.* Mexico: Fondo de Cultura Económica.
1958 *The Aztecs: People of the Sun.* Norman: University of Oklahoma Press.
1963 Land tenure among the ancient Mexicans. *American Anthropologist*, vol. 65, pp. 863-878.
1965 Sculpture and mural painting of Oaxaca. In *Handbook of Middle American Indians*, vol. 3, edited by R. Wauchope and G. R. Willey, pp. 849-870. Austin: University of Texas Press.
1966 El culto al sol. *Traducciones Mesoamericanas*, vol. 1, pp. 177-190. Mexico: Sociedad Mexicana de Antropología.
1967 *Lost Calendarios Prehispánicos.* Mexico: Instituto de Investigaciones Históricas.
1971 Calendrical systems of Central Mexico. In *Handbook of Middle American Indians*, vol. 12, edited by R. Wauchope and H. F. Cline, pp. 324-369. Austin: University of Texas Press.

Casteel, Richard
1972 Two static maximum population density models for hunter-gatherers: a first approximation. *World Archaeology*, vol. 4, pp. 19-40.

Castile, George Pierre
1980 Purple people eaters? a comment on Aztec elite class cannibalism à la Harris-Harner. *American Anthropologist*, vol. 82, pp. 389-391.

Castillo, Cristóbal del
1908 *Historia de los Mexicanos desde su Salida de Aztlan Hasta la Fundación de México.* Edited by Francisco del Paso and Troncoso. Florence.

Castillo F., Víctor M.
1972 *Estructura Económica de la Sociedad Mexica.* Mexico: Instituto de Investigaciones Históricas.

Castro, Cristóbal de, and Diego de Ortega Morejón
 1936 Relaçion y declaraçion del modo que este valle de Chincha y sus comarcanos se governavan antes que oviese yngas y despues q(ue) los vuo hasta q(ue) los (cristian)os e(n)traron en esta tierra (1558). In *Quellen zur Kulturgeschichte des Präkolumbischen Amerika*, edited by H. Trimborn, pp. 236-246. Studien zur Kulturkunde, vol. 3. Stuttgart: Strecker und Schröder.
Chadwick, Robert
 1971 Native pre-Aztec history of Central Mexico. In *Handbook of Middle American Indians*, vol. 11, edited by G. Ekholm and I. Bernal, pp. 474-504. Austin: University of Texas Press.
Chagnon, Napoleon, and R. B. Hames
 1979 Protein deficiency and tribal warfare in Amazonia: new data. *Science*, vol. 203, pp. 910-913.
Chavero, Alfredo
 1880 Explicación del códice geroglífico del Mr. Aubin. In *Historia de las Indias de Nueva España y Islas de Tierra Firme*, by Diego Durán, vol. 2, Appendix. Mexico. Imprenta de Ignacio Escalante.
Childe, V. Gordon
 1936 *Man Makes Himself*. London: Watts.
 1954 *What Happened in History*. Baltimore: Penguin.
 1957 *The Dawn of European Civilization*. New York: Knopf.
Chimalpahin Cuauhltehuanitzin, Don Francisco de San Antón Muñón
 1958 *Das Memorial Breve Acerca de la Fundación de la Ciudad de Culhuacan*. Translated by Walter Lehmann and Gerdt Kutscher. Stuttgart: W. Kohlhammer Verlag.
 1965 *Relaciones Originales de Chalco Amaquemecan*. Mexico: Fondo de Cultura Económica.
Cieza de León, Pedro de
 1922 *La Crónica del Peru* (1553). Los Grandes Viajes Clásicos, no. 24. Madrid: Calpe.
 1943 *Del Señorío de los Incas: Segunda Parte de la Crónica del Perú, que Trata del Señorío de los Incas Yupanquis y de sus Grandes Hechos y Gobernación* (1553). Buenos Aires: Ediciones Argentinas Solar.
 1959 *The Incas of Pedro de Cieza de León* (1553). Translated by Harriet de Onis and edited by Victor W. von Hagen. Norman: University of Oklahoma Press.
Claessen, Henri, and Peter Skalnik
 1978a The early state: theories and hypotheses. In *The Early State*, edited by H. Claessen and P. Skalnik, pp. 3-29. The Hague: Mouton.
 1978b Limits: beginning and end of the early state. In *The Early State*, edited by H. Claessen and P. Skalnik, pp. 619-635. The Hague: Mouton.
Clavijero, D. Francisco S.
 1826 *Historia Antigua de Megico*. 2 vols. London: R. Ackermann.
Cobean, Robert H.
 1979 The Pre-Aztec Ceramics of Tula, Hidalgo, Mexico. Ph.D. dissertation, Department of Anthropology, Harvard University.
Cobo, Bernabé
 1890-95 *Historia del Nuevo Mundo* (1653). Edited by Marcos Jiménez de la Espada. 4 vols. Seville: Sociedad de Bibliófilos Andaluces.
 1979 *History of the Inca Empire: An Account of the Indians' Customs and Their Origin Together with a Treatise on Inca Legends, History, and Social Institutions* (1653). Translated and edited by Roland Hamilton. Austin: University of Texas Press.
Codex Aubin
 1893 *Codex Aubin: Histoire de la Nation Mexicaine Depuis le Départ d'Aztlan Jusqu'à*

l'Arrivée des Conquérants Espagnols. Edited by J.M.A. Aubin. Paris: Ernest Leroux.

Codex Boturini
1944 *Codex Boturini (Tira de la Peregrinación).* Mexico: Librería Anticuaria.

Codex Ramírez
(See Tovar 1944)

Coe, Michael D.
1962 *Mexico.* New York: Praeger.
1964 The *chinampas* of Mexico. *Scientific American,* vol. 211, pp. 90-98.

Cohen, Mark N.
1977 Population pressure and the origins of agriculture: an archaeological example from the coast of Peru. In *Origins of Agriculture,* edited by C. A. Reed, pp. 135-178. The Hague: Mouton.
1978 *The Food Crisis in Prehistory.* New Haven: Yale University Press.
1981 The ecological basis for New World state formation: general and local model building. In *The Transition to Statehood in the New World,* edited by G. D. Jones and R. R. Kautz, pp. 105-122. Cambridge: Cambridge University Press.

Cohen, Ronald
1978 State origins: a reappraisal. In *The Early State,* edited by H. Claessen and P. Skalnik, pp. 31-75. The Hague: Mouton.
1981 Evolutionary epistemology and human values. *Current Anthropology,* vol. 22, pp. 201-218.

Cohen, Y. A.
1969 Ends and means in state control: state organization and the punishment for adultery, incest, and violation of celibacy. *American Anthropologist,* vol. 71, pp. 658-687.

Conrad, Geoffrey W.
1977 Chiquitoy Viejo: an Inca administrative center in the Chicama Valley, Peru. *Journal of Field Archaeology,* vol. 4, pp. 1-18.
1980 Platformas funerarias. In *Chanchán: Metrópoli Chimú,* edited by R. Ravines, pp. 217-230. Fuentes e Investigaciones para la Historia del Perú, no. 5. Lima: Instituto de Estudios Peruanos.
1981a Cultural materialism, split inheritance, and the expansion of ancient Peruvian empires. *American Antiquity,* vol. 46, pp. 3-26.
1981b Reply to Paulsen and Isbell. *American Antiquity,* vol. 46, pp. 38-42.
1982 The burial platforms of Chan Chan: some social and political implications. In *Chan Chan: Andean Desert City,* edited by M. E. Moseley and K. C. Day, pp. 87-117. Albuquerque: University of New Mexico Press.
ms. The Central Andes (Peru-Bolivia). In *Chronologies in South American Archaeology,* edited by C. Meighan and G. R. Willey. Los Angeles: UCLA Latin American Studies Center Press. In press.

Cook, Sherburne F.
1946 Human sacrifice and warfare as factors in the demography of pre-Colonial Mexico. *Human Biology,* vol. 18, pp. 81-102.

Cordero Miranda, Gregorio
1971 Reconocimiento arqueológico de Pucarani y sitios adyacentes. *Pumapunku,* no. 3, pp. 7-27. La Paz.

Covarrubias, Miguel
1957 *Indian Art of Mexico and Central America.* New York: Knopf.

Cowgill, George L.
1975a On causes and consequences of ancient and modern population changes. *American Anthropologist,* vol. 77, pp. 505-525.
1975b Population pressure as a non-explanation. In *Population Studies in*

Archaeology and Biological Anthropology: A Symposium, edited by A. C. Swedlund, pp. 127-131. Society for American Archaeology Memoirs, no. 30.

1979 Teotihuacan, internal militaristic competition, and the fall of the Classic Maya. In *Maya Archaeology and Ethnohistory*, edited by N. Hammond and G. R. Willey, pp. 51-62. Austin: University of Texas Press.

Davies, Nigel

1968 *Los Señoríos Independientes del Imperio Azteca*. Mexico: Instituto Nacional de Antropología e Historia.

1972 The military organization of the Aztec empire. *Atti del 40 Congresso Internazionale degli Americanisti*, vol. 4, pp. 213-221. Rome.

1973 *Los Mexicas: Primeros Pasos Hacia el Imperio*. Mexico: Instituto de Investigaciones Históricas.

1974 *The Aztecs*. New York: G.P. Putnam's Sons.

1977 *The Toltecs: Until the Fall of Tula*. Norman: University of Oklahoma Press.

1979 Mixcoatl: man and god. *Actes du 42e Congrès International des Américanistes*, vol. 6, pp. 19-26. Paris.

1980 *The Toltec Heritage: From the Fall of Tula to the Rise of Tenochtitlan*. Norman: University of Oklahoma Press.

Day, Kent C.

1973 Architecture of Ciudadela Rivero, Chan Chan, Peru. Ph.D. Dissertation, Department of Anthropology, Harvard University.

Demarest, Arthur A.

1976 The ideological adaptation of the Mexica Aztec. Advanced Seminar on Mesoamerican Archaeology, edited by G. R. Willey. Department of Anthropology, Harvard University.

1981 *Viracocha, the Nature and Antiquity of the Andean High God*. Monographs of the Peabody Museum, no. 6. Cambridge: Peabody Museum Press.

ms. Mesoamerican human sacrifice in evolutionary perspective. In *Ritual Sacrifice in Pre-Columbian Mesoamerica*, edited by E. Boone and J. Soustelle. Washington: Dumbarton Oaks. In press.

Devereux, George

1967 A typological study of abortion in 350 primitive, ancient, and pre-industrial societies. In *Abortion in America: Legal, Anthropological, and Religious Considerations*, edited by H. Rosen, pp. 97-152. Boston: Beacon Press.

Díaz del Castillo, Bernal

1956 *The Discovery and Conquest of Mexico*. Translated by A. P. Maudslay. New York: Farrar, Straus, and Cudahy.

1964 *Historia Verdadera de la Conquista de la Nueva España*. Mexico: Editorial Porrúa.

Diehl, Richard

1971 *Preliminary Report: University of Missouri Archaeological Project at Tula, 1970-71 Field Seasons*. Columbia: University of Missouri.

Diehl, Richard (editor)

1974 *Studies of Ancient Tollan: A Report of the Missouri Tula Archaeological Project*. Columbia: University of Missouri.

Diener, Paul

1980 Quantum adjustment, macroevolution, and the social field: some comments on evolution and culture. *Current Anthropology*, vol. 21, pp. 423-443.

Diener, Paul, Kurt Moore, and Robert Mutaw

1980 Meat, markets, and mechanical materialism: the great protein fiasco in anthropology. *Dialectical Anthropology*, vol. 5, pp. 171-192.

Diener, Paul, Donald Nonini, and Eugene Robkin
1978 The dialectics of the sacred cow: ecological adaptation versus political appropriation in the origins of India's cattle complex. *Dialectical Anthropology*, vol. 3, pp. 221-238.
1980 Ecology and evolution in cultural anthropology. *Man*, vol. 15, pp. 1-31.

Diener, Paul, and Eugene Robkin
1978 Ecology, evolution, and the search for cultural origins: the question of Islamic pig prohibition. *Current Anthropology*, vol. 19, pp. 493-540.

Diez de San Miguel, Garci
1964 *Vista Hecha a La Provincia de Chucuito por Garci Diez de San Miguel en el Año 1567*. Documentos Regionales para la Etnología y Etnohistoria Andinas, vol. 1, pp. 1-287. Lima: Casa de la Cultura del Perú.

Dodson, M. M.
1975 Quantum evolution and the fold catastrophe. *Evolutionary Theory*, vol. 1, pp. 107-118.

Donnan, Christopher B., and Carol J. Mackey
1978 *Ancient Burial Patterns of the Moche Valley, Peru*. Austin: University of Texas Press.

Drummond, D. E., and Florencia Muller
1972 Classic to Post-Classic in highland Central Mexico. *Science*, vol. 175, pp. 1208-1215.

Durán, Diego
1964 *The Aztecs: The History of the Indies of New Spain*. Translated by D. Heyden and F. Horcasitas. New York: Orion Press.
1967 *Historia de las Indias de Nueva España y Islas de Tierra Firme*. Edited by Ángel Garibay. 2 vols. Mexico: Editorial Porrúa.
1971 *Book of the Gods and Rites and the Ancient Calendar*. Translated by F. Horcasitas and D. Heyden. Norman: University of Oklahoma Press.

Durkheim, Émile
1915 *The Elementary Forms of the Religious Life*. Translated by Joseph W. Swain. London: Allen and Unwin.

Dutton, Bertha P.
1955 Tula of the Toltecs. *El Palacio*, vol. 62, pp. 195-251.

Duviols, Pierre
1967 Un inédit de Cristóbal de Albornoz: La instrucción para descubrir todas las guacas del Pirú y sus camayos y haziendas (ca. 1582). *Journal de la Société des Américanistes*, n.s., vol. 56, pp. 7-39. Paris.
1973 Huari y llacuaz, agricultores y pastores: un dualismo prehispánico de oposición y complementaridad. *Revista del Museo Nacional*, vol. 39, pp. 153-191. Lima.
1976 Punchao, idolo mayor del Coricancha: historia y tipología. *Antropología Andina*, no. 1-2, pp. 156-183. Cuzco.
1979 Un symbolisme de l'occupation, de l'aménagement et de l'exploitation de l'espace: le monolithe 'huanca' et sa fonction dans les Andes préhispaniques. *L'Homme*, vol. 19, no. 2, pp. 7-31.

Earls, John
1976 Evolución de la administración ecológica Inca. *Revista del Museo Nacional*, vol. 42, pp. 207-245. Lima.

Eldredge, Niles
1976 Differential evolutionary rates. *Paleobiology*, vol. 2, pp. 174-177.
1979 Alternative approaches to evolutionary theory. In *Models and Methodologies in Evolutionary Theory*, edited by J. H. Schwartz and H. B. Rollins, pp. 7-19. Bulletin of the Carnegie Museum of Natural History, no. 13.

Eldredge, Niles, and Stephen Jay Gould
1972 Punctuated equilibria: an alternative to phyletic gradualism. In *Models*

in Paleobiology, edited by T. J. M. Schopf, pp. 82-115. San Francisco: Freeman, Cooper.

Engel, Frédéric
1963 *A Preceramic Settlement on the Central Coast of Peru: Asia, Unit 1.* Transactions of the American Philosophical Society, n.s., vol. 53, pt. 3.

Engels, Friedrich
1972 *The Origin of the Family, Private Property, and the State.* New York: International Publishers.

Erdheim, Mario
1978 Transformaciones de la ideología Mexica en realidad social. In *Economía, Política e Ideología en el México Prehispánico*, edited by P. Carrasco and J. Broda, pp. 221-255. Mexico: Centro de Investigaciones Superiores.

Espejo, Antonieta
1944 Algunas semejanzas entre Tenayuca y Tlatelolco. *Memorias de la Academia Mexicana de la Historia*, vol. 3, pp. 522-526.

Evans-Pritchard, E. E.
1937 *Witchcraft, Oracles, and Magic Among the Azande.* Oxford: Clarendon Press.
1956 *Nuer Religion.* Oxford: Clarendon Press.

Feldman, Robert A.
1977 Life in ancient Peru. *Field Museum of Natural History Bulletin*, vol. 48, no. 6, pp. 12-17.
1980 Aspero, Peru: Architecture, Subsistence Economy, and Other Artifacts of a Preceramic Maritime Chiefdom. Ph.D. Dissertation, Department of Anthropology, Harvard University.

Ferdon, Edwin N., Jr
1981 Holocene mangrove formations on the Santa Elena Peninsula, Ecuador: pluvial indicators of ecological response to physiographic changes. *American Antiquity*, vol. 46, pp. 619-626.

Firth, Raymond
1981 Spiritual aroma: religion and politics. *American Anthropologist*, vol. 83, pp. 582-601.

Fisher, Lawrence, and Oswald Werner
1978 Explaining explanation: tension in American anthropology. *Journal of Anthropological Research*, vol. 34, pp. 194-218.

Flannery, Kent V.
1972 The cultural evolution of civilizations. *Annual Review of Ecology and Systematics*, vol. 3, pp. 399-426.
1977 Review of Eric R. Wolf (editor), *The Valley of Mexico. Science*, vol. 196, pp. 759-761.

Flannery, Kent V. (editor)
1976 *The Early Mesoamerican Village.* New York: Academic Press.

Flannery, Kent V., and Joyce Marcus
1976 Formative Oaxaca and the Zapotec cosmos. *American Scientist*, vol. 64, pp. 374-383.

Flores Ochoa, Jorge A. (editor)
1978 Organización Social y Complementaridad Económica en los Andes Centrales. *Actes du 42e Congrès International des Américanistes*, vol. 4, pp. 7-156. Paris.

Fortune, Reo F.
1932 *Sorcerers of Dobu.* London: George Routledge and Sons.

Freidel, David A.
1979 Culture areas and interaction spheres: contrasting approaches to the emergence of civilization in the Maya lowlands. *American Antiquity*, vol. 44, pp. 36-54.
1981 Civilization as a state of mind: the cultural evolution of the lowland

Maya. In *The Transition to Statehood in the New World*, edited by G. D. Jones and R. R. Kautz, pp. 188-227. Cambridge: Cambridge University Press.

Friedman, Jonathan
1974 Marxism, structuralism and vulgar materialism. *Man*, vol. 9, pp. 444-469.
1975 Tribes, states, and transformations. In *Marxist Analyses and Social Anthropology*, edited by M. Bloch, pp. 161-202. New York: John Wiley and Sons.

Friedman, Jonathan, and M. J. Rowlands
1978 Notes toward an epigenetic model of the evolution of civilization. In *The Evolution of Social Systems*, edited by J. Friedman and M. J. Rowlands, pp. 201-276. London: Duckworth.

Garcilaso de la Vega, 'El Inca'
1945 *Comentarios Reales de los Incas* (1609). 2 vols. Buenos Aires: Emecé Editores.
1966 *Royal Commentaries of the Incas and General History of Peru* (1609-17). Translated by Harold V. Livermore. 2 vols. Austin: University of Texas Press.

Garibay K., Ángel María
1958 *Veinte Himnos Sacros de Los Nahuas*. Mexico: Universidad Nacional Autónoma de México.

Garn, Stanley M.
1979 The noneconomic nature of eating people. *American Anthropologist*, vol. 81, pp. 902-903.

Garn, Stanley M., and Walter D. Block
1970 The limited nutritional value of cannibalism. *American Anthropologist*, vol. 72, p. 106.

Gasparini, Graziano, and Luise Margolies
1980 *Inca Architecture*. Translated by Patricia J. Lyon. Bloomington: Indiana University Press.

Gibson, Charles
1971 The structure of the Aztec empire. In *Handbook of Middle American Indians*, vol. 10, edited by G. Ekholm and I. Bernal, pp. 376-394. Austin: University of Texas Press.

Gilman, Antonio
1981 The development of social stratification in Bronze Age Europe. *Current Anthropology*, vol. 22, pp. 1-23.

Godelier, Maurice
1973 *Horizon, Trajets Marxistes en Anthropologie*. Paris: Maspero.
1977 *Perspectives in Marxist Anthropology*. Cambridge: Cambridge University Press.
1978a Economy and religion: an evolutionary optical illusion. In *The Evolution of Social Systems*, edited by J. Friedman and M. J. Rowlands, pp. 3-12. London: Duckworth.
1978b Politics as 'infrastructure': an anthropologist's thoughts on the example of classical Greece and the notions of relations of production and economic determinism. In *The Evolution of Social Systems*, edited by J. Friedman and M. J. Rowlands, pp. 13-28. London: Duckworth.
1978c Infrastructures, societies, and history. *Current Anthropology*, vol. 19, pp. 763-771.

González Holguín, Diego
1608 *Vocabulario dela Lengua General de Todo el Peru, Llamada Lengua Quichua, o del Inca*. Lima.

González Torres, Yólotl
1976 La esclavitud entre los Mexica. In *Estratificación Social en la Mesoamérica*

Prehispánica, edited by P. Carrasco and J. Broda, pp. 78-87. Mexico: Centro de Investigaciones Superiores.

Gould, Stephen Jay, and Niles Eldredge
1977 Punctuated equilibria: the tempo and mode of evolution reconsidered. *Paleobiology*, vol. 3, pp. 115-151.

Guaman Poma de Ayala, Felipe
1936 *Nueva Corónica y Buen Gobierno...* (ca. 1610-15). Travaux y Mémoires de l'Institut d'Ethnologie, no. 23. Paris.

Hammel, Eugene A.
1965 Review of R.T. Zuidema, *The Ceque System of Cuzco: The Social Organization of the Capital of the Inca. American Anthropologist*, vol. 67, pp. 780-785.

Harner, Michael
1977a The ecological basis for Aztec sacrifice. *American Ethnologist*, vol. 4, pp. 117-135.
1977b The enigma of Aztec sacrifice. *Natural History*, vol. 86, pp. 47-52.

Harris, Marvin
1964 *The Nature of Cultural Things*. New York: Random House.
1968 *The Rise of Anthropological Theory*. New York: Thomas Y. Crowell.
1974a Reply to Azzi. *Current Anthropology*, vol. 15, pp. 323-324.
1974b *Cows, Pigs, Wars and Witches: The Riddles of Culture*. New York: Random House.
1974c Why a perfect knowledge of all the rules one must know in order to act like a native cannot lead to a knowledge of how natives act. *Journal of Anthropological Research*, vol. 30, pp. 242-251.
1977 *Cannibals and Kings: The Origins of Cultures*. New York: Random House.
1979 *Cultural Materialism: The Struggle for a Science of Culture*. New York: Random House.
1980 *Culture, People, Nature*. 3rd edition. New York: Harper & Row.

Harvey, Herbert R.
1971 Ethnohistory of Guerrero. In *Handbook of Middle American Indians*, vol. 11, edited by R. Wauchope, G. Eckholm, and I. Bernal, pp. 603-618. Austin: University of Texas Press.

Hemming, John
1970 *The Conquest of the Incas*. New York: Harcourt Brace Jovanovich.

Hernández Príncipe, Rodrigo
1923 Mitología andina (1621-22). *Inca*, vol. 1, pp. 25-68. Lima.

Heyden, Doris
1975 An interpretation of the cave underneath the Pyramid of the Sun in Teotihuacan, Mexico. *American Antiquity*, vol. 40, pp. 131-147.

Hicks, Frederic
1974 Dependent labor in prehispanic Mexico. *Estudios de Cultura Náhuatl*, vol. 11, pp. 243-266.
1976 Mayeque y calpuleque en el sistema de clases del México antiguo. In *Estratificación Social en la Mesoamérica Prehispánica*, edited by P. Carrasco and J. Broda, pp. 67-77. Mexico: Centro de Investigaciones Superiores.
1979 'Flowery war' in Aztec history. *American Ethnologist*, vol. 6, pp. 87-92.

Himes, N. E.
1963 *Medical History of Contraception*. New York: Gamut Press.

Historia de los Mexicanos por sus Pinturas
1941 Historia de los Mexicanos por sus Pinturas. In *Nueva Colección de Documentos para la Historia de México*, pp. 209-240. Mexico: Editorial S. Chávez Hayhoe.

Historia Tolteca-Chichimeca
    1947 *Historia Tolteca-Chichimeca: Anales de Quanhtinchan.* Edited by Heinrich
    Berlin and Silvia Rendon, prologue by Paul Kirchhoff. Mexico: Antigua
    Librería Robredo.
Histoyre du Mechique
    1961 Histoyre du Mechique. Translated by Joaquín Meade. *Memorias de la
    Academia Mexicana de la Historia,* vol. 20, pp. 183-210.
Hunt, Eva
    1977 *The Transformation of the Hummingbird.* Ithaca: Cornell University Press.
Hyslop, John
    1977 Chulpas of the Lupaca zone of the Peruvian high plateau. *Journal of Field
    Archaeology,* vol. 4, pp. 149-170.
Isbell, William H.
    1978 Environmental perturbations and the origin of the Andean state. In *Social
    Archeology,* edited by C. Redman and others, pp. 303-313. New York:
    Academic Press.
    1981 Comment on Conrad. *American Antiquity,* vol. 46, pp. 27-30.
Isbell, William H., and Katharina J. Schreiber
    1978 Was Huari a state? *American Antiquity,* vol. 43, pp. 372-389.
Ixtlilxochitl, Fernando de Alva
    1975 *Obras Históricas, Vol. 1: Relaciones Históricas.* Edited by Edmundo
    O'Gorman. Mexico: Universidad Nacional Autónoma de México.
    1977 *Obras Historicas, Vol. 2: História de la Nación Chichimeca.* Edited by
    Edmundo O'Gorman. Mexico: Universidad Nacional Autónoma de
    México.
Jérez, Francisco de
    1853 *Verdadera Relación de la Conquista del Perú y Provincia de Cuzco, Llamada la
    Nueva Castilla* (1534). Historiadores Primitivos de Indias, compiled by
    Enrique de Vedia, vol. 2, pp. 319-348. Biblioteca de Autores Españoles,
    vol. 26. Madrid: Rivadeneyra.
Jiménez Moreno, Wigberto
    1940 Signos cronográficos del códice y calendario Mixteco. *Códice de Yanhuitlan,*
    pp. 69-76. Mexico: Secretaría de Educación Pública.
    1941 Tula y los toltecas según las fuentes históricas. *Revista Mexicana de Estudios
    Antropológicos,* vol. 5, pp. 79-85.
    1953 Cronología de la historia de Veracruz. *Revista Mexicana de Estudios
    Antropológicos,* vol. 13, pp. 311-313.
    1956 Síntesis de la historia precolonial del valle de México. *Revista Mexicana
    de Estudios Antropológicos,* vol. 14, pp. 219-236.
    1959 Síntesis de la historia pretolteca de Mesoamérica. In *Esplendor del México
    Antiguo,* vol. 2, pp. 1109-1196. Mexico: Centro de Investigaciones
    Antropológicas de México.
    1961 Diferente principio del año entre diversos pueblos y sus consecuencias
    para la cronología prehispánica. *El México Antiguo,* vol. 9, pp. 137-152.
    1966 Mesoamerica before the Toltecs. In *Ancient Oaxaca,* edited by J. Paddock,
    pp. 3-82. Stanford: Stanford University Press.
Kaplan, David
    1960 The law of cultural dominance. In *Evolution and Culture,* edited by M.
    D. Sahlins and E. R. Service, pp. 69-92. Ann Arbor: University of Michigan
    Press.
Katz, Friedrich
    1966 *Situación Social y Económica de los Aztecas Durante los Siglos XV y XVI.*
    Mexico: Instituto de Investigaciones Históricas.
    1972 *The Ancient American Civilizations.* New York: Praeger.

Keatinge, Richard W., and Geoffrey W. Conrad
   ms. Imperialist expansion in Peruvian prehistory: Chimu administration of a conquered territory. *Journal of Field Archaeology*. In press.
Kelley, Ellen
   1978 The temple of the skulls at Alta Vista, Chalchihuites. In *Across the Chichimec Sea*, edited by C. Riley and B. Hedrick, pp. 102-126. Carbondale: Southern Illinois University Press.
Kelley, Isabell
   1941 The relationship between Tula and Sinaloa. *Revista Mexicana de Estudios Antropológicos*, vol. 5, pp. 199-208.
Kelley, J. Charles
   1971 Archaeology of the northern frontier: Zacatecas and Durango. In *Handbook of Middle American Indians*, vol. 11, edited by R. Wauchope, G. Ekholm, and I. Bernal, pp. 768-804. Austin: University of Texas Press.
Kendall, Ann
   1974 Architecture and planning at the Inca sites in the Cusichaca area. *Baessler Archiv: Beiträge zur Völkerkunde*, neue folge, vol. 22, pp. 73-137.
   1976 Preliminary report on ceramic data and pre-Inca architectural remains of the Urubamba Valley, Cuzco. *Baessler Archiv: Beiträge zur Völkerkunde*, neue folge, vol. 24, pp. 41-159.
   1979 The Cusichaca archaeological project (Peru): the early stages. *Bulletin of the Institute of Archaeology*, no. 16, pp. 131-157. London.
Kirchhoff, Paul
   1950 The Mexican calendar and the founding of Tenochtitlan-Tlatelolco. *Transactions of the New York Academy of Sciences*, 2nd series, vol. 12, pp. 126-132.
   1955 Quetzalcoatl, Huemac, y el fin de Tula. *Cuadernos Americanos*, vol. 14, pp. 163-196.
   1956 Calendarios Tenochca, Tlatelolca, y otros. *Revista Mexicana de Estudios Antropológicos*, vol. 14, pp. 257-267.
   1959 The principles of clanship in human society. In *Readings in Anthropology*, edited by M. H. Freid, pp. 259-270. New York: Thomas Y. Crowell.
Kohl, Philip L.
   1981 Materialist approaches in prehistory. *Annual Review of Anthropology*, vol. 10, pp. 89-118.
Kolata, Alan L.
   1982a Chronology and settlement growth at Chan Chan. In *Chan Chan: Andean Desert City*, edited by M. E. Moseley and K. C. Day, pp. 67-85. Albuquerque: University of New Mexico Press.
   1982b Tiwanaku: portrait of an Andean civilization. *Field Museum of Natural History Bulletin*, vol. 53, no. 8, pp. 13-18, 23-28.
   ms. The evolution of civilization in the South Andes. In *Ancient South Americans*, edited by J. D. Jennings. Salt Lake City: W. H. Freeman. In press.
Kosok, Paul
   1965 *Life, Land and Water in Ancient Peru*. New York: Long Island University Press.
Kowalewski, Stephen A.
   1980 Population-resource balances in Period I of Oaxaca, Mexico. *American Antiquity*, vol. 45, pp. 151-165.
Krickeberg, Walter
   1966 *Altmexikanische Kulturen*. Berlin: Safari-Verlag.
Kubler, George
   1946 The Quechua in the Colonial world. In *Handbook of South American Indians, Vol. 2: The Andean Civilizations*, edited by J. H. Steward, pp. 331-410. Bureau of American Ethnology Bulletin 143, vol. 2.

1961 Chichén-Itzá y Tula. *Estudios de Cultura Maya*, vol. 1, pp. 47-80.
1962 *The Art and Architecture of Ancient America*. Baltimore: Pelican.
Kurtz, Donald V.
    1978 The legitimation of the Aztec state. In *The Early State*, edited by
    H. Claessen and P. Skalnik, pp. 169-189. The Hague: Mouton.
Langer, William L.
    1974 Infanticide: a historical survey. *History of Childhood Quarterly*, vol. 1, pp.
    353-366.
Leach, Edmund R.
    1976 *Culture and Communication: The Logic by Which Symbols are Connected.*
    Cambridge: Cambridge University Press.
    1977 A view from the bridge. In *Archaeology and Anthropology: Areas of Mutual
    Interest*, edited by M. Spriggs, pp. 161-176. British Archaeological Reports,
    Supplementary Series, no. 19.
Lee, Richard B.
    1972 The intensification of social life among the !Kung Bushmen. In *Population
    Growth: Anthropological Implications*, edited by B. Spooner, pp. 343-350.
    Cambridge: MIT Press.
Lee, Richard, and B. Irven DeVore (editors)
    1968 *Man the Hunter*. Chicago: Aldine.
Legros, Dominique
    1977 Chance, necessity, and mode of production: a Marxist critique of cultural
    evolutionism. *American Anthropologist*, vol. 79, pp. 26-41.
Legros, Dominique, Donald Hunderfund, and Judith Shapiro
    1979 Economic base, mode of production, and social formation: a discussion
    of Marx's terminology. *Dialectical Anthropology*, vol. 4, pp. 243-249.
León-Portilla, Miguel
    1958 Itzcoatl creador de una cosmovisión místico-guerrera. *Siete Ensayos sobre
    Cultura Náhuatl*, pp. 117-143. Mexico: Universidad Nácional Autónoma de
    México.
    1959 *La Filosofía Náhuatl Estudiada en sus Fuentes*. Mexico: Instituto de
    Investigaciones Históricas.
    1960 The concept of the state among the ancient Aztecs. *Alpha Kappa Deltan*,
    vol. 30, no. 1, pp. 7-13.
    1963 *Aztec Thought and Culture*. Norman: University of Oklahoma Press.
    1968a *Quetzalcoatl*. Mexico: Fondo de Cultura Económica.
    1968b *Time and Reality in the Thought of the Maya*. Boston: Beacon Press.
Lévi-Strauss, Claude
    1963 *Structural Anthropology*. New York: Doubleday.
    1966 *The Savage Mind*. Chicago: University of Chicago Press.
    1969 *The Elementary Structures of Kinship*. Revised edition, translated by J. H.
    Bell, edited by J. R. von Sturmer and R. Needham. Boston: Beacon Press.
Leyenda de los Soles
    1975 Leyenda de los Soles. In *Códice Chimalpopoca*, translated by P. Feliciano
    Velázquez, pp. 119-142. Mexico: Instituto de Investigaciones Históricas.
Lockhart, James
    1972 *The Men of Cajamarca: A Social and Biographical Study of the First Conquerors
    of Peru*. Austin: University of Texas Press.
Logan, Michael H., and William T. Sanders
    1976 The model. In *The Valley of Mexico*, edited by E. R. Wolf, pp. 31-58.
    Albuquerque: University of New Mexico Press.
López Austin, Alfredo
    1961 *La Constitución Real de México-Tenochtitlan*. Mexico: Universidad Nacional
    Autónoma de México.

1973 *Hombre-Dios: Religión y Política en el Mundo Náhuatl.* Mexico: Instituto de Investigaciones Históricas.

Lorenzo, José Luis

1968 Clima y agricultura en Teotihuacan. In *Materiales Para la Arqueología de Teotihuacan,* edited by J. L. Lorenzo, pp. 51-72. Mexico: Instituto Nacional de Antropología e Historia.

Lumbreras, Luis G.

1974a *The Peoples and Cultures of Ancient Peru.* Translated by Betty J. Meggers. Washington: Smithsonian Institution Press.

1974b Los reinos post-Tiwanaku en el área altiplánica. *Revista del Museo Nacional,* vol. 40, pp. 55-86. Lima.

Lumbreras, Luis G., and Hernán Amat

1968 Secuencia arqueológica del altiplano occidental del Titicaca. *Actas y Memorias del 37 Congreso Internacional de Americanistas,* vol. 2, pp. 75-106. Buenos Aires.

MacNeish, Richard S.

1962 *Second Annual Report of the Tehuacan Archaeological-Botanical Project.* Andover, MA: R. S. Peabody Foundation for Archaeology.

Malinowski, Bronislaw

1922 *Argonauts of the Western Pacific.* New York: Dutton.

1927 *Sex and Repression in Savage Society.* New York: Harcourt.

1929 *The Sexual Life of Savages in Northwestern Melanesia.* London: George Routledge and Sons.

1935 *Coral Gardens and Their Magic.* 2 vols. London: Allen and Unwin.

1939 The group and the individual in functional analysis. *American Journal of Sociology,* vol. 44, pp. 938-964.

1944 *A Scientific Theory of Culture and Other Essays.* Chapel Hill: University of North Carolina Press.

1945 *The Dynamics of Culture Change: An Inquiry into Race Relations in Africa.* Edited by P. Kaberry. New Haven: Yale University Press.

1948 *Magic, Science, and Religion and Other Essays.* Glencoe, IL: Free Press.

Malthus, Thomas Robert

1926 *An Essay on the Principle of Population as it Affects the Future Improvement of Society, with Remarks on the Speculations of Mr. Godwin, M. Condorcet and Other Writers.* London: Macmillan.

Mamdani, Mahmood

1974 The myth of population control. *Development Digest,* vol. 12, pp. 13-28.

Marquina, Ignacio

1951 *Arquitectura Prehispánica.* Memorias del Instituto Nacional de Antropología e Historia, no. 1. Mexico.

Martínez del Río, P.

1946 Tlatelolco a través de los tiempos. *Memorias de la Academia Mexicana de la Historia,* vol. 5, pp. 148-176.

Martínez Marín, Carlos

1964 La cultura de los Mexicas durante la migración. *Actas y Memorias del 35 Congreso Internacional de Americanistas,* vol. 2, pp. 113-123. Mexico.

1976 Historiografía de la migración Mexica. *Estudios de Cultura Náhuatl,* vol. 12, pp. 121-135. Mexico.

Marx, Karl

1965 *Pre-Capitalist Economic Formations.* New York: International Publishers.

1971 *A Contribution to the Critique of Political Economy.* London: Lawrence and Wishart.

1975 *Capital: A Critique of Political Economy.* New York: International Publishers.

Matos Moctezuma, Eduardo
  1974 *Proyecto Tula, Primera Parte.* Colección Científica, no. 15. Mexico: Instituto Nacional de Antropología.
  1976 *Proyecto Tula, Segunda Parte.* Colección Científica, no. 33. Mexico: Instituto Nacional de Antropología.
Means, Philip A.
  1931 *Ancient Civilizations of the Andes.* New York: Charles Scribner's Sons.
Meillassoux, Claude
  1972 From reproduction to production. *Economy and Society*, vol. 1, pp. 93-105.
Mendelson, Jack
  1979 On Engels' metaphysical dialectics: a foundation of orthodox 'Marxism'. *Dialectical Anthropology*, vol. 4, pp. 65-73.
Menzel, Dorothy
  1959 The Inca occupation of the south coast of Peru. *Southwestern Journal of Anthropology*, vol. 15, pp. 125-142.
  1964 Style and time in the Middle Horizon. *Ñawpa Pacha*, no. 2, pp. 1-105. Berkeley: Institute of Andean Studies.
Middleton, John, and E. H. Winter
  1963 *Witchcraft and Sorcery in East Africa.* New York: Praeger.
Millon, Clara
  1973 Painting, writing, and polity at Teotihuacan, Mexico. *American Antiquity*, vol. 38, pp. 294-314.
Millon, René
  1973 *Urbanization at Teotihuacan, Mexico, Vol. 1: The Teotihuacan Map, Part 2: Text.* Austin: University of Texas Press.
  1976 Social relations in ancient Teotihuacan. In *The Valley of Mexico*, edited by E. R. Wolf, pp. 205-248. Albuquerque: University of New Mexico Press.
Mishkin, Bernard
  1946 The contemporary Quechua. In *Handbook of South American Indians, Vol. 2: The Andean Civilizations*, edited by J. H. Steward, pp. 411-470. Bureau of American Ethnology Bulletin 143, vol. 2.
Molina, Cristóbal de
  1913 Relación de las fábulas y ritos de los Ingas (1575). Edited by Tomás Thayer Ojeda. *Revista Chilena de Historia y Geografía*, vol. 5, pp. 112-190.
Monzón, Arturo
  1949 *El Calpulli en la Organización Social de los Tenocha.* Mexico: Instituto de Historia.
Moore, Sally Falk
  1958 *Power and Property in Inca Peru.* New York: Columbia University Press.
Moreno, Manuel
  1931 *La Organización Política y Social de Los Aztecas.* Mexico: Universidad Nacional Autónoma de México.
Morgan, Lewis Henry
  1877 *Ancient Society.* New York: Henry Holt.
Morley, Sylvanus G.
  1956 *The Ancient Maya.* 3rd edition, revised by George W. Brainerd. Stanford: Stanford University Press.
Morris, Craig
  1972 State settlements in Tawantinsuyu: a strategy of compulsory urbanism. In *Contemporary Archeology: A Guide to Theory and Contributions*, edited by M. P. Leone, pp. 393-401. Carbondale: Southern Illinois University Press.
  1974 Reconstructing patterns of non-agricultural production in the Inca economy: archaeology and documents in institutional analysis. In *Recon-*

structing Complex Societies: An Archaeological Colloquium, edited by C. B. Moore, pp. 49-68. Supplement to the Bulletin of the American Schools of Oriental Research, no. 20.

Morris, Craig, and Donald E. Thompson
1970 Huanuco Viejo: an Inca administrative center. *American Antiquity*, vol. 35, pp. 344-362.

Morris, Earl H., Jean Charlot, and Ann A. Morris
1931 *The Temple of the Warriors at Chichen Itza, Yucatan.* Carnegie Institute Publication, no. 406. 2 vols. Washington: Carnegie Institute of Washington.

Morúa, Martín de
1922-25 *Historia de los Incas, Reyes del Peru, de sus Hechos, Costumbres, Trajes y Manera de Gobierno* (ca. 1600). Colección de Libros y Documentos Referentes a la Historia del Perú, edited by Horacio H. Urteaga and Carlos A. Romero, 2nd series, vol. 4, pp. 1-253, vol. 5, pp. 1-72. Lima: Sanmartí.

Moseley, Michael E.
1975a Chan Chan: Andean alternative of the preindustrial city. *Science*, vol. 187, pp. 219-225.
1975b *The Maritime Foundations of Andean Civilization.* Menlo Park, CA: Cummings.
1975c Prehistoric principles of labor organization in the Moche Valley, Peru. *American Antiquity*, vol. 40, pp. 191-196.
1977 Waterways of ancient Peru. *Field Museum of Natural History Bulletin*, vol. 48, no. 3, pp. 10-15.
1978 The evolution of Andean civilization. In *Ancient Native Americans*, edited by J. D. Jennings, pp. 491-541. San Francisco: W. H. Freeman.

Moseley, Michael E., and Kent C. Day (editors)
1982 *Chan Chan: Andean Desert City.* Albuquerque: University of New Mexico Press.

Moser, Christopher L.
1973 *Human Decapitation in Ancient Mesoamerica.* Dumbarton Oaks Studies in Precolumbian Art and Archaeology, no. 11. Washington: Dumbarton Oaks.

Motolinía, Toribio de Benavente
1971 *Memoriales, o Libro de las Cosas de la Nueva España y de los Naturales de Ella.* Mexico: Instituto de Investigaciones Históricas.

Murra, John V.
1958 On Inca political structure. In *Systems of Political Control and Bureaucracy in Human Societies*, edited by V. F. Ray, pp. 30-41. Proceedings of the 1958 Annual Spring Meeting of the American Ethnological Society.
1960 Rite and crop in the Inca state. In *Culture in History*, edited by S. Diamond, pp. 393-407. New York: Columbia University Press.
1962 An archaeological restudy of an Andean ethnohistorical account. *American Antiquity*, vol. 28, pp. 1-4.
1964 Una apreciación etnológica de la visita. In *Visita Hecha a la Provincia de Chucuito por Garci Diez de San Miguel en el Año 1567*. Documentos Regionales para la Etnología y Etnohistoria Andinas, vol. 1, pp. 419-444. Lima: Casa de la Cultura del Perú.
1966 New data on retainer and servile populations in Tawantinsuyu. *Actas y Memorias del 36 Congreso Internacional de Americanistas*, vol. 2, pp. 35-45. Seville.
1968 An Aymara kingdom in 1567. *Ethnohistory*, vol. 15, pp. 115-151.
1972 El 'control vertical' de un máximo de pisos ecológicos en la economía de las sociedades andinas. In *Visita de la Provincia de León de Huánuco en 1562*,

Iñigo Ortiz de Zúñiga, visitador, edited by J. V. Murra. Documentos para la Historia y Etnología de Huánuco y la Selva Central, vol. 2, pp. 427-476. Huánuco: Universidad Nacional Hermilio Valdizán.

1975 The conquest and annexation of Qollasuyu by the Inka state. Paper presented at the 40th Annual Meeting of the Society for American Archaeology, Dallas, Tx.

1980 *The Economic Organization of the Inka State.* Greenwich: JAI Press.

Murra, John V., and Craig Morris

1976 Dynastic oral tradition, administrative records, and archaeology in the Andes. *World Archaeology*, vol. 7, pp. 269-279.

Murúa, Martín de

(See Morúa 1922-25)

Nardi, Bonnie Anna

1981 Modes of explanation in anthropological population theory: biological determinism vs. self-regulation in studies of population growth in Third World countries. *American Anthropologist*, vol. 83, pp. 28-56.

Nichols, Deborah L.

1982 A Middle Formative irrigation system near Santa Clara Coatitlan in the Basin of Mexico. *American Antiquity*, vol. 47, pp. 133-144.

Nicholson, Henry B.

1955 Native historical traditions of nuclear America and the problem of their archaeological correlation. *American Anthropologist*, vol. 57, pp. 594-613.

1957 Topiltzin Quetzalcoatl of Tollan: A Problem in Mesoamerican Ethnohistory. Ph.D. dissertation, Department of Anthropology, Harvard University.

1971a Religion in prehispanic central Mexico. In *Handbook of Middle American Indians*, vol. 10, edited by G. Ekholm and I. Bernal, pp. 395-445. Austin: University of Texas Press.

1971b Major sculpture in prehispanic Central Mexico. In *Handbook of Middle American Indians*, vol. 10, edited by G. Ekholm and I. Bernal, pp. 92-134. Austin: University of Texas Press.

1978 Western Mesoamerica: A.D. 900-1520. In *Chronologies in New World Archaeology*, edited by R. E. Taylor and C. W. Meighan, pp. 285-329. New York: Academic Press.

1979 Ehecatl Quetzalcoatl vs. Topiltzin Quetzalcoatl of Tollan: a problem in Mesoamerican religion and history. *Actes du 42e Congrès International des Américanistes*, vol. 6, pp. 35-47. Paris.

Oakes, Guy

1981 The epistemological foundations of cultural materialism. *Dialectical Anthropology*, vol. 6, pp. 1-21.

Offner, Jerome A.

1981 On the inapplicability of 'oriental despotism' and 'the Asiatic mode of production' to the Aztecs of Texcoco. *American Antiquity*, vol. 46, pp. 43-61.

Olson, Robert E. (editor)

1975 *Protein-Calorie Malnutrition.* New York: Academic Press.

Origen de los Mexicanos

1941 Origen de los Mexicanos. In *Nueva Colección de Documentos para la Historia de México*, pp. 256-280. Mexico: Editorial S. Chávez Hayhoe.

Orlove, Benjamin S.

1980 Ecological anthropology. *Annual Review of Anthropology*, vol. 9, pp. 235-273.

Orozco y Berra, Manuel

1877 Dedicación del Templo Mayor de México. *Anales del Museo Nacional de México*, serie 1, vol. 2, pp. 60-74.

1880 *Historia Antigua de la Conquista de México*. Mexico: Tipografía de Gonzalo A. Estera.

Ortiz de Montellano, Bernard R.
1978 Aztec cannibalism: an ecological necessity? *Science*, vol. 200, pp. 611-617.

Ortiz de Zúñiga, Iñigo
1967 *Visita de la Provincia de León de Huánuco en 1562*. Edited by J. V. Murra. Documentos para la Historia y Etnología de Huánuco y la Selva Central, vol. 1. Huánuco: Universidad Nacional Hermilio Valdizán.

Padden, R. C.
1967 *The Hummingbird and the Hawk*. Columbus: Ohio State University Press.

Palerm, Ángel
1972 *Agricultura y Sociedad en Mesoamérica*. Mexico: Centro de Investigaciones Superiores.
1973 *Obras Hidráulicas Prehispánicas en el Sistema Lacustre del Valle de México*. Mexico: Instituto Nacional de Antropología e Historia.

Palerm, Ángel, and Eric R. Wolf
1957 Ecological potential and cultural development in Mesoamerica. *Social Science Monographs*, vol. 3, pp. 1-32. Washington: Panamerican Union.

Parsons, James T., and William M. Denevan
1967 Pre-columbian ridged fields. *Scientific American*, vol. 217, no. 1, pp. 91-100.

Parsons, Jeffrey R.
1968a An estimate of size and population for Middle Horizon Tiahuanaco, Bolivia. *American Antiquity*, vol. 33, pp. 243-245.
1968b Teotihuacan, Mexico, and its impact on regional demography. *Science*, vol. 162, pp. 872-877.
1971 *Prehispanic Settlement Patterns in the Texcoco Region, Mexico*. Memoirs of the Museum of Anthropology, no. 3. Ann Arbor: University of Michigan.
1974 The development of a prehistoric complex society: a regional perspective from the Valley of Mexico. *Journal of Field Archaeology*, vol. 1, pp. 81-108.
1976a Settlement and population history of the Basin of Mexico. In *The Valley of Mexico*, edited by E. R. Wolf, pp. 69-100. Albuquerque: University of New Mexico Press.
1976b The role of chinampa agriculture in the food supply of Aztec Tenochtitlan. In *Cultural Change and Continuity*, edited by C. E. Cleland, pp. 233-262. New York: Academic Press.

Patterson, Thomas C.
1981 *Archaeology: The Evolution of Ancient Societies*. Englewood Cliffs, NJ: Prentice-Hall.

Paul, Robert, and Paul Rabinow
1976 Bourgeois rationalism revived. *Dialectical Anthropology*, vol. 1, pp. 121-134.

Paulsen, Allison C.
1976 Environment and empire: climatic factors in prehistoric Andean culture change. *World Archaeology*, vol. 8, pp. 121-132.
1981 The archaeology of the absurd: comments on 'Cultural materialism, split inheritance, and the expansion of ancient Peruvian empires'. *American Antiquity*, vol. 46, pp. 31-37.

Pease, Franklin
1973 *El Dios Creador Andino*. Lima: Mosca Azul Editores.

Peterson, David A., and Thomas MacDougall
1974 *Guiengola: A Fortified Site in the Isthmus of Tehuantepec*. Vanderbilt University Publications in Anthropology, no. 10. Nashville, Tn.

Pike, Ruth L., and Myrtle L. Brown
1967 *Nutrition: An Integrated Approach*. New York: Wiley.

Pimentel, David, William Dritschilo, John Krummel, and John Krutzman
1975 Energy and land constraints in food protein production. *Science*, vol. 190, pp. 754-761.

Pizarro, Pedro
1844 *Relación del Descubrimiento y Conquista de los Reinos del Perú, y del Gobierno y Orden que los Naturales Tenían* (1571). Colección de Documentos Inéditos para la Historia de España, compiled by Martín Fernández Navarrete, Miguel Salvá, and Pedro Sainz de Baranda, vol. 5, pp. 201-388. Madrid: Imprenta de la Viuda de Calera.
1921 *Relation of the Discovery and Conquest of the Kingdoms of Peru* (1571). Translated by Philip A. Means. Documents and Narratives Concerning the Discovery and Conquest of Latin America, no. 4. 2 vols. New York: The Cortés Society.

Plog, Fred T.
1975 Systems theory in archaeological research. *Annual Review of Anthropology*, vol. 4, pp. 207-224.

Polgar, Steven
1971 Culture history and population dynamics. In *Culture and Population: a Collection of Current Studies*, edited by S. Polgar, pp. 3-8. Chapel Hill: Carolina Population Center.
1972 Population history and population policies from an anthropological perspective. *Current Anthropology*, vol. 13, pp. 203-211.
1975 Birth planning: between neglect and coercion. In *Population and Social Organization*, edited by M. Maz, pp. 174-203. The Hague: Mouton.

Polo de Ondegardo, Juan
1916a *Los Errores y Supersticiones de los Indios, Sacadas del Tratado y Averiguación que Hizo el Licenciado Polo* (1559). Colección de Libros y Documentos Referentes a la Historia del Perú, edited by Horacio H. Urteaga and Carlos A. Romero, vol. 3, pp. 1-43. Lima: Sanmartí.
1916b *Relación de los Fundamentos Acerca del Notable Daño que Resulta de No Guardar a los Indios sus Fueros* (1571). Colección de Libros y Documentos Referentes a la Historia del Perú, edited by Horacio H. Urteaga and Carlos A. Romero, vol. 3, pp. 45-188. Lima: Sanmartí.
1917a *Del Linaje de los Incas y Como Conquistaron* (1567). Colección de Libros y Documentos Referentes a la Historia del Perú, edited by Horacio H. Urteaga and Carlos A. Romero, vol. 4, pp. 45-95. Lima: Sanmartí.
1917b *Translado de un Cartapacio a Manera de Borrador que Quedo en los Papeles del Licenciado Polo de Ondegardo...* (1567). Colección de Libros y Documentos Referentes a la Historia del Perú, edited by Horacio H. Urteaga and Carlos A. Romero, vol. 4, pp. 95-138. Lima: Sanmartí.
1940 Informe del Licenciado Juan Polo de Ondegardo al Licenciado Briviesca de Muñatones sobre la perpetuidad de las encomiendas en el Perú (1561). *Revista Histórica*, vol. 13, pp. 125-196. Lima.

Pomar, Juan Bautista
1941 Relación de Tezcoco. In *Nueva Colección de Documentos para la Historia de México*, pp. 1-64. Mexico: Editorial S. Chávez Hayhoe.

Ponce Sanginés, Carlos
1972 Tiwanaku: espacio, tiempo y cultura; ensayo de síntesis arqueológica. *América Indígena*, vol. 32, pp. 717-772. Mexico.

Porras Barrenechea, Raúl
1943 Los dos Cristóbal de Molina. In *Las Crónicas de los Molinas*, compiled by Carlos A. Romero, Raúl Porras Barrenechea, and Francisco A. Loayza, pp.87-98 (2nd paging). Los Pequeños Grandes Libros de Historia Americana, 1st series, vol. 4. Lima: Librería y Imprenta D. Miranda.

Porter-Weaver, Muriel
  1981 *The Aztecs, Maya, and their Predecessors.* 2nd edition. New York: Academic Press.
Prescott, William H.
  1847 *The Conquest of Peru.* 2 vols. New York: Harper and Brothers.
Price, Barbara J.
  1978 Demystification, enriddlement, and Aztec cannibalism: a materialist rejoinder to Harner. *American Ethnologist*, vol. 5, pp. 98-115.
Pulgar Vidal, Javier
  1972 *Geografía del Perú: Las Ocho Regiones Naturales del Perú.* 7th edition. Lima: Editorial Universo.
Radcliffe-Brown, A. R.
  1935 On the concept of function in social science. *American Anthropologist*, vol. 37, pp. 394-402.
  1946 A note on functional anthropology. *Man*, vol. 46, pp. 38-41.
  1949 Functionalism: a protest. *American Anthropologist*, vol. 51, pp. 320-323.
  1952 *Structure and Function in Primitive Society.* London: Cohen and West.
  1957 *A Natural Science of Society.* New York: Free Press.
  1958 *Method in Social Anthropology.* Chicago: University of Chicago Press.
Radin, Paul
  1920 *The Sources and Authenticity of the Ancient Mexicans.* University of California Publications in American Archaeology and Ethnology, vol. 17, no. 1.
Rappaport, Roy A.
  1967 *Pigs for the Ancestors.* New Haven: Yale University Press.
  1971 The flow of energy in an agricultural society. *Scientific American*, vol. 225, no. 3, pp. 117-132.
  1978a Maladaptation in social systems. In *The Evolution of Social Systems*, edited by J. Friedman and M. J. Rowlands, pp. 49-71. London: Duckworth.
  1978b Normative models of adaptive processes: a response to Whyte. In *The Evolution of Social Systems*, edited by J. Friedman and M. J. Rowlands, pp. 79-87. London: Duckworth.
Raymond, J. Scott
  1981 The maritime foundations of Andean civilization: a reconsideration of the evidence. *American Antiquity*, vol. 46, pp. 806-821.
Recktenwald, Mark E.
  1978 State and Economy in Moche III-IV Society. B.A. thesis, Department of Anthropology, Harvard University.
Relación de la Genealogía y Linaje
  1941 Relación de la Genealogía y Linaje. In *Neuva Coleccion de Documentos para la Historia de México*, pp. 240-256. Mexico: Editorial S. Chávez Hayhoe.
Renfrew, Colin
  1978 Trajectory discontinuity and morphogenesis: the implications of catastrophe theory for archaeology. *American Antiquity*, vol. 43, pp. 203-222.
  1979 Systems collapse as social transformation: catastrophe and anastrophe in early state societies. In *Transformations: Mathematical Approaches to Culture Change*, edited by C. Renfrew and K. L. Cooke, pp. 481-506. New York: Academic Press.
Richardson, James B. III
  1973 The preceramic sequence and the Pleistocene and Post-Pleistocene climate of northwest Peru. In *Variation in Anthropology: Essays in Honor of John C. McGregor*, edited by D. W. Lathrap and J. Douglas, pp. 199-211. Urbana: Illinois Archaeological Survey.
  1974 Holocene beach ridges between the Chira River and Punta Parinas, northwest Peru, and the archaeological sequence. Paper presented at the

39th Annual Meeting of the Society for American Archaeology, Washington, DC.

1981 Modeling the development of sedentary maritime economies on the coast of Peru: a preliminary statement. *Annals of the Carnegie Museum of Natural History*, vol. 50, no. 5, pp. 139-150.

Rivera Dorado, Miguel

1971a La cerámica Killke y la arqueología de Cuzco. *Revista Española de Antropología Americana*, vol. 6, pp. 85-123.

1971b Diseños decorativos en la cerámica Killke. *Revista del Museo Nacional*, vol. 37, pp. 106-115. Lima.

1972 La cerámica de Cancha-Cancha, Cuzco, Perú. *Revista Dominicana de Arqueología y Antropología*, vol. 2, no. 2-3, pp. 36-49.

1973 Aspectos tipológicos de la cerámica cuzqueña del Período Intermedio Tardío. *Atti del 40 Congresso Internazionale degli Americanisti*, vol. 1, pp. 353-362. Rome-Genoa.

Rodin, Miriam, Karen Michaelson, and Gerald M. Britan

1978 Systems theory in anthropology. *Current Anthropology*, vol. 19, pp. 747-762.

Romero, Carlos A.

1916 El licenciado Juan Polo de Ondegardo. *Revista Histórica*, vol. 5, pp. 452-469. Lima.

Rostworowski de Diez Canseco, Maria

1960 Succession, coöption to kingship, and royal incest among the Inca. *Southwestern Journal of Anthropology*, vol. 16, pp. 417-427.

1961 *Curacas y Sucesiones: Costa Norte*. Lima: Imprenta Minerva.

1962 Nuevos datos sobre tenecia de tierras reales en el incario. *Revista del Museo Nacional*, vol. 31, pp. 130-164. Lima.

1966 Las tierras reales y su mano de obra en el Tahuantinsuyu. *Actas y Memorias del 36 Congreso Internacional de Americanistas*, vol. 2, pp. 31-34. Seville.

1977 *Etnía y Sociedad: Costa Peruana Prehispánica*. Historia Andina, no. 4. Lima: Instituto de Estudios Peruanos.

Rounds, J.

1979 Lineage, class, and power in the Aztec state. *American Ethnologist*, vol. 6, pp. 73-86.

Rowe, John H.

1944 *An Introduction to the Archaeology of Cuzco*. Papers of the Peabody Museum of American Archaeology and Ethnology, vol. 22, no. 2. Cambridge: Harvard University.

1945 Absolute chronology in the Andean area. *American Antiquity*, vol. 10, pp. 265-284.

1946 Inca culture at the time of the Spanish Conquest. In *Handbook of South American Indians, Vol. 2: The Andean Civilizations*, edited by J. H. Steward, pp. 183-330. Bureau of American Ethnology Bulletin 143, vol. 2.

1948 The kingdom of Chimor. *Acta Americana*, vol. 6, no. 1-2, pp. 26-59.

1956 Archaeological explorations in southern Peru, 1954-1955. *American Antiquity*, vol. 22, pp. 135-150.

1962 Stages and periods in archaeological interpretation. *Southwestern Journal of Anthropology*, vol. 18, pp. 50-54.

1967 What kind of a settlement was Inca Cuzco? *Ñawpa Pacha* vol. 5, pp. 59-77. Berkeley: Institute of Andean Studies.

1976 Religión e imperio en el Perú antiguo. *Antropología Andina*, no. 1-2, pp. 5-12. Cuzco.

1979 An account of the shrines of ancient Cuzco. *Ñawpa Pacha*, no. 17, pp. 1-80. Berkeley: Institute of Andean Studies.

Ruiz de Arce, Juan
1933 Relación de los servicios en Indias de Don Juan Ruiz de Arce, conquistador del Perú (1543). *Boletín de la Academia de la Historia*, vol. 102, pp. 327-384. Madrid.

Ruppert, Karl J., Eric S. Thompson, and Tatiana Proskouriakoff
1955 *Bonampak, Chiapas, Mexico*. Carnegie Institute Publications, no. 602. Washington: Carnegie Institute of Washington.

Ruyle, Eugene E.
1975 Mode of production and mode of exploitation: the mechanical and the dialectical. *Dialectical Anthropology*, vol. 1, pp. 7-23.

Ruz Lhuillier, Alberto
1945 *Guía Arqueológica de Tula*. Mexico: Instituto Nacional de Antropología e Historia.
1962 Chichén Itzá y Tula: comentarios a un ensayo. *Estudios de Cultura Maya*, vol. 2, pp. 205-223.
1971 *Chichén Itzá en la Historia y en la Arte*. Mexico: Editora del Sureste.

Sahagún, Bernardino de
1950-69 *Florentine Codex: General History of the Things of New Spain*. Translated by C. E. Dibble and A. J. O. Anderson. 11 vols. Santa Fe: School of American Research.

Sahlins, Marshall D.
1973 Economic anthropology and anthropological economics. In *Explorations in Anthropology*, edited by M. Fried, pp. 274-288. New York: Thomas Y. Crowell.
1978 Culture as protein and profit. *New York Review of Books*, November 23, pp. 45-53.

Sahlins, Marshall D., and Elman R. Service (editors)
1960 *Evolution and Culture*. Ann Arbor: University of Michigan Press.

Sancho (de la Hoz), Pedro
1917 *An Account of the Conquest of Peru* (1534). Translated by Philip A. Means. Documents and Narratives Concerning the Discovery and Conquest of Latin America, no. 2. New York: The Cortés Society.
1962 *Relación de la Conquista del Perú* (1534). Edited by Joaquín García Icazbalceta. Biblioteca Tenanitla, no. 2. Madrid: Ediciones José Porrúa Turanzas.

Sanders, William T.
1956 The Central Mexican symbiotic region. In *Prehistoric Settlement Patterns in the New World*, edited by G. R. Willey, pp. 115-127. Viking Fund Publications in Anthropology, no. 23.
1965 The Cultural Ecology of the Teotihuacan Valley. University Park, PA: Department of Sociology and Anthropology, The Pennsylvania State University. Mimeographed.
1968 Hydraulic agriculture, economic symbiosis and the evolution of states in Central Mexico. In *Anthropological Archeology in the Americas*, edited by B. J. Meggers, pp. 88-107. Washington: Anthropological Society of Washington.
1970 The population of the Teotihuacan Valley, the Basin of Mexico, and the Central Mexican symbiotic region in the sixteenth century. In *The Teotihuacan Valley Project Final Report, Vol. 1*, by W. T. Sanders et al., pp. 385-457. Occasional Papers in Anthropology, no. 3. University Park, PA: Department of Anthropology, The Pennsylvania State University.
1972 Population, agricultural history, and societal evolution in Mesoamerica. In *Population Growth: Anthropological Implications*, edited by B. Spooner, pp. 101-153. Cambridge: MIT Press.

1976 The population of the Central Mexican symbiotic region, the Basin of Mexico, and the Teotihuacan Valley in the sixteenth century. In *The Native Population of the Americas in 1492*, edited by W. Denevan, pp. 85-150. Madison: University of Wisconsin Press.

Sanders, William T., Anton Kovar, Thomas Charlton, and Richard A. Diehl
1970 *The Teotihuacan Valley Project Final Report, Vol. 1.* Occasional Papers in Anthropology, no. 3. University Park, PA: Department of Anthropology, The Pennsylvania State University.

Sanders, William T., Jeffrey R. Parsons, and Michael H. Logan
1976 Summary and conclusions. In *The Valley of Mexico*, edited by E. R. Wolf, pp. 161-178. Albuquerque: University of New Mexico Press.

Sanders, William T., Jeffrey R. Parsons, and Robert S. Santley
1979 *The Basin of Mexico: Ecological Processes in the Evolution of a Civilization.* New York: Academic Press.

Sanders, William T., and Barbara J. Price
1968 *Mesoamerica: The Evolution of a Civilization.* New York: Random House.

Sanders, William T., and Robert S. Santley
1977 A prehispanic irrigation system near Santa Clara Xalostoc in the Basin of Mexico. *American Antiquity*, vol. 42, pp. 582-588.
1978 Review of Richard E. Blanton, *Monte Albán: Settlement Patterns at the Ancient Zapotec Capital. Science*, vol. 202, pp. 303-304.

Santacruz Pachacuti Yamqui Salcamaygua, Joan de
1879 Relación de antigüedades deste reyno del Pirú (ca. 1610-15). In *Tres Relaciones de Antigüedades Peruanas*, edited by Marcos Jiménez de la Espada, pp. 229-328. Madrid: Imprenta y Fundición de M. Tello.

Santillán, Fernando de
1879 Relación del origen, descendencia, política y gobierno de los Incas (1563-64). In *Tres Relaciones de Antigüedades Peruanas*, edited by Marcos Jiménez de la Espada, pp. 1-133. Madrid: Imprenta y Fundición de M. Tello.

Santley, Robert S.
1980 Disembedded capitals reconsidered. *American Antiquity*, vol. 45, pp. 132-45.

Santo Tomás, Domingo de
1951 *Lexicón o Vocabulario de la Lengua General del Perú* (1560). Facsimile edition published by Raúl Porras Barrenechea. Lima: Instituto de Historia, Universidad Nacional Mayor de San Marcos.

Sarmiento de Gamboa, Pedro
1942 *Historia de los Incas* (1572). Colección Hórreo, no. 10. Buenos Aires: Emecé Editores.

Schaedel, Richard P.
1978 Early state of the Incas. In *The Early State*, edited by H. Claessen and P. Skalnik, pp. 289-320. The Hague: Mouton.

Scott, John F.
1978 *The Danzantes of Monte Alban*. Dumbarton Oaks Studies in Pre-Columbian Art and Archaeology, no. 19. 2 vols. Washington: Dumbarton Oaks.

Segovia, Bartolomé de
1943 Relación de muchas cosas acaecidas en el Perú...(1553). In *Las Crónicas de los Molinas*, compiled by Carlos A. Romero, Raúl Porras Barrenechea, and Francisco A. Loayza, pp. 1-78 (1st paging). Los Pequeños Grandes Libros de Historia Americana, 1st series, vol. 4. Lima: Librería y Imprenta D. Miranda.

Séjourné, Laurette
1965 El Quetzalcoatl en Teotihuacán. *Cuadernos Americanos*, vol. 24, pp. 131-56.

Seler, Eduard
  1960-61 *Gesammelte Abhandlungen.* 5 vols. Graz, Austria: Akademischen Druk- und Verlagsanstalt.
Shady, Ruth, and Hermilio Rosas
  1977 El Horizonte Medio en Chota: prestigio de la cultura Cajamarca y su relación con el 'Imperio Huari'. *Arqueológicas,* no. 16. Lima.
Shady, Ruth, and Arturo Ruiz
  1979 Evidence for interregional relationships during the Middle Horizon on the north-central coast of Peru. *American Antiquity,* vol. 44, pp. 676-684.
Sheffer, Charles
  1971 Review of Ester Boserup, *The Conditions of Agricultural Growth. American Antiquity,* vol. 36, pp. 377-379.
Simoons, Frederick J.
  1973 The sacred cow and the constitution of India. *Ecology of Food and Nutrition,* vol. 2, pp. 281-296.
  1979 Questions in the sacred-cow controversy. *Current Anthropology,* vol. 20, pp. 467-493.
Simoons, Frederick J., and Elizabeth S. Simoons
  1968 *A Ceremonial Ox of India.* Madison: University of Wisconsin Press.
Skalnik, Peter
  1978 The early state as a process. In *The Early State,* edited by H. Claessen and P. Skalnik, pp. 597-618. The Hague: Mouton.
Smith, Jason W.
  1976 *Foundations of Archaeology.* Beverly Hills: Glencoe Press.
Smith, Michael G.
  1978 Conditions of change in social stratification. In *The Evolution of Social Systems,* edited by J. Friedman and M. J. Rowlands, pp. 29-48. London: Duckworth.
Soustelle, Jacques
  1961 *The Daily Life of the Aztecs on the Eve of the Spanish Conquest.* Translated by Patrick O'Brian. Stanford: Stanford University Press.
Steele, F., and A. Bourne (editors)
  1975 *The Man/Food Equation.* New York: Academic Press.
Steward, Julian H.
  1955 *Theory of Culture Change.* Urbana: University of Illinois Press.
Sullivan, Thelma D.
  1966 Pregnancy, childbirth, and the deification of the women who died in childbirth: texts from the Florentine Codex, book VI, folios 128v-143v. *Estudios de Cultura Náhuatl,* vol. 6, pp. 66-96.
Swanson, Guy E.
  1960 *The Birth of the Gods.* Ann Arbor: University of Michigan Press.
Tagányi, Zoltán
  1978 Comment on Godelier. *Current Anthropology,* vol. 19, pp. 770-771.
Terray, Emmanuel
  1978 Event, structure, and history: the formation of the Abron kingdom of Gyaman (1700-1780). In *The Evolution of Social Systems,* edited by J. Friedman and M. J. Rowlands, pp. 279-301. London: Duckworth.
Tezozomoc, Fernando Alvarado
  1943 *Crónica Mexicana.* Mexico: Universidad Nacional Autónoma de México.
  1975 *Crónica Mexicayotl.* Mexico: Instituto de Investigaciones Históricas.
Tolstoy, Paul
  1975 Settlement and population trends in the Basin of Mexico (Ixtapaluca and Azcatenco phases). *Journal of Field Archaeology,* vol. 2, pp. 331-349.

Tolstoy, Paul, Suzanne Fish, Martin W. Boksenbaum, Katherine B. Vaughn, and C. Earle Smith
1977 Early sedentary communities of the Basin of Mexico. *Journal of Field Archaeology*, vol. 4, pp. 91-106.

Tolstoy, Paul, and Louise I. Paradis
1970 Early and Middle Preclassic culture in the Basin of Mexico. *Science*, vol. 167, pp. 344-351.

Torquemada, Juan de
1975 *Monarquía Indiana*, vols. 1-5. Mexico: Instituto de Investigaciones Históricas.

Tosi, Joseph A., Jr
1960 *Zonas de Vida Natural en el Perú*. Boletín Técnico, no. 5. Lima: Instituto Interamericano de Ciencias Agrícolas de la Organización de Estados Americanos, Zona Andina.

Tovar, Juan de
1944 *Códice Ramírez: Relación del Origen de los Indios que Habitan esta Nueva España, Según sus Historias*. Mexico: Editorial Leyenda.

Townsend, Richard F.
1979 *State and Cosmos in the Art of Tenochtitlan*. Dumbarton Oaks Studies in Pre-Columbian Art and Archaeology, no. 20. Washington: Dumbarton Oaks.

Tozzer, Alfred M.
1957 *Chichen Itza and Its Cenote of Sacrifice: A Comparative Study of Contemporaneous Maya and Toltec*. Memoirs of the Peabody Museum, vols. 11 and 12. Cambridge: Harvard University.

Trigger, Bruce
1978 Inequality and communication in early civilizations. In *Time and Traditions: Essays in Archaeological Interpretation*, by B.G. Trigger, pp. 194-215. New York: Columbia University Press.

Trimborn, Hermann
1975 Sama. *Zeitschrift für Ethnologie*, no. 100, pp. 290-299.
1977 Excavaciones en Sama (Dpto. Tacna, Perú). *Indiana: Beiträge zur Völker- und Sprachenkunde, Archäologie und Antropologie des Indianischen Amerikas*, vol. 4, pp. 171-178.

Trimborn, Hermann, Otto Kleemann, Karl J. Narr, and Wolfgang Wurster
1975 *Investigaciones Arqueológicas en los Valles del Caplina y Sama*. Studia Instituti Anthropos, no. 25. Estella, Navarre.

Tschopik, Marion H.
1946 *Some Notes on the Archaeology of the Department of Puno, Peru*. Papers of the Peabody Museum of American Archaeology and Ethnology, vol. 27, no. 3. Cambridge: Harvard University.

Uchmany, Eva A.
1978 Huitzilopochtli, dios de la historia de los Azteca-mexitin. *Estudios de Cultura Náhuatl*, vol. 13, pp. 211-238. Mexico.
1979 Las características de un dios tutelar Mesoamericano: Huitzilopochtli. *Actes du 42e Congrès International des Américanistes*, vol. 6, pp. 49-62. Paris.

Valcárcel, Luis E.
1946 The Andean calendar. In *Handbook of South American Indians, Vol. 2: The Andean Civilizations*, edited by J. H. Steward, pp. 471-476. Bureau of American Ethnology Bulletin 143, vol. 2.

Vargas Ugarte, Rubén
1936 La fecha de la fundación de Trujillo. *Revista Histórica*, vol. 10, pp. 229-239. Lima.

Vayda, Andrew P.
1976 On the 'New Ecology' paradigm. *American Anthropologist*, vol. 78, pp. 645-646.
Vayda, Andrew P., and Bonnie T. McCay
1975 New directions in ecology and ecological anthropology. *Annual Review of Anthropology*, vol. 4, pp. 293-306.
Vreeland, James M., Jr
1980 Prácticas mortuorias andinas: perspectivas teóricas para interpretar el material textil. *Actas y Trabajos del III Congreso Peruano 'El Hombre y la Cultura Andina'*, 2nd series, vol. 3, pp. 141-154. Lima.
Vreeland, James M., Jr, and Aidan Cockburn
1980 Mummies of Peru. In *Mummies, Disease, and Ancient Cultures*, edited by A. Cockburn and E. Cockburn, pp. 135-174. Cambridge: Cambridge University Press.
Wagley, Charles
1973 Cultural influences on population: a comparison of two Tupi tribes. In *Peoples and Cultures of Native South America*, edited by D. R. Gross, pp. 145-156. Garden City: Doubleday.
Wallace, Anthony F. C.
1956 Revitalization movements. *American Anthropologist*, vol. 58, pp. 264-281.
1966 *Religion: An Anthropological View*. New York: Random House.
1970 *The Death and Rebirth of the Seneca*. New York: Knopf.
Waterlow, J. C., and P. R. Payne
1975 The protein gap. *Nature*, vol. 258, pp. 113-117.
Watson, Patty Jo, Stephen A. LeBlanc, and Charles L. Redman
1971 *Explanation in Archaeology*. New York: Columbia University Press.
Weber, Max
1930 *The Protestant Ethic and the Spirit of Capitalism*. Translated by Talcott Parsons. New York: Scribner's.
West, Robert C.
1964 Surface configuration and associated geology of Middle America. In *Handbook of Middle American Indians*, vol. 1, edited by R. C. West, pp. 33-83. Austin: University of Texas Press.
White, Daryl
1979 Genesis as ideology. *Dialectical Anthropology*, vol. 4, pp. 329-338.
White, Leslie
1959 *The Evolution of Culture*. New York: McGraw-Hill.
Whitebook, Joel
1976 Reflections on the evolutionist controversy. *Dialectical Anthropology*, vol. 1, pp. 181-185.
Whitecotton, Joseph W.
1977 *The Zapotecs: Princes, Priests, and Peasants*. Norman: University of Oklahoma Press.
Whyte, Anne
1978 Systems as perceived: a discussion of 'Maladaptation in social systems'. In *The Evolution of Social Systems*, edited by J. Friedman and M. J. Rowlands, pp. 73-78. London: Duckworth.
Willey, Gordon R.
1971 *An Introduction to American Archaeology, Vol. 2: South America*. Englewood Cliffs, NJ: Prentice-Hall.
1976 Mesoamerican civilization and the idea of transcendence. *Antiquity*, vol. 50, pp. 205-215.

Wilson, David J.
  1981 Of maize and men: a critique of the maritime hypothesis of state origins
    on the coast of Peru. *American Anthropologist*, vol. 83, pp. 93-120.
Wittfogel, Karl
  1957 *Oriental Despotism: A Comparative Study of Total Power*. New Haven: Yale
    University Press.
Wolf, Eric R.
  1959 *Sons of the Shaking Earth*. Chicago: University of Chicago Press.
  1975 Review of Maurice Godelier, *Horizon, Trajets Marxistes en Anthropologie*.
    Dialectical Anthropology, vol. 1, pp. 99-104.
Wolf, Eric R. (editor)
  1976 *The Valley of Mexico*. Albuquerque: University of New Mexico Press.
Woodcock, Alexander, and Monte Davies
  1978 *Catastrophe Theory*. New York: Dutton.
Wrigley, Edward A.
  1969 *Population and History*. New York: McGraw-Hill.
Xérez, Francisco de
  (See Jérez 1853)
Zantwijk, Rudolf van
  1963 Principios organizadores de los Mexicas. *Estudios de Cultura Náhuatl*, vol.
    4, pp. 187-220.
  1966 Los seis barrios sirvientes de Huitzilopochtli. *Estudios de Cultura Náhuatl*,
    vol. 6, pp. 177-187.
  1976 La organización social de la México-Tenochtitlan naciente. *Actas del 41
    Congreso Internacional de Americanistas*, vol. 2, pp. 188-208. Mexico.
  1979 El parentesco y la afiliación étnica de Huitzilopochtli. *Actes du 42e Congrès
    International des Américanistes*, vol. 6, pp. 63-68. Paris.
Zorita, Alonso de
  1941 Breve y sumaria relación de los señores de la Nueva España. In *Nueva
    Colección de Documentos Para la Historia de México*, pp. 65-205. Mexico:
    Editorial S. Chávez Hayhoe.
  1963 *Life and Labor in Ancient Mexico (Breve y Sumaria Relación de los Señores de
    Nueva España)*. Translated by B. Keen. New Brunswick: Rutgers University
    Press.
Zuidema, Reiner Tom
  1958 The kinship system of the Inkas, and some of its implications. *Proceedings
    of the 32nd International Congress of Americanists*, pp. 300-305. Copenhagen.
  1962 Reflections on Inca historical conceptions. *Akten des 34 Internationalen
    Amerikanistenkongresses*, pp. 718-721. Vienna.
  1964 *The Ceque System of Cuzco: The Social Organization of the Capital of the Inca*.
    Translated by Eva M. Hooykaas. International Archives of Ethnography,
    Supplement to vol. 50. Leiden: E. J. Brill.
  1973 Kinship and ancestorcult in three Peruvian communities: Hernández
    Príncipe's account of 1622. *Bulletin de l'Institut Français d'Etudes Andines*, vol.
    2, no. 1, pp. 16-33.
  1977a La imagen del Sol y la huaca de Susurpuquio en el sistema astronómico
    de los Incas en el Cuzco. *Journal de la Société des Américanistes*, n.s., vol. 63,
    pp. 199-230. Paris.
  1977b The Inca calendar. In *Native American Astronomy*, edited by A. F. Aveni,
    pp. 219-259. Austin: University of Texas Press.
  1977c The Inca kinship system: a new theoretical view. In *Andean Kinship and
    Marriage*, edited by R. Bolton and E. Mayer, pp. 240-281. American
    Anthropological Association Special Publications, no. 7.
  1977d Mito e historia en el antiguo Perú. *Allpanchis*, vol. 10, pp. 15-52. Cuzco.

Zuidema, Reiner Tom, and U. Quispe M.
  1968 A visit to God: the account and interpretation of a religious experience in the Peruvian community of Choque-Huarcaya. *Bijdragen tot de Taal-, Land-en Volkenkunde*, vol. 10, pp. 22-39.
Zuidema, Reiner Tom, and Gary Urton
  1976 La constelación de la Llama en los Andes Peruanos. *Allpanchis*, vol. 9, pp. 59-119. Cuzco.

INDEX

CPSIA information can be obtained
at www.ICGtesting.com
Printed in the USA
LVHW041153190722
723851LV00003B/154

9 780521 318969